HANDBOOK OF
ACCOUNTING
COMMUNICATIONS

HANDBOOK OF OF ACCOUNTING

ADDISON-WESLEY PUBLISHING COMPANY

JEREMIAH J. SULLIVAN

School of Business
University of Washington

COMMUNICATIONS

Reading, Massachusetts • Menlo Park, California • London
Amsterdam • Don Mills, Ontario • Sydney

To my wife Barbara,
for her interest,
her companionship,
and her communications skill.

Library of Congress Cataloging in Publication Data

Sullivan, Jeremiah J., 1940–
  Handbook of accounting communications.

  Bibliography: p.
  Includes index.
  1. Communication in accounting.   I. Title.
HF5657.S83   657'.0141   82-3953
ISBN 0-201-07508-3   AACR2

ISBN 0-201-07508-3
ABCDEFGHIJ-AL-898765432

Preface

The primary functions of accounting are measurement and communication—the getting and giving of information. This book concerns itself with the communications function in public and corporate accounting. It is intended for practitioners and for senior and graduate-level accounting students in colleges and universities.

The book has two purposes: (1) to develop an understanding of the communications behavior of accountants and (2) to build oral and written accounting communications skills. In writing the text, I consulted the literature of business communications, social and cognitive psychology, organizational behavior, management theory, rhetoric, general semantics, management accounting, behavioral accounting, and auditing. In addition, I surveyed senior corporate executives and managing audit partners and followed up my survey with interviews in New York City, Chicago, and Seattle.

Among the many people who gave me advice, encouragement, funding, and examples, the following deserve special mention: Gerhard Mueller, Gary Sundem, and Fred Mueller, Accounting Department, University of Washington School of Business; Robert May, Accounting Department, University of Texas at Austin; Jack Jorgenson, Unigard Insurance Group; Jack Henry, Randy O'Neil, Arthur Andersen and Company; Keith Larson, John Hoverson, Price Waterhouse and Company; Robert Boyd, William Kuntz, Matt Mangino, Deloitte Haskins and Sells; Frank McCord, William Conroy, Peat, Marwick, Mitchell; Robert Sack, John Clearman, Touche Ross; Robert Ingram, University of South Carolina; Leonard Haba, PACCAR, Inc.; Virgil Harder, Douglas MacLachlan, Marketing Department, University of Washington.

v

Contents in Brief

CONTENTS

What Happens When Accountants Communicate

chapter **1**

To communicate efficiently and effectively, an accountant must know something about communicating, the most complex of all human activities. If makers and senders of financial messages are to prosper, the act of making an accounting communication must be clearly understood. In this chapter we attempt to create such understanding. Specifically, we discuss the reasons why accountants communicate. We also describe the communications process and its parts, detail the barriers to successful accounting communications and note how they can be overcome, point out the benefits of a decisionmaker orientation to communicating, delineate the kind of planning that goes into an accounting communication, and list the criteria for evaluating the communication. We will take up some of the important themes introduced in this chapter and explore them more fully in the next two chapters.

WHY ACCOUNTANTS COMMUNICATE

To consider why accountants communicate may seem like asking why chickens cross roads (to get to the other side). Yet there are less than obvious reasons for communicating. Accountants need to be aware of what they are doing and of what goals they are seeking if they want to control the communicating process.

▲ To begin with, the most obvious goal of an accountant's communicating is *to transmit observations, measures, facts, inferences, evaluations, judgments, preferences, suggestions, and requests* to clients and managers. They will use such information to make financial decisions regarding the future or to make judgments evaluating the past.

▲ Another obvious goal is *to affect the behavior of others*. Such communicating is usually referred to as persuasion. Although accountants must be careful to engage in persuasive communicating only under appropriate conditions, they do employ persuasion regularly.

▲ A third, less obvious goal is *to open or to maintain a communications channel*. All corporate accountants know that many of their routine reports will go unread and unused. Nevertheless, these messages still must be sent regularly to maintain communication links within the organization. If the information stopped flowing, many of these links would weaken or disappear. Such links then would not be available when they were needed. For example, consider the accountant who stopped sending accounts receivable information to the credit manager because age-of-accounts information was not being used or even considered in determining the payment period for a credit sale. When a severe recession occurred and customers prolonged their payments, the impact of the age-of-accounts data on a planned restructuring of the payment period became obvious, and the data was sought. But too much time elapsed while the flow of information was restarted, and the company suffered a cash flow problem. If the communications channel had been kept open in the first place, the cash flow problem would not have occurred.

▲ A fourth important goal of an accountant's communicating is *to establish or to maintain a trust relationship*. The reality of life is that people who have developed a relationship within or between groups tend to trust each other, and trust is crucial to successful financial activities. If an accountant is trusted by a client, for example, the accountant's work for the client will probably require less validating than if trust did not exist. Such a relationship thus increases the efficiency of the accountant, in that efforts for other clients can be increased because of the validating time saved with a client who has a strong trust relationship with the accountant. Naturally, accountants usually work quite hard to communicate so as to develop such relationships.

▲ A less important but no less real communications goal is *to ritually express a sense of belonging to a community*. Such communications are ceremonial, in that they are conventional or customary. Take the case of a phone call or letter of congratulations to a client who has obtained a new contract. The purpose of such a letter might be to express the accountant's genuine happiness at the client's good fortune. The accountant is in a sense proclaiming that the client's joy is shared because of their relationship. Their two firms are a community, and the letter reaffirms the community.

▲   Accountants also communicate at times *to express emotions*. Of course, a calm, professional tone is the mark of a good accountant; but, human needs being what they are, sometimes a practitioner is compelled to "unload" personal feelings with some force to a colleague, a superior, a client, or a subordinate—or to the SEC regulator. While there are obvious risks of such expression, the benefit of gaining increased attention to one's position sometimes outweighs the costs.

▲   A little-discussed goal is *to effect word magic*. What we mean by this phrase is best interpreted as "saying makes it so." Thus a simple accounting report concerning a financial condition can, in the absence of other information or of objections, create its own validity. In other words, the report may be seen not as an aid to determining financial conditions but rather as *the* statement of financial condition. The mere utterance of the measures was all that was necessary to establish the condition.

The technical term for this word magic is *rationalizing*—the report provides a satisfactory but not necessarily correct answer to the question, "What is the financial condition?" Look at the issue this way: Suppose the company president asked the controller the question, and the controller, after research and deliberation, sent a memo report containing only this sentence:

> I think that the financial condition of the company is swell.

The president, who was looking for a satisfactory but not necessarily correct answer, accepted the report and proclaimed the strong condition of the firm to stockholders and bankers alike. Delighted, they deluged the company with added capital. Everyone prospered, and the wise controller's salary was raised.

We have given an extreme example as an illustration rather than a proof of our point: Accountants occasionally rationalize in their communications because they often are rewarded for doing so. Moreover, such behavior, while generally reprehensible, is not always wrong (either morally or managerially). The teacher who tells backward children that they are undoubtedly doing quite well in class may be engaging in word magic in the hope that saying something will lead to the existence of that something. Educational research strongly suggests that teachers can indeed improve performance simply by telling students that they are doing well and should continue to do well. Such rationalizing communications, then, can be quite useful. While accountants must, for the sake of professional credibility, almost always avoid rationalizing, most accountants will admit to the rare employment of word-magic rationalizing for the purpose of fostering the general good of their organizations.

In sum, then, we see that once we get beyond the obvious goals of communicating, the issue becomes quite complex and even controversial. Indeed, the communicating that accountants do is a more difficult task than the information gathering that they do.

THE TWO DIMENSIONS OF ACCOUNTANCY
How does communicating fit into the process of accounting? Bedford and Baladouni (1962) identify two dimensions to accounting activities:

▲ *Observing data*—Receiving and recording data regarding the economic events of an organization; interpreting the data; selecting information to transmit to decisionmakers.

▲ *Producing information*—Putting the information in message form; sending it along a selected channel to its destination.

The first activity involves information processing, whereas the second is communication processing.

These two activities require fundamentally different kinds of behaviors and perceiving on the part of the accountant:

▲ *Getting versus giving*—Getting information involves pulling; giving information requires pushing. Getting information is the acquiring of a resource, knowledge; giving information is the allocating of knowledge.

▲ *Self-satisfaction versus decisionmaker satisfaction*—When accountants get information, they satisfy their own need to do a good job. When they give information, they satisfy someone else's need.

The shift of focus from getting and self-satisfaction to giving and the satisfaction of others is probably the hardest task faced by an accountant—which is to say that preparing to communicate and then actually communicating require skills of a high order. In the long run, then, the goals of an accounting communicator described earlier cannot be achieved with any certainty of success until he or she learns to make the shift from information gathering to information transmitting. Exhibit 1.1 illustrates a failure to transmit information.

In the exhibit the accountant provided information—and in fact provided it in rather admirable graphic form—but his communication goal of transmitting information was muted by his self-focus as an information gatherer rather than an information provider. It isn't that he hasn't done a good job of communicating. He has. Rather the point is that he hasn't done the best job possible. In the nonroutine occurrence described, he needs to make a nonroutine communication to help management decide what to do. In the long

Exhibit 1.1   **INFORMING IS NOT NECESSARILY COMMUNICATING**

1.   A cost accountant sends the following chart to management as part of a routine monthly report.

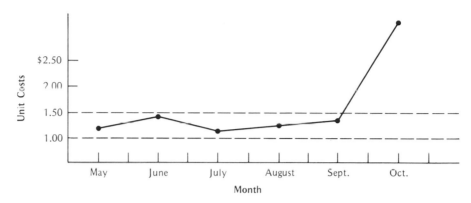

2.   The horizontal dotted lines represent the acceptable range of unit costs, which the October costs have far exceeded.

3.   Without any accompanying discussion, the chart has several alternative meanings.

Meanings	Implied Actions
A. An element(s) of cost has increased.	A. Identify the element and try to control it better.
B. Managerial oversight has failed	B. Change managers or alter the managerial oversight process.
C. An economic downturn in demand has affected economies of scale.	C. Increase marketing effort.
D. A random fluctuation has occurred.	D. Do nothing, but closely monitor future costs.

run the ability to make such communications, which indicates the ability to shift from a data-collecting focus to a knowledge-providing focus, will identify the successful accounting communicator from the not so successful one.

MODEL OF THE COMMUNICATION PROCESS   Exhibit 1.2 describes the process of an accounting communication. We will describe it in detail throughout the rest of this chapter. Such description will enable us to point out skill-building techniques that should improve communicating. Before doing so, however, several statements need to be made about the way accountants (and most people) view communicating.

Exhibit 1.2 **THE PROCESS OF COMMUNICATING**

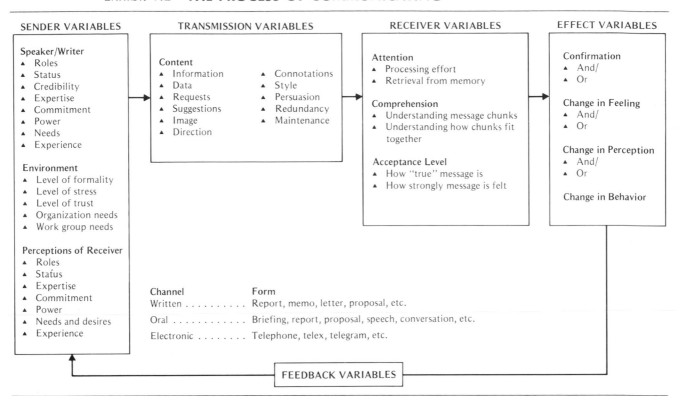

Accountants' View of Communicating

Like most people, accountants generally see the process of communicating as easier to do than it in fact is. Certainly they know that writing is hard and making an oral report difficult, but these kinds of communicating are even more complex than they are seen to be. Indeed, communicating is so complex that no one really understands it in anything but a superficial way.

What are the consequences of accountants seeing communicating as easier than it is? There are at least three. First, accountants don't usually allocate enough effort to communicating. They tend to think that because it's easy to do most of the time, they can reallocate their efforts to information gathering. Second, they tend to expect more of communications than can be delivered. Thus the immense financial edifice of General Motors cannot be explained in an annual report or even in a thousand internal accounting reports; yet accountants often act as if it can. Third, accountants often ask more of reader/listeners of accounting communications than they have a right to.

If they committed themselves to realizing how terribly hard it is to communicate financial information, accountants would spend less time gathering data and more time putting messages together. They would not expect anything more of financial reporting than a rough approximation of financial reality—an approximation that they would always be trying hard to move closer to the truth. Finally, they would communicate to help readers and listeners understand and would not simply dump data on them. A number of fine accounting professionals have built their reputations on these activities; their success should serve to make them models for the rest of the profession. Note that the first step is for accountants to admit to themselves just how difficult communicating really is.

The Model

As shown in Exhibit 1.2, five variables are used to classify the parts of the communication process:

▲ *Sender*—Who is communicating, in what environment, and with what perceptions about the receiver?

▲ *Transmission*—What is the content of the message? In what form and across what channels is it traveling?

▲ *Receiver*—Who is receiving the message? What effort will they make to pay attention? How successful will they be at understanding what was intended by the sender? How "true" will they perceive the message to be? How strongly will they feel its "truth"?

▲ *Effect*—Will something they feel or do or know be confirmed or justified? Will their feelings change? Will the way they see things change? Will their beliefs change? Will their behavior change?

▲ *Feedback*—What messages are received by the sender? Do they confirm that her message was received as intended? Do they confirm that the desired effect has occurred, is occurring, or is likely to occur?

Throughout the rest of this chapter, we will discuss these variables within the context of accounting communications.

THE ACCOUNTANT AS MESSAGE SENDER The objectives of any accounting communication are (1) to get the receiver of the message to understand it as intended by the accountant; (2) to obtain the desired effect; and (3) to expend the least possible amount of time, energy, and money in getting the intended understanding and desired effect. These goals require accountants to decide how characteristics of their own behavior, of their environment, and of their perceptions of the message receivers will affect the process. For routine communicating this analysis is done in a moment, whereas for nonroutine messages or for important messages it is a conscious effort. Let's look at the major issues that accountants need to consider about themselves before communicating.

Roles

A role is a set of behaviors that a person performs to which a name is attached. What then is the role of an accountant? Before discussing this topic, we need to identify several key terms that will help us in describing the impact of roles on successful communicating:

- *Role expectations*—Behaviors that clients, peers, superiors, subordinates, and the public expect of an accountant (Katz and Kahn, 1978);
- *Communication expectations*—Messages that the groups named above expect an accountant to send;
- *Assigned role*—Set of behaviors prescribed by rules, policies, standards, and conventions or by the directive of superiors;
- *Evolved role*—Set of behaviors that results from the interaction of prescribed behaviors with the various situations and groups encountered by the accountant.

These definitions allow us to state some of the common communication decisions that an accountant must make daily:

- *Should I communicate with a group in terms of my assigned or my evolved role?* For example, an accountant is discussing SEC requirements with a client regarding carrying noncancelable capital lease costs as debt. In her assigned role she might cite the requirements and tell the client how to account for the costs—nothing more. In her evolved role of accountant as confidante, she might also want to discuss the whole issue of sale-leasebacks.

- *Should I meet the communications expectations of my superiors or of my clients?* If a senior expects a junior to tell clients facts and to avoid opinions, should an accountant respond to a client who says, "What's your personal opinion?" There is no right thing to do in this situation. The important point is to realize that role issues raise communication problems.

- *Should I try to make uniform the communications expectations of all the groups I serve?* Although such an achievement is virtually impossible, many accountants act as if they have accomplished it. For example, some accountants, regardless of the situation or the group with whom they are communicating, will play the role of dignified and conservative professionals. They will communicate as if the whole world expected them to speak in sonorous, measured tones. They will be wrong, because some groups will see their communicating as cold, formal, pompous, and indifferent.

The plain fact is that communications expectations based on role expectations differ across groups. One group will expect an accountant's words to be chiefly reliable, while another will expect them to be chiefly relevant. Accountants must learn to satisfy both groups: they must learn to play different roles for different groups and even different roles for the same group at different times.

Status, Credibility, Expertise, and Power

How much clout do accountants have with message receivers? The answer depends on several factors. If the accountants have higher status (real or perceived as real by the receivers), they can add more recommendations to their conclusions than if they had lower status. If they have more credibility (in comparison with other accountants or with some standard), they can express greater certainty about their statements. If they have more expertise, they need not provide as much support for their conclusions. If they have more power over reader/listeners, they need not persuade or request as often but simply direct. Accountants, then, with high status and credibility who are perceived by reader/listeners to be experts and to have power over them can usually make communications that are unsupported, high-impact prescriptions. Life at the top is indeed sweet!

Credibility and the Role of Professional

The success of an accounting firm is based on the professional nature of the staff. They are professional in the sense that they share a deep commitment to a discipline, are often licensed, and can lose their license if they behave in ways that the discipline cannot sanction. This professional status gives accountants a credibility that, for example, management consultants (who could do most of the work accountants do) do not possess because they lack a recognizable discipline and a licensing procedure.

A problem can exist, however, in terms of the role behaviors engaged in by accountants in organizations. Most organizations sanction behavior that is mostly based on actions required to accomplish tasks. These required behaviors are communicated as rules. Yet professionals do not follow the rules of an organization so much as the rules of their profession. For accountants role conflict may occur; for example, an organizational rule may require certain work to be done rapidly to keep costs low and clients happy, but a professional rule may require the same work to be done slowly and painstakingly. Inevitably, the organizational rule is followed, and over time the professional status of the accountants—who may be compelled to behave in ways their discipline cannot sanction—declines. They come to see themselves less and less as professionals, and they tend to signal this self-perception to the community.

If the community comes to see accountants as not really professional, then the credibility of the accountants diminishes, and they take on the status of management consultants. Indeed, management consulting has become ever more important in accounting firms over the years.

Nevertheless, accounting organizations must always be seeking to communicate the credibility of their accountants to clients if they are to remain in business. Hence efforts are always under way to upgrade the professionalism of accountants. The price to be paid is a never-ending role conflict in which the accountants' *assigned* role as professionals sometimes conflicts with their *evolved* role as salaried, rule-obeying workers. This role conflict can lead to communications difficulties within a firm, particularly regarding superior-subordinate communications, as well as to credibility problems with clients.

Needs and Commitment

Generally speaking, ambitious and dynamic accountants will be better communicators than those who are not. Their need to succeed will lead to a commitment to communicating well, which will bring forth the extra effort needed for the complex communicating that makes up so much of accounting. But there is an even greater benefit to being highly motivated. Consider this formula:

$$
\begin{array}{l}
\text{Reader/Listener's} \\
\text{Judgment of} \\
\text{Accountant's} \\
\text{Performance as a} \\
\text{Communicator}
\end{array}
=
\begin{array}{l}
\text{Reader/Listener's} \\
\text{Perception of} \\
\text{Accountant's} \\
\text{Communication} \\
\textit{Effort}
\end{array}
\left(
\begin{array}{l}
\text{Reader/Listener's} \\
\text{Perception of} \\
\text{Accountant's} \\
\textit{Ability} \text{ as a} \\
\text{Communicator}
\end{array}
-
\begin{array}{l}
\text{Reader/Listener's} \\
\text{Perception of} \\
\text{the } \textit{Communication} \\
\textit{Task's Difficulty}
\end{array}
\right)
$$

The formula describes the process by which a reader/listener decides just how well an accountant is communicating. Notice that *effort,* because it is multiplied by each of the two other variables, is the most important element in a person's judgment about an accountant's communication performance. Thus not only will an accountant's commitment bring out better communicating, but also clients and other message receivers will tend to recognize the improvement.

Experience

Experienced accountants know what to say and when to say it. Even more important, they know what channel to choose to carry a message. Take the case, for example, of the client who has complained about the costs of an audit. Should the senior respond by telephone, in person, by writing, or by some combination of these channels? There is no one solution, but an experienced senior will have learned the best approach. This knowledge of channel selection is probably one of the major experience-based skills an accountant can develop.

Level of Formality

Experience also teaches accountants how to respond to the formality of the communications situation. If some kind of rule or ritual exists that governs a communication, the degree to which the rule governs the making of the communication is the degree to which the communication is formal. Many public accounting firms wisely require a good deal of formality in their accountants' communications. Their hope is that the resulting messages will have a certain uniformity that will tend to increase a reader/listener client's sense of their reliability. This hope is well founded, since consistent communicating creates an image of steadiness, soundness, and credibility. The accounting communicator, then, departs from a required formality only in extreme circumstances, such as a crisis, when getting a message through immediately in any form is more important than following the communication rules.

Level of Stress

Stress is the anxiety accountants feel when the demands on them outstrip their resources. Typically, they will act to reduce demands (e.g., holding incoming telephone calls) or to increase resources (e.g., assigning a junior to handle routine client requests), or do both. What they should also do is recognize that communicating under stress is dangerous. Rules tend not to be followed, momentary opinions get expressed with more certainty than they deserve, and a motivated communicator turns into simply an aggressive, unpleasant careerist. Accounting firms and divisions usually try to help accountants deal with communicating under stress by providing training and, more important, by creating formal or implied rules governing what kinds of communications must occur during stress and what can be put off. In one firm, for instance, routine flash reports have to be delivered on time each month no matter what, but the delivery date for following up reports based on the flash report is a range of days of the month rather than a specific date. The statement of the date as a range gives the accountants some ability to put off delivery during periods of stressful demands on them for other work.

Level of Trust

Trusted accountants are seen as predictable, sincere, honest, helpful, friendly, competent, and hard working, among other things. Accountants who are labeled as trusted enjoy valuable advantages while communicating. Their assertions need not be strongly supported because their validity will easily be perceived by reader/listeners. The conflicts they may have with clients, peers, superiors, and the like, will easily be resolved and often avoided. Indeed, trust is what creates efficiency in accountants' work and in their communicating. When they are trusted, they do not have to work as hard at either job as they ordinarily would.

Communicating to build trust is one of the most important tasks accountants undertake, and we will return to this topic again and again in this book. For now we need simply state that if message-sending accountants perceive that they are trusted, they can reduce their communications effort somewhat and redirect it to communications in situations where their trustworthiness is still being established.

Organizational and Work Group Needs

Accountants must know what their firms, colleagues, and clients expect them to say and write. We will take up these issues in later chapters; suffice it to say here that professionals communicate to serve their firms as well as to serve whoever happens to be receiving their messages.

Message Receivers' Needs

Classic and contemporary theories of rhetoric agree on one thing: One of the prime determinants of what is said and how it is said by a message sender is the nature and needs of the message receiver. This statement is more controversial than it looks. Consider the client who one morning wants a quick telephone response to a certain complex question. The firm's policy requires that a senior partner approve such responses before they are made—but no partner is available that day. According to the reader/listener theory of rhetoric, the most effective communication decision would be to get back to the client that day with the answer, justifying the action later on to the partner. But such responsiveness to receiver needs would violate a rule establishing formality in the firm's communications. If these violations became widespread, the image of the firm as reliable might suffer.

Nevertheless, even though there are risks at times in being reader/listener oriented, one theme of this book is that *most* accounting communications will be successful and effective if accountants decide what to say and how to say it in terms of the needs, desires, and nature of message receivers. One must, of course, give heed to rules, conventional procedure, organizational needs, and the needs of others not involved in the communication.

Being reader/listener oriented is another topic we will take up later in this chapter. But we should note here that accountants need to assess the reader/listeners' roles, status, expertise, and so on, while focusing on their own roles, status, and the like. Of crucial importance is the accountants' recognition of just what role their communication will ascribe to the message receiver. Should it be the assigned or the evolved role? Should an accountant, for example, communicate with the controller as if the controller were the chief information processor of the company (assigned role) or as if he were one of the chief decisionmakers in the company (evolved role)? In the first case a report might emphasize the analysis of data, whereas in the second the same report might stress suggested actions based on the data and a plan of implementation.

The whole issue of roles is extraordinarily complex. Exhibit 1.3 shows what happened to a young accountant who didn't think about his own role and the role of his boss.

CONTENT AND FORM   Content is the words and numbers that make up a message. Form can be thought of as the container in which content is stored.

Content

As Exhibit 1.2 suggests, the content of content can be many things. Certainly content includes data and information (which we will discuss in Chapter 3); but also included are requests, suggestions, directives, and persuasion—all action-seeking kinds of messages.

Exhibit 1.3 **COMMUNICATING IN ASSIGNED AND EVOLVED ROLES: HOW TO GET BETWEEN A ROCK AND A HARD PLACE**

Situation

Jim Preston was assigned by Mr. Mason, the controller, to be an analyst for an ad hoc group formed to make a step-by-step evaluation of the company's internal controls. Ed Baker was the project manager for whom Jim was to provide data and analyses on control procedures and tests.

For six weeks all went smoothly: Jim made weekly reports to Ed, who made progress reports every three weeks to Mr. Mason. One day, however, Mr. Mason called Jim on the phone and requested the current data. Jim sent it off, providing a report to Ed in the usual manner. Soon Mr. Mason was on the phone to Jim two or three times a week, seeking data. Ed was aware of Mr. Mason's interest but was seemingly unconcerned, so Jim complied without worrying.

After a time Mr. Mason began to request not only data from Jim but also recommendations for improving controls. Again Jim eagerly complied. This went on for several weeks, but finally Ed barged in on Jim one day and complained that Jim was undercutting him by sending recommendations to Mason. He demanded that Jim stop.

Jim's communications problem is this: His assigned analyst role requires providing only data, but his new evolved managerial role requires providing recommendations. If he continues to play the evolved role, his communications will please Mason but offend Baker. If he switches back to his assigned role, he pleases Baker but offends Mason. What should he do?

Solution

There is none. He must suffer no matter what he does. All he can do is try to soften the blow before it comes by explaining the situation to both parties.

Moral

Be aware (1) of the role you play, the role you are asked to play, and the role your boss plays and (2) of how roles determine communications. If you are aware, you can often avoid getting trapped between a rock and a hard place by not accepting an evolved role (and thus by continuing to communicate in the assigned role) or by getting the evolved role formalized.

Connotations

Less visible are connotations, the hidden messages implied in the communication. Americans tend to be unsophisticated about using connotations to communicate, which is unfortunate. By sending implied messages, accountants can tell reader/listeners many things they would not want to include in the overt words and numbers. For example, an auditor says, "We feel that an opportunity exists for the company to establish review procedures for monitoring control systems on an ongoing basis." The implied message may be, "You've got a control problem that you've got to do something about." An astute manager will pick up the implication, probe a bit to make sure that she got the implication in the sense intended, and then act to resolve the problem.

Auditors often communicate with connotations, and they recognize the risks involved in not getting a hidden message across. But the benefits can outweigh the costs, especially when a client can be told that he has a problem without the word *problem* having to be used. Other elements of content are style, redundancy, and maintenance.

Style

The sense the reader/listener gets of the accountant's thought and of the confidence he has in his thought constitutes the style of the message. Style reflects the accountant's self-image or the image he wants the world to see. It is born in the way words and numbers are arranged together, but it does not die when the words are forgotten. Style survives in the minds of readers and listeners just as a footprint of some ancient human can survive in soft lava. Like the modern anthropologist reconstructing what our ancestor looked like from a footprint, the accountant's reader or listener can reconstruct an image of the accountant based only on a sense of his communications style and tone.

Redundancy

When accountants say something twice to make sure that their messages are received, they are practicing redundancy. If not overused, redundancy is a valuable tool for reducing the risk of making a poor communication (one that is not received or is not received as intended). Many professionals are virtuosos of the telephone, for example, as they make calls to repeat messages already sent in writing. By the same token, good communicators will follow up important conversations with summary memos. The appropriate use of redundancy is a skill learned by experience. Young accountants may worry that their redundant messages are simply boring repetition rather than a form of effective communications insurance. All in all, however, the chance of being a bore is offset by the improved chance of communicating well.

Maintenance

Sometimes accountants will call clients or managers whom they haven't talked to lately. Their purpose is not to convey meaning in words, but rather to keep the communications channel open. In a sense, such messages ought to have contentless content, since their purpose is to ensure that the communications channel is open and functioning rather than to send any meanings across it. We may refer to such communicating as *small talk,* but it is just as necessary as important talk.

Form

We turn now to form, which we referred to as the container of content. Less graphically, form is the mode of presentation. Written forms include reports, memos, letters, and the like. Oral forms are face-to-face conversation, speeches, and group interacting, among others, while electronic forms involve such things as telephone conversations, telex communicating, and teleconferencing.

Experienced accountants know that a good presentation of information is like money in the bank. It builds goodwill, impresses clients, conveys a professional image, and, when used repeatedly, conveys a sense of predictability and trustworthiness to readers and listeners. Accountants spend much time and effort developing suitable written forms, but they often lack knowledge of oral and electronic forms.

To drive home the importance of content and form, the following display recounts Patrick Matthew's development of the theory of natural selection— certainly the most powerful and most influential scientific theory in human existence—nearly thirty years before Darwin published *On the Origin of Species* (1859):

	Content	Form
Matthew	Scattered comments in an appendix	A book on naval timber
Darwin	A systematic presentation, supported by data and reason	A book devoted solely to developing the theory

Yet who remembers Patrick Matthew? The plain fact is that Charles Darwin's immortality rests not on his being the first to develop the theory but on his ability to mold his words in a proper form. Appropriate content and form— which is to say, good communicating—is the base on which immortality rests.

CHOOSING A COMMUNICATIONS CHANNEL

Communications channels are the paths across which messages travel. We have identified three channels: written, oral, and electronic. Exhibit 1.4 describes channels that are available when an accountant wants to send a message to a selected person or group in a particular time. Every professional

Exhibit 1.4 **COMMUNICATION CHANNEL AVAILABILITY IN TERMS OF TRANSMISSION TIME AND POTENTIAL MESSAGE RECEIVERS**

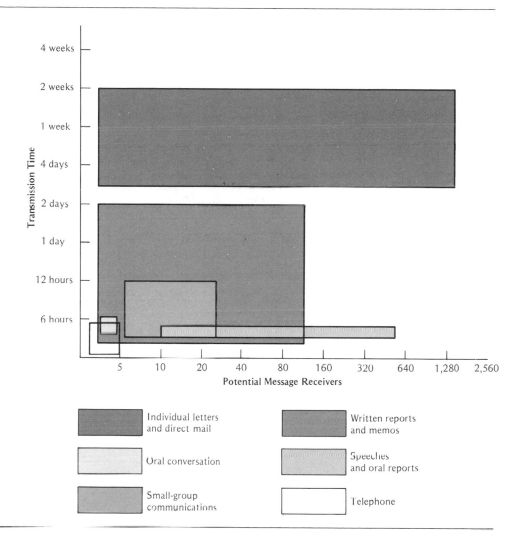

ought to plan a communication in terms of the variables listed in the exhibit. For example, let us assume that an accountant has prepared an elaborate cash budget for the coming year. She is somewhat startled to discover that projected bank loans for June and July are almost double what was forecast in the last cash budget, six months ago. She decides to communicate her discovery to the company treasurer and to four senior vice presidents—a total of five message receivers. Next, instead of rushing out the door to their offices or grabbing for the telephone, she sits back and asks herself, "How rapidly do I want to make this communication, and how should I make it?" She begins to consider her options.

Here is where the exhibit comes in. Assume that she wants to make her communication that same day. Obviously there are several channels available to her:

▲ Written memo to all five persons
▲ Oral conversation with each person
▲ Telephone conversation with each person
▲ Small-group meeting with all five persons

She has wisely chosen to consider her choice of channel (or mix of channels, such as telephone calls followed by a memo). Underlying her wisdom is the realization that *the channel employed to send a message can have a great impact on the level of acceptance of the message.*

Notice that most channels are available for what accountants need to do most of the time: communicate with one or a few persons within a time span of a few minutes to a few days. Conversely, no channel is available for most accountants to communicate with many people rapidly. Some large corporations, however, are now purchasing elaborate communications systems to fill the gap. Thus an analyst who wanted to get out a flash report straight from the computer conceivably could press a button and have the report appear on a CRT display screen for proofing. Then another button could be pressed, and the report would travel across telephone lines to printers or to storage at subsidiaries nationwide. The time from report completion to reception would be only a few minutes.

There is a potential problem here. These reports, for all the electronic wizardry going into them, are still written. If we expand the channel availability of written reports to include the lower right portion of Exhibit 1.4, then virtually the whole space is covered. In effect, channel availability becomes biased in favor of writing, and indeed many accountants put pen to paper or finger to button without considering whether writing is the channel they ought to be using. Just because a bridge exists is no compelling reason to cross it. The solution to this bias, needless to say, is also electronic, since teleconferencing as a way of conducting electronic face-to-face conversations, group interactions, and oral reports has already arrived. But it too has its problems, particularly since it gives the benefit of immediate feedback (like face-to-face conversation) at the high cost of lost intimacy and easy informality.

Let us return to the decision facing the wise accountant whom we encountered above. She must decide which of four channels to use to make her communication about the need for more bank loans. To help her, we have suggested several criteria that can apply in choosing a channel (see Exhibit 1.5).

Exhibit 1.5 **CRITERIA FOR CHOOSING A COMMUNICATIONS CHANNEL**

▲ Need for an exact record

▲ Need for an immediate response

▲ Need for communication to appear formal

▲ Reader/listener's need to remember the communication

▲ Need of message sender to present an organized and thorough image

▲ Need to communicate with a large number of people all at the same time

▲ Need to communicate with a large number of people fast

▲ Need to show friendliness, empathy, or other feelings

▲ Perceived reader/listener's difficulty in understanding quantitative, highly technical, or otherwise difficult information

▲ Perceived ease of getting reader/listeners to accept the information

▲ Need to support message statements with data and evidence

▲ Need to communicate several messages at the same time

▲ Need to qualify statements to avoid misinterpretation

▲ Need to communicate at low monetary cost

The criteria that seem to apply to her deciding are these:

▲ Need for a record

▲ Need for some formality

▲ Prevalence of quantitative information

▲ Need for reader/listeners to remember

▲ Need to support statements

Given these criteria, which of the available channels should the accountant choose? The choice is certainly not clear-cut, but the needs for a record, for formality, for supporting evidence, and for aids to comprehension because of the difficult quantitative nature of the data seem to require a written memo. To get the receivers to keep in mind the message she sends, the accountant might also want to convene a short meeting after sending the memo. At the meeting she could stress the importance of her findings in their deliberations concerning financial planning for the next year. Through her careful decision about the communications channel, then, the accountant probably has increased her chances of getting her message across and of having it be influential (in comparison with her chances if she had simply grabbed at the closest available channel—the telephone).

BEING READER/LISTENER ORIENTED

As we noted earlier, the first goal of an accountant ought to be the satisfaction of reader/listener needs. Thus an accounting communication must accomplish three tasks:

▲ It must get the attention of the reader/listeners.

▲ It must get them to understand the message in the way intended by the accountant.

▲ It must get them to accept the message as informative, suggestive, persuasive, friendly, or whatever is intended.

Getting attention means getting reader/listeners to make the effort to process the information and to store it in memory. Getting comprehension means getting them to establish the meaning of message chunks and to fit the message chunks together in a coherent whole. And getting acceptance means getting them to acknowledge the message as satisfying their needs (1) for information to reduce uncertainty, (2) for suggestions (stated or implied) concerning future judgments and actions, (3) for direction in terms of orders or influential persuasions, or (4) for maintenance of communication channels or personal relationships.

Being reader/listener oriented is something on which accountants have not generally concentrated. It is a focus that is time-consuming and for which they are untrained. To illustrate this point, consider the "Case of the Japanese Bookkeeper" in Exhibit 1.6.

In a slightly altered form, the incident in the exhibit really happened. Why did it happen? What could have been done to prevent the unpleasant result? To begin with, the accountant did not communicate the right message. From his point of view the message was designed to recommend a helpful action regarding a client. If he were oriented to his reader, the senior partner, however, he would have designed his message to reaffirm the policy and to persuade the partner to accept a minor change this one time. Essentially, then, a persuasive memo was called for, but he supplied a simple recommendation memo instead. The memo was then understood by the senior to imply an abandonment of the policy—not what was intended.

One might object that the basic policy was strongly reaffirmed at the end of the memo. Nevertheless, research has shown that *the first information attended to in a message tends to get remembered and is more influential than is information provided in the message's middle or its end.* Thus for all practical purposes, the "top" of the memo signals the message, no matter what is at the bottom.

To avoid the misunderstanding and consequent failure of the senior partner to accept the message, the accountant could have chosen to communicate initially through a face-to-face channel. This channel allows a message sender's persuasive arguments to have greater impact than does a written

Exhibit 1.6 **CASE OF THE JAPANESE BOOKKEEPER**

The head of auditing in a public accounting firm was approached by a Japanese client who asked for the firm's help in setting up the bookkeeping of the Japanese company's New York office. The auditor realized that his firm's policies specifically stated that the firm would avoid performing bookkeeping services, but in this special case of a foreign client's need, he decided to recommend that the firm make an exception. The memo he wrote to the senior partners requesting approval is outlined as follows:

Introduction:	A. Client's problem and need.
	B. Opportunity to offer the service.
Recommendation:	We should help out our client.
Discussion:	A. Our current policy.
	B. Why we should make an exception in this case.
	C. Other cases in which we may want to make exceptions.
	D. Strong reaffirmation of the basic policy.

Within an hour after sending the memo, the auditor received a telephone call from the partner who had recommended the original policy. He was furious that the policy was now to be abandoned.

The auditor was bewildered. He tried to point out that the memo strongly reaffirmed the policy. But before he could do so, the partner had hung up.

channel. Moreover, in a follow-up memo he could have focused on the policy, its importance, and a minor exception to it instead of the needs of the Japanese, the importance of helping them, and the exception to the policy.

A speaker/writer must always first ask, "What do the reader/listeners need to receive?" rather than "What do I need to communicate?" Look at how each of these approaches leads to messages with different foci:

	"What do I need to communicate?"	"What do the reader/listeners need to receive?"
A Request	I want action to be taken. I will state my request clearly and briefly.	They need background, details, and some discussion so that they can fit the request into the framework of their experience and their goals.
A Directive	I want swift compliance. I will state my directive as a concrete "You will" order.	They need a discussion of procedures to use and to avoid, as well as a time frame and perhaps a sense of the costs and benefits of compliance.

Clearly the decision of accounting communicators as to whether or not to be reader/listener oriented is an important one. Indeed, it should be a conscious commitment. If it is not a deliberate decision, then we can predict that the implied decision will always require being self-oriented. While there is nothing wrong with being self-oriented—one does, after all, have to achieve one's communications goals—our point is (and will be in this book) that being reader/listener oriented is the better way to achieve goals. In serving their readers and listeners, accountants serve themselves.

SEEKING FEEDBACK To evaluate the impact of a communication, an accountant seeks feedback, either a response from another person or a collective response from the group or the organization. Feedback can be directed at evaluating performance (a past orientation) or at securing information useful in making decisions about future communications and future actions (Koehler, Anatol, and Applbaum, 1976). The accountant needs to decide which kind of feedback he or she needs. Pitfalls can occur, such as when an accountant who has made an important report on a proposed budget seeks feedback on her performance from her superiors (past-oriented feedback) instead of directions about further changes in the proposal (future-oriented feedback).

By the same token, the accountant who provides first-rate tax information to a client in a haphazard, garbled format may find that (after the client untangles the gobbledygook) he eventually receives excellent feedback about how to prepare the client's future taxes (future-oriented feedback)—but also that he is out of a job for next time. In this case he should have sought past-oriented feedback as he went along instead of seeking "How can I do it better next time" feedback at the end. "How am I doing?" is here a better question than "What do I do next?"

The best feedback occurs under conditions where mutual trust prevails. Thus accountants need to work to build up the kinds of interpersonal relations that foster trust. With trust comes information that reduces uncertainty about past performance and about future actions that are needed.

READER/LISTENER COMMUNICATION BARRIERS If an accounting communication is effective, it will result in one or both of the following:

▲   A confirmation of the reader/listener's perceptions, beliefs, feelings, knowledge, or behavior;

▲   A change in the nature or level of a reader/listener's perceptions, beliefs, feelings, knowledge, or behavior.

Many accountants routinely confirm what their clients already know. This kind of communicating is more important than it sounds. In common parlance it amounts to "hand-holding" or "stroking." Clients often require such messages, since they provide support for positions taken or for procedures under way. Most accountants, however, earn their keep by communicating to change their readers or listeners in one way or another. These changes can involve changes in the way clients or superiors see the financial world about them (perceptions), the inferences they make about what they see (beliefs), the attitudes and opinions they derive from their inferences (feelings), the additions they make to their storage of information (knowledge), and the financial decisions they make and implement (behavior).

In achieving the confirmations or changes he seeks, an accountant will find that his reader/listeners are not as cooperative as he would wish. They don't pay attention to what he says; or if they do, they misunderstand him; and if they understand him, they may not believe him; and if they believe him, they still may not use their newly gained information appropriately. These problems in attention, understanding, belief, and application add up to communications barriers of formidable proportions. In this section we discuss several of these barriers and will return to the discussion in the next chapter.

Leveling

When Captain James Cook became the first white man to visit Australia, he found to his amazement that the aborigines at first continued to go about their business as if he were not there. His words and actions were ignored. After a few days, the native people soon learned that the visitors were men like themselves, and communications began. This astonishing incident is an extreme example of what is called leveling, the refusal of reader/listeners to attend to messages or parts of messages that are incompatible with their perceptions, feelings, beliefs, or knowledge.

Many accountants could probably recount incidents of their encounters with English-speaking equivalents of Cook's aborigines. For example, an auditor asks a client for information on EDP data collection, data validation, and batch file updating procedures. The client supplies information only on data collection and batch file updating—nothing is said about data validation. The client has engaged in leveling: he has no data validation procedure and has never considered the subject. Thus he simply does not attend to that part of the accountant's request.

The antidote to leveling—or, to mix metaphors, the way to overcome the barrier—is to learn what the client knows and believes before making complex requests or statements. The auditor could have sat down with the client and discussed EDP activities first and then described data validation techniques before making her request. Then she would have been told of the lack of such a procedure. This response is much better feedback for the accountant than is silence born of leveling.

Sharpening

When reader/listeners magnify part of a message into an importance it does not deserve, they are sharpening.

Example 1

Senior to junior:	"In our new system the variance accounts may or may not be closed at the end of the accounting period."
Senior's meaning:	We'll decide whether to close them or not after more planning.
Junior's sharpening:	I am at liberty to close some variance accounts and to leave others open as I see fit.

Here the junior's desire for freedom of action got the best of her. She magnified the phrase "may or may not" into an importance it did not deserve.

Example 2

Accountant to client in engagement letter:	"We will provide guidance to meet management needs for system documentation."
Accountant's meaning:	We will tell you the general procedures to follow to set up the system documentation.
Client's sharpening:	The accountant will set up the system documentation.

In example 2 the client sharpened part of the message so that the word *guidance* was defined differently by him than it was by the accountant. This situation, when an important word is defined one way by a message sender and another by a receiver without either one realizing it, is a form of sharpening called *bypassing* (Haney, 1979). Bypassing is one of the more dangerous communications problems faced by accountants, and we will return to a discussion of it in Chapter 14.

The way to prevent sharpening is for the accountant to anticipate it. In the first example the senior could have added, "We'll decide later." In the second, the accountant could have added a discussion as to what *guidance* involves.

Assimilation

Assimilation occurs when receivers hear or read a part of a message that was not in the message. Assimilation is not simply sharpening but rather the tacking on of meanings, as in the following example:

Accountant to treasurer:	"If we don't increase cash flow next month to $500,000, we will be in bad shape."
Accountant's meaning:	We will need to seek more bank credit.
Treasurer's assimilation:	We will need to seek more bank credit, but we probably won't be able to get it. Thus we are about to go under.

Once again, the way to prevent assimilation is to anticipate it. The accountant should have added, "By 'bad shape' I mean that we'll need more bank credit, but I think we'll pull through." This sentence would have cut off any opportunity for the treasurer to include in the message received a fear from within himself. Such assimilations are all too common.

Overcoming Reader/Listener Barriers

Get to know clients. Get to know the supervisor. Get to know colleagues. Practice anticipating ways in which they might misinterpret vague words or perhaps add their own fears or desires to messages you have communicated to them. These are the ways in which a reader/listener-oriented accountant communicates effectively to overcome barriers.

ANALYZING AN ACCOUNTING COMMUNICATION

We turn now to a discussion of the ways a communication can be analyzed. The value of understanding how to analyze a communication is that such understanding will enable an accountant to plan a communication so that maximum effectiveness can be achieved, which is to say that the accountant's goals, the reader/listener's needs, and the demands of the situation are met as much as possible.

Criteria for Analyzing a Communication

A communication can be categorized in terms of five criteria:

▲ *Specificity of intent*—The degree to which the communication is planned. A planned communication will be receiver oriented and will embody clearly defined sender goals. An unplanned communication will usually be sender oriented and will embody no thought-out sender goals. Most conversation, for example, is unplanned.

▲ *Reality*—The degree to which the message reflects psychological or physical reality.

▲ *Authenticity*—The degree to which the communication transmits signs or cues that the receiver can identify as dealing with reality as he knows it. A communication can represent reality but lack authenticity if the reader/listener doesn't sense the reality. By the same token, an authentic communication still may not deal with reality; such a message, if intended to be authentic but unreal, is a lie.

▲ *Ambiguity*—The degree to which the message is open to different interpretations by the receiver.

▲ *Congruency*—The degree to which the message is relevant to the needs, values, and desires of the receiver.

The perfect communication is a planned, unambiguous, authentic representation of reality that is congruent with the receiver's needs. Unfortunately, such a communication is exceedingly rare in accounting. Consider the following problems:

Reality versus Congruency

Problem.   A communication that represents reality may be incongruent with the receiver's values or needs. Thus a report showing that a control system is seriously flawed may not be congruent with the beliefs of the manager who developed it (and who receives the report).

Partial Solution.   Increase specificity of intent so that the arguments are well delivered. Also increase authenticity through use of quotes from experts or from colleagues trusted by the manager.

Ambiguity versus Authenticity

Problem.   A simple, unambiguous, but hasty memo to a production manager that the unit cost of a product this quarter is 30 percent higher than last quarter may be labeled as unclear because it is not authentic—in that the hasty-memo format does not look like the format for most cost accounting communications. Since it doesn't look right, it is perceived to contain doubtful or unclear information.

Partial Solution.   Increase congruency by making the argument that the manager has much to gain and nothing to lose if she assumes that there is some merit to the message. Also show that the costs to the manager of rejecting the message outweigh the benefits.

Authenticity versus Reality

Problem.   The same information as above is presented to the production manager in a report format identical to those routinely sent every quarter.

The important information on unit cost for the product in question is buried within a mass of statistical data on other product costs. The message is authentic in that it will be recognized by the manager as dealing with reality; but in fact the message will lack a degree of reality because a sense of the importance of the finding will not be communicated. To gain authenticity, the accountant gave up much reality—and an unintended deception will occur.

Partial Solution. Reduce ambiguity by revealing the unit cost data at the top of the report, where important data is usually perceived by readers to be important, under a special heading labeled "Important Finding." The reader will be compelled to interpret the data as important. (The solution is partial, however, because if the practice of using such a heading is followed *every* time the accountant wants the manager to sense the importance of something, the manager will soon accept the information under "Important Finding" as simply more routine data.)

Ambiguity versus Specificity of Intent

Problem. A thoroughly planned analysis of wage rates contains many conclusions and recommendations that cover the whole wage structure of the organization. However, the involved analysis and complex set of conclusions open the report up to different overall interpretations as to what must be done, what can be done, or what can be put off. The high specificity of intent led to ambiguity.

Partial Solution. Increase authenticity by adding a discussion of the feasibilities involved in the recommended changes.

Congruency versus Authenticity

Problem. The same information about wage rates is developed in a series of studies. As each study of an element of the wage structure is finished, the accountant sends it off to senior management because he feels that such action is congruent with their need to know important information as soon as possible. However, senior management, which is used to receiving highly controlled information flows in recognizable formats at predictable times, will be unable to see the importance of the accountant's information and will thus label it as lacking authenticity.

Partial Solution. Increase specificity of intent by planning to prepare management to receive information in a form with which it is not familiar. A series of telephone calls prior to sending the first report might help, as would the cultivation of a senior mentor who could act as a legitimizing agent for the reports.

In sum, reality can conflict with congruency and authenticity; ambiguity can conflict with authenticity, specificity of intent, and congruency; and so on. These clashes make communications less than ideally effective. Indeed the effort to make a perfect accounting communication is probably doomed.

The Maximizing Process

The real focus of accountants should be to maximize the effectiveness of their communications rather than to create perfect messages. The maximizing process involves, first, the analysis of a communication one intends to make in terms of the five criteria noted earlier. Second, the potential conflicts must be listed. Third, partial solutions must be developed, usually by increasing one's effort to improve the adherence to a nonconflicting criterion. As we saw above, the problems caused by trying to adhere to the demands of two conflicting criteria could be partially resolved by redirecting attention to another criterion. Finally, the accountant should consult Accounting Communications Checkoff 1.1 during the maximizing process.

Checkoff 1.1 **ACCOUNTING COMMUNICATIONS: WHAT HAPPENS WHEN ACCOUNTANTS COMMUNICATE**

PLANNING EFFECTIVE COMMUNICATIONS	YES	NO
1. Have I avoided overplanning so that the message doesn't contain too much material?	____	____
2. Have I avoided underplanning so that the message isn't solely oriented to my own needs?	____	____
3. Does the information of the message parallel the existing beliefs of the reader/listener?	____	____
4. Have I avoided making the communication too inconsistent with past communications? Is it predictable in its form?	____	____
5. Have I avoided letting the form and structure of the communication mask important contents (e.g., are trivial recommendations based on my opinions in a separate part of the communication from important recommendations based on observations)?	____	____
6. Is the message unambiguous?	____	____
7. Does the communication meet the reader/listener's goals?	____	____

How Financial Decisionmakers Process

chapter 2 **Accounting Information**

In the first chapter we described the communications goals of the accountant and stressed that the best way to accomplish these goals is to be reader/listener oriented. In the present chapter we describe the ways in which decisionmakers receive and process financial information. Our aim is twofold: (1) to increase the accountant's understanding of what being reader/listener oriented involves and (2) to identify perception problems that can bias the responses of decisionmakers to the information that accountants supply them. As we will see, accountants can engage in a number of communications activities to head off faulty perceptions of and responses to financial communication.

FINANCIAL INFORMATION-PROCESSING BEHAVIOR

One thing not discussed in this chapter is persuasion, which is the communicating of arguments and reasons why decisionmakers should believe or do something that accountants want them to do or believe. Rather our concern here is with getting decisionmakers to process information adequately so that the accountant's message, be it persuasion or whatever, is received as intended (Chapter 19 discusses persuasion). The plain truth is that most people do not process information very well and, worse yet, many accountants tend to assume that they do. Indeed some accountants appear to communicate as if they were addressing some sort of ideal reader or listener who can process and respond to communications of financial information in a rational, analytical way. Luckily, many message receivers will behave in this way. Unfortunately, many will not.

Exhibit 2.1 drives home the point that the receivers of accounting messages are too varied in the way they process information to allow for the creation of an ideal receiver. Notice that we are not talking about the needs or motivations of decisionmakers. Every accountant knows that decisionmakers with different needs will respond differently to messages. What we are emphasizing is that even a group of decisionmakers *with the same needs* could process the same information differently and arrive at different responses and decisions.

Look at the axis marked "External Financial Information." Assume that some kind or amount of information from among a whole range of financial information along the axis has been communicated to five decisionmakers, all with the same needs and desires. Further assume that some of the message

Exhibit 2.1 **POTENTIAL RESPONSES TO A COMMUNICATION IN TERMS OF EXTERNAL FINANCIAL INFORMATION PROVIDED AND INTERNAL PROCESSING METHOD EMPLOYED BY AN INDIVIDUAL DECISIONMAKER**

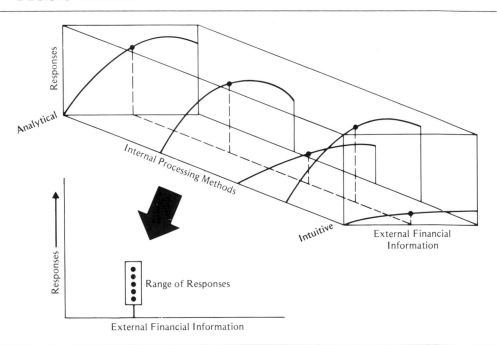

receivers process the information in an analytical manner and respond as the accountant expects. The rest, however, process in what could be called an intuitive or less analytical manner, and their responses are not predicted. In fact, when the accountant lists the responses to his message (say a corporate internal audit report sent to a board of directors presumed to have a uniform need to maximize the effectiveness and efficiency of internal controls), he finds that five separate responses have occurred—only one of which, the response based on thoroughgoing analytical processing of the information, was he able to predict. By assuming an ideal reader, he failed to anticipate the consequences of his communications. Ironically, the accountant's assumption of an ideal analytical reader was a failure of analysis on his part.

Model of Internal Processing

The reader/listener-oriented accountant must therefore not only analyze the needs and motivations of decisionmakers prior to communicating with them, but she must also analyze the range of ways decisionmakers might process the information and the range of responses they might make. In particular, she must anticipate the faulty processing in which decisionmakers could engage and must try to communicate so that she influences the message receivers to process financial information in a rational, analytical manner instead of a quasi-rational, intuitive way.

The first step in learning how to influence decisionmakers to process rationally is to learn what the processing of financial information involves. Exhibit 2.2 describes a model of a so-called black box, an internal mechanism within which the complex processing of external information occurs so that

Exhibit 2.2 **MODEL OF A DECISIONMAKER'S INTERNAL PROCESSING OF FINANCIAL INFORMATION**

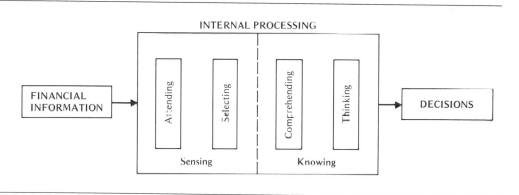

responses and decisions can be made. The box contains apparatus for *sensing information,* which requires attending and selecting activities, and for *knowing about information,* which requires comprehending and thinking activities.

Sensing

Decisionmakers are the depository for immense quantities of marketing, financial, production, economic, organizational, and personal information. They cannot possibly handle all of it. Here is where the sensing part of their minds comes in. It tells decisionmakers (1) how much processing effort to devote to a given body of information (attending) and (2) how much of that information, if any, to transfer from short-term memory into long-term memory for further processing. A large body of research suggests that information attended to in short-term memory will be completely forgotten if it isn't transferred. Indeed, this phenomenon explains the behavior of Captain Cook's aborigines (and their financial equivalents in the United States and Great Britain) that was discussed in Chapter 1. They attended to the information—since it was right before their eyes, they had no choice—but they could not select it. The result was that Captain Cook, for a short time at least, simply did not exist for them.

Since the aborigines can be assumed to have been (and still are for all we know) reasonably intelligent human beings competent to adapt to their changing environment, the pressure of Captain Cook's overwhelming presence eventually compelled the natives to acknowledge his presence intelligently and to begin to understand what they were seeing, to think about it, and to make some decisions. Like their modern financial counterparts facing up to strange data, they probably decided to respond in a number of ways: flight, fight, curious investigation, confusion, and so on—depending on how each one of them processed the information. Our point here is, however, that *sensing* activities have a great deal to do with whether or not information will be responded to; *knowing* activities will determine the nature of the response.

Knowing

Once financial information is attended to and selected by a decisionmaker, it goes into long-term memory, where it is understood (comprehending) and evaluated (thinking). *Comprehension* is thought to involve a matching process, in which the financial information is matched against information, beliefs, attitudes, and the like, already in memory. Meaning, then, is determined largely by what the decisionmaker knows. This point is important and will be repeated often in this book. Accountants do not determine the meaning of their messages; decisionmakers do. The accountant's task is to help the decisionmaker arrive at a meaning that parallels the accountant's meaning. So accountants need to know what clients, superiors, and other receivers of their messages know. The less they know about the people with whom they communicate, the harder it is for them to help decisionmakers arrive at the intended meaning of messages. In fact, the less accountants know about the knowledge of their message receivers, the more likely they are to assume an ideal reader of the kind described above and to risk unforeseen responses to their financial data.

Thinking, on the other hand, is a process of assessing the significance of data and determining the reasonableness of the assertions made or implied. The information is labeled "accepted" or "rejected" or is assigned some kind of uncertainty value in between. A response is made and stored in memory to aid future processing. Some kind of overt, measurable behavior, such as a feedback communication or a decision act, may or may not occur.

Let us assume that a response is communicated and a decision made that parallels the reasonable actions implied or stated in the accountant's original message. Look at the four barriers the accountant had to hurdle in getting his message accepted:

1.   First he had to get the decisionmaker to pay attention to his data.
2.   Next he had to get her to select the data for further processing.
3.   Then he had to present the data in such a way that it could be matched against the decisionmaker's knowledge so that comprehension could occur without too much effort.
4.   Finally he had to make assertions in such a way that the decisionmaker would find them reasonable and significant and therefore useful in making decisions.

Many accountants are not reader/listener oriented, in the sense that they concentrate on coping with barrier 4 and devote almost no attention to barriers 1, 2, and 3.

Analytical versus Intuitive Processing

The box in Exhibit 2.2 contains no arrows showing the direction of processing within the mind. In fact, the mind can process information in many ways, ranging from analytical to intuitive (see Exhibit 2.1). In the section above we discussed the processing as if it were analytical, with information being sensed and then developed into knowledge by being matched against what the person already knows. The process is logical in that the new financial information is a premise tested by the mind's experience (such as experience of past financial information) so that a conclusion can be reached.

However, as Exhibit 2.3 makes clear, the mind of a financial decisionmaker need not process information analytically and logically. The mind can

Exhibit 2.3　**MODEL OF A DECISIONMAKER'S DUAL SYSTEM FOR PROCESSING FINANCIAL INFORMATION**

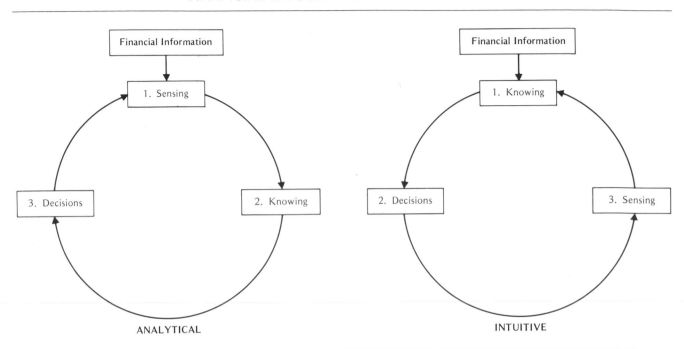

employ a whole range of quasi-rational "rules of thumb" to bypass arduous and time-consuming analysis. These short-cut rules are usually quite helpful to busy clients and managers; but as we will see below, they can at times lead people astray into faulty interpretation. Every accountant who has ever thought, "How could they ever conclude *that* from *that?*" will understand this problem. It is the problem of intuitive processing.

In contrast to the analytical model, the intuitive model of the processing system in Exhibit 2.3 shows financial information not being attended to and selected (sensing) in the first step; in fact, sensing is the last step. We can understand the meaning of this model if we begin with decisions. The model shows financial decisions as the result of what the mind already knows. What the mind knows in intuitive processing are rules of thumb. One such rule, which we discuss below, is "The long run will look like the short run." If this rule is "known" to the decisionmaker and is used to guide decisions, then the new financial information coming in is not as important as the rule already known for arriving at decisions. This is why we have put knowing at step 1 and decisions next.

There is, however, more to say about why sensing is put at step 3. When decisionmakers process analytically, they base their financial decisions on what they read, see, and hear. But if they switch to an intuitive process, then their past decisions will tend to govern what they read, see, and hear. Their sensing will simply be an act to confirm past decisions rather than to determine future decisions. Accountants who communicate to individuals processing information in this way will find that their messages are being used not to help carry out the firm's goals but rather to legitimize the status quo.

Assume, for example, that a manufacturer of diesel engines has been purchasing pistons from a supplier. After some analysis, she decides that she can manufacture the part herself at a lower cost than she is paying for them. She switches to piston production. After three months the accountant makes a report on unit production costs, which he finds are higher than the supplier's price. The manufacturer refuses to accept the report until the allocated overhead costs are adjusted downward. The accountant complies, although he views the new allocation basis as somewhat unconventional. A new report is issued, showing that piston production costs are lower than the supplier's price. In this example the manufacturer sought data to confirm what she had already decided rather than to process the information so that she could make new decisions.

In sum, then, the benefits of an intuitive mode of processing information can sometimes involve a reduction of time-consuming information-attending and selecting efforts as decisions become based on in-place knowledge. If such benefits did not often exist, financial decisionmakers would not process intuitively. The costs of such processing, however, can involve a redirection of focus on the past rather than on the future—a potentially dangerous situation. The accountant communicating financial information to an intuitive message processor must deal with a reality-versus-authenticity conflict of the kind described in Chapter 1.

FINANCIAL INFORMATION-PROCESSING SHORT CUTS

Accountants usually communicate as if the receivers of financial information will process it analytically. While there is nothing wrong with this approach— many pronouncements of the AICPA, FASB, and others, seem to suggest such a communications process—the reality of the financial world is that financial managers must often resort to short-cut, quasi-rational, nonanalytical, rule-of-thumb processing if they are to get any decisions made at all.

Intuitive Processing Rules

There simply is not enough time in the day for rigorous analysis of financial information, involving careful attending and selection followed by a determined effort to fully comprehend and a thoroughly logical evaluation of the data before a conclusion is reached and a decision made. Instead, message receivers must sometimes resort to the use of intuitive knowledge structures and rules of thumb that quickly guide them in their comprehending and thinking. Recent research has revealed just what some of these rules of thumb are (Tversky and Kahneman, 1974; Nisbett and Ross, 1980):

1. *Descriptive Information Can Take Precedence over Quantitative Information.* If the results of a quantitative financial report are augmented with a verbal description of the results in nonquantitative terms, the description may have the greatest impact on the decisionmaker's forming of conclusions. The reason for this intuitive rule may be that processing of descriptive information requires less attending and selecting effort. Data can be hard on the *eyes*; description isn't. Whatever the case, we should be clear about what we are claiming for the rule. Financial managers and decisionmakers who are processing analytically will not resort to such a simplistic guideline, and even intuitive processors *need* not resort to it. Nevertheless, enough evidence exists for us to assert that message receivers of financial information can and do use such a guideline. Exhibit 2.4 provides an example of descriptive information taking precedence over quantitative information.

Exhibit 2.4 **EXAMPLE OF INTUITIVE PROCESSING RULE 1**

Jane Tomkins was assigned to prepare a projected cash flow analysis for the coming year. In doing the projection, she based her calculations of labor expenses on current wage rates, although she had a feeling that labor would demand and win substantial gains in rates within the next six months. However, since she had no evidence to support her feeling, she did not incorporate expected changes in her work. But she estimated that the cash shortfalls projected and the consequent recommended bank financing had only about a 50–50 chance of being valid. To cover herself, she footnoted the projected labor costs and explained the estimation problem in the footnotes.

When she had finished, she sent the statistical data to her immediate superiors. For senior management she covered the data with a memo in which she described the financial operations for the next year. For the sake of brevity, she omitted from the memo the qualifications expressed in the statistical presentation. Thus her description had a greater air of certainty about it than did the statistical presentation.

Two days later she found herself engaged in conversation with her immediate superior. He expressed reservations about her labor estimate and, like her, saw the financing requirements as having only a 50–50 chance of coming out as projected. That same day, however, she received the following memo from a senior vice president:

> I've read your cash flow projections carefully, particularly your discussion of how hard it is to forecast wage rates. Nevertheless, your projections seem to me to have an 80–20 chance of coming out. We're going to seek credit accordingly. Nice job.

Within a few days she had received similar memos from other senior people.

In the example the accountant's assertive description had taken precedence over her tentative data. The senior people had not ignored the statistical discussion; in fact, they had carefully examined it. Then, being busy men and women, they simply consulted the intuitive rule and put their faith in the descriptive cover memo.

2. *Means Are Often the Preferred Statistic for Making Predictions.* Let us say that an accountant has been asked to calculate quickly the expected percentage of accounts receivable that will be bad debts next year. The accountant looks at the data for the last ten years and draws up the following table:

Year	Bad Debt Accounts as Percent of Total Accounts for Year
1982	4%
1981	6
1980	5
1979	4
1978	1
1977	3
1976	3
1975	4
1974	2
1973	1
Mean	3.3%

When reporting the table to management, the accountant provides a discussion of recent government forecasts that indicate an impending credit crunch and high interest rates. Thus further analyses may be in order and the bad-debt percentage could be as high as 7 percent. The accountant is mildly upset upon finding that management eventually concludes that the bad debt percentage will be about 3.5 percent.

Here management found the mean to be a persuasive influence on its thinking, even though information existed suggesting that a more analytical effort be made to estimate the percentage.

3. *Vivid Data from a Single Case Can Take Precedence over Nonvivid Data from a Large Sample.* Public relations experts have known for decades that a single vivid example can be more influential on decisions than can volumes of statistics. Thus an accountant for a large restaurant calculates cash

disbursements per month for the firm's operations last year. The disbursements (about two million dollars) have been routine and consistent with expectations, with the exception of the food and supplies figure for March, which was exceptionally large. The accountant notes that in March the restaurant prepaid for a $10,000 order of frozen steaks, which, since the meat wholesaler had gone bankrupt, were never delivered. In the rush to maintain steak inventories, the chief steward had been forced to purchase the needed meat at $15,000. Thus $10,000 worth of meat had cost $25,000. The accountant considers cash-disbursing procedures to be operating smoothly, with only the one unpleasant exception. The restaurant owner, however, concludes that disbursing must be better controlled and requires that the chief steward obtain the owner's approval before instituting any purchase order for the accountant.

4. *The Long Run Will Look like the Short Run.* Even in the fast-paced modern era, things don't change as rapidly as certain gurus of the future would have us believe. Thus financial decisionmakers usually exercise intuitive good sense when they conclude that short-run events are a sensible indicator of what the long run will look like. If we can control costs now, we can probably do so in the future. If we have been successfully audited this year, we can expect to be successfully audited next year. Unfortunately, financial reality is not quite so predictable, and often dramatic changes can occur that are totally unforeseen. Sometimes financial communications can signal such changes, but accountants can count on some message receivers ignoring the communication and instead assessing the future in terms of rule 4.

5. *Redundancy Increases Confidence.* Two firms have net incomes for the last six years ranging from "high" to "medium" to "low":

	Firm A	Firm B
Year 1	Medium	Medium
Year 2	Medium	High
Year 3	Medium	Low
Year 4	Medium	High
Year 5	Medium	Low
Year 6	Medium	Medium

If we assume that medium is the midpoint between high and low, which firm will probably have medium profits next year? Actually our level of confidence should be about the same for both firms, since the mean net income is the medium figure for both. In this case the mean is not only the intuitive choice for a processing tool, it is also the best analytical tool available. Yet many, perhaps most, decisionmakers will exhibit more confidence in firm A having medium profits, because the information for it is more redundant and thus assumed to be more reliable.

6. *Extreme Information Inputs May Lead to Expectations of Extreme Outputs.* Sometimes accountants are required to submit overwhelmingly detailed reports to managers and clients, reports that contain more information than can be processed by the decisionmakers. It may be that the message receivers are following an intuitive guideline telling them that extremely large information inputs will lead to extremely large increases in financial performance. Since this result often does occur, decisionmakers are usually acting wisely when they demand ever larger amounts of information from accountants. However, an information-processing rule that the bigger the cause, the bigger the effect is too global to be always valid. Consider, for example, the potential client who receives a 250-page proposal from a Big Eight firm and a 50-page proposal from another, smaller public firm. If he processes the information intuitively following rule 6, he might choose the Big Eight firm because they have supplied him with 200 more pages of detailed proposal. He will expect the work proposed by the Big Eight firm to be four times more likely to be successful. Such reasoning is obviously faulty, but one suspects that some firms do indeed see an occasional potential client who processes information in this way.

Another example: A new firm is having trouble with computer-generated invoices for sales transactions being recorded in the sales journal and the accounts receivable subsidiary ledger. End-of-the-month sales are being recorded during the next month at an unacceptable rate. Thus during the past year an average of 10 percent of the transactions in a month were not being recorded during that month. A consultant from a public accounting firm is hired to report on a procedure for speeding up the recording so that a smaller percentage of total transactions is carried over to the next month. The report is delivered in June, a month when the rate is only 5 percent. The recommended changes are implemented immediately, but the July rate is 8 percent, 3 percent greater than in June. The client is upset with the consultant and says so in a letter sent to the consultant's firm on August 10.

The client is following intuitive processing rule 6: he has received a rapidly generated, large information input; now he expects a large, speedy effect, such as a 1 or 2 percent rate. Although the rate is 2 percent below the mean and gives signs of dropping further, the client chooses to see a failure since the rate went from 5 percent in June to 8 percent in July.

The irony here is that the accountant's success in speedily preparing a long, admirable, information-laden report for the client may have triggered the client to process the information in the same way so that he responded to the report by expecting the rate to drop fast and far. Extreme information inputs triggered the expectation of extreme outputs.

7. *What Gets Mentioned Frequently May Be Deemed to Occur Frequently.* A chief purchasing agent with thirty buyers working for her is notified in a memo that buyer A has exceeded internally developed price estimates on five occasions during the previous month. It so happens, however, that buyer B has also exceeded estimates on five occasions in the month and with equivalent dollar amounts involved. But the chief purchasing agent has, for no particular reason, received the accountant's memo *each time* B exceeded estimates (five memos) in comparison with the one memo for A. The agent intuitively senses that B has a bigger problem than A does, even though they are equal in every way.

8. *Estimates of Financial Risk Depend Largely on the Ease with Which Financial Success or Failure Can Be Described.* Let's assume that a large corporation is preparing pro forma balance sheets for the first five years of a new investment. An accountant is assigned to calculate annual working capital estimates, which are to be used as a measure of the risk of the investment. His report is to include a qualitative discussion of the likelihood and nature of sales-generated cash inflows that will be available to discharge liabilities. Because the economy is currently on an upswing, with consumer spending high and consumer credit rates low, he finds it easy to describe hypothetical situations in which heavy sales will lead to large revenues. Because he has no experience of severe recession and/or the effects of Federal Reserve attempts to cut consumer demand by stimulating high interest rates, he finds it difficult to describe situations in which sales do not respond to the company's best marketing efforts. Nevertheless, he does his best and submits what he considers a balanced assessment to management, which falsely sees forecast events that are easy to describe as more likely to occur than events that are not so easy to describe. Management's estimates of financial risk may turn out to be too low in the light of subsequent developments.

9. *Information Chunks That Occur Together Are Often Seen to Be Related.* Researchers refer to this rule as illusory correlation or false association. Information elements that are processed together tend to be seen as related by intuitive message receivers. Say a cost accountant sends out a monthly report to senior management in which she discusses (1) a minor increase in the allocation of labor-related costs to the basic wage rate, mostly due to increases in social security taxes and (2) important overall increases in unit costs of production. Even though section (2) of the report makes it clear that raw material cost increases are the prime candidate for the cause of unit

cost increases, some managers will intuitively decide that steps to control unit costs will require steps to control labor-related costs (in addition to raw material—related activities). The association these managers see is an illusory one in the sense that the focused-on correlation between labor costs and unit costs is real but trivial, whereas the played-down relationship between raw material costs and unit costs is also real but important.

10. *Starting-Point Information May Be Insufficiently Adjusted.* This rule is employed in several ways by intuitive message receivers. To begin with, financial information in the beginning of a report is likely to be influential, even though it may be strongly qualified within the body of the report. Annual report preparers often show their knowledge of this rule by placing summary data on the first page of the report and highly important qualifying information in the notes on the last page. Beyond single-report data, however, the rule can be employed by people who process information over time. Thus the book value of an asset can stick in a decisionmaker's mind as an important figure long after its significance has diminished. By the same token the initial estimate of expenses in an account's pro forma income statement may be the major determinant of the final estimate by a manager. A low initial estimate might lead to a low final estimate, a high to a high, and so on. All in all, accountants need to exercise great care in choosing what information to present first to clients and managers.

Need for Accountants to Know the Rules

Accountants who are familiar with these ten rules are in a position to exercise great power both for good and for bad results over financial clients and managers to whom they report. Virtually all message receivers process information heard or read intuitively at times, and they will use the rules or variations of them to speed up their sensing and knowing activities. Reputable professionals will manipulate their communications to such people so that the decisionmakers' needs are served—both their need to learn about financial entities and their need to learn rapidly. Exhibit 2.5 summarizes the rules and suggests communicating techniques that respond to the behavior of message receivers who seem to be processing intuitively. There are two caveats worth mentioning:

▲ People probably use different rules at different times to help their intuitive processing. Accountants may have difficulty in deciding which intuitive rule is being employed.

▲ Accountants are never relieved of their professional duty to provide rigorous analyses of financial data. Their use of techniques that respond to anticipated intuitive processing should be an addition to and not a substitute for rational analyses.

The guidelines followed by intuitive message processors apply not only to the receivers of accounting information. Accountants, too, are often put in a position where they must resort to gaining knowledge of financial reality in a less than analytical way. Chapter 12 discusses intuitive processing mainly from the point of view of the accountant being the message receiver. In addition, this chapter develops further strategies that an accountant can follow to influence the message processing of decisionmakers in an appropriate manner.

Exhibit 2.5 COMMUNICATIONS TECHNIQUES FOR RESPONDING TO ANTICIPATED INTUITIVE MESSAGE PROCESSING

INTUITIVE PROCESSING RULES	COMMUNICATIONS TECHNIQUES
1. Descriptive information can take precedence over quantitative information.	Provide cover memos that describe statistical data in words.
2. Means are often the preferred statistic for making predictions.	Provide means only when the mean is the best estimate of future events. If other bases exist for better and different estimates, avoid providing means. Avoid means if a sample size is small.
3. Vivid data from a single case can take precedence over nonvivid data from a large sample.	If data from a single case supports the overall message, emphasize it. If such data contradicts the overall message, omit it or take steps to warn decisionmakers not to be influenced by it.
4. The long run will look like the short run.	Emphasize the value of short-run projections only for the short run. When such data is also a good indicator of the long run, stress its long-run value.
5. Redundancy increases confidence.	To gain the greatest impact, list similar results from different financial analyses in one communication rather than in several.
6. Extreme information inputs may lead to expectations of extreme outputs.	Do not employ long, complex analyses to make minor points; conversely, avoid simple analyses to make important points. Make the input parallel the output.
7. What gets mentioned frequently may be deemed to occur frequently.	Make sure that important points receive more frequent mention than minor points. Make sure that sets of financial data of equal importance are allocated an equal number of communications.
8. Estimates of financial risk depend largely on the ease with which financial success or failure can be described.	Take care to balance qualitative analyses in which successful and unsuccessful financial activities are described. Do not let the nature of the description, rather than the nature of financial reality, determine managerial or client responses.

Exhibit 2.5   *(concluded)*

INTUITIVE PROCESSING RULES	COMMUNICATIONS TECHNIQUES
9. Information chunks that occur together are often seen to be related.	Break up unrelated parts in a report with dividers or different-color pages. In oral communicating interject filler material between parts of the conversation that might be mistakenly related by the listener.
10. Starting-point information may be insufficiently adjusted.	Withhold initial financial estimates from decisionmakers until the probability of their being close to final estimates is high.

Checkoff 2.1 **ACCOUNTING COMMUNICATIONS: HOW DECISIONMAKERS PROCESS ACCOUNTING INFORMATION**

UNDERSTANDING INFORMATION PROCESSING	YES	NO
1. Am I aware that my message receivers, even though they all have similar needs and will receive similar information from me, may process information differently and reach different conclusions or responses?	____	
2. Are my message receivers likely to process the information in a rational, analytical way?		
3. If my message receivers are likely to process intuitively, do I have a sense of the processing rule or rules they might follow?	____	____
4. Do I try to help my message receivers to perceive meaning rather than assume that my meaning will enter their minds fully formed?	____	____
5. Do I try to help my message receivers devote attention to my communication and select for further processing?	____	____
6. Do I try to help my message receivers comprehend and think about my communications content?	____	____

Professional

chapter 3 # Accounting Communications

Who are the readers of and listeners to accountants' communications? To auditors, consultants, and tax accountants, they are clients. To management accountants they are managers. To financial accountants they are managers as well as employees, directors, and owners. External to a company, the readers of and listeners to financial communications are lenders, suppliers, potential lenders and owners, customers, analysts, brokers, underwriters, lawyers, economists, regulators, tax officials, legislators, journalists, union officials, trade association representatives, and researchers. All these people want messages that will help them, in one way or another, (1) make decisions; (2) develop plans; (3) implement controls; (4) document assets, liabilities, revenues, and the like; and (5) evaluate performance.

In this chapter we examine professional accounting communications in detail. First, we discuss the communications task that dominates all tasks: to provide data, information, and knowledge to reduce uncertainty in the minds of decisionmakers (or those planners, controllers, documenters, and evaluators who also must eventually make decisions). Second, we describe the kinds of measures accountants use or ought to use to develop uncertainty-reducing communications. Third, we discuss the detailed communicating of financial, auditing, management, and consulting accountants. Finally, we list a number of communications problems that accountants have identified and with which they must cope.

COMMUNICATIONS AND UNCERTAINTY REDUCTION

Every client wants messages from accountants that result in an increase in hope, a reduction in anxiety, or both. In short, they want financial information to reduce uncertainty. They want the content of the messages to appear in three forms (Bedford and Onsi, 1966):

- ▲ *Data*—Directly observed facts without elaboration, such as a balance sheet or other financial statement;
- ▲ *Information*—Data plus evaluation, analyses, and comment, such as a routine corporate monthly report;
- ▲ *Knowledge*—Accumulated data and information from the past, such as an annual report.

Most accountants develop data and draw from knowledge to present information to their reader/listeners. Thus information is the key content of accounting communications. Data alone is often not assimilable by managers, and knowledge alone may not be useful in making decisions about the future.

Information and Uncertainty

The amount of information decisionmakers need is a function of the amount of uncertainty that plagues them:

Amount of Information Needed $= f$ {Amount of Uncertainty}

In turn the amount of managers' uncertainty is a function of the number of choices available to them:

Amount of Uncertainty $= f$ {Number of Possible Choices}

Thus the amount of information needed by managers is a function of the number of choices that can be made, the number of options available, the number of potential controls that could be implemented, and so on:

Amount of Information Needed $= f$ {Number of Possible Choices}

Information that reduces the number of possible choices for decisionmakers also reduces uncertainty. The more choices eliminated, the greater the reduction in uncertainty and the more effective the message. Exhibit 3.1 describes two staff accounting reports, one of which reduces a manager's uncertainty more than the other does.

Report 2 was the most informative, even though report 1 was longer. Thus report length ought not to be a prime consideration in determining how well received an accountant's work will be. Unfortunately, however, here we run up against the intuitive processing rule described in Chapter 2 stating that decisionmakers will often expect important output (information) to be characterized by large input (number of words). The accountant needs to keep this rule in mind when reporting information that reduces uncertainty—but reducing uncertainty is always more important than producing extremely long financial reports.

Uncertainty and Overload

Decisionmakers' preferences and capacity for information often do not coincide (Driver and Mock, 1975). They will demand more information from accountants than they can possibly process. Why does this overload situation occur? Probably because decisionmakers sense that they can somehow reduce financial uncertainty to the barest minimum with ever increasing amounts of financial information. Moreover, they may invoke the intuitive rule that many words mean much information.

Whatever the case, accountants may be required to supply managers and clients with enormous amounts of *data* that will never be examined. The information value of this data is zero, since it cannot reduce uncertainty if it cannot be processed. But the cost of the data remains the same as if it were useful. From a benefits/costs viewpoint, then, overload data is enormously expensive. Accountants have a responsibility to try to cut down on the communicating of such data, but they will inevitably find that managers and clients, seeking to reduce financial uncertainty, will resist their efforts.

Information and Certainty

Exhibit 3.2 describes the attitudes of accountants and decisionmakers toward information under conditions of certainty and uncertainty. Decisionmakers who feel uncertain about what to do or what judgment to make will feel favorable toward accounting information that they believe will reduce uncertainty; but they may view financial data less favorably if they know exactly what must be done or what judgment to make—they may see such data as expensive frills. Accountants, on the other hand, feel more favorable toward

Exhibit 3.1   **EXAMPLE: INFORMING TO REDUCE UNCERTAINTY**

Situation.   Management wants to increase profit and profitability. Seven possible courses of action can be undertaken:

A.   Cut unit costs of current production.
B.   Increase sales of current production.
C.   Develop new products and sell them.
D.   A and C.
E.   A and B.
F.   B and C.
G.   A, B, and C.

Two accountants are assigned to do two reports.

Report 1.   A 5,000-word cost study. Finding: Costs cannot be cut much below current levels. Choices A, D, E, and G are thus eliminated, leaving choices B, C, and F.

Report 2.   A 2,000-word analysis of markets for current and new products. Finding: Increased sales of current products are unlikely, and capital to develop new products is unavailable. Choices B, C, D, E, F, and G are eliminated, leaving choice A to be considered.

Question.   Which report is the most informative?

Answer.   Report 2 is the most informative, since it reduced uncertainty the most by cutting available courses of action to one.

Note.   Both reports together eliminate all possible courses of action. Management can decide to do nothing or to restudy the problem.

---

the information they communicate in situations where certainty prevails (such as data in support of a decision already taken and successfully implemented). There is no risk of being wrong with such data. When great uncertainty exists, however, accountants feel less favorable toward their data, since they often cannot be sure that it will be helpful.

In organizations where great certainty prevails, such as in defense companies with big government contracts in a period of international tension, managers and clients will be much less well-disposed toward accounting information than accountants will be. Accounting information should be kept cost effective. In periods of uncertainty, such as when a company's revenues are threatened by new competition in the marketplace, managers and clients will be more well-disposed toward accounting information than accountants will be. Although accountants may be worried about the usefulness of their data, they should provide all the data sought from them and should warn managers about the high net costs of overload data.

Exhibit 3.2 ATTITUDES OF ACCOUNTANTS AND DECISIONMAKERS DURING FINANCIAL CERTAINTY AND UNCERTAINTY

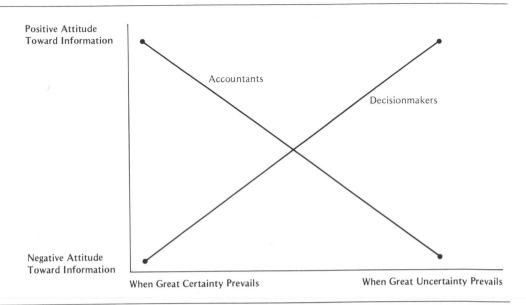

THE ISSUE OF FINANCIAL MEASUREMENT

In mathematics, when there is a one-to-one correspondence between two sets of symbols (such as numbers and letters), so that manipulation of one set corresponds to and thus reveals meaning about the other set, an *isomorphism* exists. This awkward word describes what accountants try to do when they manipulate financial numbers to reveal meaning about financial reality. Financial measurement and its interpretation constitute the isomorphic process of accounting.

The development of this process over the past few hundred years can justly be called one of the glories of Western culture, but it is nevertheless a flawed glory. Financial measures do not always exhibit a one-to-one correspondence to financial reality. The isomorphism—the mapping, as it were—is not and can never be perfect. This imperfection has a great impact on the way accountants communicate and on what they communicate.

Financial Measures: Purpose and Types

The purpose of a financial measure is to aid rational financial decision making regarding (1) evaluations of what has occurred financially, (2) judgments of what is occurring, and (3) forecasts of what will occur. The use of measures

Exhibit 3.3 **FINANCIAL-INFORMATION/FINANCIAL-REALITY ISOMORPHISM: NET INCOME EXAMPLE**

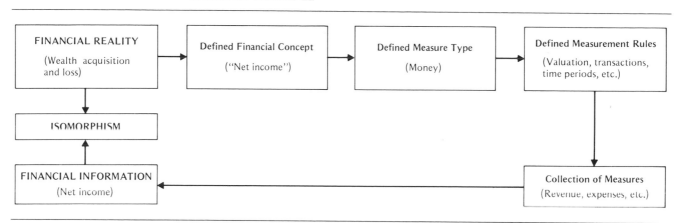

must be purposeful in that one seeks to affect future behavior—but not in any predetermined way. The choice of a financial measure of performance, for example, such as return on investment, sales growth, or ratio of profit to sales, should be made not to support an accountant's feeling, attitude, or opinion but rather to facilitate some financial manager's or client's decision-making process.

Some of the types of financial measures employed are:

▲ Quantifiable equivalent values of economic exchange—money;

▲ Quantifiable real values of economic exchange, such as people, units, or buildings;

▲ Nonquantifiable descriptions, statements, assertions, inferences, or explanations.

Although numbers usually appear as a more exact isomorphism in financial communications than words, both sets of measures are in fact only rough approximations of financial reality. They take the form of estimates, classifications, assigned values, allocated values, and so on, which in turn are generated in accord with certain professional rules, conventions, definitions of concepts, and habits. Let's look at Exhibit 3.3 for an example of the measurement process.

Measuring Net Income

Exhibit 3.3 describes the process by which accountants create an isomorphism between the financial reality of wealth acquisition and loss and the financial information known as net income. The reality and the measure, because of the imperfect mapping process, are not the same thing. If we defined different measurement rules for, say, depreciating assets, stating cash flows at a present value, or valuing inventory, we would get different measures of net income. We could not say which measure *exactly* corresponds to the reality because we could not determine which combination of rules and measuring procedures would be required to derive an ideal measure. Accountants are thus compelled to do the best estimating of which they are capable and to communicate the results to decisionmakers. But what should be the contents of such a communication?

Net income and similar financial information can be communicated in the following ways:

▲ As a single-value measure—the current approach;

▲ As a range between the highest and the lowest estimates;

▲ As a series of measures, with each measure described in terms of the measurement rules and assumptions on which it was based (Chen and Summers, 1977).

Virtually all modern financial communications provide single-value measures that are judged by the accountant to best represent financial reality. These figures are simple and easy to comprehend, but they have the disadvantage of appearing as more exact representations than they in fact are. They give reader/listeners the sense that they can be more certain than they have a right to be.

To counter the problems of single-value measures, current financial communications often present high-low estimates or, as is the case with net income in annual reports, several measures with an explanation for each. Thus along with conventional net income is presented inflation-adjusted net income figures based on both book and replacement values of certain assets. The preparation and communication of other kinds of financial data in the form of ranges and multiple measures will undoubtedly increase in coming years. As it does, accountants will be required to spend more effort explaining procedures for developing the financial measures they communicate.

Measuring and Evaluating

With the measures accountants provide them, financial decisionmakers derive judgments, preferences, attitudes, choices, and decisions. In essence they make evaluations. To help them evaluate, they require accountants to provide:

▲ Comparison data,

▲ Standards data,

▲ Required levels or conditions data.

Thus evaluation can occur in terms of (1) a comparison of the measures with past measures or with measures from another entity in the present, (2) meeting a standard set by the organization or by some professional or regulatory body, and (3) meeting an ad hoc levels requirement set by the organization. Most accounting communications contain financial measures as well as knowledge of past performance, of other entities' performance, of fixed standards, and of desired levels of performance.

FINANCIAL ACCOUNTING COMMUNICATIONS

Financial accounting generally involves providing useful data and information to present and potential investors, creditors, and others to aid their making of investment, credit, and other decisions (Financial Accounting Standards Board, 1978). The kinds of data, information, and knowledge provided, in the form of both qualitative and quantitative measures, include the following:

▲ Sources, amounts, timing, and uncertainty of the firm's cash inflows and outflows as indicators of liquidity and solvency;

▲ Economic resources of the firm, claims against them, and the effect on resources and claims of transactions, events, and circumstances;

▲ Present performance compared to past performance through measures of earnings and the components of earnings;

▲ Management activities on behalf of the firm.

Useful Information

Useful information should be both relevant and reliable. *Relevant* information (1) helps a decisionmaker assess the probability of some future event related to the attainment of the firm's financial goals and (2) goes on to aid the decisionmaker in reducing the uncertainty associated with the occurrence of some future goal-related event. Relevance depends on the following factors:

▲ Needs of the decisionmaker (the information should be congruent with those needs),

▲ Quality and quantity of past information,

▲ Attending and selecting ability of the decisionmaker,

▲ Comprehending and evaluating ability of the decisionmaker,

▲ Timeliness of the communication,

▲ Consistency of the communication with past communications of similar information,

▲ Comparability of the information with similar information from other firms.

The relevance of a financial accounting communication cannot be evaluated until one knows a good deal about the readers and listeners at whom it is aimed: what they need, what they know, whether they are able to sense the communication input (which may involve how busy they are), and whether they will process it analytically or intuitively. Accountants cannot ignore these kinds of assessments without risking irrelevant and thus useless financial communicating.

A *reliable* financial communication is real and authentic; it gives the reader/listener an accurate and accurate-appearing representation of financial reality that avoids ambiguity. The attainment of reliability in a financial communication depends on three qualities:

▲ *The verifiability of the information*—Would independent measurers using similar rules and standards arrive at the same measures? If a question exists, the accountant should report the results of several measurements with an explanation of each.

▲ *The representationally faithful quality of the information*—Does the information correspond to financial reality and seem to do so to the decisionmaker? If reality cannot be known (e.g., a very uncertain future performance) *or* if the information will not look real to the decisionmaker (because it departs radically from expectations), the accountant can improve the reliability of the information by providing a range of data point estimates with a discussion of how they probably include financial reality within them. After the publication of the famous *FAS 33* regarding financial accounting for inflation, the representational faithfulness of reliable financial information has become a major issue in financial accounting.

▲ *The completeness of the information*—Is the information capable of having a material impact on decision making? If not, it should not be considered reliable.

Material Information

Material financial information is defined as information that affects the judgment of decisionmakers or is significantly likely to affect their judgment. Material information is illustrated by the following examples:

▲ A dramatic increase in inventory value above historical cost
▲ A highly profitable transaction
▲ A readjustment of past reported earnings
▲ A pending SEC investigation
▲ Negotiations to sell significant assets
▲ Accounting changes and error that change net income more than 5–10 percent

Material information is assumed to be both relevant and reliable.

Reliability versus Relevance

Financial communications should be both relevant and reliable, but this is not always possible. For example, to make information as verifiable as possible by other accountants (and thus reliable), practitioners will often present data and information in a conventional but highly complex manner (e.g., a consolidated balance sheet). Such a presentation serves the needs of the profession; but, because of comprehension problems, it may not serve the needs of decision-makers who are not accountants (relevance). Here, then, the striving for reliability in financial communicating leads to a conflict with the goal of relevance.

By the same token a communication that is reliable in the sense of being complete (say a 500-sheet printout) may not be relevant to a decisionmaker who has no time to process it before a decision is due. The decisionmaker may instead process intuitively and depend on one of the rules of thumb discussed in Chapter 2. Thus the financial communication invokes a nonanalytical response. Accountants, as was noted earlier, should try to avoid triggering such responses.

Relevance/Reliability versus Conservatism

In addition to being relevant and reliable, financial communications are usually conservative. The information should, if the accountant has a choice, understate rather than overstate such measures as net income and net assets (*APB Statement 4,* para. 171). Yet such an approach may call into question the relevance or reliability of the information. A better approach is to describe the uncertainty that surrounds information. Rather than understating inventory valuation, for example, a range of values could be presented with the probability of the validity of each measure assigned. The most likely measure would appear in the report, with the description of uncertainty in a note. Far better to describe uncertainty than to adopt a rigidly conservative and unrealistic point of view.

Reliability/Relevance versus Comparability

Financial communications should strive for comparability. In this way information regarding one activity can be evaluated in terms of information regarding another activity. However, the striving for comparability can lead to problems with relevance.

Consider a company in which cost accounting reports are designed to allow comparability of cost-to-volume relationships across product divisions. In most divisions nonvariable costs do not vary at all with volume, and variable costs vary directly and proportionately with volume. The cost reports thus describe variable and nonvariable costs so that costs in divisions are comparable. In one division, however, where indirect labor and clerical costs are high, nonfixed costs vary directly, but less than proportionately, with volume. Yet the striving of management for comparability has led it to require the reporting of these semivariable costs within a variable costs framework.

The benefit of this comparability is that all divisions report estimated costs in the same format—resulting in rapid, easy processing by senior management. The problem is that the cost estimates for the division with the semivariable costs estimates have a greater likelihood of being either too high or too low in terms of financial reality than do the other divisions' estimates. This division's reports will be full of information that is more uncertain and less real (but no less authentic) than the other divisions' reports. In sum, they will be less relevant.

Standardizing reporting practices to ensure comparability can also affect reliability of information. Let's say a company uses current ratios for each of its units as measures of liquidity. Two units may have the same current ratios but in fact differ in liquidity because one unit has a greater proportion of cash in current assets than the other. Here the desire for simple measures allowing comparability leads to the choice of a measure lacking in representational faithfulness to reality and thus lacking reliability.

Comparability is a tool for aiding decisionmakers to evaluate information, but it can have negative effects on the relevance and reliability of information. Any reporting done by accountants should be uniform if possible—over time, such reports foster congruency by living up to reader/listener expectations—but not at the expense of relevance or reliability. A concentration on the presentation of information should never be allowed to damage the isomorphism between financial reality and financial information.

AUDITING COMMUNICATIONS

The bulk of financial communications are written, and indeed the most important audit communications are written. But auditors spend about 80 percent of their time in oral communicating—questioning, probing, and interviewing people to obtain information—and only about 20 percent in writing reports and memos. The following section briefly reviews the oral communications of the auditor (a subject taken up again in Chapter 15) and then concentrates on the forms and contents of written audit communications.

The Audit Communications Process

Auditors collect information (a "getting" process of the kind described in Chapter 1) to enable them to communicate an opinion (a "giving" process) as to whether or not a company's financial statements were prepared in accordance with generally accepted accounting principles (GAAP). All their communications must demonstrate *independence;* that is, they must show "judicial impartiality" (AICPA, 1980). This phrase implies that all their questions asked and discussions held in getting information, as well as their subsequent reports, must show fairness to owners, management, creditors, and other involved parties. This professional standard essentially requires auditors to be reader/listener oriented, in the manner discussed in earlier chapters, while planning the audit work, collecting information, evaluating the information, and compiling working papers (the permanent file of the work done). We will see that the same is true in making reports.

Planning

The auditor's communications in planning the work include the following activities:

▲ Discussing the examination of internal controls with relevant persons in the firm;
▲ Requesting previous reports, files, correspondence, and statements;
▲ Gathering information about current business developments affecting the firm;
▲ Preparing a memo setting forth the audit plan.

Collecting Information

Data is collected from interactions with computers and similar files, but the most important information is derived from oral interviews with the client's employees and from requests made in writing to creditors and customers, among others.

Evaluating Information

In deciding on the extent to which financial procedures and statements are in accord with GAAP, auditors ask the following questions:

▲ How much information do I have?
▲ How did I get it?
▲ Who gave it to me?
▲ Is the information corroborated?
▲ How certain can I be that the information is accurate?
▲ How likely are errors or irregularities?

The answers to these questions will provide the background and support for subsequent opinions and reports.

Compiling Working Papers

Auditors gather information together in files called working papers. These provide a resource for current and future work and act as support material for reports. The files include records of procedures followed, tests performed, information obtained, and conclusions and inferences reached. Specifically, the working papers may involve the following items (Chapter 9 describes specific working-paper memos):

▲ Work programs

▲ Analyses and tests

▲ Memos regarding inventory, accounts receivable, exceptions, weaknesses, irregularities, and the like

▲ Letters of confirmation and representation from persons outside the firm

▲ Abstracts of company documents

▲ Schedules prepared and obtained by the auditor

▲ Check lists

Audit Reports: Primary Communications

When an audit is finished, the audit firm issues a report, called the auditor's standard report or sometimes the short-form report, which is published in the company's annual report. The report is addressed to the board of directors of the company and to the shareholders. Its purposes are (1) to state an opinion as to whether or not the financial statements of the company have been prepared in accord with GAAP and (2) to state the scope of the examination that led to the opinion (see Exhibit 3.4, p. 58).

The opinion can be unqualified, as in the example, or qualified, in which case the phrases "except for" or "subject to" may be included, followed by a description of the qualification and the reasons for noting it. Qualified opinions can result from at least four situations:

▲ Differences of opinion between the client and the auditor regarding the application of GAAP;

▲ Uncertainty that cannot be resolved;

▲ Limitations on the scope of the examination;

▲ Insufficient information.

The long-form report, which will be illustrated in Chapter 11, may take the place of, but usually supplements, the short-form report. In general it covers the following material:

▲   Information on the internal control system of the company and the extent to which current procedures depart from the system;

▲   Information on errors or irregularities;

▲   Recommendations for improving the system of internal controls.

During the examination, an auditor sometimes discovers a material weakness in the firm's internal controls. Either at the time of discovery or at the end of the examination—and either in writing or orally, or both—the auditor will inform senior management as to the nature of the weakness. If the report is in written form, it will sometimes include recommendations for correcting the weakness and perhaps a description of management's response to the recommendation. Section 323 of the *AICPA Professional Standards* describes the material weakness communication in detail.

The primary reports made by auditors deal with internal control issues and whether the controls are such that the financial statements of the firm present fairly the financial position of the company. However, many readers clearly see the reports as evaluations of the financial *position* of the company. A reader/listener-oriented auditor ought to state within a report that the contents represent an evaluation of the company's financial information-gathering and processing activities, not of its wealth-generating abilities.

Auditing Language

The following list defines a number of words that embody important auditing concepts. Auditors must use these terms with care; if they do not, they risk implying opinions and other evaluations that are not intended.

▲   *Accounting change*—A change in an accounting principle (such as the depreciation method), an accounting estimate (such as service life), or a reporting entity (such as a subsidiary).

▲   *Accounting principle*—An accounting rule, standard, policy, convention, guideline, or assumption and the procedure for applying it to measurement. Generally accepted accounting principles are broad guidelines as well as detailed procedures developed by the profession.

▲   *Contingency*—A situation involving uncertainty regarding a future gain or loss. A contingency is often described as either probable, reasonably possible, or remote.

▲   *Error*—Unintentional mistakes, such as might occur in misinterpreting facts or in making a math/clerical error while applying an accounting principle

Exhibit 3.4   **EXAMPLE OF AUDITOR'S STANDARD REPORT**

Opinion.   In our opinion, the accompanying consolidated balance sheet and the related consolidated statements of income and retained earnings and of changes in financial position present fairly the financial position of Ajax Manufacturing Company on September 28, 1982, and September 29, 1981, and the results of their operations and the changes in their financial position for the years then ended, in conformity with generally accepted accounting principles consistently applied.

Scope.   Our examination of these statements was made in accordance with generally accepted auditing standards *and* accordingly included such tests of the accounting records and such auditing procedures as we considered necessary in the circumstances.

▲   *Fairness*—The degree to which the presentation of financial statements is based on GAAP. A fair presentation contains information that is (1) appropriate in the circumstances, (2) informative regarding the application of GAAP, (3) neither too detailed nor too condensed, (4) presented consistently with past presentations, and (5) reasonably adequate.

▲   *Full disclosure*—The providing of information in accord with GAAP and with regulations of government bodies. The goal of full disclosure can conflict with the goal of making decisionmaker-oriented communications when an accountant simply dumps data on a message receiver to comply with a regulation.

▲   *Internal controls*—Methods and measures adopted by an organization to help decisionmakers safeguard assets, check the accuracy and reliability of accounting data and information, promote operational efficiency, and adhere to organizational policies. These controls can be (1) accounting controls or (2) administrative controls.

▲   *Irregularity*—The intentional distortion of financial information.

▲   *Management integrity*—The degree to which management effectively operates internal control procedures and avoids misstatements in financial information.

▲   *Weakness*—Anything that limits the effectiveness of control procedures. A *material* weakness is one that would substantially diminish the fairness of the presentation of financial information. Such a weakness would involve the failure to employ GAAP or the misapplication of GAAP.

Audit Reports, Letters, and Memos: Secondary Communications

At the request of a client or as they deem necessary, auditors may issue other reports in addition to the short- or long-form reports or in place of them when no opinion is to be made.

Internal Control Reports

Internal control reports describe the nature and effectiveness of a client's internal controls. They are used (1) as a basis for determining the future reliability of unaudited financial statements and (2) as evaluations of management performance. The reports are not opinions, but they could lead decisionmakers to treat them as such and thus to put too much reliance on unaudited financial statements. In writing such reports, then, auditors need to state clearly just what the report is and what it is not. Section 640.12 of the *AICPA Professional Standards* provides a model format.

Reviews of Interim Financial Information

Without stating an opinion, an auditor may review interim financial information. These reports may be attached to required SEC filings, added as a note to audited financial statements, or presented as a separate document. The format for the reports is as follows:

1. An introductory statement on the purpose of the review and the need for such reviews (contained in Section 721 of the *Professional Standards*);
2. A description of the information reviewed;
3. A description of the review procedures;
4. A statement that the scope of the work was less than for an audit;
5. Recommendations on material modifications, if any.

Special Purpose Reports

Auditors may do other reports for clients, regulatory agencies, and the Internal Revenue Service. These special purpose reports include (1) reports prepared in accord with accounting principles other than GAAP; (2) reports that focus on only a part of a financial statement, such as a report on royalties applicable to a product; (3) financial forecasts; (4) studies on compliance with contracts; and (5) studies on compliance with regulatory requirements. Section 621 of the *Professional Standards* covers these reports and provides model formats.

Letters

If the company is involved in litigation regarding contingencies that management deems material, the auditor will write to the firm's attorneys requesting, first, information about a possible gain or loss. Specifically, the *lawyer's letter* (Section 337A) will seek a response describing the nature of the case, the

Exhibit 3.5   **NEEDS OF SENDERS AND RECEIVERS OF INTERNAL AUDIT REPORTS**

SENDER/RECEIVER	NEEDS
Concerned manager	Needs to know about *every* deficiency to be reported by auditor in order to prepare a defense. *Past oriented.*
Internal auditor	Needs to stress what should be changed rather than defended. *Future oriented.*
External auditor	Needs details on both deficiencies and suggested changes. *Description oriented.*
Audit committee	Needs brief, nondetailed recommendations on which to base decisions about companywide changes. *Decision oriented.*

progress to date, what management has decided to do about the case, and an estimate of the potential gain or loss, if any. Included with the request will be a description of management's representations concerning the matter. A second request in the letter will be for an assessment as to whether the lawyer's representation matches that of management. Finally, the letter will also request advice concerning the matter of full disclosure in the financial statements.

Other letters that may be sent are those seeking confirmation of receivables, inventories, and the nature of the company's long-term investments.

Last, the auditor may send out *comfort letters* to underwriters or their legal counsel. These are informative letters that give what is called "negative assurance," a statement that nothing came to the auditor's attention that led to a belief that the financial statements were not prepared under GAAP. However, before issuing a negative assurance, Section 630 of the *Professional Standards* recommends that the client, the auditor, and the client's legal counsel confer. This letter may include such things as the following:

▲ A statement regarding the independence of the auditor,

▲ A statement that the financial statements comply with the accounting and auditing requirements of the Securities Act of 1933,

▲ Unaudited financial statements contained in the registration statement,

▲ Any changes in the financial statements since they were last prepared,

▲ Statistical data,

▲ A description of accounting procedures followed.

Memos

When auditors need to employ a specialist, such as an engineer, an actuary, or anyone else possessing a special skill that can be applied in examining financial statements and internal controls, they write a *memo of under-*

standing for all concerned parties and for the working papers. The memo covers (1) the objectives and scope of the specialist's work; (2) the specialist's relationship to the client, if any; (3) the methods and assumptions to be used by the specialist and how they compare with those used in the previous period; (4) the ways in which the specialist's findings will be used by the auditor; and (5) the form and content of the report to be done by the specialist.

Auditors will also write other memos for the working papers, and other letters and reports as necessary. Some of these may take the form (1) of responses to queries from the client or from legal entities or (2) of file data for documentary purposes.

INTERNAL AUDIT REPORTING

Among all accountants, a company's internal auditors have the most difficult communications task. They must analyze the internal controls of a work unit and then inform the concerned manager about problems encountered, make conclusions to the audit committee about control procedures in the whole organization, and alert the external auditors to control areas on which they might focus.

As Exhibit 3.5 notes, the needs of the relevant senders and receivers of the internal control communication can conflict. The manager wants to defend himself; the internal auditor wants change; the external auditor wants depth of detail; and the audit committee wants breadth of focus. Chapter 11 will take up the form and content of internal audit reports. In this section, we want to describe the difficult nature of such report-writing activities and briefly list some techniques with which internal auditors can satisfy their own needs as well as the needs of their message receivers. Internal auditors can do the following:

▲ *Satisfy themselves* by placing recommendations for changes at the top of the report, where they will get maximum attention. The report thus emphasizes change;

▲ *Satisfy the audit committee* by briefly noting how and whether the suggested changes could be implemented companywide;

▲ *Satisfy the concerned manager* by allowing his rebuttals to form a part of the report's discussion section;

▲ *Satisfy the external auditors* by describing the relevant standards and procedures in detail in an appendix.

MANAGEMENT ACCOUNTING COMMUNICATIONS

Management accounting communications help management plan, implement, and monitor decisions. Planning may involve such things as long- and short-run profit projections as well as capital investment planning (Corr, 1977).

Implementing and monitoring activities require reports on how to carry out plans and on whether or not objectives have been met.

Planning, Implementing, and Monitoring Communications

Planning communications from accountants usually take the following forms:

▲ *Summaries* of past performance regarding capital investment, product lines, and so on;

▲ *Analyses* of cost-volume-revenue-profit relationships over time, in comparison with standards or in terms of forecasts;

▲ *Forecasts* of such things as internal rates of return, expected cash flows, asset lives, salvage values of assets, and degrees of uncertainty for some possible future event;

▲ *Evaluations* of financial decision alternatives.

Implementing communications from management accountants are usually concerned with the kinds of financial measures that must be made and the amount of financial information that needs to be collected during the step-by-step implementation process. Of greater importance, however, are the monitoring communications that accountants prepare to inform management about the effect of financial decisions. Specifically, these reports often take the form of *exceptions* to standards, norms, past trends, or similar bases. The goal of exception reporting is to alert management (1) to changes needed in planning or (2) to changes needed in implementing. In the first case, for example, reports of revenue figures for a product that do not meet forecasts would lead to new marketing plans. In the second, reports highlighting the inadequacy of unit cost measures would lead to changes in the way unit costs are measured rather than to changes in management plans for controlling costs.

Content Goals: Understanding and Significance

The content of management accounting communications should be formulated in terms of the criteria described in Chapter 1: specificity of intent, description of financial reality, recognition by the message receiver that the message is authentic (that it does in fact deal with reality), unambiguous interpretation, and congruency with receiver needs and expectations. Moreover, the need to make the message easily comprehended, described in Chapter 2, must also be satisfied. These criteria usually assert themselves in either of two approaches: a concentration on achieving reader/listener understanding or a focus on creating an authentic, significant document (Jordan, 1969). The two approaches can be distinguished as follows:

Focus on Reader/Listener Understanding

Accountant's goal—To achieve easy reader/listener comprehension of the content.

Nature of content—Short sentences; concrete, nontechnical language; concise presentation. Example: a budget memo highlighting major changes in plans.

Focus on Creating a Significant Document

Accountant's goal—To make the content correspond to significant financial reality.

Nature of content—Description of all information collected and all possible significant interpretations and outcomes. Example: a forecast of net income based on historical costs, replacement costs, and CPI-adjusted costs with an explanation of the significance of each.

In terms of the need for reader-oriented accounting proposed in Chapter 1, the focus on gaining understanding is the appropriate one. However, no general can say that in the heat of battle an officer should load his gun with such and such ammunition—the nature of the enemy will determine that. So it is with the content (the ammunition) of management accounting communications. The accountant should always consider a reader-oriented report first, but must choose whatever the situation demands.

Form Goals: Uniformity and Flexibility

The importance of the form of accounting messages was noted in Chapter 1. We will concentrate here on the form of written messages, since they are the most common in management accounting reports. Forms can involve short memos or long reports, depending on the nature of the situation and of the reader. Of crucial importance is consistency of form. The accountant must consider several questions: How consistent should my report formats be? Should they all be uniform and thus predictable, or should they be flexible and thus adaptable to specific situations? The choice depends on the accountant's goal.

Focus on Uniformity of Form

Accountant's goal—to lessen the chances of misinterpretation due to unfamiliarity with the format (a negative focus).

Nature of form—Reports all look alike, so readers can predict what each page will contain; to achieve a middle ground, the report format will be neither too long nor too short.

Focus on Flexibility of Form

Accountant's goal—To increase the chances of correct interpretation by adapting the format to the needs of the readers and of the situation (a positive focus).

Nature of form—Reports all look different: short reports for less important situations; long reports for important situations; short reports for senior management; long, detailed reports for junior management.

The choice of uniformity or flexibility is a difficult one. Both are reader oriented, although one takes a negative and the other a positive approach. In terms of criteria such as specificity of intent, the focus on flexibility is preferred. But if one chooses to emphasize a criterion such as congruency with reader needs and knowledge, then uniformity is preferred. There is no focus on form that is clearly preferable.

Uniting Form and Content in Management Accounting

Exhibit 3.6 describes the types of reports that will result from each combination of form and content foci. The greatest dichotomy is between uniform, understandable reports that a manager can easily process and flexible, significant reports that require much processing effort but cover financial issues in depth. Accountants who send the first kind of reports will create an image of themselves as competent and decision oriented. Those who send the second kind will be viewed as hard working and planning/analysis oriented. Although many modern accountants want to be decision oriented, a substantial number remain committed to accounting as an information-processing planning activity—and thus analytical in our sense here—rather than a decision-making activity. No one can say whether the decision approach or the planning approach is the right one regarding the nature of report form and content. What we can say is that accountants should study the approach they take and be willing to change it if management requests a change. *Business Week* and other magazines are full of stories of accountants who deluge management with long, incomprehensible reports that do not clearly point to a decision. Yet many managers, who do not talk to *Business Week* reporters, want such reports from accountants so that they can do their own decision-making formulations.

One point made in the exhibit needs highlighting. Uniform, significant reports can be the most difficult to understand, often because accountants

Exhibit 3.6 **UNITING FORM AND CONTENT IN MANAGEMENT ACCOUNTING COMMUNICATIONS**

ACCOUNTANT'S GOALS FOR FORM	ACCOUNTANT'S GOALS FOR CONTENT	
	Understanding	Significance
Uniformity	Short reports; all look alike; content easily comprehensible to readers; single topic; emphasis on manager need to process information rapidly.	Can be least comprehensible of all; long reports, always in same format; rigid format will demand little processing effort from managers.
Flexibility	Highly comprehensible reports; may be short or long; varied formats will require extra processing effort from managers.	Long reports; all look different; many topics, all covered in depth; emphasis on thoroughness of analyses and content.

have tried to force information into a rigid, unsuitable format. Yet this rigid format is so predictable for managers that they skim through it easily. While they will not understand some of the report, they will still have no problem zeroing in on the parts that concern them. Such reports are probably the most common of all in companies today, because they require little processing effort but contain much information. They are ugly, but they work, and they work because they hold the middle ground. They aim for complex, in-depth significance, but their uniformity eases the processing burden for managers. Chapter 11 will describe these and the other types of reports in more detail.

COMMUNICATIONS OF MANAGEMENT ADVISORY SERVICES

The consulting arm of professional accounting, called management advisory services, has grown to the point where the AICPA has felt compelled to issue standards for the communications made by a public accountant performing consulting services for a client (AICPA, 1979). These standards cover the contents of memos of understanding with clients, interim reports, and final reports.

Memo of Understanding

The memo of understanding, which can be a letter or a file document, constitutes the agreement between the accountant/consultant and the client. Although it is a contract, it is also a protocol—a guideline that should be referred to as the work progresses. If a deviation from the memo of understanding occurs, a new agreement should be drawn up. This memo should be included behind the title page of the final report. The memo should contain the following:

▲ Objectives of the engagement,

▲ Extent and nature of the work,

▲ Constraints and limits on the work,

▲ Roles and responsibilities of the parties,

▲ Description of the major work tasks,

▲ Time line for the tasks,

▲ Expenses and fees,

▲ Reports to be made.

Interim Report

As the tasks get done, the accountant delivers written or oral progress reports. The AICPA suggests that these reports contain the following:

▲ Findings to date;

▲ Tentative recommendations;

▲ Discussion of tasks done compared with tasks outlined on the memo of understanding;

▲ Problems encountered, if any;

▲ Reassessment of priorities, if needed;

▲ Client decisions that are or may be needed, if any.

Final Report

The final report is usually delivered both in writing and orally. The contents of both reports are similar, but the accountant should never read the written report to the client during the oral presentation. We will discuss oral reporting and its differences from written reporting in Chapter 13. The general contents of both reports in the case of consulting cover these items:

▲ Findings;

▲ Recommendations;

▲ Statement of purpose, objectives, and tasks of the engagement;

▲ Scope of and limits on the work;

▲ Discussion of how the tasks were accomplished;

- ▲ Why alternative findings and recommendations were not accepted;
- ▲ Suggested ways of implementing the report's recommendations;
- ▲ Further work that may be needed.

ACCOUNTING COMMUNICATIONS PROBLEMS

No matter what accounting function is performed—be it tax, management, financial, audit, or consulting accounting—an accountant will meet with a set of communications problems common to the profession. The following discussion of these problems is based on a survey of and follow-up interviews with a number of accountants nationwide.

Finding Common Ground

For a communication to be effective, both sender and receiver must have some common ground (recall again Captain Cook's natives, who did not respond because they had no common ground with the whites). Thus the reader of a financial statement seeks information to aid in planning, implementing, and decision making. The accountant seeks to present financial information in such a way that it can be used for these purposes. Both are decision oriented and on common ground.

But what if the accountant seeks to present a massive amount of data (not information) as evidence of the effort he has made? He is now seeking to communicate an image, to create an impression, rather than to aid decision making. The concerns of the accountant and the manager or client are no longer mutual. They are not on common ground. The client may sense that the message content needed for decision making is harder to comprehend than it should be. Thus the client may resort to quasi-rational rules of thumb, as described in Chapter 2, which do not lead to the best decision.

The lack of common ground, then, can foster less than optimal decision making. To avoid this outcome, accountants need to identify the purposes of their communications and to make sure that they are in common with those of the client.

Making Truth Meaningful

The statements an accountant makes must be *meaningful* and *true,* but these two qualities are not always present together. Consider the following:

> The auditor received written and oral representations from management during the examination that were usually supported by other evidence.

PROFESSIONAL ACCOUNTING COMMUNICATIONS

This statement has meaning and is true. But we can make it meaningful yet untrue by removing the word *usually* from the sentence. Now the statement says that *every* representation was supported by evidence—a claim that most auditors would label as false.

More important, we can by the same token make the statement true but not meaningful:

> The auditor received written representations from management during the examination and oral representations that were usually supported by other evidence.

Here the statement is true enough, but it does not adequately function to make it clear to the reader that written representations also were usually supported by other evidence. The reader cannot tell what *that* refers to—either oral representations alone or both oral and written. Without knowing the referent of *that,* the reader cannot construct a reasonably certain meaning. In this sense the statement is not meaningful.

The distinction between truth and meaning is not an academic one. Some accountants have learned to concentrate only on making true financial statements, statements that correspond to financial reality but may allow for multiple interpretations because of sloppy or illogical writing or speaking. Such persons need to learn that communicating true approximations of reality must be followed by communicating to foster appropriate meanings in the minds of decisionmakers. Put another way, the creation of a good isomorphism may lead to the reality of the communication, but the task of creating authenticity, congruency, and nonambiguity still remains.

Communicating While Disclosing

Often accountants must write and speak with one eye over their shoulder to see if their communication will receive a nod of approval from the SEC, the FASB, the IRS, or some other regulatory or standard-setting body. To put the matter more concretely, they must sometimes, while communicating, anticipate some legal or professional entity's reaction to their message. The needs of their real reader/listeners, their clients and managers, can become dismissed or even forgotten in these situations, and meanings may be unfathomable beneath an ocean of what is called *full disclosure* information—but what can be referred to as "C.Y.A." ("Cover Your A——") information, loophole-plugging information, jargon, and gobbledygook. There is rarely any excuse for placing the demands of a regulation ahead of the legitimate needs of a client for a simple, straightforward communication.

Keeping Informing from Becoming Evaluating

When data is transformed by the accountant, the result is supposed to be information (what is or has been or what might be). Sometimes, the outcome is not information but evaluation (what is supposed to be or what ought to be). Accountants easily slide off from informing into evaluating. Thus they must discipline themselves to avoid evaluating unless asked to do so.

Validating Information Prior to Communicating

How do accountants know the truth of the information they are communicating to clients of one kind or another? If accountants are uncertain of their information's validity, they cannot exhibit professional confidence and strength of assertion in their communications. Some validation strategies, ordered from the most to the least appropriate, are as follows:

- ▲ Comparison of data collected from one source with similar data collected from other sources;
- ▲ Double-checking data collected through formal channels by inquiries made through informal channels;
- ▲ Employing sophisticated interviewing techniques when collecting data from people—for example, requesting the same information in different ways or summarizing interviewees' responses for them to check for misinterpretation;
- ▲ Establishing a climate of trust with information providers and then depending on their integrity;
- ▲ Associating the status or experience of an information provider with information validity—the higher the status, the higher the validity;
- ▲ Adherence to routine—if the information fits in with past experience, it is considered valid.

Certainly the first four validation strategies are appropriate and ought to aid accountants to communicate confidently. The last two, however, while not appropriate, are certainly used. Accountants must learn not to use them.

Evaluating the Communications of Subordinates

Accountants must assimilate vast amounts of data, data often provided to them by subordinates. It is imperative for them to provide useful evaluations to subordinates regarding their communications. This feedback will ensure that future communications are improved to the point where they can be assimilated rapidly and thoroughly. When asked what they tell subordinates and similar data sources to help them communicate better, a number of accountants respond that they say:

▲ Don't confuse me.

▲ Express to me; don't try to impress me.

▲ Don't overload me with details.

▲ Give me something I can understand in *one* reading.

▲ Give me something I can act on.

Checkoff 3.1 **ACCOUNTING COMMUNICATIONS: PROFESSIONAL ACCOUNTING COMMUNICATIONS**

	YES	NO
INFORMATION AND UNCERTAINTY		
1. Have I avoided supplying only data when in fact information was requested?	____	____
2. Have I communicated to reduce uncertainty by reducing the number of financial choices that a decisionmaker must consider?	____	____
3. Have I realized that the quantity of information that I provide is not always positively related to an increase in information and certainty?	____	____
Have I concentrated instead on the quality of my information?	____	____
4. Am I aware that clients will often demand more costly data from me than they can process? Have I educated them regarding their needs?	____	____
5. Do I know that in periods of high financial certainty, managers and clients may demand that my accounting information be cost effective?	____	____
6. Do I know that in periods of high financial uncertainty, managers and clients may be the most well-disposed to my accounting information?	____	____
FINANCIAL MEASUREMENT		
7. Do I understand that financial measures rarely exhibit a perfect correspondence (isomorphism) to financial reality?	____	____
8. Have I chosen to employ certain financial measures because they serve the client's or the manager's needs for aids in decision making?	____	____
9. Have I used nonquantifiable measures when appropriate, such as opinions, assertions, or judgments?	____	____

Checkoff 3.1 *(continued)*

	YES	NO
10. Have I avoided treating quantified measures, which are only approximations of reality, as if they were in fact reality?	___	___
11. Have I evaluated the possibility of communicating a range or a series of financial measures instead of a single-value measure?	___	___
12. Have I educated my clients and managers so that they do not become more certain about the future than they ought to be after receiving a communication of single-valued measures?	___	___

FINANCIAL ACCOUNTING COMMUNICATIONS

13. Have I made my information useful by making it relevant and reliable?	___	___
14. Is my information relevant by being reader/listener oriented, congruent, comprehensible, timely, consistent over time, and comparable?	___	___
15. Is my information reliable by being authentic and unambiguous, verifiable, representationally faithful, and complete?	___	___
16. Do I understand that relevance and reliability criteria are often in conflict?	___	___
17. Have I avoided conservative understating and instead described the likelihood of both high and low financial measures?	___	___
18. In my eagerness to communicate comparable information, have I avoided making its relevance or reliability questionable?	___	___

AUDITING COMMUNICATIONS

19. Do I understand that independence requires a reader-oriented focus?	___	___
20. Have I made it clear to reader/listeners of my opinion and reports that I am evaluating the financial statements of the company and not its financial position?	___	___
21. Have I made it clear when my internal control and other reports are not opinions?	___	___

INTERNAL AUDIT REPORTING

22. Have I communicated to satisfy the needs of managers, the audit committee, and the external auditors?	___	___

MANAGEMENT ACCOUNTING COMMUNICATIONS

23. Do my monitoring communications stress exceptions to routines or standards rather than compliance?	___	___

(continued)

Checkoff 3.1 (*concluded*)

		YES	NO
24.	Is the content of my messages focused, first, on reader/listener understanding and, second, on communicating in-depth financial data?	___	___
25.	Have I decided whether my report formats should all be uniform for the sake of consistency or flexible and thus adaptable to specific situations?	___	___
26.	Have I realized that I create an image of myself as competent if I send reports that are consistent in form and understandable in content?	___	___
27.	Have I realized that I create an image of myself as hard working if I send reports that are flexible in format and highly detailed in content?	___	___

COMMUNICATIONS OF MANAGEMENT ADVISORY SERVICES

		YES	NO
28.	If the nature of the consulting work changes as it progresses, have I drawn up a new memo of understanding for the client?	___	___
29.	Have I avoided reading my final report to the client during my oral report?	___	___

COMMUNICATIONS PROBLEMS COMMON TO ALL ACCOUNTANTS

		YES	NO
30.	Are my purposes in communicating parallel to the receiver's needs?	___	___
31.	Are my communications not only true but also meaningful?	___	___
32.	Have I made full disclosure a secondary rather than a primary goal of my communications?	___	___
33.	Have I avoided evaluating when informing?	___	___
34.	Have I validated the data that makes up the information in my communications?	___	___

chapter 4 Writing to Increase Understanding

We turn now to a discussion of the various written communication activities of the accountant. Writing is certainly the most studied of all accounting communications; indeed, scores of training packages and seminars are offered by national, local, and in-house experts. In this and the next three chapters, we analyze writing skill and describe the writing process.

Exhibit 4.1 sets out the three writing goals of the accountant in any situation—gaining reader understanding, avoiding an unfavorable image, and communicating a favorable image—and suggests the means for achieving them. A chapter is devoted to each goal, and the fourth chapter ties the discussion together. Notice the logical simplicity of the goals. The accountant's first job is to get the reader to pay attention and then to understand the communication. The second goal is to avoid making any writing mistakes that could lead the reader to develop unfavorable feelings about the writer. Finally, the third goal is to employ a style that helps to create favorable feelings about either the accountant or the organization, or both.

The accountant cannot choose to seek only one or two of these goals. However, many young or unsophisticated accountants work only to create understanding and to avoid error by following grammatical rules. They neglect the third goal of creating a favorable image through the

Exhibit 4.1 **WRITING GOALS OF THE ACCOUNTANT**

GOAL	HOW GOAL IS ACHIEVED
To gain reader understanding	▲ By serving the reader's needs so as to get the reader's attention.
	▲ By employing writing techniques that aid perception and comprehension.
To avoid creating an unfavorable self-image	▲ By following the rules of grammar.
	▲ By spelling correctly.
	▲ By employing proper mechanics.
To develop a favorable image of the writer or the organization	▲ By employing an acceptable, pleasing, and reader-oriented writing style.

use of an appropriate style. The results, as often as not, are reports, opinions, and memos that transmit messages adequately but develop credibility inadequately. The problem is this: a reader who has formed only a neutral or no image of the writer will attach less credibility to a piece of information than will a reader who has formed a favorable image. If a communication lacks credibility, it may not be believed. If it is not believed, it is not useful and thus fails as a professional accounting communication.

SERVING READER NEEDS AND INTERESTS

The accountant's first writing task is to reduce to a minimum the effort a reader must make to pay attention to accounting information. Such a reduction involves a shift of focus in which the writer no longer looks inward and asks:

What do I need to say?

Instead the writer looks outward and asks:

What do my readers need to know?

This shift is the fundamental task of the reader-oriented writer.

Consider the assistant to the controller of a large corporation who is preparing a report on the property taxes of the firm. He discovers that assessed valuation has been constant and that rates have risen slowly. Expected changes are minor. This information is really all the controller needs to know; yet the assistant's report describes the valuation model in great detail, offers a long discussion of the relationship of tax rates to expected county budgets, and ends by employing a sophisticated decision model to predict the minor future changes that were a certainty to begin with. Somewhere along the way that assistant undoubtedly answered the question "What do I need to say?" in the following fashion:

> I need to give the controller enough information to demonstrate that I have done a thorough investigation. I need to show her that I can be trusted to handle more complex assignments than this one. I need to validate my image of competence.

The assistant is indeed an admirable young man. He is hard working, he is trustworthy, and he is competent. What's more, he is sophisticated—he knows that he must blow his own horn in one way or another. If he doesn't, who will?

Unfortunately, this admirable, sophisticated fellow is a poor communicator. He is self rather than reader oriented. If he is lucky, the controller will overlook the deluge of impressive data, force herself to pay attention to what she needs to know, sigh, and go on. If he is unlucky, he will be chewed out in no uncertain terms—or, even worse, ignored.

The anecdote of the controller's assistant makes an important point: smart accountants often are not reader oriented for quite good reasons. If they don't impress their bosses with excessively detailed reports, how will they advance their careers? If they don't use obscure accounting jargon, how will they cue people as to their professional status? If they don't surround opinions with a tangled thicket of qualifiers, how will readers learn that they are conservative in their judgments? The sad fact, then, is that career-oriented accountants need not be reader-oriented writers. We can hope that they will realize the *added* career benefits of improved communications, but we must note that many accountants can survive quite nicely without writing to help their readers pay attention and thus understand with the least possible effort.

Saying all this is to admit reality, but it is not to submit to reality. Accountants *must* become reader oriented in their writing. They serve a valuable public function, and their various publics deserve writing that is easy to understand. How then does one write to serve reader needs and to get reader attention? The answer to this question requires the answers to several other questions:

▲ What do expected readers currently know and what do they want to know?
▲ Is what the readers want to know different from what they need to know (as the accountant assesses those needs)?
▲ What is the readers' attitude toward the situation or toward the accountant?
▲ What do the readers expect from the accountant's communication?

We must examine each of these questions in turn, for the answers to them will give accountants the information they need to tailor their messages so that readers are helped as much as possible to pay attention in order to learn what they need to know.

Assessing Reader Knowledge

What do the readers know, or better yet, what do the readers know they know about the subject of the accountant's communication. Many corporate executives are supposed to know what a financial statement of sources and uses of funds contains; but if tortured severely, they would admit that the statement mystifies them. They know they don't know how to interpret it fully. This knowledge constitutes *true knowing* versus *theoretical knowing* (what they are supposed to know). Good accountants assess true knowing and provide explanations and definitions accordingly. They describe background details in some depth to place statistical data within a context, and they provide some indication of what the future seems likely to hold if the data is accurate and predictive.

In supplying needed knowledge, the *desires* of the readers must also be considered. Here we encounter complexity, for some managers and clients will be offended if the accountant's detailed communications imply that the reader's true knowledge is vastly inferior to his or her theoretical knowledge. None of us likes to be told subtly that we don't really know what we are supposed to know. Furthermore, what readers want from accountants may not have much to do with increasing knowledge and reducing uncertainty. In reasonably stable business environments the accountants' reports, opinions, or letters may serve as a kind of ritual affirmation that business life goes on. The reports themselves are what is important, not the information in them. Professional accountants who spend much time on formats, colors, and graphics of reports intuitively realize this noninformational dimension to reporting. They know what their readers want.

Distinguishing Reader Wants from Reader Needs

The really good accounting communicator goes beyond data dumping and format finagling and makes some kind of estimate of differences between what a reader *wants* and what the reader *needs* to know. All clients and managers need information to reduce uncertainty, be it uncertainty about taxes, acquisitions, revenues, or whatever. However, these people are often uncertain about uncertainty. In other words, they sometimes don't know what they need to know, and their wants will not parallel their needs. The job of the accountant here is twofold. The accountant must give the information that satisfies the uncertainty-reducing need of the decisionmaker, but must first *persuade* the reader to want more and perhaps different information in comparison with what was initially desired. This persuasive communication will require giving what has not been asked for and discussing the benefits of the additional information. This process is sometimes described as "giving a little extra." It is not! "Extra" in our terms is absolutely necessary if reader needs are to be served.

Improving Reader Attitudes

Is the reader ready to accept what the accountant has to say? If so, the communication will be an easy one. The information will be received and used to serve needs. But if for some reason the reader is primed to reject the information, the accountant's task becomes more difficult. The causes of the reader's hostility must now be examined and counterarguments devised to neutralize it. Otherwise—although few accountants like to do this sort of thing—the information may not be accepted and reader needs will not be served.

Some of the possible causes for a propensity to reject accounting information may involve situational and personal issues. Take, for example, the case of the manager who must make an important decision regarding the prices to charge for a line of products in a bad economic environment. The manager wants to price on the basis of marginal cost, letting the price be slightly higher than this cost. The accountants have been supplying full-cost data, because they assume that the economic crisis is not as stressful for the company as the manager believes it to be. In normal times the company engages in full-cost pricing, and the accountants have not received instructions from senior management to change to the marginal pricing used in bad times. Thus the manager will continue to receive full-cost data and price estimates from the accountants, but is primed to reject the communication.

How can the accountants serve the manager's needs? In other words, how can they communicate reader-oriented information—information that is easily understood, that can be used, and that will be used? The answer requires the accountants to do two things *before* sending their report:

▲   The accountants must convince the manager that they are not ignoring the need for marginal-price data but that senior management has not yet defined the situation as requiring a shift to marginal-cost reporting. Reporting policy requires uniform-cost reporting under the direction of the controller. The convincing will probably require several face-to-face visits, from which may emerge either the manager's acquiescence or perhaps some sort of compromise.

▲   The accountants also must convince the manager that mutual understanding and empathy should exist between them. They must have a firm personal relationship of the kind that allows conflict yet controls it. Specifically, the manager must come to feel well-disposed to the accountants' communications. When disagreeing, therefore, the manager will not adopt a rejecting manner but will instead work to develop a compromising attitude. The accountants will act in the same way.

Writing is not readable, then, until the reader is disposed to make the effort to read, and it is the accountant's job to see to it that the reader develops a favorable attitude toward accounting communications. The accountant is not reader oriented—is not serving reader needs—until he or she does so.

Identifying Reader Expectations

The writer often must fall short of totally serving the reader's needs. Accountants who do their best for their clients or managers may still fall short of their readers' expectations. In this common situation the accountants' task is to show in what way they have partially served needs and what can or must be done in the future to serve them fully. In this way the writer serves the reader's need to know what's missing from the picture.

The cost accountant who provides overhead allocation data in a report may find that the data does not fully serve the manager's goal of evaluating cost control across several departments. The reason is that allocation methodology is inherently flawed; therefore, no perfect cost evaluation tool exists. In the report, then, the accountant ought to define several methods, choose one, say why it has been chosen, reveal its flaws, and offer some discussion of alternative actions the manager can take to evaluate costs. Otherwise, the manager's expectations for the communication will be denied without explanation. It is far better for the accountant to explain—not so much for self-defense (that, too, of course) but more to define the level of service being given and the service still to be provided (if possible).

WRITING TO HELP READER COMPREHENSION When readers have realized—hopefully after the first paragraph or two—that their needs are being served, their attention will increase and they will make a serious effort to process the accountant's communication. That effort involves a "scanning-plus-reviewing" process (Hirsch, 1977):

- ▲ *Scanning* is the perception of a sequence of linguistic elements.
- ▲ *Reviewing* is the matching of what is perceived against a series of meanings hypotheses stored in the mind until a likely match is hit upon and comprehension occurs.

The accountant must write in such a way that scanning is made easy and reviewing both easy and accurate.

Exhibit 4.2   **USE OF HEADINGS, WHITE SPACE, LISTING, AND PARALLEL VERB FORMS TO FACILITATE SCANNING**

A PROCEDURE

In emergencies, prepare Form 134 in the same manner as directed under A above, and forward it to the SM & M Section on any workday; or, at locations outside the General Office, if the emergency necessitates shipments from the General Office on the same day as that on which the requisition is being made, telegraph or telephone (as appropriate) the requisitions of the location to the supervisor involved at the General Office, who will prepare Form 134 covering the telephone or telegraph request in the same manner as directed under A, above, forwarding the last copy to the location originating the request, and all other copies to the Comptroller, Attention: SM & M Section.

EMERGENCY PROCEDURES

General Office
1. In emergencies prepare Form 134 as shown above in A.
2. Send the form to the SM & M Section on any workday.

Locations Outside General Office
1. Follow steps 1 and 2 above, unless the emergency requires shipments from the General Office on the same day as the requisition is being made.
2. If the shipment date and the requisition date are the same, telephone or telegraph the involved General Office supervisor. The supervisor will:
    A. Prepare Form 134 as directed in A above,
    B. Forward the last copy to the request originator,
    C. Forward the form and all other copies to the Comptroller, SM & M Section.

Helping the Reader to Scan

Look at Exhibit 4.2 and read the "Procedure" at the top of the page. Hard to get into, isn't it? That's because the writer did not make any effort to help the reader scan the material. Now look at the revision, "Emergency Procedures," beneath it. Here some simple devices have made scanning easy:

Headings.   The use of headings signals the reader that two important subjects are covered and gives their names.

White Space.   By breaking up the paragraph so that the words and sentences are framed by white space instead of by the paragraph itself, the writer has made the writing seem less impenetrable to the eye. The reader's eyes will find scanning easier.

Listing. The basic steps in the procedure are listed and numbered. In this way the reader senses—before understanding—that each subject has two parts and that the parts are ordered in a special way. After reading, the reader will learn that the ordering was of steps to be performed first and then second.

Sometimes listings are not numbered because the writer-accountant does not want to stress the ranking of the parts. In this case a series of dashes ("—") or bullets ("▲") can be used. No matter what listing technique is used, however, the first items in the list will get scanned first. Thus they will receive more reviewing time before comprehension than the others. Naturally, then, the accountant would want to place the most important items first so they have the best chance of being comprehended.

Parallel Verb Forms. Each step in the procedure is signaled to the reader by a similar verb form (*prepare, send, follow, telephone, telegraph, prepare, forward, forward*). When the reader has read a few steps, the scanning mechanism of the reader's brain will begin to look for similar verb forms that signal the remaining steps. Use of listing and white space helps the search for these verbs.

Some other techniques that help the reader to scan the writing for key words and phrases crucial to the reviewing process are underlining, placing the key phrases at the front of sentences and paragraphs, pruning verbiage, and writing sentences of appropriate length:

Underlining. The only <u>point</u> to <u>make</u> here is that too much <u>underlining</u> diminishes its <u>pointing-out</u> <u>power</u>.

Leading with Key Words and Phrases. As we saw above with items in a list, what gets scanned first gets more reviewing. By the same token, those words and phrases that cue the reader to the points being made ought to be in the front of sentences and paragraphs for initial scanning:

▲ *Wrong*—The depreciation found by applying a rate to the book value of the asset at the beginning of that year rather than to the asset's original cost is called the *double declining-balance* depreciation.

▲ *Right*—*Double declining-balance* depreciation is found by applying a rate to the book value of the asset at the beginning of that year rather than to the asset's original cost.

Pruning Verbiage. Scanning is improved by clearing a paragraph of the excess words that simply clutter it:

▲ *Wrong*—All invoices that are received after the last day of the month but that pertain to purchases during the month must be given the special handling that is described in Internal Control Procedure I–17.

▲   *Right*—Invoices for a month received after that month must be handled in accord with Internal Control Procedure I–17.

Writing Sentences of Appropriate Length.   Sentences with about ten to twenty words are relatively easy to scan. When they get longer, the reader may have trouble picking out the important elements. However, when sentences get very short, the reader may find that too many stop-and-start eye movements are required and may tire of scanning:

▲   *Wrong*—The plant superintendent usually maintains a continuous labor tabulation report based on the weekly reports furnished to the foremen from the daily summary reports that are collected by the accountant every other day.

▲   *Right*—The plant superintendent usually maintains a continuous labor tabulation report. This report is based on the weekly reports furnished to the foremen. All the reports are based on the daily summary reports collected every other day by the accountant.

▲   *Wrong*—Management must understand something. Differences between cost and estimated replacement value occur. These differences can be significant. The determination of production and pricing policies are affected by them.

▲   *Right*—Management must understand that cost-estimated replacement value differences occur. These differences can significantly influence the determination of production and pricing policies.

Helping the Reader to Review

After scanning the material to inventory the linguistic elements—words and phrases, mostly—the reader then matches these elements against personal memory, experience, habits, and knowledge of language. Meaning results and comprehension occurs.

This reviewing process can be easy or hard, depending on the extent of the reader's abilities and the writer's skills. To help the reader, the writer has available a number of techniques, some of which are described below and the rest discussed in the next three chapters.

Using Consistent Verb Tenses.   Verbs are the most "reviewed" of all linguistic elements; when the reader has "got" them, perhaps one-half of the reviewing process is completed. Why is this so? The answer is simple: verbs tell what action is happening. After acquiring a sense of the event occurring, the reader can easily fill in details of what, when, where, and so on. We will see in a later chapter on writing that verbs telling little about action (*is, are, was,* etc.) damage good writing if used excessively. For now we simply want to point out the needless obstacles to comprehension that are imposed by writers who do not control the tenses of their verbs:

▲ *Wrong*—Wages *will be* an important factor in the company's higher operating ratio. They *have absorbed* about 36 percent of total revenues. When we *look* at similar companies in our industry, we *are seeing* an 18 percent rate.

▲ *Right*—Wages *are* an important factor in the company's higher operating ratio. They *absorb* about 36 percent of total revenues. When we *look* at similar companies in our industry, we *see* an 18 percent rate.

Making Relationships Clear. It's the little things that can kill you! So it is with writing, where the use of *and* instead of *or* or *but* instead of *yet* can destroy a reader's sense of the relationship between two or more statements. Consider first, however, the following example of *hot commas,* which often make relationships unclear:

In emergencies follow procedures X, Y, or Z.

The sentence seems simple enough, but we cannot understand its true meaning because it can be interpreted in two ways:

1. Do X and Y. If you don't do them, do Z.
2. Do X or Y or Z.

Three sentences may be required:

In emergencies follow procedures X and Y. If both of these cannot be followed, follow procedure Z. If either X or Y can be followed, do not follow procedure Z.

If hot commas can muddy the waters, *hot adjectives* like the following can hurt careers:

The current accounting staff has performed in an excellent manner.

Assume that an accountant in charge of a department writes this message regarding her department to her senior, the former head of the department. That person could fix his reviewing on the word *current* and interpret the sentence as meaning that the excellent performance has occurred in comparison with the poor performance of the department under *his* supervision. Needless to say, no such meaning was intended, but to remove the hint of an unintended meaning the accountant should have removed *current*.

Now let us turn to those little words that kill:

▲ *Wrong*—Prior to September 30, the amounts of prebilling were insignificant, *and* by October 30 the amount was $530,000.

▲ *Right*—Prior to September 30, the amounts of prebilling were insignificant. *However,* by October 30 the amount was $530,000.

The word *however* helps the reader to understand that $530,000 is related to the word *significant*. The word *and* tells the reader, erroneously, that the $530,000 is still insignificant.

▲ *Wrong*—June sales have been quite low, *and* the line of credit has not been extended.

▲ *Right*—June sales have been quite low, *yet* the line of credit has not been extended.

The *yet* conveys a powerful signal to the reader to expect the unexpected, in this case management's ability to avoid borrowing in the face of poor revenues. The *and* is not as favorable in signaling management's achievement, since it could just as easily suggest the bank's decision not to grant an extension.

We will see other examples of the crucial importance of little words, but for now the point is that they help the reader to see relationships between cause and effect; part and subpart; past, present, and future; the expected and the unexpected; and statement and qualification.

Keeping Statements in Proper Sequence. The presentation of statements can be random or it can be ordered. Ordered is best for reader comprehension:

▲ *Wrong*—In planning our capital budget, we need to consider building a new plant, which will involve a study of the earnings it will create over its life. The operating costs of such a plant will be lower than those of our current plant because of technology improvements. However, a capital budget consideration to acquire an existing modern plant also ought to give us the earnings we seek. That plant's costs, of course, will have to be compared with the costs of a newly constructed one. The earnings study will consider these things.

▲ *Right*—In planning our capital budget, we need to consider building a new plant or acquiring a new one. In either case technology-induced cost reductions below our current old plant's costs should lead to increased earnings. Of course, we will need to conduct a study of the costs, revenues, and earnings of all possible alternatives.

The ordered presentation describes either-or decision alternatives and discusses criteria for making the decision. In the random presentation a disorderly mix of alternatives and criteria occurs.

Anticipating Reader Difficulties. The reader's effort in reviewing and matching the linguistic inventory against the mind's inventory of experience and knowledge ought to be the writer's constant preoccupation. How, asks the writer, can I help make the effort easier? One way is to anticipate reader matching difficulties and to reduce the likelihood of incomprehension through the following techniques:

▲ Identify information that is complex and make it as simple as possible.

▲ Consider the reader's knowledge and experience and decide whether the information will be familiar or unfamiliar. If unfamiliar, provide background, definitions, and whatever else is needed to get the reader familiar.

▲ Estimate the reader's expectations. If the information is unexpected, provide explanations and descriptions until the reader is ready to review the unexpected. Remember that accounting communications are not like horror movies—very little of the unexpected should occur.

CHECKING FOR COMPREHENSIBILITY If the accountant has gotten readers to pay attention by serving their needs, has helped readers to scan easily, and has fostered the reviewing process, comprehension will occur and the communication will be effective. We can learn just how comprehensible our writing is by observing the actions and responses of our readers. However, techniques exist for making a rough estimate of the understandability of writing *before* communicating.

One technique, so the story goes, is to keep a dumb accountant on the staff and to have him read every report or client communication. If he can understand it, anyone can. This approach, however, usually gives way to the use of a nonhuman test of comprehensibility—a readability formula (comprehensibility and readability are the same thing).

Currently over fifty readability formulas exist. Some are good measures but hard to use. Others are easy to use but give only a moderately good measure of the comprehensibility of a piece of writing. One, the Flesch Reading Ease Formula (REF), provides a good measure and is easy to use (Flesch, 1948).

Calculating the REF

The Flesch Reading Ease Formula provides a quantitative measure of the difficulty a reader will have in understanding a written message. The measure is calculated as follows:

1. *Pick a Sample.* If the material to be measured is short, all of it can be used. If not, 100–300-word samples are taken. A five-page report probably should be measured by testing two or three samples. Naturally the more samples tested, the greater the reduction in the writer's uncertainty about the report's readability.

2. *Count the Words in Each Sample.* Contractions (*shouldn't, can't*) are counted as one word, as are hyphenated words (*right-hand*), numbers ($53,000,000), and abbreviations (*e.g., etc.*).

3. *Count the Number of Sentences in Each Sample.* Independent clauses joined by conjunctions (*and, or*) are counted as one sentence, but independent clauses separated by periods, colons, or semicolons count as two sentences.

4. *Calculate Average Sentence Length for Each Sample.* Simply divide the number of words by the number of sentences.

5. *Calculate Syllables per 100 Words for Each Sample.* A syllable is identified by reading the passage aloud. Thus $50,000 counts as six syllables (*fif-ty thou-sand dol-lars*). The syllables for a sample are added up and the syllables per 100 words calculated:

$$\text{Syllables per 100 Words for a Sample} = \frac{\text{Total Syllables}}{\text{Total Words}} \times 100$$

6. *Calculate the Reading Ease Score.*
A. Multiply the sample's average sentence length by 1.015 _____
B. Multiply the sample's rate of syllables per 100 words by 0.846 _____
C. Add A and B _____
D. Subtract the sum of A and B from 206.835. The result is the REF _____

Interpreting the REF

Exhibit 4.3 describes the likely range of REF measures that can be obtained and the various degrees of readability for selected intervals within the range. The REF scores for all the samples of a piece of writing are compared to the table, and an assessment is made of the level of readability. If the samples yield widely divergent scores, more sampling should be done until a representative mean score can be calculated.

The readability score of a typical annual report will probably lie between 10 and 40, although a score above 50 would be more appropriate for stockholders. Internal corporate reports might score from 0 to 40, depending on the subject matter, and audit letters probably ought to score above 30 if they are to serve a client adequately.

Exhibit 4.3   **INTERPRETATIONS OF FLESCH READING EASE FORMULA SCORES**

REF SCORE	UNDERSTANDABILITY OF THE SAMPLE	COMPARABLE PROFESSIONAL AND MASS MEDIA WRITING
91–100	Very easy	Comics
81–90	Easy	Pulp fiction
71–80	Fairly easy	Slick fiction
61–70	Standard	Digests, *Time*
51–60	Fairly difficult	*Harper's, Atlantic*
31–50	Difficult	Academic, scholarly
0–30	Very difficult	Scientific, technical

Assessing the Utility of the REF

All researchers agree that the REF gives no indication of whether or not one is writing in a style that creates a favorable image. Nor does it tell whether the writer is following the rules of grammar. Its chief task rather is to suggest how hard a reader will find a piece of writing to read. Even here, however, disagreement exists. Klare (1963) concluded that REF is probably a valid and reliable measure of readability, but others have pointed out real weaknesses in the measure. Generally, the Flesch REF:

▲   Assumes a reader of average reading ability. It does not take into account exceptionally good or bad reading ability.

▲   Ignores the reader's prior experience with the material discussed in the writing. Highly experienced readers will have less trouble comprehending than will other readers.

▲   Copes poorly with highly technical writing. It treats short, highly abstract words with complex meanings as easily understood words.

How useful, then, is REF to accountants? Sullivan (1980) conducted research on the power of the Flesch REF and concluded that it is accurate to within ±14 on the REF scale. Thus a set of samples with a mean score of 30 is probably less readable than a set with a mean score of 45. An accountant who wants a report to be understandable at a fairly difficult or better level (above 50) would do well not to assume that the criterion was met unless the mean score of a sample set was above REF 64. With scores above 64 the accountant could be 95 percent certain that the report was understandable at a fairly difficult level or above.

Accountants preparing important proposals for prospective clients or reports for clients or managers ought to use the Flesch REF to test the readability of their writing. As long as they allow ±14 points to account for the inherent limitations of the formula, it yields useful information that reduces the accountant's uncertainty regarding the comprehensibility of the report to the reader.

Checkoff 4.1   **ACCOUNTING COMMUNICATIONS: WRITING TO INCREASE UNDERSTANDING**

	YES	NO
SERVING READER NEEDS AND INTERESTS		
1. Am I writing what the readers need to read as well as what I need to say?	___	___
2. Am I defining the readers' needs in terms of what they truly know rather than what they are supposed to know?	___	___
3. If the readers' desires are different from their needs, have I convinced them beforehand or in my writing that their needs ought to be uppermost in their minds as they read?	___	___
4. Have I created a favorable attitude in the readers so that they will give my writing their full attention and thus see that their needs are being served?	___	___
5. Is the information I am providing fully meeting reader expectations?	___	___
6. If I am not able to provide all the expected information, have I clearly described what the readers still need to know and made an effort to show how such information might be forthcoming?	___	___
HELPING READERS TO SCAN		
7. Have I used headings to identify subjects?	___	___
8. Have I used white space to make the writing seem penetrable?	___	___
9. Have I listed items to signal the parts of some whole?	___	___
10. Have I used parallel verb forms to identify similar linguistic elements, such as instructions in a control process?	___	___
11. Have I used underlining (sparingly) to signal words needing scanning?	___	___
12. Have I begun sentences with words and phrases that tell the reader what is being discussed?	___	___
13. Have I pruned excess verbiage that clutters sentences and impedes scanning?	___	___
14. Have I generally used sentences of about ten to twenty words that are more easily scanned than shorter or longer sentences?	___	___

(continued)

Checkoff 4.1 (*concluded*)

	YES	NO
HELPING READERS TO REVIEW		
15. Have I kept my verb tenses consistent to improve the readers' sense of the action occurring?	——	——
16. Have I avoided hot commas and made clear the meaning of items separated by commas?	——	——
17. Have I eliminated hot adjectives that could trigger reader comprehension that I did not intend?	——	——
18. Have I included the *and's, or's, but's, yet's,* and so on, that tie statements together so that relationships can be understood?	——	——
19. Have I made statements in some sort of orderly fashion, avoiding the scatter-shot approach that my mind will employ if the order is not controlled?	——	——
20. Have I anticipated and simplified information that readers will find complex?	——	——
21. Have I anticipated information that readers will find unfamiliar and made it more familiar?	——	——
22. Have I anticipated information that readers will find unexpected and prepared them for it?	——	——

Writing to Avoid an Unfavorable Image: Following the Rules

chapter 5

America is a free country when it comes to sex, greed, and grammar, but virtually all Americans agree that some kinds of rules must govern these activities. Grammatical and other linguistic rules do not have the benefit of ethical, moral, or legal thinking behind them; yet they are enforced more rigidly and more widely than the rules covering sex and greed. Why is this so? The answer is simple: image. Violations of sex and greed rules can sometimes create public images of the violators that may be much admired. Grammar violators are always metaphorically hung. The hard question is, why are rules of grammar and language so strictly enforced, particularly by seniors over juniors in American accounting? The answer again is image.

Accountants who do not follow the rules of grammar, syntax, spelling, punctuation, and numbers signal to the reader their lack of writing ability—a lack that is then easily associated with a lack of professional ability in the accountants themselves and even in their organizations. This signaling can lead to readers forming unfavorable images of accountants and their superiors.

GRAMMAR AND SYNTAX

Accountants, then, must follow the rules, and the rules that govern the use of language are its *grammar*. Those rules of grammar governing the arrangement of words into sentences are called *syntax*. Most of what the accountant needs to know regarding grammar involves syntax. The following discussion deals mostly with avoiding violations of syntactical rules.

Grammatical rules have not been engraved on stone somewhere by someone dressed up to look like Charlton Heston. Yet they exist. We do not say, "The boy run." We do not say, "Runs the boy." Even though both sentences are comprehensible, neither obeys the rules that common usage has laid down over the last thousand years. This usage has by now developed into prescriptions that tell us what is acceptable and not acceptable in how we put words together.

Rather than trying to learn all the rules of English grammar, accountants can improve their writing—in the sense that they avoid bad grammar and the accompanying unfavorable image—by learning what mistakes are commonly made and by avoiding them. The most common mistakes involve:

▲ Dangling participles and gerunds,

▲ Pronoun problems,

▲ Sentence fragments,

▲ Comma splices,

▲ Subject–verb agreement.

Dangling Participles and Gerunds

Modifying phrases, often at the beginning or ending of a sentence, need a noun or pronoun to which they refer. Some common mistakes involve (1) omitting the noun or pronoun, (2) modifying the wrong word, and (3) placing the modified noun too far from the modifier:

▲ *Wrong*—Having prepared the pro forma statements, formal approval was sought.

▲ *Right*—Having prepared the pro forma statements, *the staff accountant* sought formal approval.

▲ *Wrong*—Cash expenditures are made without the manager's approval, resulting in a lack of control.

▲ *Right*—Because cash expenditures are made without the manager's approval, a lack of control results.

▲ *Wrong*—Divided into two sections, the senior partner supervised the staff.

▲ *Right*—The senior partner supervised the staff, which was divided into two sections.

A variation of the dangling participle occurs with the gerund (a verb used as a noun). These are often used as the object of a preposition, and the source of the action to which they refer usually must be mentioned:

- ▲ *Wrong*—After examining selected inventory samples, the inventory memo was written.
- ▲ *Right*—After examining selected inventory samples, *the auditor* wrote the inventory memo.
- ▲ *Wrong*—By requesting information from the credit manager, the status of bad accounts can be learned.
- ▲ *Right*—By requesting information from the credit manager, *we* can learn the status of bad accounts.

Virtually all grammatical problems with modifiers can be avoided if the writer rereads what is written and asks, "Who did what to whom and when?" If the writing makes the *who* clear, then dangling modifiers ought not to be much of a problem.

Pronoun Problems

The easiest pronoun mistake to make is overuse of *it*:

- ▲ *Wrong*—It is not likely that our accountants will be able to agree on the value of goodwill. Its importance, however, makes it imperative that it be measured.
- ▲ *Right*—Our accountants may be unable to agree on the value of goodwill. The importance of goodwill, however, requires that they measure it.

It [*sic*] is such an easy mistake because a writer's mind will generate small, familiar words quicker and with less effort than it [*sic*] can generate long, concrete words. Indeed, a writer who is tired runs the risk of falling back on little, vague words such as *it*.

Equally common, but due more to sloppiness than to fatigue, is faulty noun–pronoun agreement:

- ▲ *Wrong*—Each manager needs to submit *their* expenses promptly.
- ▲ *Right*—Each manager needs to submit *his or her* expenses promptly.
- ▲ *Wrong*—The firm is divided into three divisions: operations, administration, and research. *They* give the most attention to operations.
- ▲ *Right*—The firm is divided into three divisions: operations, administration, and research. *It* gives the most attention to operations.

In the first example the writer ignored the key word *each,* which should have signaled that the subject was singular. Similar words are *either, neither, one, anyone,* and *everybody.* They are all singular. In the second example the writer referred to the firm as *they.* Not only does one not refer to firms as *they,* but also one does not use *they* when the reader could easily see it as referring to the objects of the previous sentence instead of the subject of that sentence

Sentence Fragments

Incomplete sentences, or sentence fragments as they are called, usually result from hasty rather than unskilled writing. The most frequent kind are subordinate clauses separated from their main clause by a period:

▲ *Wrong*—Our staff has been issuing the reports weekly. Although the time pressures have been great.

▲ *Right*—Although the time pressures have been great, our staff has been issuing the reports weekly.

Also common is the following:

▲ *Wrong*—This *being* the third month in a row an unfavorable variance occurred. The supervisor decided to conduct a special study of the item.

▲ *Right*—After experiencing unfavorable variances in the item for three straight months, the supervisor decided to conduct a special study.

Here the word *being* was made to serve as a main verb, a violation of most of what is sacred and holy in English grammar.

Comma Splices

The term *comma splice* refers to the use of a comma instead of a period between sentences:

▲ *Wrong*—The firm expects to be drawing on its line of credit this month, therefore, the proposed investment expenditure can be made.

▲ *Right*—The firm expects to be drawing on its line of credit this month. Therefore, the proposed investment expenditure can be made.

The requirement for a period or a semicolon before *therefore* will probably come as a shock to many readers, since this form of comma splice is perhaps the most common syntax mistake one sees. Nevertheless, it is a mistake, and similar comma splices with *however, furthermore, moreover,* and *nevertheless* are also mistakes.

Subject–Verb Agreement

Another mistake due mostly to hasty writing without rereading is the use of a verb that agrees with an intervening noun rather than with the subject of the sentence:

▲ *Wrong*—The categorization of products by product lines *are* helping the staff to analyze profitability more accurately than before.

▲ *Right*—The categorization . . . *is* . . . .

▲ *Wrong*—Revenue from sales *are* recorded by the bookkeeper on the day after the transaction.

▲ *Right*—Revenue . . . *is* . . . .

Sometimes inexperienced writers will incorrectly make the verb agree with a predicate noun instead of with the subject:

▲ *Wrong*—The only large asset the company owns *are* ten Kenworth trucks.

▲ *Right*—The . . . asset . . . is . . . .

Even experienced writers, however, have trouble with multiple subjects joined by *or* or *nor*. Here are two rules: (1) *Two or more singular subjects joined by* or *or* nor *take a singular verb:*

▲ *Wrong*—Neither the partner nor the manager *were* aware of the audit problem.

▲ *Right*—. . . the partner nor the manager *was* . . . .

(2) *Two or more subjects mixing singular and plural nouns take a verb governed by the nearest subject:*

▲ *Wrong*—Neither the partner nor the managers was aware of the audit problem.

▲ *Right*—. . . the partner nor the managers *were* . . . .

Confusing, isn't it!

Finally, and a lot simpler to remember: *each, either, someone, everyone,* and similar words take a singular verb:

▲ *Wrong*—Everyone on the staff *are* instructed to report material weaknesses to the in-charge.

▲ *Right*—Everyone . . . *is* . . . .

SPELLING In Finland a child learns to spell correctly at the age of seven or eight and rarely misspells words thereafter. In America virtually *everyone* has trouble with spelling. Why? To begin with, in Finland words are spelled the way they are sounded, while in America the spelling of words is often insanely different from the sounds. For example, one would ordinarily spell *through* as *thru*, *rough* as *ruf*, and *thorough* as *thuhrow*. But we don't, and the irrationality of English spelling is manifest when we realize that -*rough* in these three words stands for three different pronunciations:

-*rough* = *ru* (*through*) = *ruf* (*rough*) = *row* (*thorough*)

English spelling, then, is often irrational. We can learn it only (1) by memorizing the spelling of words that are commonly misspelled and (2) by learning the rules that—with numerous exceptions—govern spelling.

The question comes up, Why bother? Wouldn't it be easier if all of us simply spelled as we wished? In time this process would eventually result in a rational and mostly uniform spelling of words. The problem, however, is that no one, particularly accountants, wants to initiate the movement to uniform spelling. What accountant would dare write:

The lees akwisishun proseedjer wil bee deeskribd n part tou uv this reeport.

Until the millennium occurs, then, all of us must learn to spell. Numerous studies show that American business culture will not tolerate unconventional spelling. Indeed, spelling is often listed as the major writing problem of young businesspeople.

To improve in spelling, the accountant needs helpful peers and superiors who will review draft memos and reports and point out misspelled words. Then by keeping a list of these words and consulting it when writing, the accountant will soon cut errors dramatically.

Another approach is to consult a dictionary when even the slightest doubt occurs about the spelling of a word.

Still another approach is to memorize a list of the 500 most misspelled words. Such lists can be found in most grammar books. One of the most common is J.C. Hodges and M.E. Whitten, *Harbrace College Handbook,* which is available in its umpteenth edition at any bookstore.

Finally, the accountant can memorize a few rules that should help to cut spelling problems considerably:

▲ Place *i* before *e*, except after *c*, or when sounded like *a* as in *neighbor* and *weigh.*

▲ Add a prefix to a root word without dropping letters (*unnecessary, dissatisfied*).

▲ If a suffix begins with a vowel, drop the final *e* of the root word (*coming, famous*).

▲ Before adding a suffix beginning with a vowel (-*er, -ed, -en*), double the final consonant of the root word if it is preceded by a single vowel (*occurred, planned*). If not, don't (*lender, defaulted*).

▲ When a root word ends in *e*, drop it if the next syllable begins with a vowel (*movable*).

PUNCTUATION The most difficult punctuation for an accountant involves commas, semicolons, and colons. Below are listed a few rules that, if followed, ought to eliminate most punctuation problems.

Commas

Of the many rules governing the use of commas, here are some of the most helpful:

1. *Commas separate the items in a series. Always place a comma before the* and *or the* or *to avoid unclear lists.* Consider this sentence:

> We divided debts into short term, medium term and long term and calculated debt-to-equity ratios for each.

Were there two classifications or three? Probably three, but the insertion of a comma after *medium term* ensures clarity.

2. *Commas separate two independent clauses joined by* and, or, but, nor, *and* for. *Commas do not separate two verbs within a sentence or a subject from its verb.*

3. *Commas separate introductory dependent clauses from the main part of the sentence. Introductory phrases don't usually need to be set off by commas.*

4. *If an adjectival clause or phrase follows a noun and gives nonessential information, set it off with commas. If it contains essential information, don't:*

> The Ajax food processing investment, which was approved on December 20, will yield a 20 percent return on investment next year.
>
> The investment that we discussed yesterday regarding Ajax Foods will yield a 20 percent return on investment next year.

In the first example the clause is not needed to identify the investment; since its information is nonessential, commas are required. In the second example the clause identifies the investment and thus is attached to the subject without commas.

5. *Transitional words, such as* however, moreover, furthermore, *and* nevertheless, *are separated from the rest of the sentence by commas:*

> Moreover, the review procedures for the monitoring system must be revised. The revision, however, need not be a lengthy process.

Here are three examples of sentences with misused commas. *Avoid* this usage:

> The next step, is to calculate the average life of the asset and to divide that into the cost of the asset.
>
> The next step is, to calculate the average life of the asset and to divide that into the cost of the asset.
>
> The next step is to calculate the average life of the asset, and to divide that into the cost of the asset.

Semicolons

These two rules cover the most frequent use of semicolons:

1. *A semicolon joins two independent clauses.*
2. *Semicolons divide items in a series when at least one item contains a comma:*

> The report includes inventory valuation; accounts receivable financing; and short-term, medium-term, and long-term debt information.

Colons

The chief use of a colon, outside of letters (Dear Sir:), *is to introduce lists of explanations or examples:*

> There are three possible depreciation methods: straight line, sum-of-years digits, and accelerated.

NUMBERS There are no hard and fast rules for determining when to state numbers as figures or as words, but conventional usage over the years provides several rules of thumb that will serve most accounting needs.

1. *At the beginning of a sentence, numbers are best stated as words:*

▲ *Wrong*—July was a good month. $10,000,000 in revenue was taken in.
▲ *Right*—July was a good month. Ten million dollars in revenue was taken in.

2. *State numbers in the same series as either figures or words. Don't mix figures with words:*

- ▲ *Wrong*—We have five inventory controls, 15 performance measures, and twenty production controls.
- ▲ *Right*—We have five inventory controls, fifteen performance measures, and twenty production controls.

3. *Use words for numbers 1 through 99 (1 through 9 in technical writing); use figures for other numbers except isolated round numbers.* (Note: Numbers under 99 that are exact amounts of money or exact dimensions are usually written as figures. Thus money is almost always expressed as figures.)

- ▲ *Wrong*—The first half of the production program was forecast at about 5 million units.
- ▲ *Right*—The first half of the production program was forecast at about five million units.
- ▲ *Wrong*—The price of each unit will be five dollars.
- ▲ *Right*—The price of each unit will be $5. [Note: The decimal point and the double zero here may be omitted.]

4. *If a sentence contains two series of numbers, use figures for one series and words for the other:*

- ▲ *Wrong*—In June revenues were $1.3 million on sales of 10,000 units. In July revenues were $1.5 million on sales of 12,000 units.
- ▲ *Right*—In June revenues were $1.3 million on sales of ten thousand units. In July revenues were $1.5 million on sales of twelve thousand units.

5. *When two different numbers appear next to each other, differentiate them by using words and figures or by using a comma:*

- ▲ *Wrong*—We recently purchased 12,900 3-inch bolts.
- ▲ *Right*—We recently purchased 12,900 three-inch bolts.
- ▲ *Wrong*—In 1982 73 new units were produced.
- ▲ *Right*—In 1982, 73 units were produced.

6. *When expressing money as decimals, be consistent:*

- ▲ *Wrong*—Our prices are $15.50, $10.30, and $11, respectively.
- ▲ *Right*—Our prices are $15.50, $10.30, and $11.00, respectively. [Note: Add the double zero after $11 to be consistent.]

▲ *Wrong*—The unit costs are $0.47, $0.32, and 63 cents, respectively.

▲ *Right*—The unit costs are $0.47, $0.32, and $0.63, respectively.

7. *Use figures for the following:*

8:27 P.M. (*eight o'clock* or *eight in the evening* is acceptable also)

47% (47 percent is acceptable)

¾ (or three-fourths)

Figure 9

Table 5

Chapter 4

page 17

8. *Express the plural of a figure by adding s without an apostrophe:*

The production was in 100s.

Checkoff 5.1   **ACCOUNTING COMMUNICATIONS: WRITING TO AVOID AN UNFAVORABLE IMAGE: FOLLOWING THE RULES**

	YES	NO
GRAMMAR AND SYNTAX		
1. Have I avoided dangling participles by asking *who* is doing the action referred to in the participial phrase?	____	____
2. Have I cut down on the use of vague *it?*	____	____
3. Have I avoided sentence fragments by looking for subjects and verbs in each sentence?	____	____
4. Have I avoided comma splices by using semicolons or periods instead of commas between independent clauses?	____	____
5. Have I read over my work to make sure that verbs agree with subjects?	____	____
SPELLING		
6. Have I checked my spelling in a dictionary?	____	____
7. Have I compiled a list of words I sometimes misspell?	____	____
8. Do I ask people to check my work for misspelling before I submit it?	____	____
9. Do I know and follow the basic spelling rules?	____	____
PUNCTUATION		
10. Do I use commas appropriately in lists and between clauses?	____	____

(*continued*)

Checkoff 5.1 (*concluded*)

		YES	NO
11.	Do I avoid needless commas between subjects and verbs?	____	____
12.	Do I set off clauses between subjects and verbs with commas only when the clause contains nonessential information?	____	____
13.	Do I use semicolons between independent clauses and to set off items in a complex series (one that also includes commas)?	____	____
14.	Do I introduce series and lists with colons?	____	____

NUMBERS

		YES	NO
15.	Do I state numbers as words: at the beginning of sentences, in lists where other related numbers are in words, and in situations where two numbers as figures together can be confusing?	____	____
16.	Do I state numbers as figures: when exact amounts of money are stated, to be consistent with other related numbers, when numbers over ninety-nine are stated, and to avoid confusion with numbers stated as words?	____	____

chapter 6 Writing to Create a Favorable Image

In this chapter we concentrate on the steps that accountants can take to develop favorable images of themselves or of their organizations. This task involves first asking, "How can I sound competent, thorough, reliable, effective, and efficient?" The answer is to employ a writing style that cues readers to develop favorable attitudes toward the writer. Notice that *being* competent, thorough, reliable, effective, and efficient is not enough. One must also *appear* to have these attributes. An appropriate style creates that appearance and goes a long way toward guaranteeing the acceptance of the accountant's communication as credible.

BREVITY In America sex novels have to be 800 pages, even though a writer can describe most known sexual practices quite graphically in 200 pages. Why? There are two governing rules:

▲ Nothing succeeds like excess.
▲ Quantity is more important than quality.

These rules, almost cultural values, apparently are learned by young accountants early in their training. Indeed, they seem to feel that every document ought to be a monument, often to themselves. Unfortunately they fail to realize that a piece of writing intended to impress others rather than to communicate accounting messages—a monument—can end up as their memorial!

The first rule for brevity in writing, then, is this:

▲   Seek to express, not to impress.

Accountants must realize that a concise, tightly organized presentation is more effective than a long, rambling discourse. No one is impressed by the accountant who fills his or her dump truck with odds and ends of data and then offloads it onto the reader. In fact, to extend the metaphor, the reader will feel smothered rather than impressed.

Reducing Wordiness

Are accountants more wordy than others in their writing? Are they too wordy? Certainly some people would say yes; for example, accountants tend to use needless pairs of words like the following:

> To identify and designate
> Debts and obligations
> Liquidation or payment
> Use and demand
> Character and integrity
> Excellence and worth

They also tend to turn verbs into nouns, such as the following:

> Our validation indicated (instead of: we validated).
> The implementation of the policies is being carried out (instead of: the policies are being implemented).

Look at the following sentences, which contain both needless pairs of words and also verbs turned into nouns:

> Our review validated the excellence and worth of the new policies governing liquidation or payment of debts and obligations. The implementation of the policies is being carried out by this department.

Now look at this less wordy revision:

> We validated the worth of the new policies governing debt payments. The policies are being implemented by this department.

Thirty-one words in the first example became only nineteen in the second.

Accountants can check for excessive nominalizations (verbs turned into nouns) by examining the subjects and verbs of sentences in first drafts of documents. Simply circle each subject ending in *-ment* or *-ion* and each verb that is a form of the verb *to be.* If more than three or four circles per typewritten page are found, then rewriting to cut down wordiness is called for.

Cutting Glue Words

Some experts claim that there are two kinds of words: *working words,* which carry meaning, and *glue words,* which hold the working words together. Look at the circled working words and boxed glue words in the following sentence:

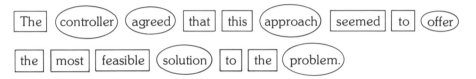

There are six working words and ten glue words. By rewriting to eliminate glue words, which do not earn their keep to the extent that working words do, we get this result:

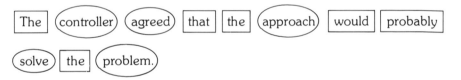

Here there are five working words and only six glue words—an elimination of 40 percent of the glue words. The sentences have the same meaning, but the second one is shorter and more readable because of the glue word reduction.

Turning Clauses into Phrases

Look for clauses beginning with *who, which,* and *that.* Such clauses can often be reduced to phrases:

▲ *Clause*—The president emphasized that the company was controlling inventories very carefully.
▲ *Phrase*—The president emphasized the carefully controlled inventories.
▲ *Clause*—The standard, which had been put into effect by the AICPA, required the procedure.
▲ *Phrase*—The standard enacted by the AICPA required the procedure.

Avoiding *It, There,* and *This*

One way to ruin the smooth flow of information in a document is to burden it with vague or indefinite words such as *it, there,* and *this* used as subjects of sentences:

▲ *Wrong*—*It* will be shown below that the complexity of the proposed procedure does not provide for easy installation of the required control mechanism. *This* is a methodology that has never proved itself in practice. *There* is sufficient reason, therefore, to recommend a revised procedure.

▲ *Right*—The complexity of the proposed procedure, described in detail below, does not provide for easy installation of the required control mechanism. This procedure has never proved itself in practice. Therefore, sufficient reason exists to recommend a revised procedure.

All the accountant needs to do is to take out the *it is* and *this is* subject–verb combinations and to put in their places subjects that name something and verbs that describe some action. These changes (notice that we didn't say *this*) will aid readers in threading their way through the prose easily and quickly.

Discarding Preambles

Some accountants love to employ long preambles to introduce some kind of action or proposed action:

> In furtherance of the corporate goal of reducing nonmonetary expenses, we recommend . . . .
> In accord with the regulations of the Securities and Exchange Commission, the prospectus . . . .

These and similar preambles can be eliminated if one section of the communication sets out the justification for the actions or recommendations that will appear in another section. In this way a preamble will not be required for each action. Of course, we should note that preambles in themselves are not harmful to a fluid writing style—only the excessive use of them as hurdles over which the reader must leap before getting to the message of the sentence.

Pruning Unnecessary Words and Phrases

Unnecessary words make the reader expend more energy than needed to comprehend a message:

▲ *Wrong*—We would like to request the preparation of quarterly reports describing the nature of the revenues in terms of kinds of products for the perusal of managers in analyzing the type and amount of customers' needs.

▲ *Right*—We request a quarterly revenue report, by products, for management analysis of customers' needs.

Notice that the big words are not causing the wordiness. Rather a whole bundle of *would's, like's, to's, in's, of's, and's,* and the like, are responsible. In fact, researchers have found that significant differences in the comprehensibility of a passage can be achieved simply by revising it to lessen the number of prepositions.

Reader comprehension will also be served by removing pretentious words and phrases inserted by some accountants in the mistaken belief that such words are part of a professional writing style:

Pretentious	**Simple**
Exactitude of conformance	Care
Conditions obtaining at this time	Existing conditions
100 percent	All
To render a certification	To certify
Successful attainment	Success

Finally, the repetition of ideas is a rhetorical device for making transitions or for persuading. But repetition for its own sake is both boring and harmful to understanding:

▲ *Wrong*—The total expense is not above $10,000 in amount.

▲ *Right*—The total expense is not above $10,000.

▲ *Wrong*—The provision in Section 4 provides that . . . .

▲ *Right*—Section 4 provides that . . . .

▲ *Wrong*—We certify that in our opinion . . . .

▲ *Right*—In our opinion . . . .

COMPLETENESS Even while being brief in writing, the accountant must make the reader feel that the job has been adequately done, that the writing contains all that the reader needs or desires to know. All this seems simple enough, except that often readers of accounting communications do not know what they want. Consider the case of the marketing manager who needs market segment information to help her allocate her sales force. Should the sales force be sent mostly to Wisconsin or to Illinois? The accountant who wants to create an image of completeness will give the information requested *and* will explain the impact of concentration in either area on shipping costs. The accountant will make this explanation even though no one has asked for it.

A style, then, that creates the favorable image of completeness does the following:

▲　All information needed by the reader is given. If some information cannot be provided, the accountant explains why and describes what he will do to acquire the missing data.

▲　A discussion of how the information can be used is provided. Even though a reader may not have asked for such a discussion, she probably needs it and will be grateful for it.

Hemming and Hawing

Sometimes accountants will inject phrases and statements into their writing to establish a proper note of caution to the reader:

> It may be that . . . .
>
> We can safely theorize that . . . .
>
> These findings should be interpreted cautiously.

While these qualifiers are all well and good in many cases, they can create the wrong image of the writer if overused. The reader who sees a management letter full of words such as *perhaps, seems, cautiously, appears,* and the like, may conclude not that the writer is admirably careful to avoid extreme conclusions and recommendations but rather that the letter reflects a job not completely done.

Eliminating "Would"

Worth special mention is the overuse of the word *would:*

> It would appear that . . . .
>
> We would think that . . . .

The word is used to hedge statements that have an aura of probability rather than fact to them. By using the bland word *would,* writers avoid the risk of making factual statements for which they can be held responsible. Moreover, they also avoid the necessity of using words such as *probability* and *possibility,* words that they feel might signal to the reader that they lack confidence in their own statements.

Too many *would's,* however, can create a credibility-ruining image just as easily as can the use of such qualifiers as *probable.* Then why bother to use them? The *would's* don't help; they can even create an image of deceitfulness if used frequently. Far better to tell the reader that information is probably accurate and that further confidence in the data can be gained if certain future actions are taken. This kind of admission is honest writing, and honesty breeds credibility no matter how tentative the assertions.

PARAGRAPH PATTERNS

Paragraphs are not on the page just to make it look nice. They serve a useful purpose. As we saw in Chapter 4, they aid comprehension by breaking up the page into manageable chunks for scanning and reviewing. They signal to the reader that a step in the communications process is about to occur or has occurred. Perhaps an introduction is finished and a discussion is to begin. Or it could be that one topic has been dealt with and another one is coming on.

Whatever the case, paragraphs are stylistic devices as well as comprehension aids. Their skillful use by an accountant creates a favorable image of deliberate, orderly progression. Crucial to the creation of that image is the employment of the various paragraph forms common to English. The forms, or patterns, shown in Exhibit 6.1 subtly tell the reader that a mind is at work behind the words, shaping them in ways that are familiar and conventional.

Accountants should check their writing to see whether they have been using the paragraph patterns described in the exhibit. If they cannot recognize any patterns in their work, they can be sure that their readers won't either. Readers will sense that something is not quite sound in the writing. They will see the writer as somehow not quite thoughtful enough about the material. To avoid this unfavorable image, then, accounting communicators must employ one of the conventional modes of organizing written thoughts in English.

PARALLEL CONSTRUCTION AND TRANSITIONS

Readers expect a subsequent event to resemble closely a preceding event (Hirsch, 1977). When no changes occur and resemblance exists, the writer signals the fact of resemblance by using *parallel construction.* When a change does occur and the reader must be signaled to expect nonresemblance, the writer uses *transitions.* Transitions speed up understanding by integrating meaning.

We will be looking at both parallel construction and various kinds of transitions, but first a point needs to be made. These devices are indeed aids to comprehension, but they also aid in the exhibition of an appropriate style. Most writers do not realize this. They think that such little words cannot be of much consequence in the creating of a favorable image. *In fact, almost all*

Exhibit 6.1   **PARAGRAPH PATTERNS IN ACCOUNTING COMMUNICATIONS**

THE STORY PARAGRAPH

Form

Story or Narrative

↓

Significance of the Narrative

Example

We observed that total costs of $10,000 were incurred during the month. At the same time revenues were $12,000. After closing the balances in Sales and Cost of Goods Sold to Loss and Gain, Loss and Gain showed a net profit for the month. This net profit was the third monthly gain in a row.

THE CAUSE–EFFECT PARAGRAPH

Form

Cause–Fact–Inference 1
Cause–Fact–Inference 2

↓

Effect–Conclusion–Conclusion

Example

Over the last ten years pioneering research by our firm has led to the development of a wide range of new products. At the same time we have introduced the latest cost-cutting technology. The result has been an increase in profits averaging 10 percent a year.

THE "THEREFORE" PARAGRAPH

Form

Inference–Fact 1 leads to

↓

Inference–Fact 2 leads to

↓

Inference–Fact 3 leads to

↓

Logical Conclusion

Example

Interest rates have risen to 18 percent. This rise has led to a decrease in bond prices. Thus the bonds that our bank purchased last year at 10 percent will not sell well today. We believe, therefore, that our net income will be adversely affected this year.

THE ADVANCER PARAGRAPH

Form

Little–Particular–Minor–Least Important

↓

Big–General–Major–Most Important

Example

On December 30 Ajax made a sale to Jones, Inc. The goods were supposed to be shipped on February 28. On February 15, however, Jones canceled the order. There is reason to believe that Ajax and Jones never intended to engage in a transaction.

(continued)

107

Exhibit 6.1 (continued)

THE "FOR EXAMPLE" PARAGRAPH

Form

Significant Generalization

↓

Narrative as Example

Example

The problems faced by the company are complex. For example, the need to increase profits on the hydraulic press product line will require substantial cost reductions. However, the bank is reluctant to extend the company extra credit to purchase new machinery until increased net cash flow allows for reduced borrowing.

THE "COUNT THEM" PARAGRAPH

Form

Significant Conclusion

↓

Fact–Inference 1
Fact–Inference 2

Example

The firm's revenues are poor. In 1981 revenues were 20 percent higher than today. In 1982 the figure was 25 percent. Moreover, our most similar competitor has increased revenues 30 percent since 1981.

THE "BECAUSE" PARAGRAPH

Form

Significant Conclusion leads to

↓

Fact–Inference 1 leads to

↓

Fact–Inference 2 leads to

↓

Fact–Inference 3

Example

From 1970 to 1980 bad debts did not exceed 1 percent of outstanding accounts at any time. Our customers are reliable and honest. Such honesty warrants a reduction in credit terms and costs to them. Of course, this reduction will require us to monitor accounts receivable aging even more closely than before.

THE RECEDER PARAGRAPH

Form

Big– General– Major– Most Important

↓

Little– Particular– Minor– Least Important

Example

The company predicts a continued rapid increase in government orders. Most of this new work will be in prime contracts. However, about 25 percent will be in subcontracts. Most subcontracts will be with Summit Corporation.

(continued)

Exhibit 6.1 (concluded)

THE ATTENTION-GETTER PARAGRAPH

Form

Detail as Attention Getter
↓
Significant Assertion
↓
Details

Example

The revenues of Division A last year were the lowest of the last ten years. Division A is not contributing adequate revenues anymore. Not only are sales down, but profits have fallen also. Indeed, costs in the division are steadily rising.

THE SWITCH PARAGRAPH

Form

Ideas—Facts—Inferences
↓
But, However
↓
Ideas—Facts—Inferences

Example

To assist dealers in financing their inventory, we established a wholly owned finance subsidiary. However, the finance company was expected to produce a profit as well as to service customers. The interest charged was set at four points above prime.

THE CLASSIC PARAGRAPH

Form

Generalization or Assertion
↓
Development (in addition, moreover, yet, however, nevertheless, etc.)
↓
Recapitulation (summary)
↓
Transition

Example

The firm's costs are high. It has experienced a 50 percent increase in expenses over the last two years. Yet neither profits nor production has risen. All in all, the company faces much greater costs than in the past. What, then, can it expect in the future?

writers forget to put transitional and parallel wording in their work during their first draft. Such words are seen as simple glue words of the kind discussed above. They are not! As we saw in the section on paragraph patterns, transitional words (*however, moreover,* etc.) help signal the reader that the writing is conventional, orderly, and thoughtful. In this sense they are crucial to good style.

Parallel Construction to Show Resemblance

The major device for tying similar ideas and information together is parallelism, particularly in lists:

▲ *Wrong*—The tests employed were counting the inventory on hand in warehouse A, and *we took a sample* of the inventory in warehouse B.

▲ *Right*—The tests employed were *counting* the inventory in warehouse A and *sampling* the inventory in warehouse B.

Parallel construction signals the reader that action regarding the first item in a list is similar to action regarding the other items. Without parallelism, the reader must work harder to see the relationship of the items. With parallelism, an image of order and relationship is created.

Transitional Words to Show Nonresemblance

To cue the reader that new or opposite ideas or points of view are now to be discussed, the accountant uses the following:

Conversely	However
Nevertheless	Yet
On the other hand	Still
Nonetheless	But
On the contrary	Notwithstanding

To show that a concession or qualification is being made, the accountant uses:

Granted	Admittedly
Undeniably	Of course
Naturally	Obviously
To be sure	It is true

To introduce a new topic:

As for	With respect to
Concerning	Now

To sum up:

In short	On the whole
In sum	As has been stated

Finally, to conclude:

Consequently	Accordingly
Hence	As a result
Therefore	Thus
For this reason	It follows that

Transitional Words to Connect

A number of transitional words and phrases simply connect ideas or items in a list:

In addition	Moreover
Also	Furthermore
And	Yet another
Besides	Next

Others show similarity:

In like manner	Such
Here again	Similarly

Still others connect examples to generalizations or conclusions:

To illustrate	For instance
For example	As a case in point

Pronouns and Repetition to Tie Ideas Together

Like the little words described above, the writer can use other short words—pronouns—to refer back to an idea or a noun that signals the idea:

> The firm supplies outdoor goods and services desired by many customers—lawn mowers, garden care equipment, and hedge trimmers. *These* provide its principal sources of income.
>
> Exhibit 6 shows how production has lagged behind orders by several months. *This* problem must be solved if revenues are to be realized.

The words *these* and *this* refer back to major pieces of information in the writing and thus help to keep the information in the mind of the reader. The pronouns also relieve the writer from a boring repetition of the data to keep it fresh before the reader.

Repetition need not be boring, however, if it is carried out with the goal of brevity in mind:

▲ *Wrong*—To prepare for the November meeting of the board, we obtained additional information from the files. The information we obtained revealed that . . . .

▲ *Right*—To prepare for the November meeting of the board, we obtained additional *information* from the files, *information* revealing that . . . .

By using the word *information,* the writer can remind the reader that the rest of the document concerns material from the files. The writer need not keep telling where the information came from.

Transitions using connectives, pronouns, and repetition aid the comprehensibility of an accountant's writing and create a favorable image in the reader's mind. Other transitional devices, such as forward and backward reference in reports, will be described in the chapters on report writing. The seemingly trivial techniques discussed above, however, are among the most powerful language tools for developing a good writing style. The accountant ignores them at peril.

Checkoff 6.1 **ACCOUNTING COMMUNICATIONS: WRITING TO CREATE A FAVORABLE IMAGE**

	YES	NO
BREVITY		
1. Am I emphasizing quality over quantity?	____	____
2. Am I seeking to express rather than to impress?	____	____
3. Am I avoiding needless word pairs such as *debts and obligations?*	____	____
4. Am I avoiding turning verbs into subject-nouns with *-ment, -ion,* and similar endings?	____	____
5. Am I cutting down on the number of glue words (such as *that, the, to, a*)?	____	____
6. Have I reduced clauses beginning with *who, which,* and *that* into phrases whenever possible?	____	____
7. Have I eliminated vague subject-verb combinations of the *it is, there is,* and *this is* variety?	____	____
8. Have I cut down on the number of wordy preambles to opinions and statements?	____	____
9. Have I pruned unnecessary words, pretentious words, and repeated words and phrases?	____	____
COMPLETENESS		
10. Have I explained what information is lacking and what can be done about the lack?	____	____
11. Have I given some direction to the reader on how to use the information I have provided?	____	____
12. Have I avoided overuse of qualifying and conditional words such as *perhaps, seems, cautiously,* and *would?*	____	____
PARAGRAPH PATTERNS		
13. Do my paragraphs follow one of the patterns common to English?	____	____

(continued)

Checkoff 6.1 (concluded)

PARALLEL CONSTRUCTION AND TRANSITIONS	YES	NO
14. Have I gone back over my first draft and inserted parallel wording and transitional wording?	____	____
15. Have I used parallel wording to signal the reader that ideas, facts, or statements are related to each other?	____	____
16. Have I used transitional wording to signal the reader that new or opposite ideas or facts are now to be discussed?	____	____
17. Have I used pronouns such as *these* and *this* to connect new statements to old?	____	____
18. Have I repeated key words to remind the reader about prior assertions and statements?	____	____

chapter 7 Homing In on Good Writing

What is good writing? Certainly it is writing that is easily understood, that follows the rules of grammar and syntax, and that creates a favorable image of the writer. This definition is satisfactory, but more than a definition is in order if we are to sense the reality of one of humankind's most complex activities. We will examine writing, therefore, in comparison with thinking and talking and then describe the writing process as it takes place.

WRITING, THINKING, AND TALKING

Few people realize that thinking and writing are two different processes. As they think, so they write. Thoughts pop up and go down on the paper. Even good thinkers follow this procedure. When the disorderly nature of their writing is pointed out, they are offended. They see their writing as their thoughts, and their thoughts as themselves. An attack on their writing is an attack on them. Note what happens: The next time they will not improve their writing; they will be more guarded and circumspect in their thoughts. The result in the writing will be gobbledygook, bureaucratese, and similar writing of a kind well known to accountants.

All of this need not be. If accountants will only understand the differences between thinking and writing, they will realize that thoughts are greatly altered in writing:

Thinking		Writing
Disorderly facts		Orderly facts
Randomly selected ideas		Selected ideas
Uncensored feelings	altered	Controlled feelings
Thinker-oriented point of view	into	Reader-oriented point of view
Purposeless musing		Purposeful communicating
Unassailable ephemera		Criticizable document
Unconnected facts		Connected facts

The point is that thinking is easy, writing is not. Thinking is a messy business, writing is not. Thinking is natural, writing is highly artificial.

Another easy, messy, and natural activity is talking, and the accountant must realize that talking is also different from writing:

Talking		Writing
Repeated statements		Nonrepeated statements
Exploratory probing	altered	Statements of discovery
Digressive musings	into	Focused assertions
Nonverbal aids		Graphic aids
Retractable statements		Less retractable statements

When we examine something we have written, we should ask ourselves, *"Can I say it aloud without sounding silly or muddled?"* An honest yes answer tells us that our work will read easily and flow along smoothly. But we should not let this sensible test of good writing fool us into thinking that we should write as we talk. We shouldn't. Talking is repetitive, exploratory, digressive, often nonverbal, and retractable. Writing is none of these things. Indeed, good writing read aloud will sound sane and ordered, but it will also sound different from talking. It will sound somewhat contrived and artificial. The writing will sound, as it were, formal. We should perhaps think of good writing as speech dressed up in a tuxedo.

THE WRITING PROCESS

Writing is often said to be linear. An introduction proceeds to a middle, which leads to an ending:

This model of the process is true enough for simple memos, letters, and working papers. Complex writing, however, is more convoluted:

The looping parts involve such things as backward-looking summaries and forward-looking signals about upcoming topics. Thus writing does not move relentlessly onward. Generally speaking, *writing is not linear.* If we look at the good writer at work, we can see this looping process developing.

The Good Writer at Work

What does a good writer do? We will assume that he has defined reader needs, learned the rules of grammar, and worked to develop a favorable style. With these tasks in hand he follows a process that remains the same no matter what the writing situation.

Exploring the Information

The writer begins by touring through the information he has collected with the reader's needs and his own goals always in mind. He makes more than one tour:

Tour 1. Here he makes notes (in sentences rather than fragments) with the aim of creating communication chunks that will be the basic units of his message. Some of his notes will be more than information for his message. They will be helpful hints to himself—identifying related chunks, tentative hypotheses, possible conclusions and recommendations, likely comparisons to make, and standards useful for evaluating data.

Tour 2. The next step is to go through the notes and the information again, reading this time with the goal of labeling chunks. Some sort of one-to-five-word heading is put on each note/chunk.

Organizing the Information

Now the writer rereads his helpful hints and finds a large table. On the table he makes piles of notes with similar headings. Let's say he creates fifteen piles corresponding to fifteen headings. He then turns to his helpful hints and looks for advice regarding relationships among the headings that will allow him to create categories. He makes a list of headings and encompassing categories.

Outlining

Only now does the writer make an outline. Some people think that outlining is a first step, but in fact it cannot be undertaken without exploring and organizing. When it is done right, the result is a statement of all the major topics and subtopics in the order the reader will read about them. The order, however, is *not* the order in which the writer will write about them.

First Writing

If the writer's notes are in sentence form rather than in fragments, the first writing is easy. However, the topic written about first should be the last topic to be read by the reader. Suppose that the writing will be the recommendations in an internal audit report. The order of first writing would be:

1. Recommendations;
2. Conclusions that support the recommendations;
3. Analyses, measurements, evaluations, and the like, that support the conclusions.

This approach guards somewhat against the perils of a drifting mind. Mind drift can lead both to analyses that do not lead to the conclusions stated and to recommendations that do not follow logically from the conclusions. Although this phenomenon can occur when one writes recommendations first, the likelihood is greater that the relevant topics will be related.

Second Writing

Now the writer reads what he has written. He makes changes if he can't answer positively the following questions:

1. *Have I got a plain English topic sentence for each major paragraph?* Note that accountants with sophisticated technical skills often write in an inductive manner, with facts and assertions leading to some sort of statement at the end of a paragraph. Often this last sentence in a paragraph is really best placed as the topic-identifying first sentence:

▲ *Wrong*—At the Central Office the various reports from the divisions can be collated. Danger spots can be pinpointed and managers alerted. Moreover, control procedures can be developed from the information in the reports, which will minimize the possibilities of loss. *Each division thus should make up a monthly credit report and send it to the Central Office.*

▲ *Right*—*Each division should make up a monthly credit report and send it to the Central Office.* At the Central Office the various reports from the divisions can be collated. Danger spots can be pinpointed and managers alerted. Moreover, control procedures can be developed from the information in the reports, which will minimize the possibilities of loss.

2. *Is only one major point made in each paragraph?*

3. *Will each sentence easily be seen by the reader to be somehow related to the sentences before and after it?* If the writer has even the slightest

sense of unease about sentence relationships, he can expect the reader's bewilderment to be ten times greater. Most of us, after all, will tend to evaluate our own writing on a much higher level than others will.

4. *Does each paragraph look like one of the paragraph models common to English?*

Essentially, then, the second writing is a tightening process. Such writing is the hardest of all, because it involves our admitting to ourselves that we have made mistakes that need correcting. Few accountants seem to realize this point. They think that getting the words down on paper is the hardest writing work they have to do. But if they have explored the information and organized adequately, the words will pour onto the page in a great rush. The real agony will come with the second writing. (Note: If the words do *not* pour onto the page in the first writing, the accountant should realize that she has not explored and organized as well as she could. This problem is common, since accounting information often is highly complex and hard to understand. Bad writing, then, is more the result of bad preparation than of lack of writing skills. Indeed, the author has encountered many accountants who were all too eager to blame their own lack of skills for their bad writing instead of their lack of preparation before writing.)

Writing the Introduction

When all the discussion and terminal parts of the writing are finished, the introduction is written. It is the hardest part to write and is best left until last. In this way the writer simply needs to tell the reader what the writing is about and in what order the topics will be discussed. If the introduction is written first, the writer tells what he *thinks* the writing will cover. Unfortunately, our minds often may disagree, and what gets written may not be what was introduced. This is mind drift again, and it is avoided by writing introductions last.

Making Connections

Finally, the writer ties it all together. He goes over the work again and does the following:

▲ Adds transition words where appropriate—such words as *however, in addition,* and *indeed.*

▲ Inserts parallel language forms to indicate related items.

▲ Adds headings to the work to aid reader comprehension (if he hasn't done so already).

▲ Breaks up items in a series into a list set off by marginal white space (such as the list the reader is now reading).

▲ Inserts graphic aids—such as tables and charts—to add interest and to foster comprehension. (Note: In complex report writing, the graphic aids often are the very first things done instead of the last. We are speaking here only of general writing habits.)

▲ Inserts summary paragraphs after a long and complex analysis or discussion. These are called *backward references*. Moreover, the writer sometimes signals to the reader at the end of a paragraph the nature of the next paragraph. This signal is called a *forward reference*. We will discuss these in more depth in the chapters on reports.

ASSESSING WRITING PERFORMANCE

Once the writing is done, the accountant should set it aside, if possible, and then reread it several days later. At that time she can more objectively assess her writing performance—and perhaps check for readability with the Flesch Reading Ease Formula. Assessment immediately after writing will be faulty; the writer is too much in her work. After a few days, however, the writer has changed—ever so slightly—but the writing hasn't. It will be as if she is evaluating another person's work.

Evaluating the Thought

The primary purpose of the writing should be crystal clear right away, and the thought that developed the purpose should be adequate and appropriate.

Examining Facts and Opinions

One of the truly important activities of the accountant in assessing her writing is to examine the mix of facts and opinions. Opinions should be labeled as such with prefatory statements such as *"We feel"* or, better yet, *"We believe."* However she does it, the accountant has a duty to the reader to differentiate between what exists and what she feels. In this regard inferences, which are a mix of facts and opinions, can cause special problems. We will discuss inference making and inference communicating in Chapter 12.

Providing Enough Facts

Once opinions have been muted and inferences evaluated as logical and acceptable, the accountant turns to the facts. Are there too many, too few, or just enough facts? Many accountants tend to overload their work with data not needed to make the point stated or implied in the purpose. Such people are seeking to impress rather than express—although they may be dutifully responding to reader demands for more and more information. By the same token, a few accountants make conclusions and recommendations on the basis of inadequate supporting details.

Making a Proper Analysis

Analysis involves the following steps:

▲ Examining the data and information;

▲ Qualifying assertions when qualification is needed;

▲ Identifying and justifying assumptions employed in making inferences;

▲ Using the best analytical tool for the situation—be it statistics, logical relationships, or whatever—and not settling for the easiest tool;

▲ Making obvious conclusions—and not stating conclusions that do not emerge out of the discussion.

The reader must be able to follow the analysis with ease, and the writer must use concrete wording to help:

▲ *Wrong*—The benefits of liberalizing sales terms are shown *in the attached exhibits.*

▲ *Right*—The benefits of liberalizing sales terms are shown *in Exhibits 4 and 5.*

▲ *Wrong*—In 1982 the company adopted a plan of deferred payments for certain retail dealers. Current accounts receivable *indicate a heavy use* of this plan.

▲ *Right*—In 1982 the company adopted a plan of deferred payments for certain retail dealers. Current accounts receivable *include $15,055,790* under this plan.

▲ *Wrong*—Overtime wages are a *substantial part* of the product's labor cost.

▲ *Right*—Overtime wages are *45 percent* of the product's labor cost.

Without concrete wording of the kind shown above, the reader often must guess at the meaning of words such as *heavy, substantial, important, convenient, successful,* and similar adjectives. If the reader's guess does not match the writer's thought, the reader will be less likely to follow the analysis.

Establishing Proper Tone

Once the accountant is satisfied that her facts are separated from her opinions, that she has enough facts, and that the facts have been analyzed properly, the final assessment of her performance involves the evaluation of *tone.* This somewhat vague word is here defined to mean writing that is tactful, avoids clichés, uses the positive over the negative and the active over the passive, and avoids boring the reader.

Being Tactful

Tact involves the recognition of status differences. When an accountant is communicating to a reader above her in status, she should employ more than enough facts to support strongly any conclusions or recommendations made. This strong support embodies a connotation that she does not have the organizational clout that allows opinions to be taken as gospel.

Tact also requires a sense of role and position differences, as well as goal differences. The accountant who immerses himself or herself in crunching numbers sometimes assumes that everyone else in the organization has an equal love for statistics. Needless to say, what is precision swimming for the accountant may be unseemly drowning for another manager. In sum, then, tactful writing recognizes reader needs and is reader oriented.

Avoiding Clichés

The real problem with clichés—overused words and phrases—is not so much that they are boring, but rather that they communicate an image of the accountant as boring, or lazy, or too frightened by the specter of unexpected reader responses to write something different. Accountants, most of whom are rather interesting people, nevertheless have been stereotyped for years as boring because of, among other things, their penchant for cliché writing. Such writing must stop.

Using Positive over Negative Writing

Negative writing stimuli will elicit negative responses:

- *Negative message*—We recommend that you cease your practice of retaining bonds payable under long-term liabilities until maturity instead of placing them in current liabilities when within one year of maturity.

- *Positive message*—We recommend that you move bonds payable from long term to current liabilities when the bonds are within one year of maturity.

- *Negative response*—We did something wrong, and we must change our balance sheets.

- *Positive response*—We should change to improve our future balance sheets.

Accountants should emphasize the future, not the past; what they can do, not what they can't do; what to seek, not what to avoid:

- *Negative*—I can't have the data ready today.
- *Positive*—I can have the data ready by Thursday at noon.

▲ *Negative*—You can't compare profits at the northern plant with profits at the southern plant because of the flood last year at the northern plant.

▲ *Positive*—Because of the flood last year at the northern plant, you should adjust its profit data so we can compare it to the southern plant.

▲ *Negative*—We suggest that you avoid the use of replacement cost instead of net book value in valuing assets in your investment centers.

▲ *Positive*—We suggest that you employ net book value rather than replacement cost to value assets in your investment centers.

In substituting positive for negative messages, however, accountants must realize that they risk not getting the message across in the way intended:

▲ *Accountant's positive message*—Everything is in good shape with the exception of your valuation of inventories.

▲ *Receiver's interpretation*—The audit has turned out well except for a minor matter.

▲ *Accountant's intended interpretation*—We have have found a material weakness in inventory evaluation that will affect our opinion.

Here the auditor should have pointed out all the favorable results of the audit and then said, "However, we have encountered what we believe is an inventory situation requiring a major reevaluation."

Using Active over Passive Verbs

The use of active rather than passive verbs adds a tone of responsibility to the writing. Consider the following:

▲ *Wrong*—It was determined by the assistant controller that the cost was not traceable to that product.

▲ *Right*—The assistant controller determined that the cost was not traceable to that product.

▲ *Wrong*—The difference between the actual cost and the standard cost was determined by the accountant.

▲ *Right*—The accountant determined the difference between the actual cost and the standard cost.

In both cases the reader's sense of who did what is improved by placing the actor as subject and making the verb active. The passive-verb versions have an air of mystery about them, as if the determining person did not want anyone to grasp fully what she did. Such writing is often referred to as *camouflaged*. Accountants who engage in this writing can seriously damage their credibility.

Avoiding Needless Repetition
and Using a Thesaurus

As we have seen, words that are repeated can serve as good transitions between different statements concerning that word's referent. The needless repetition of words, however, bores the reader and creates an image of the writer as slipshod and careless:

▲ *Wrong*—The *equity ratio* has several definitions. The *equity ratio* can include current liabilities, or the *equity ratio* can exclude current liabilities.

▲ *Right*—The equity ratio has several definitions, depending on whether or not current liabilities are included.

With the use of a thesaurus, needless repetition is rarely a problem:

▲ *Wrong*—In commenting on the effect of accelerated depreciation, management *pointed out* that it had to be regarded as a temporary expedient. Furthermore, management *pointed out* that it still fell far short of wholly offsetting inadequate depreciation of the older facilities.

▲ *Right*—In commenting on the effect of accelerated depreciation, management *pointed out* that it had to be regarded as a temporary expedient. Furthermore, management *noted* that it still fell far short of wholly offsetting inadequate depreciation of the older facilities.

Checkoff 7.1 **ACCOUNTING COMMUNICATIONS: HOMING IN ON GOOD WRITING**

	YES	NO
DIFFERENTIATING WRITING FROM THINKING AND TALKING		
1. Have I realized that my thinking is generally disorderly and must be arranged and modified if it is to become writing?	___	___
2. Have I tested my writing by reading it aloud?	___	___
3. When I read it aloud, did it sound smooth and flowing but still more formal and artificial than talking?	___	___
DOING A WRITING TASK		
4. Have I visualized my writing task as a linear process with loopings?	___	___
5. Have I explored the information, making notes in sentence form, to create (1) the communication chunks of the message and (2) helpful hints to myself for final writing?	___	___
6. Have I then reread my notes and labeled every chunk?	___	___

(*continued*)

Checkoff 7.1 *(continued)*

	YES	NO
7. Have I assembled my list of labels and my helpful hints and created a heading system to serve as the outline of my writing as well as to provide the headings for the work?	___	___
8. Have I written backwards, saving the introduction as my last writing?	___	___
9. Have I then tightened my first writing, (1) inserting proper topic sentences, (2) looking for only one major point per paragraph, (3) checking that each sentence is related to those before and after, and (4) identifying each paragraph as modeled on a common pattern?	___	___
10. Have I realized that my hardest writing task is the tightening and not the first writing? (Note: If first writing seemed hardest of all, then the accountant should go back and do more exploring, organizing, and outlining.)	___	___
11. Have I then gone back and made connections, employing transition words, parallel language, lists, extra headings if needed, graphic aids if needed, and forward/backward references?	___	___

ASSESSING WRITING PERFORMANCE

	YES	NO
12. Have I set my writing aside for a few days, if possible, to let it simmer before my assessment?	___	___
13. When I look at the writing again, is the purpose crystal clear right away?	___	___
14. Have I labeled opinions by employing such devices as *"We believe?"*	___	___
15. Are my inferences sensible?	___	___
16. Have I avoided overloading the writing with data?	___	___
17. Have I qualified my assertions when (and only when) necessary?	___	___
18. Have I identified and justified my assumptions?	___	___
19. Have I used the best analytical tools—such as statistics or logic—and not settled for the easiest?	___	___
20. Have I made obvious conclusions and avoided conclusions not emerging out of the analysis?	___	___
21. Have I made abstract terms concrete to help the reader follow the analysis more easily?	___	___
22. Have I been tactful, showing that I sense the role and status differences between me and my readers?	___	___
23. Have I avoided cliché writing?	___	___

Checkoff 7.1   (*concluded*)

	YES	NO
24. Have I employed positive over negative writing, emphasizing the future instead of the past, what can be done instead of what can't, and what to seek instead of what to avoid?	____	____
25. Have I used active over passive verbs as a way of sharing and taking responsibility for the action described?	____	____
26. Have I avoided needless repetition and used a thesaurus where appropriate?	____	____

chapter 8 Accounting and Language

Language is the primary medium accountants use to communicate their perceptions of reality. Their reported perceptions, however, are only static, point-in-time observations and inferences about processes and events. They are not financial reality itself. Moreover, to communicate their perceptions accountants must employ the symbols of language. Thus their accounting communications are but a representation of a representation of financial reality (an isomorphism):

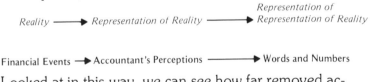

Looked at in this way, we can see how far removed accounting terminology is from reality, and we can sense the difficulty accountants face in developing useful information.

The problem is further compounded when we realize that decisionmakers often cannot observe financial reality themselves but must depend on the words and numbers of an accountant:

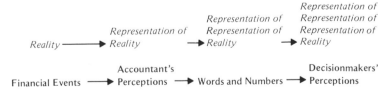

Even worse, when decisionmakers communicate decisions to managers charged with controlling the financial condition of the firm, the perceptions of those managers will be *representations of representations of representations of representations of representations of financial reality*. The likelihood of the firm responding to financial reality under such conditions is low. The key to raising the likelihood is the care that the accountant takes in perceiving and communicating. The accountant is at the beginning of the process, so if he or she does a good job, the firm's hope of doing a good job is raised.

THE MEANING OF ACCOUNTING COMMUNICATIONS

Accountants are faced with two choices:

▲ First they must choose from among all possible perceptions the perceptions to represent financial reality.

▲ Then they must choose the words and numbers (the symbols) to represent their perceptions in their communications.

The perceptions are chosen because they are:

▲ *Relevant*—They pertain to the real world.

▲ *Conventional*—A competent accountant would generally choose the same perceptions to represent reality.

▲ *Verifiable*—Most accountants would agree that these perceptions can be shown to be true representations of reality (Stanga, 1977).

The words and numbers are chosen because they will be understandable to clients and other decisionmakers.

We can see that the accountant establishes the meaning of a communication by estimating how others—accountants and decisionmakers—will react to it. This is a wise move, because the real meaning of an accounting message, a financial statement, or whatever is determined by the mind of the message receiver and not by the mind of the accountant.

The hard fact is that no accounting term—not one—has any innate meaning. Try to define the term *material*. No matter how hard we try and how elaborate the definition, there will always be an exception. Someone always could come along and point out a part of the definition that was lacking. The reason is that there is no inherent meaning of the term for us to grasp. *Meanings are not in words and numbers; they are in us.* What's more, accountants can only estimate the meanings of their terminology, because the meanings will not occur until the reader/listener's mind processes the information.

The point is that accountants are using some rather highly flawed tools to do their job. If they want to communicate financial information well, they must exercise great care in their choice of perceptions and, more important in this book, their choice of words. Such care will aid decisionmakers in creating meaning that adequately represents financial reality.

AVOIDING GOBBLEDYGOOK   Technical language in financial communications is inevitable, but it can be made meaningful to decisionmakers by the use of readable definitions and glossaries. Moreover, such language, when it precisely represents reliable and relevant accounting perceptions, is valuable and to be desired. In the case of jargon and gobbledygook, however, precise representations are not at issue. Indeed, we can define accounting gobbledygook as imprecise linguistic representation of financial perceptions. Why does such language occur so often in accounting communications?

Why Gobbledygook Occurs

Gobbledygook, or jargon, is characterized by obscure, pretentious, and unattractive technical language. It is tangled prose written by people who, without realizing what they are doing, appear pompous and stuffy to a reader. As Herman Melville observed, "a man of true science uses but a few hard words . . . whereas the smatterer in science . . . thinks that by mouthing hard words he understands hard things." Reading gobbledygook is like wading through wet sand. Every accountant knows gobbledygook when she sees it. Every accountant hates to read it and looks with scorn on the writer. Why then do so many accountants so often write it?

The causes of jargon/gobbledygook are complex and pervasive in our business culture. Sometimes an accountant deliberately chooses to write jargon for a variety of reasons. Other times jargon emerges without conscious intent to confuse and to bore. Let's look at the causes.

Poor Accounting Perceptions.   When an accountant is not in touch with the financial data and isn't sure how to analyze it and make conclusions, we can say that due to ignorance or to a complex situation, the accountant's perceptions are poor. Since precise language cannot occur if perceptions are poor, imprecise gobbledygook like the following often occurs:

> The results were that plant production is chiefly a moderate function of physical limitations, with high interactive input from labor factors.

We cannot tell whether labor or plant capacity is the most important determinant of production, probably because the accountant wasn't sure. The result of such uncertainty is sometimes gobbledygook.

128

Fear of the SEC. As we noted earlier, many accountants write with one eye over their shoulder, worried that the SEC may be gaining on them. Seriously though, SEC regulations have had a chilling effect on accounting communications as accountants write to fulfill legal requirements rather than to communicate with clients and managers. An impenetrable legal jargon results, which pleases no one except a book of regulations.

Impressing Rather than Expressing. A few people—a very few—are actually impressed by gobbledygook like this:

> The multifarious, overlapping program contributions by a myriad of individuals acting independently failed to result in a single, comprehensive program because of the fact that at their incipience they were not governed and regulated by a carefully conceived master plan under which they could have matured to a systematic singularity.

This gem of nonsense was collected by John O'Hayre for *Gobbledygook Has Gotta Go* (U.S. Government Printing Office, n.d.). The gist of it seems to be that a lack of program goals and poor coordination led to poor program performance. Simple enough, but the writer wanted to impress readers with a sophisticated analysis. The few who were impressed should be compared with the many who were outraged. (Incidently, several hundred years ago Molière built a play around a character who is terribly impressed by jargon. At one point the character says, "That must be fine, for I don't understand a word of it."—Molière, *The Physician in Spite of Himself*)

Desire to Communicate Status. Sometimes accountants employ pompous jargon to signal to the organization that they have a certain high status worthy of respect.

Belief that Presenting More Is Better. In their desire to reduce uncertainty, accountants want to present more and more financial information. Too often, however, they think only of the benefits without considering the potential costs of lapsing into windy writing that confuses rather than aids decisionmakers.

Covering Up. When accountants haven't much to report yet are required to say something, a deluge of gobbledygook can be anticipated:

> Overall parameter analysis revealed a dynamic output implementation program retarded somewhat by compatibility issues, evolving out of operational system interactions.

Avoiding Responsibility. A clear conclusion and a concrete recommendation in an accounting report are what decisionmakers seek and for which they will hold accountants responsible. Naturally some accountants will occasionally try to hedge by employing gobbledygook:

> Concerning internal inventory controls, we recommend the functional implementation of an integrated system of compliance testing. This system should be based on a highly determined set of conceptual performance criteria.

This bit of jargon could be interpreted as recommending anything from scrapping the whole compliance-testing system to simply stating the criteria on which it is based.

What Not to Do

We have seen the causes of gobbledygook and jargon to be many. With so many causes there is little wonder that it is so widespread in accounting. But gobbledygook need not be. No one likes it, and most accountants will avoid it if given some guidance. To begin with, there are a number of things to avoid.

Avoid Preposition Overload. As we saw in an earlier chapter, little words can be deadly:

▲ *Wrong*—This acquisition will be mutually beneficial *through* elimination of problems connected *with* the management *of* diverse products *by* consolidating products *into* product lines *for* each firm.
▲ *Right*—This acquisition allows us to establish product lines at each firm. Overall management will improve.

Here little words led to slow-moving, tangled writing. The writer should have read through the work and rewritten to speed it up by taking out the prepositions.

Avoid Noun Clusters. Gobbledygook through overuse of prepositions is hard to spot. Every accountant, however, recognizes big-word jargon formed by turning vague nouns into vague adjectives, which are then used to modify vague nouns:

Sequential systems support	Multiple interactive compatibility
Operational output basis	Functional capabilities area
Conceptual performance interface	Incremental input criteria

These noun clusters are meaningless globs that stain any page on which they appear. What's worse, the writer can't plead ignorance of what he was doing.

Such clusters have to be created; they don't appear fully formed in nature. Whoever uses them, therefore, is probably engaged in some kind of deception involving the apparent communication of a message that in fact has little or no meaning. An astute reader will soon begin to doubt the credibility of the accountant who employs such noun clusters.

Avoid Overelaborate Diction. Some professionals, in their desire to sound official, employ wording that is more elaborate than it need be:

▲ *Wrong*—We have *ascertained* that questionable inventory accounting was *utilized* to *enhance* net income.

▲ *Right*—We have *determined* that questionable inventory accounting was *used* to *increase* net income.

Avoid Circumlocution. Circumlocution is a big word meaning beating around the bush. Its use obscures the message:

▲ *Wrong*—At the present time our department is planning to increase revenue-generating activities and to implement cost-reduction strategies.

▲ *Right*—Currently our department is planning to increase selling and cost-cutting activities.

We are not suggesting that abrupt, curt messages are good. Rather we claim that endless getting ready to say something is not nearly as valuable as actually saying it.

What to Do

Writers who would avoid gobbledygook and jargon must commit themselves to always asking, "Would I want to read this stuff?" They must also be willing to take responsibility for making clear statements even when a risk-avoiding attitude would require the cloak of jargon. And they must realize that in writing well they will be part of a minority among some of their peers, since unfortunately jargon is often the rule rather than the exception.

RELIABLE USE OF ACCOUNTING LANGUAGE Reliable language is accurate language in which words mean the same to both senders and receivers of messages. Accountants must be careful, therefore, to be consistent in their language usage. The AICPA and other professional bodies have defined certain technical terms to foster consistent usage, but many nontechnical words deserve equal treatment. Drawing on the work of accounting communicators (Palen, 1955; Devine, 1962), we can identify a number of key words that need defining. Several of the terms discussed below are compared with similar words that nevertheless are defined differently.

Arbitrary

When an auditor notes in a report that a sample of accounts payable were arbitrarily chosen for testing, she means that the choice was based on conventional procedures. Some people, however, interpret *arbitrary* to mean purposeless or meaningless, so accountants need to clarify their usage of the word.

Biennial versus Semiannual

Biennial means *every two years*; *semiannual* means *twice a year*.

Compilation versus Review

A *compilation* is a presentation of a client's financial statements without the accountant expressing any assurance of them. A *review* implies that inquiry and analyses were performed that provide a reasonable basis for expressing limited assurance that the statements do not require material modification to make them conform to generally accepted accounting principles (AICPA, 1978).

Confirmation versus Confirmation Request

Auditors do not mail confirmation to accounts receivable customers. They mail confirmation requests. *Confirmation* does not substitute for *confirmation request*.

Consistent

The word *consistent* can have two meanings:

▲ Data provides consistent information if two opposite and mutually exclusive conclusions cannot be drawn from it.

▲ Procedures are consistent if they are done the same way each time they are required.

Notice that inconsistent procedures in analyzing data do not necessarily make the data inconsistent, and consistent analysis of inconsistent data does not make the data valid. The best thing for an accountant to do is to provide statements regarding the consistency of both data and procedures.

Could versus Should

Could means is able to; *should* means ought to or must. A directive from a senior that tells an accountant that he *could* look into the rising unit-cost data of product A is poorly written in that it leaves the decision up to the junior. The senior needed to say *"should look into"* instead.

Debt

The word *debt* is vague. It could mean all liabilities or perhaps only long-term loans and bonds. Some analysts consider preferred stock as debt. The term almost always needs defining.

Difference versus Change

A *change* can be defined as a shift in the relationship of one variable to another. If net income drops 10 percent and cash flow also drops 10 percent, it seems likely that the firm's financial condition has changed in relation to what it was in the previous period. However, if net income drops 10 percent with no corresponding change in cash flow, then perhaps no real change in the financial condition has occurred but only a *difference*. By stating the new net income figure as simply different from the previous period, the accountant is signaling the analyst or the stockholder that a random fluctuation may have occurred instead of a decline in the financial condition. If the word *change* were used, the reader or listener would be expected to conclude that a statement regarding a financial decline was being made.

The word *different* has no evaluative connotations to it—we cannot say that to be different is to be bad or good. *Change,* however, does usually connote something bad or good happening in financial reporting.

Distortion

Consider this sentence from a report:

> Past profits have been corrected for distortions resulting from historical cost accounting practices.

The word *distortions* implies that past profit figures are wrong when in fact they are simply measured differently. Accountants should avoid the word unless they provide some kind of explanation of what *distortion* means.

Equity

Although the accounting definition of *equity* as assets minus liabilities is clear enough, decisionmakers will often think of it as only the value of the common stock. There is an obvious chance for nasty mix-ups here.

Error versus Irregularity

Errors are usually misstatements or control failures where no intent to deceive exists. *Irregularities* involve deliberate intent.

Exclude versus Preclude

The probability of a large customer account being uncollectable *excludes* it (shuts it out) from a calculation of current assets, but the firm's acceptance of a similar bad debt last year does not *preclude* (prevent) litigation to recover this year's debt.

Expense versus Expenditure

Accountants have no trouble differentiating between an *expense,* which is a decrease in owner's equity, and an *expenditure,* which is a cash or equivalent outlay in exchange for an asset or a service. But nonaccountants need to be told that in any given period expenses rarely equal expenditures.

Fact

A *fact* is a verifiable observation or an accepted truth. One should not say:

> The fact of the matter is that the liabilities are excessive.

In this sentence the word *fact* is misused to signal what is an opinion.

Feel versus Believe

Both *feel* and *believe* are verbs associated with opinions and inferences. *Believe*, however, suggests a more rational approach to the opinion than *feel* does.

Former versus Latter

Accountants should avoid using the words *former* and *latter,* since readers are often confused about which item in a series is being referred to. The opportunity for misunderstanding is too great.

Imply versus Infer

Excess inventory *implies* (suggests) that production problems exist. The accountant may *infer* (conclude) that too much production is occurring. The two words have different meanings and are not interchangeable.

In Order

Consider the following statement:

> Accounts receivable were inspected and found in order.

The phrase *in order* could mean either (1) that all the accounts were in the record or (2) that all were confirmed. *In order* is too vague without elaboration.

Legalisms

Words borrowed from the legal profession often choke off any meaning that a document is supposed to transmit to a reader. Words and phrases to avoid or to use sparingly are:

Aforesaid	Party
Aforementioned	Instant
Pursuant to	Herein
Same (as a noun)	Wherein
Said (as an adjective)	Therein

Logic, Logical

Use of the word *logic* implies a series of propositions leading to conclusions that lead to further propositions, and so on. Employing logic is a way of using language to make assertions. However, such assertions are not necessarily an accurate characterization of reality. Consider the following statement:

> Thus the logic of this depreciation method is beyond dispute, and for this reason we recommend its adoption.

The depreciation method may indeed be the one the firm needs to implement, but the logic behind it may not be the reason for its choice. Its usefulness may be the reason.

Logic tends to be doubly defined: (1) as the process by which a conclusion is reached and (2) as the usefulness of the entity so described in real world terms. Thus a depreciation method is *logical* either because it is indeed useful or because the statement that it is useful is consistent with the deliberations that led to the statement. Professionals need to clarify how they are using *logic* so that readers do not see a different meaning from the one intended.

Margin

The word *margin* alone is vague. One has to say *gross margin* or *net margin* before the meaning is clear.

Merits

Consider the following statement:

> The valuation process has been judged on its merits.

Merits can be determined by comparing entities, as in a valuation process, with rules, with common practice, with desires of seniors, or with a combination of these. The writer needs to say what *merits* means.

Normal

When an internal auditor refers to the "normal control procedures" regarding employee compensation benefit allocations, she means the desirable, right, and good procedures. But when the same auditor sends a memo to the controller attaching "the normal schedules," she means the usual and conventional documents in this situation. Thus *normal* can mean either desirable or conventional, and the accountant should make it clear which meaning is intended.

Probable, Possible, Potential

What is *probable* is more likely than what is *possible*. When the accountant is reasonably certain that about 5 percent of accounts receivable will be bad debts, he speaks of probable losses on accounts receivable, not possible losses. *Possible* and *potential* are close in meaning, but *potential* has more favorable connotations. One speaks of potential revenues and possible expenses.

Presently

Presently can mean now or shortly; thus it is a vague word. Professionals should use *now* or an exact future time in place of *presently*.

Profit

Here is another one of those words that have multiple meanings to decision-makers. Profits can be:

▲   Net income (before or after taxes),

▲   Dividends,

▲   Retained earnings,

▲   Cash inflow less cash outflow,

▲   Gross margin

The only safe course for accountants is to define *profits* when they use it and to ask for a definition when they see or hear it.

Profitability

The word *profitability* requires a definition of which kind of rate of return is being employed as a measure of a company's performance:

▲   *Accounting rate of return*—Average annual net income divided by total investment.

▲   *Coupon rate*—Rate stated on a bond.

▲ *Dividend yield*—Simply stated, stock's annual dividend divided by stock's price. However, users of the measure need to be told whether stock price used is current, average, or purchase.

▲ *Internal rate of return (IRR)*—Rate such that present value of annual cash flows minus present value of annual investment equals zero. Calculation usually requires tables or a computer. Lowest possible IRR that a firm requires is called its *opportunity cost*. Lowest limit of IRR that a firm will accept is usually the cost of its capital. IRR is the best measure of profitability available but the most difficult to communicate to decisionmakers who don't understand it. Sometimes graphs are used to represent IRR, but often accountants must employ more easily grasped measures if they seek reader comprehension.

▲ *Return on equity*—Usually net income divided by equity. As we saw above, however, *equity* is a vague word and ought to be defined.

▲ *Return on investment (ROI)*—Net income divided by average investment for period covered by net income. Investment can equal (1) assets minus liabilities (*shareholders' equity* or *investment*) or (2) noncurrent liabilities plus shareholders' investment (*total investment*). Sometimes return on total investment is calculated by using operating profit (net income before income taxes plus interest on noncurrent liabilities) instead of net income. (Notice that return on equity may be the same as ROI—it all depends on the definition.)

▲ *Yield*—Investment dividend or interest on a bond divided by current market value of investment.

▲ *Yield to maturity*—IRR of a bond or long-term security. Based on annual interest, initial cost, and final sale price or maturity value. Yield to maturity is a better measure of a security's profitability than is yield or coupon rate. Once again, however, it is harder to comprehend than the simpler rates.

Realistic

When someone refers to "a more realistic basis for cost accounting" or some such phrase, a definition of the vague word *realistic* is called for.

Realize versus Incur, Sustain, or Experience

A firm can *realize* cash, revenues, or income, but it *incurs, sustains,* or *experiences* costs or losses. The two sets of terms are not interchangeable.

Revenue

Revenue is an increase in owners' equity, technically speaking. From the point of view of cultural values, however, the concept of revenue is more vague. For example, in Japan a sale may occur and "revenue" may be recorded, but at a later date the goods may be sent back and the money returned. Every sale is contingent upon the maintenance of mutual trust between sellers and buyers. If trust is threatened, the transaction is deemed inappropriate. Thus transactions are trials rather than verifiable exchanges, yet the money exchanged is called *revenue* in Japan even though it would probably not be called so in the United States. The point is that *revenue* is defined in cultural as well as technical ways; thus international accounting communicators need to be aware of differing concepts of the term in different cultures. The same could be said of such terms as *profit* and *capital*.

True

The word *true* implies a false rather than simply an alternative measure:

> The true depreciation expense is . . . .
> The true cash balance is . . . .

In these examples there is no "false" depreciation expense or cash balance as implied by *true*. Thus the word should generally be avoided.

Value

Value is often used as a verb (*"we valued the inventories at cost"*). The word is vague, however, in that it may or may not imply worth. Instead of *valued,* words such as *priced* or *stated* should be used unless the accountant genuinely wants to suggest the worth of something.

Verify

Sometimes accountants say they verified something when they only mean that they counted or examined something. To *verify* is to prove the truth of something.

Very

The word *very* is used with evaluative words such as *good, bad, excellent,* and the like. Overuse of the word, however, detracts from the accountant's image as a sober appraiser of events. The word makes the accountant seem too excited and perhaps too excitable.

Checkoff 8.1 ACCOUNTING COMMUNICATIONS: ACCOUNTING AND LANGUAGE

CAREFUL FINANCIAL COMMUNICATING	YES	NO
1. Are the observations I make relevant, conventional, and verifiable?	____	____
2. Am I expressing my observations in words and numbers that are understandable to decisionmakers?	____	____
3. Do I realize that the meaning of my financial communications will be established in the minds of decisionmakers? Have I helped them to establish the meanings I intend?	____	____
4. Have I defined key technical terms?	____	____
5. Have I avoided imprecise, obscure, pretentious, and unattractive language without sacrificing the technical precision of my terminology?	____	____
6. Am I avoiding jargon and gobbledygook by		
▲ Knowing what I am talking or writing about?	____	____
▲ Communicating for clients rather than for the SEC?	____	____
▲ Not trying so hard to communicate status?	____	____
▲ Realizing that more words are not necessarily better than few words?	____	____
▲ Avoiding needless hedging and thus taking responsibility for my conclusions and recommendations?	____	____
▲ Keeping the number of prepositions in my writing to a minimum?	____	____
▲ Avoiding noun clusters (e.g., incremental input criteria)?	____	____
▲ Avoiding wording that is more elaborate than it need be?	____	____
▲ Avoiding beating around the bush?	____	____
▲ Asking myself, "Would I want to read this stuff?"	____	____
7. Am I consistent in my word usage, avoiding vague words and defining words with multiple meanings?	____	____

140

chapter 9 Memos and Letters

In this chapter we analyze memos and letters sent by accountants. They are similar in being usually (not always) brief and usually (not always) nonroutine. Accountants write them when called on to do so or when a situation demands them, in contrast to such things as routine flash reports. Memos differ from letters in that they are internal to an organization, whereas letters are sent to people external to the company. Moreover, letters tend to be more formal than memos. We discuss memos first, then describe letter types that accountants often employ.

MEMOS People often define a memo as a short communication. This is a faulty definition. A memo is an internal document, often short. The distinction is an important one, since some accountants may try to cram a large amount of information into too short a memo under the mistaken assumption that memos must be short. If they have much to say, they should employ long memos to say it.

Memos are single-issue communications. Usually an accountant who has more than one topic to cover should send multiple memos. This procedure facilitates the filing of memos under topic headings. In addition, it avoids the problem of topics covered second in a memo not getting the processing effort they deserve from decisionmakers. Before writing a memo, an accountant needs to consider the following questions (in addition to reader needs):

▲ *What is the organizational climate?* If the organizational climate is characterized by a sense of mutual trust among members, memos can contain assertions, conclusions, and opinions with less support material than in an organization where trust is absent. As we have noted earlier, trust enhances efficient, cost-effective communicating.

▲ *Is the timing right?* When a memo is sent can be just as important as what is in it. Thus a quick response to a request for financial information may (or may not) have a greater impact than a thorough but delayed response.

▲ *What image is to be projected?* In Chapter 3 we described how an accountant can project (1) an image of competence by employing brief memos that follow predictable formats or (2) an image of hard work by sending long memos with varied formats adapted to varied subjects. The kind of image one seeks should be decided before sending memos.

▲ *How formal should the memo be?* Memos that may be read by numerous people obviously can't be chatty and informal, nor should they contain expressions of the accountant's feelings and emotions.

▲ *What responses are likely?* The accountant should consider what the receiver will do after reading the memo *and* what others will do in response to the receiver's actions. A memo is like a pebble thrown into a pond: it can cause many ripples.

▲ *Will the memo be changed as it crosses levels in the organization?* As memos travel upward in organizations, they tend to get changed. Managers lop off parts of them, delete phrases, and add their own information. Typically accountants place memo parts that might be dropped at the end of the memo, where they are easily cut.

Why Memos Are Written

Memos ought to be sent only when necessary, and then only after consideration of oral and electronic channels of communication. If they must be sent, however, the reasons for sending them ought to involve the following (assuming that serving reader needs is the first reason):

▲ A need for documentation;

▲ A communication too complex for oral or electronic channels;

▲ The provision of data, information, announcements, reminders, and clarification;

▲ The provision of feedback to oral, electronic, or written communications;

▲ A striving for redundancy—the repetition of a message already sent to increase the likelihood of reception;

▲ The need to justify past action or to seek approval;

▲ An interest in some future action through requests (*asking*), directives (*telling*), recommendations (*suggesting*), or persuasion (*arguing*);

▲ A need to open a channel of communication or to keep one open;

▲ A desire to establish or demonstrate status or hierarchical rank in the organization.

Most accountants write memos to provide requested information or to create documentation. They should recognize, however, that their organizational peers write memos for many other reasons, including the last one mentioned—showing status. Indeed, the memo wars, as the endless flow of messages in the organization is sometimes called, exist for many reasons, and not all of them involve serving organizational goals.

The Ideal Memo Format

The form of memos varies from place to place, depending on situations and needs. Exhibit 9.1, then, is an idealized (but practical) version of a memo format. The unique feature of the exhibit is the Purpose/Action section at the bottom. Here the writer can clearly indicate what the memo is about and what ought to happen next. More than one item in each column can be checked, and elaboration, if any, can be typed in next to the items checked. Some purposes, such as persuasion and justification, are not listed for obvious reasons. One would probably check "Request" and "Information" in their place.

The most important feature of the memo is the "Subject." Here the heading, which is the title of the memo, is placed. The heading often is too short. It should be long enough to make the reader understand the purpose of the memo, not simply the topic:

Overly Concise Headings	Meaningful Headings
"Labor"	"Request for Additional Labor"
"Financing"	"Recommendation for Extensions on the Company's Loan"

Exhibit 9.1 **IDEAL MEMO FORMAT**

TO:
FROM:
DATE:
SUBJECT:
REFERENCES: 1. _____
2. _____

1. Purpose of memo—what the reader needs to know.
2. Background (discussion or analysis—who, what, when, where, why, how).
3. Summary of purpose in terms of result, conclusion, opinion, preference, choice, decision, recommendation, request, or directive.
4. Statement of response desired from reader and when needed.

Purpose of This Memo   **Action Recommended**

____ Information   ____ Approval/Acceptance

____ Approval   ____ File

____ Comment   ____ Comment

____ Response   ____ Response

____ Request   ____ Action

____ Directive   ____ Study

____ Recommendation   ____ None

____ Documentation

Writing for the Files

Accountants are often asked for important information in semiformal settings, such as over the telephone or at lunch. To protect themselves from misinterpretation, they sometimes will write a memo for the files. Then if the client or manager claims that she was told something that in fact she was not, the accountant will have evidence to support his denial.

In Exhibit 9.2 the accountant describes a telephone conversation. He recounts what the client said and his responses. Each paragraph covers a separate topic in the conversation as the conversation occurred. It is written like the synopsis of a dramatic script. The reader can almost create the dialogue from the description. Moreover, the organization is linear: the memo proceeds from the beginning of the conversation to the end. This approach is better than the usual memo approach dealing with the most important topic first.

Exhibit 9.2 **MEMO FOR THE FILES**

FOR: Memorandum for the files
DATE: March 12, 1981
SUBJECT: Spring Corporation: Summary of Jane Doe call to Jim Smith

On March 11, 1980, Jane Doe called and discussed SOP 78–8. She was calling to tell me that after reviewing the SOP and Spring's facts and circumstances, she concluded that the SOP did not apply to Spring. The basis for her conclusion was that Spring does not meet all the conditions or characteristics outlined in paragraph 4 of the SOP. I told Jane that my initial reaction was that the SOP probably did not apply to Spring and that if she did not hear from me by March 24, 1981, she could assume that I concurred with her conclusion.

We also discussed what the firm's possible position might be in the event the Arrow deal is consummated and Arrow assumes a significant amount of debt. Jane was concerned that we might require separate financial statements of the subsidiary because it would be one of the highest borrowers in the consolidated group of companies within Spring. I told her that I did not think we would unless we discovered a regulatory agency or local country accounting principle requiring such separate financial statements.

I also told Jane that I had a chance to reflect on one of the matters that came up at the luncheon on March 11. The question posed to me concerned a change in accounting principles regarding providing for taxes on the unrepatriated earnings of foreign subsidiaries. In connection with the Arrow transaction, certain tax planning techniques had been suggested. To take full advantage of the foreign tax credit available through the U.S. tax laws, it might be necessary for Spring to create a dividend in Hong Kong payable to the U.S. parent. I was asked if this would cause us to change our conclusion regarding deferred taxes on foreign subsidiaries. I told Jane that conceptually I did not feel it would; however, the facts and circumstances surrounding such dividends might mean the company can no longer support its present position. In that case, it would have to change its accounting policies.

The Crucial First Paragraph

The first paragraph in most memos, with the exception of the file memo type described above, covers what the accountant thinks the reader ought to know. It should begin *with the statement of purpose, not with lead-in background material:*

A Suggestion

▲ *Wrong*—During the last year we have acquired 500,000 shares of Alpha Systems at a cost of $15 million. Alpha's CEO is a director of our company, a fact that you should note in the financial statements. Since we acquired the stock, it has risen in market value by about $2 million.

▲ *Right*—I feel that you should note the acquisition of Alpha Systems in our financial statements. During the last year, we have acquired . . . .

Information

▲ *Wrong*—This memo is to inform you of a recent development concerning the taxability, for federal income tax purposes, of sickness disability benefits and disability pensions paid under this company's plan for employees' pensions and disability benefits.

▲ *Right*—If you have received sickness disability benefits and disability pensions from our company since 1978, you may be able to get a refund on some of your taxes. This memo explains the situation and what you should do.

Asking Isn't Telling

Managers, accountants, and clients, in the rush of everyday activities, will sometimes carelessly issue directives in the form of questions:

▲ *Wrong*—Analysis revealed that allowances for bad debts have reached 5 percent of total accounts receivable. Isn't some action required to reduce this percentage?

▲ *Right*—Some action should be taken to reduce allowances for bad debts. Analysis has revealed that bad debts are now 5 percent of total accounts. Please let me have your proposed actions by May 1.

The revision in this example turns the question into a directive and, following good memo format, places the directive at the top of the message. Discussion and future action follow (refer back to Exhibit 9.1).

Opinions and Evaluations in Memos

Another memo problem caused by time pressures and stress is the substitution of evaluative words and opinions for analysis:

> Based on the enormous increase in our costs, a 15 percent increase in prices seems inevitable.

Here the words *enormous* and *inevitable* embody opinions rather than facts. The memo should begin this way:

> Based on a 5 percent increase in costs each year for the last five years—an increase that I feel is enormous—I believe that the company will be compelled to increase prices.

This introduction, which employs phrases such as *I feel* and *I believe* as well as concretely states what *enormous* means, remains evaluative and opinionated, but legitimately so.

A careful accountant ought to go over memos before sending them, circle the adjectives, and then decide whether the adjectives imply unearned or unwarranted evaluations or opinions. (We will examine this topic again in Chapter 14 on face-to-face communicating.)

Support: Reason, Expertise, or Emotion

How should accountants support their assertions in memos? With reasoned analysis, dependence on their image of expertise, or gut-level feeling based on experience? Let's look at the example in Exhibit 9.3.

Clearly the emotional response of Rumpole is not the best support of the three; *but* later on, if no one can marshal enough evidence to recommend a decision, senior management may turn to Rumpole in desperation. When standards for deciding are weak or nonexistent and when measures are hard to come by or not trustworthy, gut-level feelings tend to become important. Essentially, the short-hand intuitive analysis of Rumpole may replace reasoned analysis if reasoned analysis doesn't get anybody anywhere.

As for the reason versus expertise support, the issue is in doubt. One would like to think that reason will always win out over a pose of expertise, but this is not so. Depending on expert opinion allows decisionmakers to avoid reading hard, detailed analyses. A manager who can trust an expert will often accept the expert's recommendation. (A variation of the above example given to fifty managers, by the way, produced twenty-seven in favor of reason as support, twenty-three in favor of expertise, and none favoring emotion.) The upshot is that accountants should use reason to support statements but also build their image of expertise.

Timing, Consistency, and Accuracy

Should an accountant send memos that contain accurate or consistent data and information? That is, should subject A be covered in the same consistent way in five different memos sent out over a week's time (consistency)? Or should subject A be covered in an accurate way by including new data in the memos as it comes in and by sending follow-up memos to people who received the old data (accuracy)? Management accountants face this consistency-versus-accuracy problem all the time as they collect new data on quarterly, monthly, and even daily activities. Let's frame the question another way. What do managers need: consistent or accurate data? Consistent data fosters coordination across units and will be perceived as authentic, whereas

Exhibit 9.3 **EXAMPLE: SUPPORTING ASSERTIONS IN MEMOS**

Thornton Broadbent, CEO of Amalgamated Industries, had raised the issue of dropping the meat-packing division of the company at a senior managers' meeting. He asked the controller/treasurer, Lenora Smith, for an opinion within the next two days—nothing elaborate, just something to begin the decision process. Ms. Smith asked three of her associates for their opinions and received them within twenty-four hours. Here are the first paragraphs of those memos:

Joan Graham's Memo:
Reasoned Analysis

I believe that meat packing is a strong candidate for divestiture. Return on equity has ranged between 11 and 13 percent over the last ten years, but the return on sales has been only between 3 and 4 percent. Our long-range forecasts show a drop in these figures over the next five years.

Jim Prescott's Memo: Dependence
on Expertise

I believe that meat packing should be retained. Studies I have conducted over the last few years strongly suggest that the meat-packing division gives us and should continue to give us a moderate but predictable return. Over time, this predictability will allow us to lower the risk element of our cost of capital. Thus lower costs will offset moderate revenues. I have attached copies of several position papers written by me on the general subject of risk and costs of capital.

Edmund Rumpole's Memo: Emotional
Feeling Based on Experience

I believe that meat packing should be retained and expanded. With over twenty-five years experience as controller of that division, I know what a solid unit it is. Moreover, people I trust over there tell me that prices are probably going to soar. With our large inventory, purchased at low prices a few years ago, we should reap large profits. Of course the quality of the inventory needs checking, but I'm certain we can depend on it.

accurate data will foster appropriate responses to reality but may not be viewed as authentic because it may not be consistent with data possessed by others. Thus, do managers need consistent and authentic-looking data in memos or do they need accurate but unauthentic-looking data? Consider the scenario in Exhibit 9.4.

Exhibit 9.4 **MEMOS: CONSISTENCY VERSUS ACCURACY**

You are a new analyst for the Proteus Corporation. Each Friday morning you receive a computer printout of the firm's sales activity for the past week. You then use the data to write two memos, one to the Marketing Department and one to Financial Planning. Each memo analyzes the data with a focus on the needs of each particular department.

Today is Friday, and you receive your printout early this morning. By noon you had sent your memo to Marketing, and you expect to write and send your memo off to Financial Planning this afternoon. However, at noon another memo is received from computer operations with a new printout. It seems that the data you received this morning is flawed. Parts of it are in error, but most of the data remains accurate.

You have a decision to make regarding the memo to Financial Planning. Should you use the old data to write your memo? That way your memo will be consistent with the one to Marketing. (The two departments talk to each other all the time and will undoubtedly discuss the data.) Of course, on Monday you will have to get off new memos to both units explaining the errors and reanalyzing the data. However, your credibility as an *accurate* analyst may be threatened.

An alternative decision is to use the new data for the memo to Financial Planning. On Monday you can get off another memo to Marketing (there isn't time to do it on Friday before everyone goes home). No one could accuse you of being inaccurate, but if the two departments talk to each other late Friday afternoon, they may discover the differences in the data. You may be labeled as being *inconsistent* in the information you supply to top management.

You can't call or visit either department because you've been told to keep out of the way on Fridays—which is the day they frantically pull together data from many sources to prepare instructions that will be transmitted to field managers on Monday morning. You know that any reanalyzed data you send out on Monday will be too late to affect the morning instructions.

No particular solution exists for the accuracy-versus-consistency problems described in the exhibit. No matter which approach you choose, someone is going to be offended. To protect yourself, you probably should be accurate, but to facilitate the coordinated interaction of Marketing and Financial Planning on Friday afternoon, you probably should be consistent (after all, the errors in the first memo are only a minor part of the data). In terms of criteria of relevance, reader orientation, and decision-aiding financial information, then, you should opt for consistency. In terms of criteria of maintaining or protecting a proper image, reliability, and reality, you should choose accuracy. What is the solution?

You could have avoided this trap by considering the *timing* of your memos. If you had held the Marketing memo until the Financial Planning memo was ready, both could have been quickly revised (for accuracy) or both units could have been notified that data errors required some adjustment in the routine (for consistency). Indeed, most accountants do not need to worry about consistency/accuracy traps because they carefully consider the timing of their memos and reports as part of their system of reporting.

Gaining Compliance with Decisions

A partner in an accounting firm decided to institute a new procedure. She sent a memo describing the procedure to the staff. Two months later she investigated and found that nothing had been done. Why did her communication fail? Let's assume that the staff is generally motivated to comply. Given that, the failure must lie in the communication process, not in the receiver. Here are some reasons why people do not comply:

▲　Lack of a clear indication that a decision is being communicated. The partner's memo could have been interpreted as a casual suggestion.

▲　Lack of a time frame and a date of implementation. If nothing is said about *when* something needs to be done, it may never get done.

▲　Lack of a designation of who is to carry out the decision. Without naming names, the memo can produce endless buck-passing.

▲　Lack of preparatory communications to build up the knowledge of the staff so that they can easily process the directive when it appears.

▲　Lack of planned feedback so that questions and requests can be dealt with.

Exhibit 9.5 shows a memo that succeeds in getting people to comply with a decision. The purpose of the memo is stated as a request for help in a study. The decision to make the study and to change the system is announced in the first paragraph, and the request is made. The division managers are informed that a new management information system is to be designed and that they are to help in designing it. The controller is polite (*I request*) but clearly is implying *I order,* so no asking-versus-telling problem is occurring.

The second paragraph gives background and states the problem that led to the decision. Then the third paragraph tells what the managers are to do and when. Finally, the last paragraph describes what will happen in the future, seeks feedback, and prepares the message receivers for further communications. This memo will not be ignored. It signals to the receivers that a process is occurring of which they are to be a part. They cannot ignore it or treat it casually (assuming again that they are already motivated to comply).

FORMAL AND INFORMAL AUDIT MEMOS IN WORKING PAPERS　Audit firms employ a variety of approaches to the documentation required for each audit. Each approach, however, requires the preparation of memos— both formal and informal—to be included in the working papers at each stage of the audit process (Touche Ross International, 1978).

Exhibit 9.5   **MEMO SEEKING COMPLIANCE WITH A DECISION**

November 4, 1980

TO: Division Managers

FROM: G. G. Johnson, Controller

Clear Purpose   SUBJECT: Request for your help in a study of XYZ Corporation's Information Needs for Management and Control; implementation of a decision to design a new management information system.

**Study Goal—To Determine
Information Needs**

Decision and Request   The successful management and control of XYZ Corporation is a complex and challenging task. The senior staff commends your performance and dedication as division managers in keeping our firm operating smoothly. Recognizing that the firm's information system is a vital tool for all managers in the performance of their decision-making responsibilities, I have designed a study to analyze the firm's real information needs and data-processing requirements. The results of this study will be used to design a new Management Information System (MIS) for the use of management. I request your help in conducting the study and designing the system.

**Present Data Collection—Too Much
and Too Slow**

Background and Problem   As you well know, there is a steady flow of paperwork and reports among the various levels of this organization. I believe that some of the data collected and transmitted is not really necessary or useful for decision making and therefore should not continue to be collected. Furthermore, crucial operations information is often not processed fast enough to be of maximum benefit to managers. There is also a lack of standardization across the corporation in our data collection and interpretation procedures. Finally, our senior staff has found that current data and information flows are not adequate for profitability estimating and future-growth planning.

**Study Procedures—Based on
Cooperation**

Problem Solution   As part of the study, I will propose some information needs for XYZ Corporation on the basis of interviews with various consultants and a search of professional and

Responsibility Established   industry literature. Beyond this step, I plan to determine needs at all levels by means of a survey. I will review with senior management their own information needs. At the

Specific Requests   same time I will survey you, the division managers, regarding information you currently collect and what you need. Some of the survey items will cover our firm's current process of data analysis and interpretation and what modifications should be made. Here is where your cooperation is urgently requested. I will need support from

(*continued*)

151

Exhibit 9.5 (*concluded*)

Time Frame	your staffs when I make personal visits to your divisions for the purpose of gathering data. I also ask that you would promptly complete and return the questionnaires I will be sending you during the course of the survey. It will continue for a six-month period, beginning January 1 of next year.

Design of New Management Information System to be Based on Study Results

Future Outcome	The survey that you are being asked to support and participate in will provide a solid data foundation for the design of a new Management Information System for XYZ Corporation. This new system will bring increased compatibility, standardization, and speed to the firm's information-processing network. As one example, data will be collected so that statements of sales, earnings, and financial position can be calculated faster than at present. The system will also provide more effective selectivity in data collection, so that unnecessary information is not handled. Furthermore, information collected at lower levels of the firm will be channeled upward by the MIS in a way that better meets the needs of higher management levels. Along with the creation of this new system, criteria will be developed so that benefits realized can be related to system costs.
	After the study is completed and the results interpreted, I will draw up an implementation plan for the new system (including time frame, required equipment, personnel, investment, and expected benefits). You will be kept informed of the progress of system implementation.
Feedback Sought Implementing Date	I look forward to working with you on this task. If you have any immediate questions or advice, please get in touch with me. Otherwise, I will be contacting you again with more details by December 10.

Planning Stage

Memos written during the initial planning stage may include the following types:

▲ *Auditability of the client*—This memo or series of memos evaluates (1) the existence of sufficient audit evidence for the audit process and (2) the good faith of management in providing information.

▲ *Professional risk*—Here conditions that have a bearing on the professional risk of the engagement are discussed. Among these are economic, organizational, and managerial conditions that could create uncertainty regarding the performance of an adequate audit.

▲ *Materiality*—This memo develops guidelines on materiality that will affect the scope of the examination.

▲ *Internal-controls evaluation*—The auditor evaluates the reliability of internal controls and the extent to which the audit process may rely on them to provide information.

▲ *Audit approach design*—Based on the information, discussion, and evaluations of the working-paper memos of the planning stage, the auditor sets out the most effective, efficient, and reliable way to complete the engagement. This memo serves as the audit plan, setting forth the activities of the execution and evaluation stages.

Execution Stage

During the execution stage the various audit tests and examinations are carried out. At least two types of memo are appropriate here:

▲ *Material errors*—This memo estimates the probability of material errors in the financial statements.

▲ *Recommendations to management*—Any recommendations or information given to management regarding weaknesses in internal controls are listed in this memo.

Evaluation Stage

The evaluation stage involves the development of the opinion based on the information collected in the planning stage and on the examinations of the execution stage. During evaluation the following memos may be written:

▲ *Analytical review*—The auditor considers the reasonableness of the data collected and areas in need of additional verification.

▲ *Verification of key items*—Verification of individual transactions or account components of key importance (such as transactions exceeding the materiality guidelines or those with related parties) is described.

▲ *Post-Balance sheet review*—This memo is a description of events occurring after the balance sheet date that will affect the financial statements.

▲ *Review of the financial statements*—Here the auditor evaluates whether the financial statements present the client's financial position in conformity with applicable professional standards.

▲ *Formation of opinion*—The audit partner presents the firm's opinion.

▲ *Input for following audits*—The auditor lists recommendations made to management regarding improving the auditor-client relationship, providing additional services available, improving the efficiency of the next audit, and similar items.

These memos are representative but by no means cover all the prose found in working papers. Indeed, the above memos can be considered only

Exhibit 9.6 **WORKING-PAPER MEMO DESCRIBING RESULTS OF ACCOUNTS RECEIVABLE TEST**

COMPUTROL CORP.

A/R SUBSTANTIVE TEST

A–12–31–81

Test Done

This memo will recap the work done on Computrol's A/R.

Positive A/R circularized	R–20	$ 528,838
Negative A/R set	R–21	538,852
Add'l accounts selected for substantiation	R–22	252,145
Total per A/R T/B	36%	$1,319,835

Results of the Test

Replies to the positives were poor—only 3 of 16 replied (2 clean). Of the nonreplies, most were covered in our bad-debt review since they tended to fall within the scope of that review.

There were only a few replies to the negatives, and they did not indicate any major problem; but in view of the poor response to the positives, I don't take much comfort from the results of the negative work.

Problems with A/R

Two problems have contributed to the condition of Computrol's receivables:

1. When Computrol acquired Textmatic, there was considerable turnover in the accounting department of Textmatic; thus the personnel working the accounts tended to be inexperienced. I've noted many cases where payments that appear to be related to specific invoices (or groups of invoices) were entered as "payments on account" and not applied to the specific items. This has two effects:

Effects of the Problem

    a. It tends to improve the aging since any old items in dispute will be offset by the FIFO application of payments on accounts.

    b. It makes reconciliation more difficult since the statements become cluttered with debits and credits, and legitimate customer deductions are unrecognized.

2. Computrol had computer problems that delayed billing and cost application in the fall.

Auditor Conclusions and Action

As a result, we will be conservative in our bad-debt review and propose a healthy general reserve for billing adjustments that will almost certainly be necessary to clear up the accounts. We will also look to cash receipts in total for the period subsequent to 12/31 as a measure of the collectibility of the 12/31 receivables.

those required at a minimum. They will not always be of the "To–From–Subject" format, although a subject line ought to be employed, but they are nonetheless memos directed at senior personnel and at the files.

Writing Tips

Exhibit 9.6 describes a well-written memo concerning a test of accounts receivable during the execution stage. The test activities are listed and the results stated. Then problems—which could be material—with internal-control procedures are noted along with the effects of the problems. Finally, the conclusions and action to be taken by the auditor are set forth, including recommendations to management.

Written material of this kind must avoid vague terms. Thus *check, review,* and *scan* are not appropriate when the auditor is describing a less than 100 percent examination. The word *test* is used instead. Also, obvious and warranted test conclusions should be stated rather than left for the reader to figure out. Letting data speak for itself is not an appropriate communication strategy. Data needs to be turned into information. The conclusions should flow out of the data describing the work performed, which should be detailed enough to support the conclusions. If the conclusions are only tentative, the memo should say so and state what needs to be done (and if it is to be done) to remove the tentativeness. It is usually better to make conclusions that are not tentative.

When writers are in a hurry—and auditors are always pressed for time—they tend to let short, general words and phrases stand for specific items, actions, or descriptions. Thus in Exhibit 9.6 the auditor characterizes the replies to the positive requests for information as *poor.* Wisely, however, he goes on to state what *poor* means (only 3 of 16 replied). In his conclusion he asserts that the bad-debt review will be *conservative* and then goes on to specify the nature of the review in a more specific manner. The word *healthy* in the first line probably needs defining, but such a definition will emerge later when the proposal is made. In sum, auditors must discipline themselves to be brief in their working-paper memos, but not at the expense of clarity. Important vague words must be defined.

LETTERS Letters are formal and semiformal communications that travel from within an organization to a message receiver external to the organization. Not only does the *content* convey a message, but also the *form* of the letter says something to the reader about the organization. For these reasons accountants take a great deal of care with the composition and presentation of even routine correspondence.

Letter Format

Exhibit 9.7 displays the parts of a typical letter format discussed here.

Heading

The heading, usually printed, does more than give the return address. By being printed it tends to signal the reader that the letter is an official communication of the organization. The telephone number should be the one at which the writer can be reached. If it isn't, she should cross it out and type in her number.

Date and File Notation

The date usually should be the date of sending, not the date of composing, the letter. Sometimes it might be the date, perhaps a day or so after sending, when some action is to take place, action that is announced in the letter by phrases such as "as of today . . . ."

The file notation, an optional part of the letter, could be a documentation number, a loan number, or an account number.

Inside Address

The receiver's name is preceded by his or her courtesy title—*Mr., Ms., Dr.,* and the like—and followed on the next line by the person's official title.

Salutation

To personalize the communication, the receiver's name should follow the *Dear.* If the name isn't known and the letter is addressed to *Vice President* or some similar designation, then phrases such as *Dear Colleague* or *Dear Friend* are used. More abstract phrases such as *Dear Sir, Gentlemen,* and *Dear Madam* should be used only as a last resort.

Body

Most letter writers design the body so that the first paragraph is a short statement of purpose. The next paragraphs supply background and support, as memos do, and the final paragraph contains a brief, courteous close that touches on the future in some way.

Exhibit 9.7 **LETTER FORMAT**

Heading

CLARK MACHINE TOOL COMPANY
1406 East Pine Street
Tucker, Washington 98115
206 – 523 – 7790

Date

September 10, 1980

File Notation   2/6/Z

Inside Address   Mr. John B. Brady
Vice President
Tucker National Bank
1500 West Blount Street
Tucker, WA 98115

Salutation   Dear Mr. Brady,

Body   Enclosed are the company's August 31 financial statements that you requested in our telephone conversation of August 15.

The statements indicate a cash balance of $700,500 with working capital of $434,750. We expect to ship about $3.2 million worth of products during the current quarter and are forecasting a cash flow of $500,000 for the period.

Please contact me if you need any additional information.

Complimentary Close

Sincerely,
CLARK MACHINE TOOL COMPANY

R. G. Smith

R. G. Smith
Controller

Reference   RGS:ef
Enclosure Notation   Enclosure: Financial Statements
Copy Notation   cc: Edward Tolman

Complimentary Close and Signature

The complimentary close should be conventional. No odd or humorous phrases are appropriate. As for the signature, Exhibit 9.7 illustrates one of the most common approaches. This method covers the signature with the name of the organization and thus further drives home the point that the organization is communicating with the reader through the signer.

Reference and Notations

The reference notes first who wrote the letter and then who typed it. The enclosure notation alerts both the secretary who stuffs the envelope and the receiver that the letter is followed by attachments. Finally, the copy notation tells the secretary to whom copies should be sent and informs the letter receiver about others who will read it. An accountant who doesn't want the reader to know who got copies will put *bcc* on the rough draft instead of *cc*. Then the secretary will send copies to those noted but place no copy notation on the letter.

Letter Types

The typical kinds of letters that accountants send include informational, request, and unpleasant-decision letters.

Informational Letters

Letters that deliver information to the client may follow this form or variations of it:

Introduction
1. A statement of the information being supplied;
2. Some indication of why the information is supplied;
3. A brief signal as to the implications of the information.

Body
1. Background—what happened in the past that can help the reader understand the information;
2. Details that answer implied reader questions of the *who, what, when, where, why,* and *how* variety;
3. A more elaborate discussion of the implications of the information, including any conclusions that the accountant has reached;
4. Suggestions for actions that the reader might take in response to the information.

Courteous Close

1. A statement of appreciation;
2. An offer of help;
3. A look forward to future relations.

Exhibit 9.8 is a model of an informational letter.

The informational letters of accountants often point out weaknesses in or identify problems with a client's control systems. Sometimes it is difficult to avoid negative phrases such as the following:

You failed to	The neglect of
An improper procedure	The disregard of
We question your	We disagree that
Problems are handicapping	Results were not

Every effort should be made, however, to either soften the negative or emphasize the positive. In Chapter 7 we noted that negatives can be avoided by:

▲ Stressing opportunities, not problems.
("The opportunity exists to correct. . . .")

▲ Stressing what can be done, not what can't.
("Your efforts should be directed at. . . .")

▲ Stressing what to seek, not what to avoid.
("We suggest that you explore. . . .")

Request Letters

Request letters involve asking questions, seeking information, and making inquiries. They may be organized in the following way:

Introduction

1. Statement of a desire, a problem, a need, or an opportunity;
2. Reason for the request;
3. General statement of the request.

Body

1. Background, if needed;
2. The specific requests.

Courteous Close

1. Statement seeking a response by a certain date;
2. Expression of appreciation;
3. Expression of goodwill.

Exhibit 9-8. **INFORMATIONAL LETTER ORGANIZATION**

Dear Mr. Newell,

Reason for Information

Nature of Information

Implications of Information

     As we noted in our memo of understanding of March 15, we have undertaken a review of your cash receipts and accounts receivable system. The results of that review are briefly summarized below, as are the opportunities you have for implementing system changes.

Background

Details

     As you know, the accounts receivable clerk opens letters, endorses checks, prepares bank deposits, and posts to the subsidiary and general ledgers. Thus he functions in a receiving and recording capacity and appears to do so in a self-supervising manner. Indeed, during our review we did not notice any interactions between him and Mr. Johnson, his nominal supervisor.

Conclusion

Suggestions

     The separation of cash-receiving and posting activities is a conventional and prudent practice that most companies follow when they reach the level of sales recently attained by your company. We suggest, therefore, that you take the opportunity now (1) to increase the effectiveness of your internal control system by separating these functions. You also may wish (2) to hire an additional clerk to take over the posting duties of the current clerk. Moreover, you may want (3) to take steps to increase the supervision activities of Mr. Johnson.

Appreciation

Offer of Help

Look Forward

     We appreciate the effort you and your staff have made to assist us in our review. Please get in touch with me if you have any questions or comments. We stand eager to help and look forward to serving your needs in the future.

Sincerely,

J. J. Smithe

Exhibit 9.9 is an example of a request letter.

     To improve the comprehensibility of request letters and the speed with which the reader processes them, a few simple rules should be followed:

▲ List requests, indented, if there is more than one. The list can be numbered to indicate importance or simply set off by bullets or hyphens.

▲ Ask questions that are framed to provoke more than a yes or no answer. In this way the likelihood of an informative response is increased.

▲ List specific requests as requests, not as sentence fragments (e.g., "the requisitioning procedure"), not as informational statements ("It is important to have information about requisitioning procedures"), and not as desires ("We would like to know about the requisitioning procedure").

▲ Arrange requests so that the most important is listed first. If they are all of equal importance, list first the request that is easiest to comply with.

Exhibit 9.9 **REQUEST LETTER ORGANIZATION**

Dear Mr. Powers,

Need Implied General Request Reason	Before undertaking the review of the new purchasing accounts payable system that you requested, we are in need of some preliminary information concerning the procedures for purchasing supplies, services, and other noninventory items. With this information we can conduct the evaluation efficiently and rapidly.
Background	As you know, we have not examined the new system since it was implemented last year. We thus need to familiarize ourselves with it before beginning our work. Specifically, we would like to know the following:

Specific Requests
1. What procedures the requisitioning department follows.
2. What happens to the purchase orders once they are filled out.
3. What the purchasing department does when the merchandise is received or the services are rendered.

When Response Needed   We seek your response by July 30 so that we can be fully prepared to begin work on August 10.

Appreciation
Goodwill   On behalf of the firm I want to tell you how much we appreciate the opportunity to serve your needs. I look forward to a fruitful relationship.

Sincerely,

P. J. Kirk

Request Letters in Audits

Auditors send out several kinds of request letters during an audit. Of particular importance are accounts receivable confirmation requests and statement-of-account requests to suppliers.

Confirmation Requests. Confirmation requests ask an accounts receivable customer to confirm that he or she owes a certain sum to the audited firm. There are two types of such letters:

▲ *Positive requests*—In positives a balance is stated, and then the customer is asked whether it is correct. The customer is asked to respond to the auditor and to state whether the balance is correct or, if not, what the correct amount is. Positives are used when there are only a relatively few significant accounts balances or when some doubt exists as to the accuracy of the account balances. The letter must include the audit date, the audited firm's name and the auditor's name on the request and on any response forms, and a request number on the response form for ease of processing.

▲ *Negative Requests*—In negatives a reply is requested only if the stated balance is *not* correct. Often the letter is a form letter or card, or even a rubber stamp or sticker attached to a statement of the account. These requests are used when the auditor expects customers to comply with the confirmation requests if an incorrect balance is stated.

Statement-of-Account Requests. Statement-of-account requests seek details from suppliers regarding the audited firm's indebtedness to them. The details sought include amounts due to open accounts, notes, acceptances, loans, and contracts, as well as security, if any, and the nature of the security. The request bears the name of the audited firm and its location (especially if it is a subsidiary or division of a parent firm), the date of the statement of account requested, and the place to which the response is to be sent. Usually a self-addressed, stamped envelope is included.

Unpleasant-Decision Letters

In some classic plays the bearer of bad news is executed. Today accountants do not face the possibility of such an alarming receiver response, but unpleasant news remains one of the most difficult messages to communicate. For a historic touch, consider this letter from Baron Mulgrave (First Sea Lord) firing Admiral Jarvis of the British Royal Navy (circa 1806):

Sir:
Whereas we think fit you should haul down your flag and come on shore, you are hereby required to haul down your flag and come on shore.

The blunt letter of Baron Mulgrave is admirably brief and to the point, but it is certainly not reader oriented. A better approach requires some kind of buffering before the bad news is delivered. The following outline shows an organization that is reader oriented:

Introduction
A buffer containing appreciation, goodwill, a review of the situation, a compliment, or sympathetic understanding of the receiver's plight.

Body
1. An explanation analyzing the circumstances. Here good reasons for bad news are stated.
2. A statement of a decision, an action, or a condition that constitutes the bad news.
3. An attempt to soften the unpleasantness.
4. An attempt to rebuild goodwill, if possible.

Exhibit 9.10   **UNPLEASANT-DECISION LETTER ORGANIZATION**

Dear Mr. Snyder,

Situation Review	In our conversation of September 2 we discussed the expansion of the scope of our examination to Acme Federated, in which your firm holds a substantial minority interest. You pointed out that it would be imprudent of you to request Acme to open
Understanding	its books and records to us. I fully understand the delicate position in which you find yourself.
Explanation	In conducting the audit I am sure you will agree that our position requiring work on the underlying company is based on a reasonable standard of thoroughness. These standards require us to behave in a certain manner if we are to issue the kind of
Unpleasant Decision	opinion you seek. We feel that we must hold to our standard in this case.
Softening and Willingness to Help	I will eagerly work with you to answer your questions regarding a change of auditors. When you have chosen a new firm, you can count on me to help make the transition a smooth one. Perhaps in the future we can serve your interests in some capacity again.
Future Actions	I will call you within the next few days to work out the transition details.

Sincerely,

P. L. Partridge

Courteous Close

1. A statement of appreciation for the past.
2. A signal as to what the future is or must be.
3. An expression of interest in the receiver's situation.
4. A willingness to help, if possible.

The tone of the unpleasant-decision letter ought to be one establishing a sense of fair and reasonable behavior. If receivers can be convinced that a reasonable decision has been made, they are more likely to accept it without hostility. One thing to avoid is the blaming of the bad news on company policy. Policy doesn't make unpleasant decisions; people do. The accountant can defend adherence to a standard or a policy as the right thing to do, but that is a different communication than one that says, "Our policy compels us to. . . ."

An unpleasant decision can often be softened by offering some writer action or proposing some alternative on the reader's part. In Exhibit 9.10 the writer makes an offer to help that, if accepted, ought to ease the burden of change considerably. Moreover, the offer is personalized ("I will eagerly work with you . . ."), whereas the decision reflects the company ("we"). This shift away from the impersonal present toward the personal future tends to drive home the intended message that the reader has not been abandoned. A person, in the form of the writer, will be there to help.

Checkoff 9.1   **ACCOUNTING COMMUNICATIONS: MEMOS AND LETTERS**

MEMOS	YES	NO
1. Do I understand that memos are usually short but may be long if the situation calls for it?	____	____
2. Do I focus my memos on a single topic per memo?	____	____
3. Before writing, have I considered the organizational climate, the timing, the image I want to project, the level of formality needed, the likely responses, and the changes that might be made in the memo as it travels upward?	____	____
4. Have I considered how my memos fit in with my oral and electronic communicating?	____	____
5. Have I made the "subject" long enough to indicate the purpose of the memo and not simply the topic word?	____	____
6. Have I stated the purpose (not background) in the first paragraph?	____	____
7. Are my memos action oriented *and* reader oriented?	____	____
8. Have I framed directives as directives rather than questions?	____	____
9. Have I defined evaluative words such as *enormous, inevitable,* and the like?	____	____
10. Have I decided whether reason or expertise should be the support for my assertions?	____	____
11. Have I avoided a consistency-versus-accuracy trap by sending multiple memos on a single subject all at the same time?	____	____
12. If subordinates have not complied with my memo directives, have I considered the failure of my communication as well as their lack of motivation as a reason?	____	____
AUDIT MEMOS		
13. Have I avoided vague terms or defined them?	____	____
14. Have I stated my conclusions rather than implied them?	____	____
15. Do my conclusions flow out of the data?	____	____

(continued)

Checkoff 9.1 *(concluded)*

LETTERS	YES	NO
16. In the heading, is the telephone number my telephone number?	——	——
17. Have I employed courtesy and official titles in the inside address?	——	——
18. Have I used the copy notation effectively to tell or to keep from the reader the names of others who will see the letter?	——	——
19. Have I softened or avoided the negative?	——	——
20. Have I listed requests; asked more than yes/no-oriented questions; and avoided stating requests as sentence fragments, informational statements, or desires?	——	——
21. Have I listed the most important request first?	——	——
22. Have I buffered the bad news in an unpleasant-decision letter?	——	——
23. Have I given good reasons for the bad news?	——	——
24. Have I avoided blaming the unpleasant decision on policy without explaining the rightness of the policy?	——	——

chapter 10 Report Writing: General

Accountants write numerous reports—mostly routine but some quite specialized. In this chapter we describe general report-writing activities of which all accountants should be aware. Chapter 11 follows with a discussion of special accounting reports.

CLASSIFICATION OF REPORTS

A report is an objective, orderly presentation of information and knowledge. In terms of this definition, a report is not a personalized expression of the accountant's feelings, not data collected in the form of a schedule or a similar compilation of financial measures (although schedules may form parts of reports), not a rambling discourse on a wide range of topics, and not scattered comments. Reports involve both analysis and classification. Analysis is the breaking down of some entity into its parts, whereas classification is the assembling of entities into classes or aggregates.

The following figure illustrates the flow of a report, as analysis leads up to classification, which may spark future analysis on a higher level or analysis of another subject:

Exhibit 10.1 **Reports Classified by Purpose and Content**

CONTENT		PURPOSE: **Routine Periodic Reports** (Information)	**Special Planning Reports** (Information and conclusions)	**Special Decision-Oriented Reports** (Information, conclusions, and recommendations)
	Statistical Orientation	Monthly management reports Variance reports Financial statements	Cost analyses Short-range projections	Tax reports
	Narrative Orientation	Annual reports	Consultants' reports Long-range forecasts	Audit reports

We reaffirm here the point made in Chapter 7: Writing is not always linear; it is often better represented by a sine wave incorporating different forms of cognitive activities as they are communicated to readers.

Having briefly analyzed reports, then, we can proceed to classify them. One way to classify is by purpose; another is by type of content. Exhibit 10.1 describes several accounting reports in these terms. Another way to classify is by direction of flow:

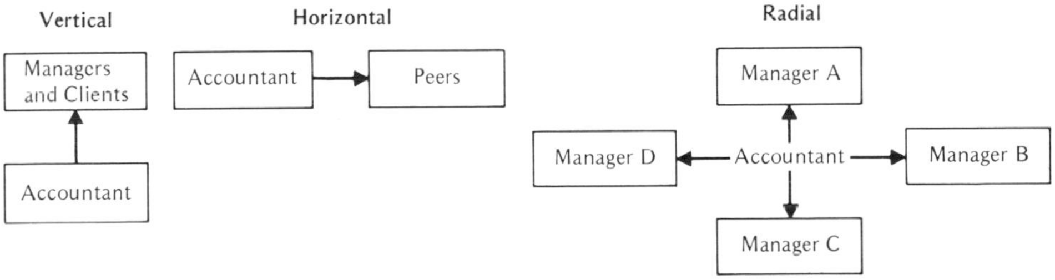

A more sophisticated version of a direction-of-flow classification combines the vertical and radial approaches:

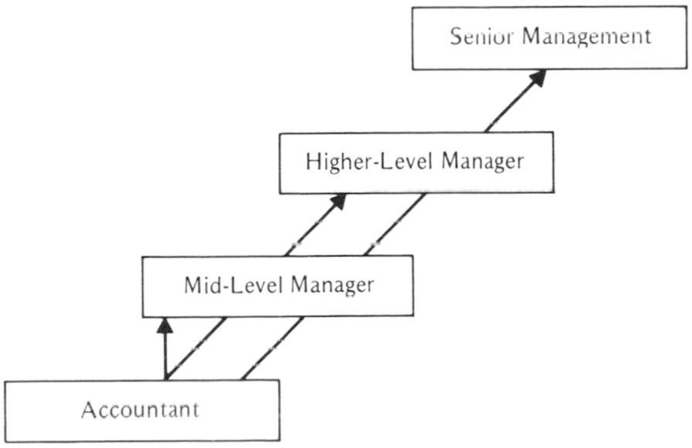

In this radial approach separate reports on the same subject are prepared and sent to each managerial level. Sometimes the reports to mid-level managers are written so that they present general analyses, conclusions, and recommendations first and more detailed discussions second. At the same time the same report, minus the details, is sent to higher and senior management. In this way reports are consistent with each other yet reader oriented. Criteria of specificity of intent, reality, authenticity, and congruency are met.

Still another way to classify is by presentation format:

Memo Report Format (see Appendix A)

To – from – subject

Conclusions and recommendations (if any)

Introduction

Discussion/analysis/categorization

Summary

Implementing information (if any)

Short Report Format (see Appendix B)

Title page

Executive summary/abstract

Introduction

Discussion/analysis/categorization

Conclusions

Recommendations

Implementing information

Letter Report Format

(Same as memo report, except the text is surrounded by letter instead of memo format)

Long Report Format

Title page

Letter or memo of transmittal

Letter or memo of authorization/ understanding

Executive summary/abstract

Table of contents

List of tables

List of figures

Introduction

Discussion/analysis/categorization

Summary

Conclusions

Recommendations

Implementing information

Appendices

Notes

Selected bibliography

Appendices A and B to this chapter illustrate memo and short reports, which are the most common.

PLANNING AND WRITING A LONG FORMAL REPORT   The writing process, which was described in Chapter 7, is preceded by the planning of the long formal report. If the accountant spends enough time and energy on this task, the writing itself ought to be relatively easygoing. The following list describes the planning and writing of a report:

1. *Determine the Report's Use and the Reader's Needs.* Reader orientation is discussed in more detail below. In general the accountant asks, "For what reason does the reader need the report?"

▲ Information only or knowledge to be stored?
▲ Guide for future action?
▲ Conclusion that answers a reader's question?
▲ Recommendation that suggests a future action?
▲ Decision that analyzes and then orders a future action?

2. *Determine the Goals.* An accountant always has three general goals in writing a report: to get the reader to understand it, to accept it, and to think favorably about the accountant and the organization. More specifically, a concrete goal is often stated in the form of a question. Writers who aren't careful can create a problem for themselves here. Look at this goal stated as a question:

▲ *Wrong*—What is the best depreciation method for our company?
▲ *Right*—What depreciation method will offer the company the largest possible expenses in the next fiscal year?

The word *best* needs defining if the report goal is to guide the writer. Moreover, the addition of a time frame (*the next fiscal year*) further specifies the goal.

Another problem with goal articulation concerns prescription versus suggestion. If a goal question contains words such as *should, must,* or *ought,* then the accountant is stating that the report will prescribe some kind of action instead of simply suggesting it:

▲ *Prescription*—What policy should the firm adopt regarding the communication of debt management information?
▲ *Suggestion*—How can the firm control the flow of debt management information?

In the prescriptive case the accountant's report will announce the optimum approach, whereas in the suggestion case it will describe a variety of approaches and suggest one that seems most suitable from among those discussed. Report writers should be clear in their minds just what they are doing before doing it.

3. *Describe the Objectives and the Tasks.* Once a general goal is stated, it is broken down into objectives and tasks:

▲   *Goal*—Should the company acquire or merge with Broadbent Utilities?

▲   *Objective 1*—To assess the costs and benefits of a purchase of Broadbent Utilities.

   Task A—Determine the benefits.

   Task B—Determine the costs.

   Task C—Evaluate benefits versus costs.

▲   *Objective 2*—To assess the costs and benefits of a pooling of interest with Broadbent Utilities.

   Task A—Determine the benefits.

   Task B—Determine the costs.

   Task C—Evaluate benefits versus costs.

These assertions of objectives and tasks should be written down in notes or even in a file memo. In this way a work plan is created to guide information-gathering activities.

4.   *Prepare a Time Chart.*   For elaborate reports, the writer usually prepares a time chart that lists each task, when it will be undertaken, and when it will be finished:

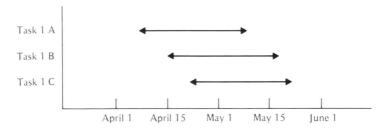

5.   *Collect Information and Identify Report Topics.*   As the tasks are carried out, the writer identifies topics and headings for the report.

6.   *Determine the Arrangement of Topics and Outline the Report.*

7.   *Write the First Draft and Prepare the Tables and Figures.*   As the first draft is written, beginning with conclusions/recommendations and ending with the introduction, the tables and figures are prepared. Indeed, a report is often built around the graphics.

8.   *Revise and Add Headings, Transitions, and Forward/Backward References.*   One of the most important activities in writing a report is tying the parts together. We will discuss headings below, and we have discussed transitions in earlier chapters. Here, however, we consider forward and backward references:

▲ *Forward reference*—This section describes the lines of responsibility within the internal control system.

▲ *Backward reference*—Once we have established lines of responsibility, we must consider the supervisory authority to be vested in key personnel. (Note: This sentence mixes a backward with a forward reference.)

▲ *Forward reference*—The new system must be cost justified. This justification requires an analysis of (1) start-up costs and (2) operating costs.

▲ *Backward reference*—In sum, then, start-up and operating-cost considerations clearly suggest that the system is practical.

These linking devices help the reader assimilate the information given and mentally prepare to process upcoming information. Forward and backward references are essential to reports and must not be left out.

    9. *Prepare Title Page, Table of Contents, and Other Front Matter.*

    10. *Prepare a Letter/Memo of Transmittal.* The letter or memo of transmittal is the vehicle that carries the report to the reader. It is simply a brief "here it is" kind of message usually placed next after a title page.

    11. *Obtain Prior Feedback.* Before a formal report is submitted, writers will often circulate preliminary copies to interested parties for comment. In this way they get the report critiqued beforehand and build support for its findings.

    12. *Submit the Written Report and Make an Oral Report.* Report writers ought to be prepared to make an oral report as a complement to their written work. The oral report is *not* simply a read version of the written work. Chapter 13 describes oral reporting.

BEING READER ORIENTED Senior accountants have pointed out a major problem they see in the reports their juniors write for clients: the junior often writes for the boss instead of for the client. The result is an out-of-focus communication that is not reader oriented. As we have noted before, accountants need to write first for their readers and then for their superiors or their governmental regulators. Indeed, writers should always assume that the reader has only a modest familiarity with the report content. Thus when highly technical or specialized terms are used, they should be defined in the text, in a footnote, in a glossary, or even (if only a few) in the report introduction. It is better to risk boring a knowledgeable reader with definitions than to risk enraging a nonknowledgeable reader without them.

Reader boredom or rage can be avoided if the accountant gathers information about the readers beforehand regarding the roles they play, their knowledge, their uses for the report, and their likely attitude toward the work. Then the finished product can be tailored appropriately. One other question the accountant needs answered concerns the way the report is to be read. Will it be skimmed, read rapidly, dipped into occasionally, or studied in depth? Obviously different reading activities of the report recipients ought to influence the content and presentation of the content:

Anticipated Reading Activity	Accountant's Responses
Skimmed	Each topic is covered in a conclusion/recommendation/discussion format; headings announce conclusions and recommendations at the top of the page.
Read Rapidly	An executive summary at the report's beginning lists conclusions and recommendations; discussion is put off until the report's middle part.
Dipped into Occasionally	Tabs and different-colored paper identify special topics; elaborate table of contents is provided.
Studied in Depth	Conventional presentation, with conclusions and recommendations stated at the top of each section and then summarized at the report's end.

A number of audit firms write "management letters" in the form of memo or letter reports with the anticipation that readers will skim or read them rapidly. Corporate accounting reports, on the other hand, are often written to be dipped into or studied in depth.

Exhibit 10.2 describes in detail the various tasks that readers face in processing an accountant's report, how they should go about accomplishing their tasks, and what the writer should do to help.

MAJOR PARTS OF A REPORT Reports are viewed as having an introduction, a body, and a terminal section. As we have seen, the terminal section, made up of a summary, a conclusion, and a recommendation (or parts of this list), is sometimes at the top of each major section and sometimes at the report's end. In this discussion, however, we describe the parts in a conventional order.

Exhibit 10.2   **READER TASKS AND WRITER STRATEGIES IN REPORT READING AND WRITING**

READER TASK	WHEN PERFORMED	READER SHOULD	WRITER SHOULD
Identifying the writer	Before reading	Ask and answer, "What is my general image of the writer? How might it affect what I read?"	Realize that the reader will have a general image or stereotype of him before reading. If possible, he should have built up over time an appropriate image of himself and his group.
Identifying the reader in the writer's eyes	During reading	Ask and answer, "What kind of person does the writer seem to suggest I am? Is it really me?"	Communicate an image of the reader that is realistic and that meets her needs and desires. The writer should make it clear that he is writing for the reader and not for someone else. He should not threaten the reader's self-image.
Determining the writer's stance	During reading	Ask and answer, "What is the writer's direction? What stand is he taking? Does he seem to know what he is talking about?"	Make it clear what conclusions he is heading for. He should show confidence, making statements assertively unless qualifiers are absolutely called for.
Identifying the writer's inferences	During reading	Look for opinions stated as facts.	Make it clear that the facts and his opinions, although parallel, are different entities.
Analyzing the interpretations of data	During reading	See if the writer is squeezing the data too hard for interpretations. The data may be weak, or else the writer hasn't collected enough.	Make data interpretations obvious. If he is squeezing the data, he should admit it and tell the reader why he is doing it.
Identifying the writer's status	During reading	Determine whether the writer is using big words, statistics, and jargon to impress the reader. Such tactics are often used (1) to communicate higher status than the reader, but also sometimes (2) to signal lower status and the need to create a favorable reader image of the writer. If the writer is not using jargon and big words to impress, his status in relation to the reader should generally be felt as equal.	Avoid attempts to manipulate status perceptions. The writer should use small words whenever possible; should define obscure terms; and should use statistics only to illustrate, to inform, to support, and to interpret.

(continued)

Exhibit 10.2 (continued)

READER TASK	WHEN PERFORMED	READER SHOULD	WRITER SHOULD
Evaluating the level of writer defensiveness	During reading	Ask and answer, "Is the writer defending his stand from attack instead of positively supporting it? Is defensiveness a sign of some weakness?"	Emphasize the supports for his position and the weaknesses of other positions, but stress the supports.
Determining the writer's interest in the report	During reading	Ask, "Does the writer seem enthusiastic about and interested in his work?" If not, the reader ought to consider why.	Show the reader that he cares about the work. The writer must communicate a sense of his own excitement.
Building rapport with the writer	During reading	Try to understand the difficulties the writer has faced.	Show the difficulty that he has faced and describe its effect on the report.
Identifying a fragmented presentation	During reading	Ask, "Does the report look as if it were done by a number of people who didn't talk much to each other? Does this fragmentation seem offensive to me? Why?"	Coordinate a team effort through the team leader or a report specialist so that it looks as if it were written by one person.
Analyzing the report's linearity	During reading	Look for a presentation that communicates an aura of a step-by-step process. If the aura is missing, the reader should look for flaws in logic and development.	Follow an extensive outline in writing and use many transitional words, phrases, and paragraphs.
Determining the value of the graphic aids	During reading	Ask, "Are the graphic aids, especially the headings, helping me to grasp quickly what I need to know?"	Make sure the graphic aids help speed comprehension. The writer should not pad the report with graphics.
Identifying valuable redundancy	During reading	Look for continuous looping back to main issues and themes.	Avoid raising important points that are then dropped, never to return. Writing is not always linear; the line may have loops in it.
Taking stock periodically	During reading	Try to stop frequently to take stock of what has been said.	Give the reader the chance to take stock by using summaries, backward references, graphic aids, occasional short paragraphs, and white space.
Projecting the reader's ideas onto passages	Reading specific passages	Attempt to project reader's own ideas onto the passage as a test of the validity of the writer's ideas.	Anticipate reader ideas and objections. The writer should raise them himself and deal with them.

(continued)

Exhibit 10.2 *(continued)*

READER TASK	WHEN PERFORMED	READER SHOULD	WRITER SHOULD
Determining the writer's goal in a passage	Reading specific passages	Ask, "What is the writer doing in this passage? What is his goal? Why does he have this goal? Why now instead of earlier or later in the report?"	Specifically, tell the reader what he is doing or at least offer understandable topic cues. The writer should assume that the reader is a part of his team who needs to be kept fully informed.
Looking for writer pointing	Reading specific passages	Ask, "Does the writer engage in *pointing*—telling me what I can expect to happen to me because of an emerging problem or solution?"	Tie problems and solutions to the reader's corporate life. The writer should show what effects the reader can expect.
Analyzing supports	Reading specific passages	Ask, "Do I feel that the writer's supports and documentation are credible, reliable, valid, and authoritative? If I don't, what would it take to make me feel it? What is missing?"	Do slightly more than is really required. Moreover, the writer should show a variety of supports and documentation and should lean on the image of his organization as competent and efficient.
Noting feedback	Reading specific passages	Look for points to raise with the writer (even if he is not available) after reading the report.	Make it clear which points will require further reader-writer communication. The writer should help the reader to formulate her feedback.
Guessing	Reading specific passages	Try to guess what the writer will do next. If the writer does something else, the reader should attempt to explain why.	Telegraph to the reader what will happen next so that she can get her mind ready.
Testing conclusions	Reading specific passages	Evaluate the conclusions not only in terms of the supporting material but also in terms of the reader's own knowledge and experience.	Evaluate the reader's knowledge and experience. The writer should not contradict that experience without strong support and an explanation for the divergence.
Listing alternatives	Reading conclusions and recommendations	Ask, "What other explanations, proposals, assertions, and actions can I come up with to replace those of the writer?"	Anticipate reader counter-arguments and show why they are not as good as the writer's argument.
Assigning blame for incomprehension	After reading	Avoid blaming herself for comprehension difficulties until she has determined whether the writer is really the one to blame.	Write readable prose. He should also try to create an image of himself as eager to communicate so that the reader will find it difficult to blame him for comprehension problems.

(continued)

175

Exhibit 10.2 (*concluded*)

READER TASK	WHEN PERFORMED	READER SHOULD	WRITER SHOULD
Determining whether change has occurred	After reading	Ask, "Do I feel that I got somewhere, that something happened to me?"	Having as a goal the changing of the reader's life, even if only in a small way. The writer might want to keep a mental image of the reader before him as he writes to remind him of his goal.
Determining whether the writer has fulfilled his goals	After reading	Ask, "Did the writer do more or less than he said he would do in the introduction?" If less, ask why. If more, ask what is the value of the excess.	Do what he says he is going to do—never less without an explanation. If the writer does more, he should describe the purpose and value of the excess.
Determining future thoughts and actions	After reading	Ask, "Does the writer make it clear what specific thought process or behavior I must either change or undertake?"	List the step-by-step specifications the reader ought to take, if any. The writer should show how the reader's thinking should or should not change.
Determining the feasibility of future thoughts and actions	After reading	Ask, "Can I do what the writer wants me to do? Can I be what he wants me to be?"	Avoid merely recommending change or action. Show the reader how to do it and when to do it. Show that it is not as hard as she might think.
Determining future reading	After reading	Ask, "Do I feel satisfied with the work but still eager to learn more because of the interesting quality of what I have read? What should I read?"	Make the reader feel that the work completes her current task but is the exciting beginning of a new task.

Introduction

An introduction may take up to 10 or 20 percent of the report's length if necessary. Typically, introductions are made up of all or part of the following:

Statement of Authorization and Purpose. The writer might begin by saying:

As authorized by Mr. Robert Cassidy of Solo Industries, we have undertaken a study of the relationship of control accounts to subsidiary ledgers in accounts receivable. The purpose of this report is to review current procedures for posting to control accounts and to suggest ways in which bookkeeper errors can be avoided.

Within this statement is the implied research goal ("What steps should the company take to reduce bookkeeper error in posting from subsidiary to control accounts?"). The purpose, then, is to answer the question posed by the goal. Often the goal includes a statement of some problem (e.g., "bookkeeper error"), but accountants typically try to avoid discussing client problems in reports unless absolutely necessary—and only then with the focus on change rather than on criticism.

Description of Scope and Limits. In this section the writer discusses what is covered in the report and, sometimes more important, what is *not* covered. If the accountant describes what wasn't done during the research and what isn't in the report, she can head off any objections that her work was incomplete. Essentially she gives reasons for the limitations and lists constraints on her work.

Statement of Methods and Sources. How was the report information developed? The writer describes what he did to collect the report material and where he obtained information. He notes whether his conclusions are based on surveys, observations, tests, interviews, or his reading of books, articles, or other reports.

Discussion of Background. Sometimes previous reports or the history of the research problem needs to be discussed to give the reader a chance to focus on the importance of the current report.

Definition of Terms. If a few key terms are to be used throughout the report, an accountant often will define them in the introduction.

Plan of Presentation. One of the writer's first forward references is the plan of presentation. She simply lists the major parts of the report in their order of treatment.

Exhibit 10.3 shows the introductory sections of a long report from management advisory services.

Body of the Report

The major text of the report may be in the middle or at the end, depending on whether or not the conclusions and recommendations lead the report. Sometimes the text is organized by topic so that each topic is like a mini report, with its own conclusions and recommendations. Whatever the case, there are a number of organizational procedures that the writer should observe.

Exhibit 10.3   **EXAMPLE OF A LONG FORMAL REPORT INTRODUCTION**

**RECOMMENDATIONS FOR PRODUCT LINE
MEASUREMENT AND ANALYSIS
FOR
KEN SHINE AND ASSOCIATES**

Introduction

Authorization

Purposes

This report concerning product-line management is submitted on June 11, 1982, to Mr. Ken Shine, president of Ken Shine and Associates. In accordance with a letter of agreement dated April 11, 1982, the report has been prepared by Janice Wald, Mark Jones, and Colleen Bruce to assist Ken Shine and Associates in the analysis of product lines by the use of weighted measures. The report will explain how such measures can be used to screen prospective product lines in order to include those most likely to attain adequate levels of sales and profits to the firm. These measures will also be used to determine the relative contribution to sales and profit of those product lines currently being marketed by Ken Shine. Finally, the report will show how the weighted measurements may signal problems in existing product lines and will make recommendations concerning the possible deletion of lines no longer profitable to the firm.

Scope and Limits

Because of time constraints, the study will not deal with market analysis, sales-force management, or cost accounting procedures. By concentrating on the one area of product management, it has been possible to cover in depth each of the five objectives stated in the letter of agreement.

Method and Sources

This study is the result of interviews with Ken Shine and his employees. Ken Shine's files and ledgers provided information concerning the company's product lines, suppliers, and sales. Secondary research yielded material on product management, distribution channels, the dynamics of planning, and purchasing. A complete bibliography is included at the end of this report. A total of approximately 200 hours of individual and group effort has been devoted to the completion of this project.

Background

Ken Shine began his business as a manufacturer's representative in 1977, working out of his home and representing only a few product lines. His business grew quickly as he continued to add new and diverse product lines from a variety of new suppliers. When the company outgrew Mr. Shine's home office, he relocated at 4200 14th Avenue in Seattle, a building occupied entirely by display rooms and offices of manufacturers' representatives. Mr. Shine now has exclusive representation of approximately twelve product lines from nearly twenty different suppliers. It appears that his business has grown beyond his present system of instinctive selection, promotion, and deletion of product lines and that his firm would benefit from a more objective system with which to monitor those activities. This report presents and recommends such a system.

Definitions

An attempt has been made in this report to use simple and understandable terminology. There are, however, a few key terms that may seem to have vague or multiple meanings. To eliminate any confusion on the part of the reader, the following definitions will hold throughout the report:

▲   *Product line*—A generic term that refers to a set of similar products, such as posters, cards, tote bags, and the like. These categories may be further divided into the individual

Exhibit 10.3 (*concluded*)

manufacturers who supply a product line, such as Thought Factory posters, Pro Arts posters, and AA Sales posters.

▲ *Marginal products or product lines*—Those products or product lines being considered for deletion due to inadequate sales performance.

Plan of Presentation   The format of this report begins with a preview of the conclusions and recommendations reached, followed by detailed discussion of how these conclusions and recommendations came about. The discussion is divided into three parts. The first deals with both the necessity and the process of seeking and screening new-product ideas for acceptance or rejection by the company. The second part develops the measures necessary to analyze current product lines, and the third and final part discusses the use of those measures developed in part two in order to reach a retention or deletion decision on product lines. Throughout the report, graphic displays emphasize particular comparisons and analyses. An appendix is attached of pertinent information deemed too detailed to be included within the body of the report. A summary of the report's findings, conclusions, and recommendations is also included at the end of the report.

Conclusions

As the result of the research conducted in compiling this report, the following conclusions were reached.

1. A systematic process for making product-line decisions is more effective than subjective analysis alone.
2. Ken Shine and Associates needs a system for seeking and screening possible new products.
3. A continuous auditing process would be beneficial for examining data necessary for making deletion or retention decisions for existing product lines.
4. The deletion or retention of product lines should be periodically examined by a systematic and objective process.

Recommendations

In light of the above conclusions, the report recommends that Ken Shine and Associates should:

1. Develop measures with which to make effective product-line decisions, rate the measures, weigh them, and compare them to absolute performance standards and to the other lines.
2. Keep records of information necessary to make product-line decisions on a regular basis.
3. Analyze the product-line performance on a regularly scheduled basis, using the recorded information.

Support for these conclusions and suggested strategies for implementing the recommendations are found in the following three sections of the report.

Look at these two outlines. Which one will be most easily understood by a reader who needs to learn which plant is experiencing problems in controlling production costs?

Organization by Plants	Organization by Costs
Plant A	Labor Costs
Labor costs	Plant A
Raw material costs	Plant B
Overhead costs	Comparison and conclusion
Plant B	Raw Material Costs
Labor costs	Plant A
Raw material costs	Plant B
Overhead costs	Comparison and conclusion
Comparison and conclusions	Overhead Costs
	Plant A
	Plant B
	Comparison and conclusion
	Summary of Conclusions

The first method, organization by plants, is probably the most reader oriented. However, if the research goal were to learn which type of production costs is the most problematical, then the second method would serve better. The point is that the research goal should determine the organizational structure of the report:

▲ If the goal is to describe what has happened, then a *chronological* past–present–future structure may be best.

▲ If the goal is to describe what happens, then a *process description* may be employed in which step 1 is followed by step 2, and so on.

▲ If the goal is to describe a thing, then a *spatial* format may be useful in which the thing is described from top to bottom, left to right, or inside to outside.

▲ If the goal is to describe a problem and offer a solution, then a *problem-solving* structure is employed. The problem is described and alternative solutions are listed. Each solution is analyzed in terms of costs and benefits. The conclusion states the best solution. The recommendation suggests how it should be implemented.

Terminal Section

The terminal section, usually made up of a summary, conclusions, and recommendation/implementation, can occur in one of several forms:

Conclusion First	Recommendation First
Conclusion	Recommendation
Recommendation	Introduction
Introduction	Body
Body	Summary
Summary	Conclusion
Implementation	Implementation
Conclusion/Recommendation for Each Topic	**Conclusion/Recommendation after Introduction**
Introduction	Introduction
Topic A	Conclusion/recommendation
Conclusion/recommendation	Body
Text	Summary
Implementation	Implementation
Topic B	
Conclusion/recommendation	
Text	
Implementation	
Summary	

Actually, not every report requires a complete terminal section. Exhibit 10.4 lists several types of reports and the terminal sections for each.

Notice that short information-only reports end simply with a brief summary. Reports that answer research questions only have summaries if the content is lengthy. Conclusions are included in most reports; they are not needed, however, when information is being reported routinely or when no research question has been asked. Recommendations are made only when they are requested, when the accountant has the status to offer them without their being requested, or when some kind of future action must be dealt with.

GRAPHIC AIDS

Information in accounting reports can be presented in textual, tabular, or visual formats (see Exhibit 10.5). In this section we discuss those tables and figures that are called graphic aids.

Purposes of Graphic Aids

What is the purpose of a graphic aid? A glance at Exhibit 10.5 shows one obvious reason for using them: they are easier on the reader's eye and thus

Exhibit 10.4 **REPORT TYPES AND TERMINAL SECTIONS COMMON TO EACH**

	Short Information-Only Report	Short Report Answering a Research Question	Long Report Answering a Research Question	Short Report Answering a Research Question and Suggesting Further Action	Long Report Answering a Research Question and Suggesting Further Action
Summary (Description of major content parts of report to aid comprehension)	■		■		■
Conclusion (Answers to questions posed by research goal; past oriented)		■	■	■	■
Recommendation/ Implementation (List of suggestions regarding future actions and decisions and how to carry them out)				■	■

easier to scan than are textual presentations. They probably are (or ought to be) easier to comprehend, too. Moreover, the form of graphic aid called a *table* can present a large amount of data in a highly condensed row-and-column format. Accounting schedules are essentially tables designed to summarize data that would take up too much space if it were described in paragraphs.

Figures, called visual presentations or charts, are not used in the way tables are—to be highly informative—although they can be. Rather their usual purpose is to dramatize a point the accountant wants to make about a trend or some relationship between entities. Moreover, figures are sometimes added to a report to brighten it or to make it look professional. Thus tables collect data, whereas figures make important points and create a professional image of the report writer. A good mix of tables and figures in a report helps define the report as a report, and it helps create a sense in the reader that an objective, orderly presentation of information has been given. Tables and figures are used in memo reports, short reports, and long formal reports.

Exhibit 10.5 **TEXTUAL, TABULAR, AND VISUAL PRESENTATION OF INFORMATION**

Textual Presentation

The Matthews plant sold 27,000 units in 1979 and 50,000 in 1980. In 1979, about 20 percent of the units sold came from inventory, and 80 percent came from production. In 1980, 40 percent came from inventory, and 60 percent came from production.

Tabular Presentation

Table 1.1. Sources of Matthews Plant Sales, 1979–1980

	1979	1980
Sales total (units)	27,000	50,000
Percent from inventory	20	40
Percent from production	80	60

Visual Presentation

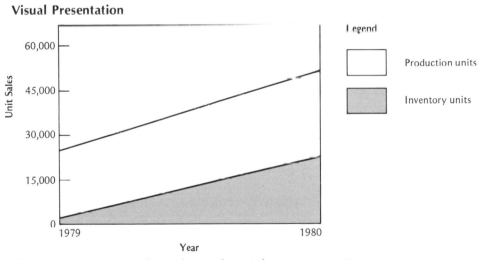

Figure 1.1. Sources of Matthews Plant Sales, 1979–1980

Tables

Tables are rows and columns of numbers or words (or both). They are placed between paragraphs, on separate pages, or on pages facing the text. Every table is numbered (so are figures, but with a separate numbering system), and the table is referenced and perhaps discussed in the text. Naturally the text

Exhibit 10.6 **EXAMPLE OF AN OPEN TABLE**

Table 1.1. Proposed Revolving Credit Facility

Time	Amount Available	Annual Interest
1/1/80– 6/30/80	$5 million	Prime plus annual fee of 0.0025 of $20 million
7/1/80– 12/31/80	$10 million	Prime plus 0.0025 of $15 million
1/1/81– 6/30/81	$18 million	Prime plus ¼% plus 0.0025 of $7 million
7/1/81– 12/31/81	$25 million	Prime plus ¼%

Source: First National Bank Proposal of August 3

should not simply repeat everything that is in the table, but the prose should highlight it. Tables are referenced with such phrases as "Table 1.1 shows that . . . ," ". . . as shown in Table 1.1," or "(see Table 1.1)."

As already noted, the purpose of a table is to present highly condensed information in a readable format. Three table formats in common use are open, ruled, and boxed. Exhibits 10.6 to 10.8 provide examples of these forms. For simple collections of data, open tables are appropriate. As data becomes harder for the reader to scan, the ruled and boxed tables are used. In the examples of the "Proposed Revolving Credit Facility," the data is best presented in a boxed table. Indeed, much accounting data in financial statements and schedules ought to be boxed instead of open, which is the current conventional format. Exhibit 10.9 shows the improvement in reader orientation where a boxed table is substituted for an open table in a financial statement.

Exhibit 10.7 **EXAMPLE OF A RULED TABLE**

Table 1.1. Proposed Revolving Credit Facility

Time	Amount Available	Annual Interest
1/1/80– 6/30/80	$5 million	Prime plus annual fee of 0.0025 of $20 million
7/1/80– 12/31/80	$10 million	Prime plus 0.0025 of $15 million
1/1/81– 6/30/81	$18 million	Prime plus ¼% plus 0.0025 of $7 million
7/1/81– 12/31/81	$25 million	Prime plus ¼%

Source: First National Bank Proposal of August 3

Exhibit 10.8 **EXAMPLE OF A BOXED TABLE**

Table 1.1. **Proposed Revolving Credit Facility**

Time		Amount Available	Annual Interest
From	To		
1/1/80	6/30/80	$5 million	Prime plus annual fee of 0.0025 of $20 million
7/1/80	12/31/80	$10 million	Prime plus 0.0025 of $15 million
1/1/81	6/30/81	$18 million	Prime plus ¼% plus 0.0025 of $7 million
7/1/81	12/31/81	$25 million	Prime plus ¼%

Source: First National Bank Proposal of August 3

Exhibit 10.9 also illustrates some number-handling techniques for improving comprehension:

▲ The overuse of zeros is eliminated by listing the figures only in thousands.

▲ The use of $ and % is cut down by inserting them only at the top of columns.

▲ Negative amounts or changes in the wrong direction are signaled by ( ).

▲ Every subcategory is totaled, and a grand total is provided at the bottom.

▲ The most recent data is listed at the left, where the reader's eye will encounter it first.

▲ The providing of percent changes from the previous year allows the reader to develop a sense of trend, if any exists.

We will describe further approaches to handling data in Chapter 11. For now, let us turn to figures.

Figures

A figure can be a chart, such as a line chart, or a photograph, a drawing, or a cartoon. Figures are numbered separately from tables and are usually listed separately in a "List of Figures" at the beginning of formal reports. Their purposes involve making a point—usually only one point per figure—and

Exhibit 10.9   **EXAMPLES OF FINANCIAL INFORMATION IN AN OPEN AND BOXED FORMAT**

Table 1.1. Capital Expenditures, 1981–1983 ($ thousands)

Type of Expenditure	1983	Change from 1982	1982	Change from 1981	1981	Change from 1980
Offshore						
Exploration	$165,170	134%	$ 70,550	27%	$ 55,350	16%
Development	80,700	(11)	90,650	115	42,186	15
Total offshore	245,870	52	161,200	65	97,536	15
Onshore						
Exploration	36,616	44	25,283	66	15,191	15
Development	5,233	(15)	6,141	13	5,444	35
Total onshore	41,849	33	31,424	52	20,635	26
Total expenditures	287,719	49	192,624	63	118,171	30

Table 1.1. Capital Expenditures, 1981–1983 ($ thousands)

Type of Expenditure		1983		1982		1981	
Location	Activity	Amount	Change from 1982	Amount	Change from 1981	Amount	Change from 1980
Offshore	Exploration	$165,170	134%	$ 70,550	27%	$ 55,350	16%
Offshore	Development	80,700	(11)	90,650	115	42,186	15
Total Offshore		245,870	52	161,200	65	97,536	15
Onshore	Exploration	36,616	44	25,283	66	15,191	15
Onshore	Development	5,233	(15)	6,141	13	5,444	35
Total Onshore		41,849	33	31,424	52	20,635	26
Total Expenditures		287,719	49	192,624	63	118,171	30

creating a favorable image of the accountant and the organization. Most report figures are easily drawn by a competent secretary, but elaborate charts for annual reports are drawn by graphic artists. Accountants employing computer graphics packages can produce professional-looking figures faster and cheaper than either artists or secretaries can.

Exhibit 10.10   **COMMON PRESENTATIONS OF LINE GRAPHS**

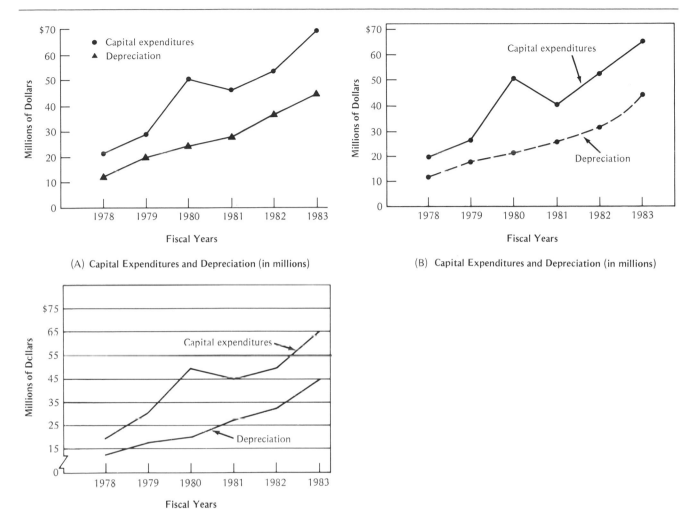

(A) Capital Expenditures and Depreciation (in millions)

(B) Capital Expenditures and Depreciation (in millions)

(C) Capital Expenditures, 1978-1983 (in millions)

Line Charts

Exhibit 10.10 describes several types of line charts. Some techniques used in drawing line and other charts, as illustrated in Exhibit 10.10, are:

▲ *Horizontal and vertical scale labels*—Notice the placement of "Million Dollars"; the preferred presentation is usually horizontal.

▲ *Use of a grid*—In presentation (c) a horizontal grid helps the reader to assign vertical scale values to points on the lines.

▲ *Scale break*—In (c) the vertical scale is broken so that the scale can begin at the zero point. Virtually all figures should have vertical scales beginning at zero.

▲ *Use of symbols to mark data points*—In (a) the data points on which the line is drawn are clearly marked, and a legend below the chart identifies the marks. Notice that when a legend is not used, the lines are identified by labeling them on the chart itself.

▲ *Curves*—In (b) the points on the "Depreciation" line are connected by a curve instead of a straight line. Curves are visually appealing, but any reader attempt to pick off values on the vertical scale will yield inaccurate data.

▲ *Dashed lines*—In (b) the points are connected in a solid and a dashed format to identify clearly the different variables. Dashed lines (or curves) are particularly useful when lines cross; if all the lines were solid, the reader would have difficulty following them after they had crossed.

▲ *Figure titles*—In (a) and (b) the titles do not indicate the dates covered. A better approach occurs in (c), where "1978–1983" is added.

Bar Charts

Bar charts are probably the most versatile and most dramatic of all graphic aids. They emphasize relationships, although they can be used to show trends over time when the bars are presented vertically. Exhibit 10.11 describes (a) a horizontal bar chart, (b) a deviation bar chart, (c) a component bar chart, and (d) a 100 percent component bar chart. All four of these figures present the same information, but each makes a different point or points. In (a) the large revenue from the carriage of steel (the data is from a rail carrier) is highlighted, as perhaps is the large increase in 1982 coal revenues. In (b) the deviation of actual revenues from planned revenues in 1981 and 1982 is noted; the increasing and unplanned-for demand for coal is highlighted. In (c) the increase in total revenue from 1981 to 1982 is stressed, while in (d) the change in the relationships of the components of revenue over the two years is illuminated. An accountant could use one or even all of these figures, depending (1) on the points she wanted to make in the report text and (2) on reader needs.

Surface and Silhouette Charts

When the writer simply shades in the area of a line chart under the line, he has created a surface line chart. This presentation is probably not used much by accountants, but a variation, the so-called staircase surface chart, is of some importance. This figure is a component bar chart with the bars run together, as in Exhibit 10.12(a). The top line is the grand total of the components. Surface charts should be distinguished from overlapping-line charts (called silhouette charts), in which one category overlaps another of which it is a part. Thus in Exhibit 10.12(b) net income overlaps the revenues from which net income was obtained, so the top line is not a grand total of component

Exhibit 10.11 **COMMON TYPES OF BAR CHARTS**

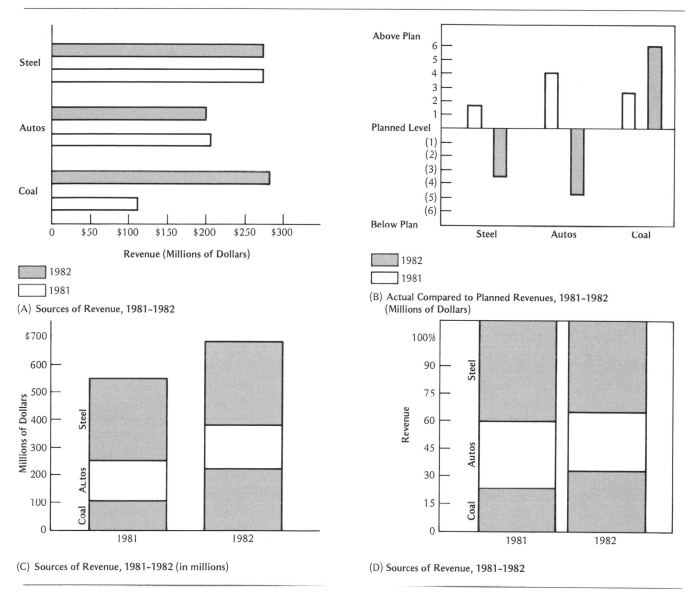

(A) Sources of Revenue, 1981–1982

(B) Actual Compared to Planned Revenues, 1981–1982
(Millions of Dollars)

(C) Sources of Revenue, 1981–1982 (in millions)

(D) Sources of Revenue, 1981–1982

values. The textual discussion of the figure should clarify the distinction between surface and silhouette charts if there is any chance that the reader might misinterpret the nature of the top line.

Semilogarithmic Charts

Assume that an accountant collects production data for the first six months of the year as shown in the following table (p. 190).

Exhibit 10.12   **EXAMPLES OF (A) STAIRCASE SURFACE AND (B) SILHOUETTE CHARTS**

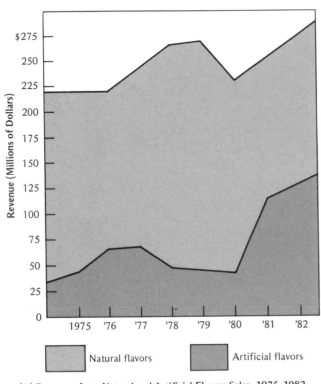

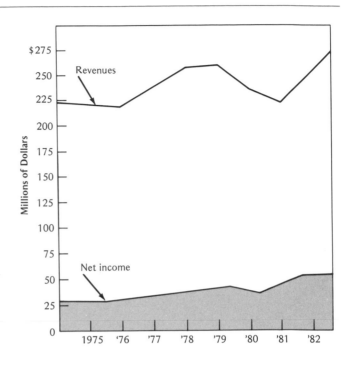

(A) **Revenues from Natural and Artificial Flavors Sales, 1975–1982**   (B) **Revenues and Net Income from Flavors Sales, 1975–1982**

Month	Units Produced	Increase from Previous Month
January	200,000	90,000
February	280,000	80,000
March	350,000	70,000
April	410,000	60,000
May	460,000	50,000
June	490,000	30,000

If she wants to make the point that production is increasing, she will present the data in Exhibit 10.13(a). However, if her concern is with the decreasing rate of production increase, she would employ Exhibit 10.13(b). If she is following reader-oriented criteria having to do with presenting specific, unambiguous data congruent with reality, she will probably want to present *both* figures. Whatever the case, the use of a semilogarithmic scale in (b) allows her to make an important information-laden point dramatically. Accountants

190

Exhibit 10.13 **EXAMPLE OF A (A) LINEAR CHART AND (B) SEMILOGARITHMIC CHART SHOWING RATE OF CHANGE**

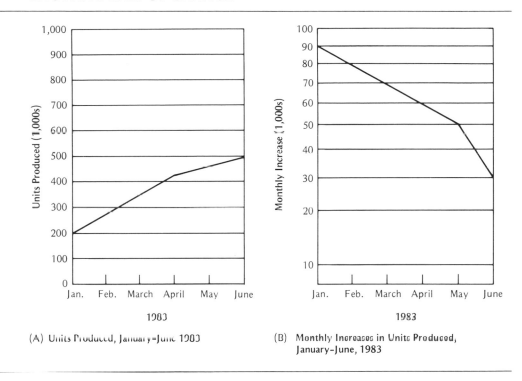

(A) Units Produced, January–June 1983

(B) Monthly Increases in Units Produced, January–June, 1983

ought to employ "semilog" graphs often in their reports when trends in rates of change of increases or decreases could influence financial decision making.

Pie Charts

Pie charts, like component bar charts, are used to compare parts of some whole. But unlike component bar charts, different wholes cannot easily be compared. In Exhibit 10.14, the accountant would *not* want to add a pie representing the previous year's current liabilities so that 1983 could be compared to 1982. The appropriate figure would include two component bars.

Other Charts

Accountants also use organization charts, flow charts, pictograms, and variations of the charts described above. If possible, each chart should appear in the report before it is discussed in the text. When many charts are shown, however, this is not always possible. Charts are rarely placed in appendices, since they would lose their dramatic impact if buried at the end of reports. The advantages and disadvantages of the charts we have described are summarized in Exhibit 10.15.

Exhibit 10.14 **EXAMPLE OF A PIE CHART**

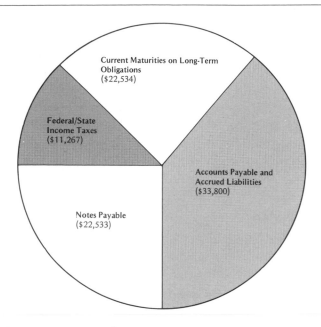

Current Liabilities, December 31, 1983 ($1,000)

Do's and Don'ts

Below are listed a few "do's" and "don'ts" that will help a writer make important points and create a favorable professional image:

▲ Do use transparent overlays to superimpose new relationships on existing charts for eye-catching comparisons.

▲ Do show running twelve-month totals as data points instead of single-month totals. The resulting trend line will be more reliable.

▲ Do footnote charts at the bottom, if necessary. The footnotes of charts are indicated by raised small arabic letters rather than numerals. In this way chart or table numbers and footnote indicators are distinguished.

▲ Do list the source of each table or figure at the bottom.

▲ Don't leave blank spaces in tables without explanation. A hyphen is not explanatory, and neither is "n.a." without definition. The designation "n.a." can mean "not available," "not appropriate," "not accurate," and the like.

▲ Don't use line charts to display discrete data (such as sales revenue for several products during a single accounting period). Use bar charts instead.

▲ Don't run bars together in a bar chart.

▲ Don't add information, such as value labels, to figures at the expense of eye-appeal.

▲ Don't break a vertical scale to allow beginning at zero if only one or two lines or bars will also be broken. Break all lines or bars or break none.

Exhibit 10.15   **ADVANTAGES AND DISADVANTAGES OF FIGURES**

FIGURE TYPE	ADVANTAGES	DISADVANTAGES
Line chart	▲ Shows trend over time. ▲ Shows frequency at different levels. ▲ Shows movement or direction rather than absolute amounts.	▲ Can show only a few lines. ▲ Easy deception through choice of vertical scale. ▲ Lines are not suitable for only a few data points.
Bar charts	▲ Shows parts of a whole at a given time. ▲ Easy to compare variables at a given time or point. ▲ Highly dramatic presentation. ▲ Easy to present percent information.	▲ Number of bars must be kept small. ▲ Variables that are enormously different in magnitude are hard to depict together.
Surface chart	▲ Shows trends and relationships of parts to whole at the same time. ▲ Eye-catching.	▲ Easy to confuse with an overlapping-line chart.
Semilogarithmic chart	▲ Presents rates of change as straight lines.	▲ Special vertical scale needed.
Pie chart	▲ Shows parts of a whole. ▲ Can represent about five parts.	▲ Hard to compare different pies representing wholes of differing magnitude.

HEADINGS   The headings used in reports are a form of graphic aid. They serve as (1) forward reference devices, (2) reader-oriented aids to scanning and comprehension, (3) pleasant breaks in the text, and (4) signals to the reader that the work is a "report," involving all the formality and objectivity that the word implies. Headings, it should be noted, are *not* substitutes for paragraph topic sentences. The writer should never begin a paragraph that has a heading such as "Cost Problems in the Textile Division" with a sentence beginning, "This is a problem that . . . ."

Exhibit 10.16 describes a heading system in common use. Four types of degrees of heading are noted, and thus four divisions of content are allowable. First-degree headings are reserved for titles and heads of major sections. Second degrees are used for subsections. Third degrees are for sub-subsections, and so on. Rarely does one need more than four degrees of heading. The rules for using the system are as follows:

▲   *Any degree may be used for the title or for a major section* (e.g., second or third); *but if a degree is not used for a major section, it cannot then be used at all.* If the writer begins with a second-degree head, a first-degree head cannot be used in the report—and thus the information can be broken down into only three classifications (second, third, and fourth degrees).

▲   *The writer cannot employ the system in reverse.* Therefore, a third-degree heading cannot have two subparts identified by second-degree headings.

▲   *A section must be broken down into more than one subsection.* A third-degree heading must thus be followed by at least two fourth-degree headings (if the section is divided into subsections).

▲   *If one section has subsections, a same-degree section need not have a similar subsection breakdown.* For example, a third-degree heading followed by three fourth-degree headings can be followed by another third-degree heading with no fourth-degree subparts at all.

▲   *When subparts to a section exist, they should be introduced in the same way (but condensed) that the whole report was introduced* (see Exhibit 10.16).

Headings should be as informative as possible within a concise format. Thus "talking" headings are usually preferable to "nontalking" headings:

Talking Headings	Nontalking Headings
Contribution of U.S. Segment to Improvement in Working Capital Position	U.S. Segment Working Capital
Poor Performance of Consumer Segment	Consumer Segment Performance

Here the talking headings tell the reader more about what is to follow than do the nontalking headings.

Another characteristic of headings is their parallel format:

Parallel Headings	Nonparallel Headings
Need for Increased Financing	Need for Increased Financing
Drive for Research Payoff	Research Payoff

Of course, not all headings in a report can be parallel, but certainly headings of the same degree should all be in a similar grammatical form. This uniformity of degree helps a reader to distinguish major from minor parts.

Exhibit 10.16 **REPORT HEADING SYSTEM**

First Degree

**COST ACCOUNTING PROBLEMS
IN THE WILSING DIVISION**

Second Degree

Introduction

Second Degree

Problems in the Alpha Plant

Introduction to Third
Degrees

Third Degree (1) **Product 1**

Introduction to Fourth
Degrees

Fourth Degree (1) **Direct Labor Costs.**

Fourth Degree (2) **Material/Overhead Costs.**

Third Degree (2) **Product 2**

STATISTICS IN ACCOUNTING REPORTS

An accounting statistic is a number that represents some kind of financial reality. If the representation is perfect (what Chapter 3 called *isomorphic*), the statistic is a fact—a verifiable truth. Less than perfect representations are estimates or predictions. When an accountant gets beyond simple reports of counting and enumerating, she leaves the realm of statistical facts and enters the realm of statistical estimates.

As noted in earlier chapters, the accountant must take care to differentiate between statistics that are facts and those that are estimates. To say that "73.2 percent of our inventory may be undervalued" is to communicate an estimate that seems to be a fact since the percent is given with such exactness. Instead, the accountant should say, "Roughly 60 to 80 percent of our inventory may be undervalued." In the same vein, an opinion should not be stated as a unitary statistic:

▲ *Wrong*—We feel that 50 percent of the short-term notes will be retired next year.

▲ *Right*—We feel that up to one-half of the short-term notes will be retired next year.

In this way the reader is less tempted to regard an opinion as a fact.

In addition to identifying statistics as (or as associated with) facts, estimates, or opinions, the accountant should make the statistic meaningful:

▲ *Not meaningful*—We examined 758 accounts receivable and found none doubtful.

▲ *Meaningful*—In past examinations about 10 percent of accounts receivable were usually found doubtful. However, we examined . . . .

The meaningful statement offers a perspective and a sense of a criterion against which to evaluate the information.

Kinds of Statistical Measures

Statistical measures can be of several kinds:

▲ *Aggregates*—Provide data based on counting and assumption. These measures are observations of and inferences about money, time, units, and people on which further analyses, inferences, estimates, and predictions are based.

▲ *Rates and percentages*—Standardize aggregates by turning them into parts of 100 so that information-laden comparisons can be made across items or over time.

▲ *Scales*—Describe an action or a person (1) by ranking the subject among similar items (ordinal scales) or (2) by assigning the subject some kind of designator— such as yes/no or acceptable/unacceptable (nominal scales).

Accountants must choose the kind of statistical measures they employ with care, and they must also be careful to avoid unintentional deception. This care is particularly needed when citing percent or ratio measures. Take the case in which fuel expenses rose $250,000 (from $1 million) while maintenance expenses went up $50,000 (from $25,000). The important aggregate figure is $250,000. Thus one would want to emphasize it. However, a careless writer might say:

> While fuel expenses increased only 25 percent last year, maintenance expenses rose by 100 percent.

The statement is true but not meaningful because the use of percentages masks the real problem, which is how to cope with a quarter-of-a-million-dollar increase in fuel expenses. If percentages say something different from aggregates, then only the more important kind of measure should be cited.

The use of percentages poses other problems. For example, a profitability change from 3 percent of investment in one year to 6 percent in the next can be referred to as a 3 percent increase *or* a 100 percent rise. The first increase is simply the aggregate change in percentage points, whereas the second is the percentage change in percentages. An accountant can avoid these interpretation problems by describing the base from which the percentage is calculated. Thus he would say that there was a 100 percent increase in profitability, from 3 to 6 percent, between year one and year two. (Of course, since the aggregate change is probably quite small, he might only want to quote it and not use any percentage information at all.)

Conclusions and Statistical Measures

A conclusion in a report is an inference that answers the question, "So what?" about the statistical measures and other information provided. *So what?* means that the conclusion should make a difference. It should be a statement answering the report's research question that, given the data, is inescapable. Notice that summaries in reports do not answer the question. They simply condense the substance of the report as a backward reference to aid comprehension. There is nothing inferential or conclusive about them.

Exhibit 10.17 describes the two logical methods used to make conclusions. (See Chapter 12 for a discussion of psychological ways of making conclusions.) In the *inductive* method data is observed and collected. Then it is analyzed (broken down into parts) and classified (built up into greater wholes) through processes based on logical reasoning, our own experience, and the expert testimony of others. We then state a conclusion that is probably valid.

Exhibit 10.17 **LOGICAL METHODS OF MAKING CONCLUSIONS**

METHOD	BASIS	ANALYSIS	NATURE OF CONCLUSION
Inductive	Data (often statistics)	Based on expert opinion, experience, reasoning	Probable
Deductive	Incontestable facts	Reasoning	Certain

This is as far as we can go, since induction can lead to support for a statement but can never prove it.

An example of the inductive method is a cost accounting report. A mass of cost data is broken down into its parts (plant A, process 1; plant B, process 1; plant A, process 2; etc.). Then the data is built up (labor costs, raw material costs, overhead costs). Transformed now into usable information, the data is examined and tested against our experience, expert knowledge, and logic. We may then conclude that costs in plant A are unacceptably higher than in plant B. This conclusion must be considered only probable, since observation we didn't make could conceivably make a case for saying that costs are acceptably high. However, the more data we collect, the greater the likelihood of our conclusion.

The other method of making a conclusion is *deduction*. Here we begin with incontestable facts, which are statements no one would deny. We then study the facts, making logical relationships, and state a conclusion that is certain. If facts A and B occur, we reason that conclusion C must occur. For example, if we report on our firm's accelerated depreciation practices, we may list the following facts:

▲   Faster write-off has led in the near past to lower taxes than with straight-line depreciation.

▲   If we want to continue to have lower taxes, we will have to buy new equipment sooner with accelerated depreciation than with straight-line depreciation.

Combining these facts, we can conclude that accelerated depreciation leads to greater equipment investment over the short term than does straight line. Assuming that all other things remain the same and that everyone agrees on the definition of vague wording such as *short term*, the stated conclusion ought to be accepted by everyone as a certainty.

Auditors are required by professional standards to form their opinions in an inductive manner. There is a paradox here in that induction, which leads to probability, is preferred over deduction, which arrives at certainty. However, there are many logical pitfalls on the way to certainty, and auditors, being averse to risky behavior, take the less certain but safer road of induction. We saw above that all report readers must define *short term* similarly if the deduction is to be considered certain. Only a very rash accountant would assume that such a vague term would be so defined. Thus he or she would either define the term as concretely as possible ("within the next two years") or else would resort to the inductive process (data from the past or from other firms analyzed by expert opinion to yield the same conclusion as above).

Deductive conclusions are quite useful in situations where laws, regulations, standards, or mathematical relationships prevail. These are the *if—then* situations. Thus *if* the law says that the investment tax credit can be applied in a certain condition and we are in that condition, *then* we can reduce our taxes. We can see that the tax accountant probably tends to make conclusions deductively, whereas the auditor, burdened by weak or vague standards, must depend on induction. Corporate accountants, who use both processes at different times, must always reflect before they write their reports on just what concluding process they ought to employ.

GROUP REPORT WRITING

Accountants, often in management advisory services, may work on projects in teams. The reports produced by the work team can provide a wealth of information to clients; but if the group activities in doing the task and producing the report are poorly coordinated, a disaster can occur.

Management Team Assignments

Management must take care in assigning accountants to task groups so that it does not doom the effort from the start. In Exhibit 10.18 specific activities to foster good group reports are described. Adequate planning involves a determination not only of the minimum time the group will need to do its work and produce a report, but also a designation of a maximum time limit. If groups are given more time than they need, Parkinson's Law (*"Work expands to fit the time allocated for it"*) comes into play. The result can be an inflated, padded report. Planning also involves assigning team members with an eye on new research questions that may arise as the job progresses. For example, if the group is to make an informational report on the management information system needs of a client, then MIS experts will be assigned.

However, if seniors anticipate a request from the client during the work for a second report recommending MIS interaction with regulatory agency

Exhibit 10.18 **MANAGEMENT TACTICS TO FOSTER GOOD GROUP REPORTS**

1. Plan adequately:
   ▲ Determine the time needed by the group. Giving the group too much time can lead to padded reports.
   ▲ Assign group members so that the group can adapt to new goals that evolve during its work.
   ▲ Assign a report writer to the group who will write the report independently and who is not the team leader.

2. Give the group specific instructions:
   ▲ Describe the behaviors and roles of each assigned member.
   ▲ State the nature of the report as informational, conclusive, or recommendatory.
   ▲ Detail the format of the report in terms of an outline and the kinds of citations required.
   ▲ Give examples of jargon words and gobbledygook passages to avoid.

3. Meet with the group before it begins:
   ▲ Go over behaviors required and possible role conflicts.
   ▲ Discuss the issue of different professional procedures.

required communications, then an accountant familiar with regulatory requirements might also be assigned or else held in readiness. Good planning also may require not burdening the team leader with the actual writing of the report. Depending on the amount of the team's budget, seniors may assign a skilled writer—often another accountant who has shown a flair for and an interest in writing—to put the report together under the direction of the team leader. Although the initial cost may be high, time and expense may be saved later on when the report is produced. If each team member were to produce a report section, the team leader would have to ensure that the writing style of each section flowed smoothly into that of the next section. Many rewrites could occur. If one person wrote the report, however, rewrite time to smooth out style could be cut. Moreover, the team leader would be available to work with the client on last-minute tasks.

Management must also tell the team members what their roles are, what the purpose of the finished report is to be, what the report outline generally should look like, and what the report text should *not* look like (what jargon and gobbledygook to avoid). Possible conflicts should be discussed, such as might occur between a disclosure-oriented accountant and a reader-oriented accountant or between a financial analyst and an accountant. If team members are alerted to the different ways specialists focus on procedures and issues, they can adapt their behaviors during the work.

Exhibit 10.19 **COMMON MISTAKES IN THE ORGANIZATION OF GROUP REPORTS**

MISTAKE CATEGORY	SPECIFIC TYPES OF MISTAKES
Data handling	Using the report as a data dump; failure to fully analyze the data; making assertions not warranted by the data; using data to impress instead of to aid understanding.
Omissions	Failure to point out problems in the work of the group; failure to explain why certain topics were or were not covered; leaving out full introductions and terminal sections; leaving out forward and backward references (which are used as transitional devices); failure to define key terms; failure to discuss ideas that are introduced.
Excesses	Use of windy and pretentious language; injection of irrelevant material; extensive use of qualifiers to avoid taking a stand.
Confusions	Lack of parallel formats in similar parts of the text; unsupported assertions mixed in with supported conclusions; discussion of elements whose importance has not been introduced; unexplained contradictions of earlier assertions and conclusions.

Group Report Production

Throughout the group's task activities someone, either the team leader or the assigned report writer, should be collecting notes, schedules, memos, and so on, from the team members for the final report. This activity should *not* occur only at the end of the task, when everyone is rushed. Also early in the task activities, the team members should meet to go over the rough report outline provided by management. They should analyze the tasks and decide on a more refined outline of the report. (Note that we are discussing the report outline, not the outline of tasks. The two will often be similar, but not always.) The team leader will then draw up the outline and distribute it to team members, with their writing assignments if a report writer is not in the team, for critique and agreement.

With the outline in hand, each specialist on the team writes his or her section of the report after completing the tasks (we will assume that a report writer is not assigned). The team leader receives their drafts; smooths them out; develops an appropriate heading system; and writes transitions, forward and backward references, recommendations, conclusions, summaries, and finally the introduction. This backward style of writing will help guarantee that introductions lead into the text and that conclusions point toward recommendations.

Exhibit 10.19 describes what can go wrong when group production of reports is not well coordinated. Generally, these problems are faulty handling of data as it becomes transformed into information, careless omissions, unprofessional excesses, confused writing, and conflicting assertions. These mistakes can be avoided if management plans the team assignment process adequately and if the report production process is coordinated.

PROPOSALS Public accounting firms often make unsolicited or solicited proposals to clients or potential clients. A proposal is a report that is factual but not necessarily objective. Indeed, a proposal is a persuasive request for some kind of allocation of resources to perform some kind of task that will benefit the resource allocator. Notice that it is a *request*. Proposals do not direct, suggest, or recommend. They ask for something.

When a government unit or perhaps a large corporation wants some kind of accounting, financial, or managerial task accomplished, such as the design of a control system, it may send requests for proposals (RFPs) to various public accounting firms. These requests are important, since their format determines the format of the proposal sent back in response. Exhibit 10.20 shows a typical outline for an RFP.

With an RFP in hand (if one has been sent out), the accounting firm prepares a proposal. Some proposals can run up to 300 pages, but most are shorter. The length depends on the nature of the task and on the format requirements of the RFP. While no single proposal form exists, the following outline will probably serve in most cases:

1. *Foreword.*   After a title page, a letter of transmittal or a foreword is inserted. This brief document identifies the proposer, describes the nature of the proposal, and assures the reader that the proposal follows RFP guidelines. Of greatest importance (because awards often depend on past relationships), the foreword reviews the previous work done by the proposer for the reader.

2. *Table of Contents.*   The contents are often cross-referenced with the RFP phase/objective/task numbers.

3. *List of Tables.*

4. *List of Figures.*

Exhibit 10.20   **OUTLINE OF A REQUEST FOR A PROPOSAL**

1. Introduction
    - ▲ *Brief mention of the task* to be accomplished.
    - ▲ *Background,* including function of the unit issuing the RFP and general standards governing its operation.
    - ▲ *Research problem,* describing a current condition (A), a desired condition (B), and the need to get from A to B.
    - ▲ *Statement of purpose,* describing the task requested in detail; specifically, the purpose requires an effort such that condition B is achieved within the context of the unit's function and under the guidance of its governing standards.

2. Objectives
    - ▲ *List of objectives,* employing verbs such as *develop, estimate, evaluate, produce, recommend,* and so on.
    - ▲ *Phases and subtasks,* listing chronological phases of the work and tasks to attain objectives in each phase:

        Phase 1
Objective A:	Task 1A.1
	Task 1A.2
Objective B.	Task 1B.1
	Task 1B.2

        Phase 2
Objective C:	Task 2C.1
	Task 2C.2

3. Project schedule and deliverables
    - ▲ *Schedule,* describing dates of initial briefings, project description by the firm awarded the contract, progress reports, interim formal reports, and final task completion and report.
    - ▲ *Deliverables,* describing in detail the format of reports and the documentation of expenses required for payment.

4. Responsibility of the contractor, describing what resources the contractor must provide in return for its fee.

5. Instructions for preparing proposal
    - ▲ *General instructions,* especially for preparing required parts of proposal.
    - ▲ *Due date.*

6. Criteria for award
    - ▲ *Criteria,* usually including price of contract, soundness of approach, capability of the proposer, past performance, experience of the staff.
    - ▲ *Evaluator,* describing who shall determine the award of the contract.

5. *Proposal Summary.* A brief description tells what the proposer intends to do and the benefits to the reader of her doing it.

6. *Introduction.* The purpose of the proposal is described in terms of the reader's problems, which have created needs that require the proposed solution.

7. *Review of the Past.* The proposer recounts efforts to solve the reader's problems in the past as well as reasons why the problem still exists and why it needs solving.

8. *Justification.* The proposer tells why he or she (or it) should be given the opportunity to solve the problem. The RFP criteria should guide the proposer's remarks here.

9. *Task Procedure.* Again guided by the RFP, the proposer describes each proposed step of the proposed work, the reasons for each step, and how the steps relate to each other. Often a chart is provided to illustrate the tasks and the time required for them.

10. *Task Material Resources.* The start-up and operating resources are listed. If a question exists about the availability of resources, a discussion is provided on how to obtain them.

11. *Task Personnel Resources.* The résumés of the key people are provided, along with a description of their experience. If key personnel are yet to be hired, a discussion is provided on where to find them.

12. *Costs.* The price of the contract is broken down into start-up and operating costs, with an appropriate breakdown of each kind and a schedule of when the costs will be incurred and when funds from the reader will be required.

13. *Reports.* The oral and written, formal and informal, and progress and final reports are listed and described. The proposer tells when he will make reports.

14. *Outcomes.* The proposer recounts what will have happened when the work is finished. This discussion instructs the reader on how to decide whether the task has been successfully accomplished. Thus it provides clear and easily applied standards, procedures, and measurements to employ in evaluating the success of the work.

15. *The Future.*   Here the proposer forecasts what benefits will occur for the reader after the successful accomplishment of the task. The proposer may suggest steps to take to maximize those benefits.

Proposals must be reader oriented. They must show understanding of the reader's problem and offer a practical solution in terms of the reader's situation. They must persuade the reader that, of all the firms available, the proposer's firm should be given the job. Their presentation should be realistic, clear, responsible, comprehensive, and focused on the specifics of the RFP. What they should *not* contain is boilerplate, vague generalities, last year's proposal recycled, excessive claims of competence and experience, impossible cost estimates, and attractive packaging at the expense of substance.

Example of a
Memo Report

TO: P. K. Downing

FROM: Susan Johnson

SUBJECT: Report on Financial Analysis of Dubuque Electric Power Company System during 1982

DATE: February 23, 1983

The following is the report you requested analyzing the financial status of Dubuque Electric Power Company System. I have based this report on the information given in the Uniform Statistical Report for the year ended December 31, 1982. In this report I have used the term *sales* to mean sales of therms to consumers, as opposed to *revenues,* which are measured in dollars. The report is divided into four parts. Part one is my conclusions. Part two is an analysis of the pattern that our sales and revenues followed during the year 1982. Part three analyzes the pricing policy of Dubuque Electric. And part four compares our different groups of customers in terms of how they contributed to sales and revenues.

Conclusions

▲   Sales and revenues for Dubuque Electric came from three main sources—residential, commercial, and industrial. These sales and revenues were greatest during the winter months, when demand was high, and subsequently they were lowest during the summer months, when demand was low.

▲   Dubuque Electric charged lower rates during the winter months than in the summer months.

▲   When demand for gas from Dubuque Electric was high, sales and revenues from residential customers were greater than those from the other groups.

▲   Dubuque Electric's industrial group provided the most total sales of all groups of customers. Moreover, sales in 1982 to the industrial group did not fluctuate as much as sales to the other groups.

Exhibit 10.A.1   **DUBUQUE ELECTRIC COMPANY SALES AND REVENUES, 1982**

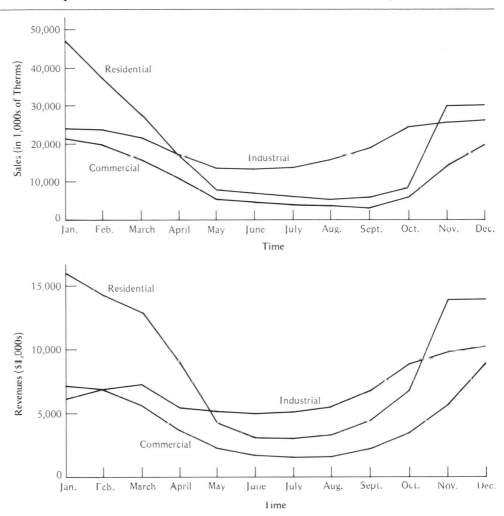

▲   Residential customers provided Dubuque Electric with more revenues in 1982 than any other group.

Fluctuations of Sales and Revenues over the Year 1982

Dubuque Electric Company experienced seasonal fluctuations in the demand for gas from its customers. Therefore, our sales and revenues also varied during the year.

Dubuque Electric's sales and revenues were at their lowest during the months of June through September. The greatest drop in both sales and revenues occurred in the residential-customers group. As Exhibit 10.A.1

207

shows, sales and revenues increased for all types of customers during the remainder of the year.

Also, in the months of May through October, the exhibit shows that the industrial customers made up the largest portion of both sales and revenues. However, during the remainder of the year, our largest group of customers was residential.

Prices Charged by Dubuque Electric

Since the demand for gas from Dubuque Electric varied during the year, the prices charged also varied. These prices fluctuated according to the time of year and type of customer.

Prices During the Year. The prices charged, in terms of revenues per sale, appear to have varied inversely with the amount of sales. In other words, from June through September when sales were at their lowest, prices were at their highest. This was especially true of residential customers and can be seen in Exhibit 10.A.2. (Note: A rate increase occurred for all types of customers in November.)

Prices to Different Customers. As the exhibit illustrates, Dubuque Electric charged higher prices to some customers than to others. The average price of 33¢ charged to residential customers was higher than the average price of 27¢ and 24¢ charged to commercial and industrial customers, respectively.

Exhibit 10.A.2   **DUBUQUE ELECTRIC COMPANY PRICES, 1982**

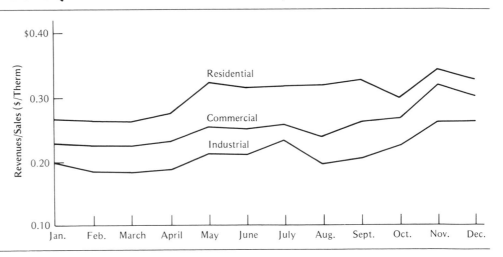

Exhibit 10.A.3 **DUBUQUE ELECTRIC COMPANY COMPARISON OF SALES AND CUSTOMERS, 1982**

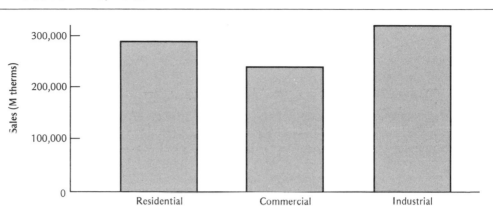

Customer Contributions to Sales and Revenues

Dubuque Electric's three main sources of sales and revenues—residential, commercial, and industrial—contributed in different proportions to both sales and revenues. Together, these customers made up more than 99 percent of our gas business.

Sales. During the year, Dubuque Electric's largest customer, in sales of therms, was the industrial sector, as illustrated in Exhibit 10.A.3. Sales to industrial customers exceeded sales to residential customers by approximately 20.1 million therms, or 7.7 percent.

Revenues. Even though the residential sector did not provide Dubuque Electric with the largest amount of sales, it did provide the largest amount of revenues. As Exhibit 10.A.4 shows, revenues from residential customers during 1982 exceeded those from industrial customers (by approximately $12.5 million, or 19.1 percent).

Finally, residential customers are the largest group and therefore have the smallest ratio of revenues per customer, as indicated in Exhibit 10.A.5.

The implications of these charts are such that a $0.05 increase in revenues per residential customer would require an equivalent increase of $9.13 in revenues per industrial customer to provide the same amount of total revenue.

If you need any clarification of these issues or if I can be of further assistance, please call me.

Exhibit 10.A.4 **DUBUQUE ELECTRIC COMPANY COMPARISON OF REVENUES AND CUSTOMERS, 1982**

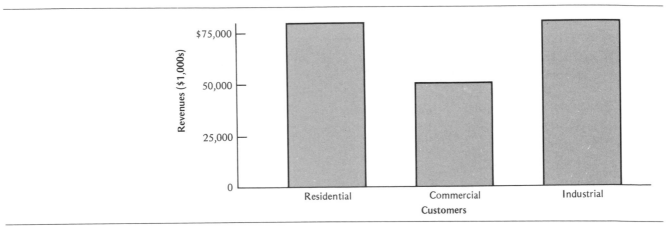

Exhibit 10.A.5 **DUBUQUE ELECTRIC COMPANY CUSTOMERS AND REVENUES PER CUSTOMER, 1982**

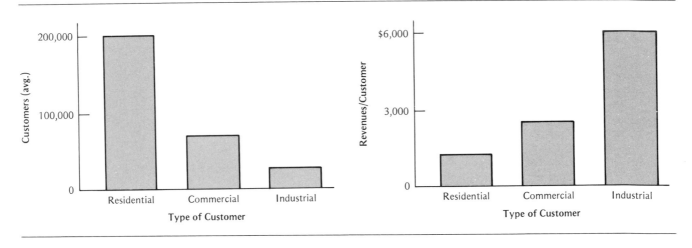

Example of a Short Report

RECOMMENDATIONS FOR IMPROVING THE EFFECTIVENESS
OF THE ANNUAL REPORT BASED ON A SURVEY OF
USERS OF THE ANNUAL REPORT

**Prepared for
J. B. Collins, President
J. B. Collins, Inc.**

Prepared by
J. C. Loewen, Staff Accountant
J. B. Collins, Inc.

November 18, 1982

MAJOR POINTS OF THE REPORT

This report was prepared by the Accounting Staff for J. B. Collins, president of J. B. Collins, Inc.

Surveys of company stockholders and security analysts across the country provided the data for this report. These surveys were used to find out (a) how effective current annual reports are in communicating information about a company and (b) how important these annual reports are in comparison with other related sources of information. Also, the surveys revealed relationships among sections in an annual report and how these sections added to or detracted from the effectiveness of the annual report.

The surveys led to the following conclusions:

▲ Annual reports of a company are not the primary source of information to an investor.

▲ Shareholders are primarily interested in tangible, monetary results of a company, while security analysts are interested in the long-range profitability of a company.

▲ Shorter annual reports and more detailed interim reports are preferred by all annual report users.

▲ All users are satisfied with the single annual report and do not want separate reports for stockholders and security analysts.

This report recommends that authors of annual reports:

▲ Place photographs of executives near the end of the annual report.

▲ Discuss earnings per share and dividend data near the beginning of the report.

▲ Simplify all textual discussions in the report.

▲ Place more accounting information in interim reports and less in annual reports.

▲ Discuss future prospects in greater detail and reduce the public relations aspect in the report.

▲ Arrange the financial information so that the data is first, the notes are second, and the auditor's statement is third.

▲ Use more charts and fewer numbers when presenting statistics.

RECOMMENDATIONS FOR IMPROVING
ANNUAL REPORT EFFECTIVENESS

Orientation to the Problem

Purpose of the Report

This report was requested on August 1, 1982, by J. B. Collins, president of J. B. Collins, Inc., because he and other managers questioned the effectiveness of the company's annual report in providing information to stockholders and security analysts. The purpose of this report is to provide recommendations for improving the annual report's effectiveness.

Collection of Data

Data for this report was collected through surveys conducted by the Department of Marketing and Economic Research. Two groups were identified as being the primary users of annual reports. One group consisted of J. B. Collins, Inc., shareholders. The other group included security analysts from throughout the country.

Survey questionnaires were sent to 500 of the company's shareholders and 200 of the security analysts. Of these, 287 shareholders and 141 security analysts responded to the questionnaire. This report assumes that the responses received accurately represent the two user groups sampled.

Format of the Report

The report first discusses the findings of the survey of shareholders. Next, the report reviews the needs of the security analysts surveyed. Finally, the report presents conclusions from the surveys and makes recommendations for improving the effectiveness of annual reports.

Survey of Company Shareholders

Shareholders of company stock were asked how much time they spent reading an annual report and what items in annual reports were most interesting to them. In addition, the shareholders were asked to give yes or no responses to a series of questions.

Time Investment Is Small

Exhibit 10.B.1 shows the distribution of how much time shareholders spend reading an annual report. Two-thirds of the shareholders spend less

Exhibit 10.B.1 **PERCENT DISTRIBUTION OF SHAREHOLDERS BASED ON MINUTES SPENT READING AN ANNUAL REPORT**

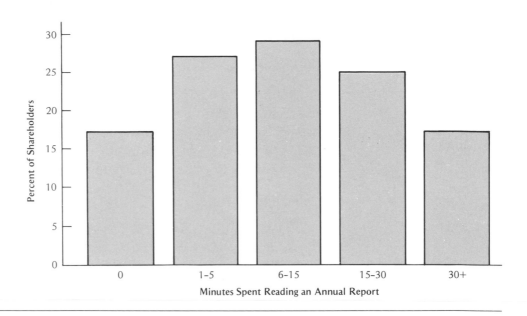

than fifteen minutes reading an annual report. Only 14 of every 100 shareholders spend more than thirty minutes reading an annual report.

The exhibit indicates that most owners of stock are interested only in an overview of the company whose stock they own. Since most annual reports take about thirty minutes to read completely through without analysis, the average shareholder apparently reads only those sections deemed interesting or understandable.

Items of Interest Are Ranked

Shareholders were given a list of sections commonly found in an annual report. Each shareholder selected one section that was of least interest and one section that was of most interest. Exhibit 10.B.2 shows the relative importance of the sections on the list the shareholders were given. In the exhibit, a large positive value means the section had many ratings of high interest and few ratings of low interest. A large negative value means the section had many ratings of low interest and few ratings of high interest.

Exhibit 10.B.2 implies that shareholders are most interested in those sections of an annual report that relate directly to them. These sections include the discussion of earnings per share, the letter to the shareholders, the discussion of future prospects, and the financial highlights. Technical sections of an

214

Exhibit 10.B.2   **RELATIVE INTEREST OF ANNUAL REPORT SECTIONS TO SHAREHOLDERS**

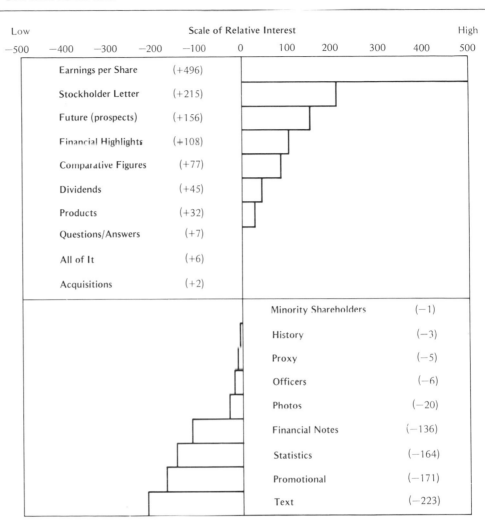

annual report seem to be of least interest to stockholders. These sections include the financial notes, statistical analyses, promotional material, and textual discussion.

Specific Responses Are Tallied

Each shareholder responded to eight specific questions. Their responses are tabulated in Exhibit 10.B.3.

The following conclusions can be drawn from the shareholders' responses:

Exhibit 10.B.3 **STOCKHOLDER RESPONSES TO SPECIFIC QUESTIONS**

	QUESTION ASKED	TYPE OF RESPONSE		
		Yes	No	Other
1.	Do you think annual reports are written in a way that the average investor can understand?	36%	53%	11%
2.	Is the annual report important to you when you are making a decision to buy or sell a stock?	32	58	10
3.	In general, do pictures in annual reports help you to understand the company?	51	39	10
4.	Do you think companies should put out two different annual reports—one written specifically for the average investor and the other for professionals such as security analysts and brokers?	35	54	11
5.	Do you know the names of the top officers, such as the president, of the companies you invest in?	21	59	20
6.	Do you think it would be helpful for you if companies cut down on the size of the annual report but put out larger, more extensive interim reports?	47	44	9
7.	Do you know what earnings per share were on any of your stocks?	43	49	8
8.	Do you know the dividend on your stocks?	74	19	7

▲ About one-third of the shareholders understand annual reports the way they are written. One-half of the shareholders feel the annual reports are too hard to understand.

▲ More than half of the shareholders don't refer to annual reports when making decisions to buy or sell stock. Only one-third of the shareholders do refer to the annual reports.

▲ Pictures in an annual report do tend to help shareholders understand a company.

▲ Half of the stockholders feel one annual report for both average investors and professional investors is sufficient, while one-third of the stockholders feel two separate reports would be beneficial.

▲ Only one-fifth of the shareholders know the names of top officers in the companies they invest in.

▲ Shareholders were split on whether to cut down the size of the annual report and increase the size of interim reports, or to keep the present relative sizes of both types of reports.

Exhibit 10.B.4 **RELATIVE IMPORTANCE OF INFORMATION SOURCES TO SECURITY ANALYSTS**

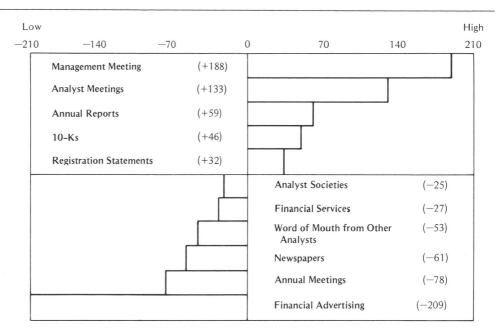

▲ Half of the shareholders did not know the earnings-per-share figures for any of the stocks they owned.

▲ Three-fourths of the shareholders did know the dividends on their stocks.

Survey of Security Analysts

The security analysts were asked questions to determine which sources of information were most (least) important to them in finding out about a company, which sections of the annual report were read first, and which of these sections were most interesting to them. In addition, the analysts responded to several general questions concerning annual reports.

Annual Reports Rank Third

According to security analysts, annual reports were ranked the third most important source of information about a company. The ranking of information sources is shown in Exhibit 10.B.4. In this exhibit the scale of importance was determined in a manner similar to that used for Exhibit 10.B.2.

As can be seen in Exhibit 10.B.4, management meetings and analyst meetings rated high as important sources of information. Annual reports fol-

Exhibit 10.B.5 **PERCENTAGE DISTRIBUTION OF ANNUAL REPORT SECTIONS READ FIRST BY SECURITY ANALYSTS**

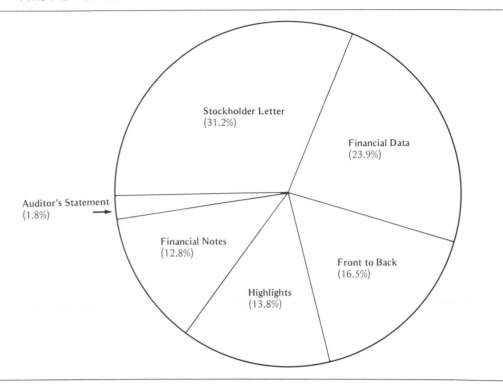

lowed in third place. Financial advertising, on the other hand, was judged by far to be the least important source of information.

The exhibit implies that a security analyst wants information from the most reliable source available. Since corporate managers and other analysts have the most recent information about a company, it follows logically that the managers and analysts are important sources of information. Conversely, financial advertising, possibly being viewed as very unreliable, is considered a very unimportant source of information, as the survey reveals.

Analysts Read the Letter to Stockholders First

The letter to the stockholders is read first by the largest percentage of security analysts. The percentage figure of 31.2 is shown in the pie chart of Exhibit 10.B.5. Over half of the analysts read either the letter to the stockholders or the financial data first. Note that less than 2 percent of the security analysts read the auditor's statement first.

The letter to the stockholders may be of concern to analysts because it can be viewed as an indicator of any changes in management policy or style.

Exhibit 10.B.6 **PERCENTAGE DISTRIBUTION OF ANNUAL REPORT ITEMS CHOSEN LEAST INTERESTING BY SECURITY ANALYSTS**

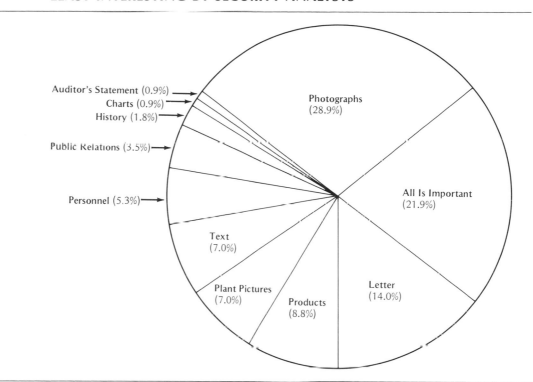

Auditor's Statement (0.9%)
Charts (0.9%)
History (1.8%)
Public Relations (3.5%)
Personnel (5.3%)
Text (7.0%)
Plant Pictures (7.0%)
Products (8.8%)
Photographs (28.9%)
All Is Important (21.9%)
Letter (14.0%)

Such changes would influence the security analysts' views of the company's profit potential and their conception of the investment risk involved.

Photographs of Executives Are Least Interesting

As Exhibit 10.B.6 shows, over 28 percent of the security analysts polled said photographs of executives were the least interesting part of an annual report. A small percentage of the analysts said the auditor's statement, accompanying charts, and historical discussion were uninteresting. In contrast, however, nearly 22 percent of the analysts said no portion of an annual report was uninteresting.

Analysts Respond to Several Questions

The following summaries are based on answers the security analysts gave to specific questions about annual reports:

219

▲ *Separate annual reports* for shareholders and professional investors were not recommended by 46 percent of the analysts. Only 44 percent did recommend separate reports, while 10 percent answered neutrally to this question.

▲ *Pictures of officers and directors* were favored by 56 percent of the analysts. Thirty-six percent said they preferred not to have these pictures included, and 8 percent said they sometimes liked the pictures.

▲ *More complete interim reports* and less complete annual reports were recommended by 82 percent of the respondents. Only 15 percent said they preferred the present reports, while 3 percent were neutral on this choice.

▲ *Rating of management,* said 95 percent of the security analysts, is not based on publication of an expensive, elaborate annual report. The other 5 percent said such a report is important, but only to a slight degree.

Conclusions from the Surveys

Results of both surveys indicate that annual reports are not the primary source of information to investors when they decide to buy or sell a particular company's stock. Small investors, the individual stockowners, seem to use annual reports only to get an overview of a company. Professional investors, the security analysts, appear to use the annual reports to get specific information that may or may not be available elsewhere.

One can also conclude from the surveys that the two groups have different primary purposes for reading an annual report. The stockowners tend to be interested in the current profitability, what's-in-it-for-me type of information. The analysts, in contrast, appear to be interested in the long-range outlook of the company, the prospects of long-term investment in the company, and present performance based on financial data.

Both groups of annual report users agreed that annual reports should be trimmed and interim reports should be expanded to include more detail. In addition, both the shareholders and the security analysts were satisfied with the present single-report system, as compared to separate annual reports for each group.

Recommendations for Improving the Effectiveness of Annual Reports

Authors of the company's annual report should implement the following recommendations in order to improve the effectiveness of annual reports in communicating information about the company:

▲ Use just enough pictures to help the reader visualize the company's products and facilities.

▲ Place photographs and descriptions of corporate officers near the end of the annual report.

▲ Discuss earnings per share and dividend data near the beginning of the report, as well as in the financial statements.

▲ Prepare the textual discussions (history, products, letter to shareholders, etc.) with reader understandability in mind. Avoid technical jargon and use an easy-to-read writing style.

▲ Place more emphasis on financial-data presentation and discussion in interim reports and less emphasis on these details in annual reports.

▲ Discuss the future prospects of the company in greater detail.

▲ Reduce the public relations aspect of the report.

▲ Continue publication of a single annual report, for use by all readers.

▲ Organize the report so that the financial data is followed by the financial notes, which in turn are followed by the auditor's statement.

▲ Reduce the amount of numerical statistics and increase the amount of graphic statistics in the report.

Checkoff 10.1 **ACCOUNTING COMMUNICATIONS: REPORT WRITING: GENERAL**

PLANNING REPORTS	YES	NO
1. Have I determined the reader's need for and likely use of my reports?		___
2. Have I written the report so that it is understandable and acceptable and creates a favorable image of me and my organization?	___	___
3. Have I planned my report goals so that they contain a time frame, avoid vague words, and focus on either prescription or suggestion?	___	___
4. Have I broken my goals down into objectives and tasks?	___	___
5. In writing the report have I written my introduction last?	___	___
6. Have I added transitions, headings, graphic aids, forward references, and backward references?	___	___
7. Is my report client rather than supervisor oriented?		
8. Have I tailored the report for either skimming, rapid reading, dipping into, or in-depth study?	___	___
REPORT PARTS		
9. Are my introductions thorough and complete?	___	
10. Does my purpose focus on change rather than on criticism?	___	___
11. Have I protected myself from later criticism by describing the limits of my report and why these limits exist?	___	___

(continued)

Checkoff 10.1 *(concluded)*

	YES	NO
12. Do my research goals and objectives influence the organizational structure of the report?	___	___
13. Have I chosen an appropriate terminal section arrangement for the report?	___	___
14. Have I used tables to condense information and aid comprehension?	___	___
15. Have I chosen my graphic figures to add eye-appeal and to make important points?	___	___
16. Have I referenced and discussed the tables and figures in the text?	___	___
17. Have I employed a sensible heading system and followed system rules?	___	___

REPORT STATISTICS

18. Are my statistical facts distinguished from my statistical estimates and opinions?	___	___
19. Have I provided criteria or a perspective to help make my statistics meaningful?	___	___
20. If percentage information stresses something different from aggregate information, have I discussed the differences?	___	___
21. Have I described the base from which percentages were calculated (20 percent of what?)?	___	___

CONCLUSIONS

22. Are my conclusions clearly *not* summaries? Do they answer the question, *"So what?"*	___	___

GROUP REPORT WRITING

23. Has the group been assigned in a way that increases its likelihood of issuing an acceptable report?	___	___

PROPOSALS

24. Is my proposal drafted in response to the RFP?	___	___
25. Is my proposal realistic and tailored to the reader's needs?	___	___

chapter 11 Report Writing: Specific

Chapter 10 described general standards and procedures for report writing. In this chapter we focus on specific accounting reports—namely, reports of public and internal auditors, corporate reports, and annual reports.

EXTERNAL AUDIT REPORTS

In Chapter 3 the highly formal short form of auditors' reports was described. Here our emphasis is on the long form, as well as on the management letter and on other special reports issued by auditors.

Long-Form Reports

The standard long-form auditor's report is a follow-up communication to the short form, which is little more than a statement of the auditor's opinion about the extent to which the client's financial statements fairly and accurately represent the financial condition of the firm. However, all the connotations of the short form should also be expressed or implied in the long-form report. These connotations imply that:

▲   The auditors are proficient;

▲   They are independent;

▲   They used due professional care;

▲   They planned the audit carefully;

▲   They carried the audit out themselves or supervised others who helped in the examination;

▲   They conducted enough audit tests (also called "studies of internal controls" and generally referred to as the "audit program") to form a relevant and reliable evaluation of internal controls.

Professional Standards

In general both long and short forms signal to the reader that the following professional standards have been applied to the communication:

▲   *Clarity*—The report does not mislead or allow the data to mislead a reader.

▲   *Completeness*—The report is based on sufficient information.

▲   *Emphasis*—The report points out (1) client departures from generally accepted accounting standards, principles, or procedures and (2) auditor omissions from generally accepted audit standards or procedures.

▲   *Objectivity*—The report exhibits the auditor's independence of mental attitude toward the audit.

▲   *Historical background*—The report reviews the nature and structure of internal controls instituted by the client.

▲   *Analytical procedure*—The report shows evidence (1) of research based on observations, interviews, inspections, samples, confirmations, and inquiries and (2) of processing of the evidence through logical, rational, statistical, or acceptable methods of inference making to reach an opinion.

▲   *Conventional format*—The report should not make radical departures in form and coverage from previous reports. It should exhibit consistency.

▲   *Consequential focus*—The report should concern itself with significant issues and not dwell on trivial matters. An issue or a measure may be considered consequential if, among other things, (1) the dollar amounts involved are large—either absolutely or relative to something (e.g., current assets); (2) the reader's response to the report will be materially affected; (3) something unstable or unusual is occurring; (4) an error or deception exists; or (5) future earnings will be affected.

Format

The formats of long-form reports vary enormously, some being quite long and others quite short. For a large corporation, which has paid the audit firm up to $500,000, the long-form report ought to be substantial. Recall the intuitive information-processing rule noted in Chapter 2: Extreme information inputs may lead to expectations of extreme outputs. In many cases, a common presentation format would look like the following:

1. Title page
2. Letter of transmittal
3. Table of contents
4. List of financial statements and schedules
5. Opinion
6. Introduction: scope of the examination
7. Financial statements and schedules
8. Explanations
9. Exceptions
10. Report to management (comments)
11. Index of topics covered

Long-form reports should be similar in form from year to year so that comparisons can be made. This does not mean that they should be full of boilerplate. On the contrary, they should be clear and easily read.

Account Titles. The auditor would want to make the account titles as clear as possible (Palen, 1955):

Unclear Titles	Clear Titles
"Securities Borrowed"	"Deposits on Account of Securities Borrowed"
"Securities Loaned"	"Deposits of Other Brokers for Securities Lent to Them"
"Foreign Exchange Sold"	"Accounts Receivable for Foreign Exchange Sold"

Terms. Clarity is also improved when the auditor defines, explains, or comments on vague terms and terms with multiple meanings. Exhibit 11.1 lists a number of important terms and comments on each one.

Opinion. The nature of the opinion is a complex technical topic that will not be discussed here except in general terms. Generally, then, the opinion is an informed judgment, an inference based on facts collected and attitudes formed during the examination. The opinion should refer to the fairness of the representations made in the financial statements covered in the report and not to any statements collected somewhere else. It is not a description of what was examined but rather an evaluation. There are many complex ways in which an opinion can be qualified, but a reader-oriented accountant would avoid long, complex qualifications. Although they add a measure of protection to the

Exhibit 11.1 **VAGUE AUDIT TERMINOLOGY**

TERM	COMMENT
Assets	Make it clear which are available or not available for satisfaction of claims and which are the most liquid.
Book value	Vague. Instead write *cost* or *cost less amortization.*
Capital	Define. State whether it is different from contributed capital.
Cost of goods sold	Also called *cost of sales, cost of production.*
Deferred	Tell whether it means applicable to future operations *or* held in suspension awaiting final status.
Exhibits	These are statistical statements, also called *supplemental statements.* When in percentages, they may be referred to as *common-size statements.*
Finished goods	Also called *finished products, manufactured goods.*
Fixed assets	Avoid *plant, property, intangibles,* and the like. Instead, write *land, buildings, equipment,* and so on.
Gross sales	Vague. Be specific.
Income	Differentiate income from operations from other income.
Liabilities	Make it clear which are secured, which are subordinated, which are due to affiliates, which are short or long term, and which are contingent.
Long-term debt	Define in chronological terms.
Other assets	Avoid or keep the dollar amounts small.
Schedules	These are breakdowns of complex entities on the balance sheet, income statement, and so on.
Shareholders' equity	Avoid vague terms such as *surplus.*
Sources of working capital	Also called *additions to working capital, transactions increasing working capital,* and *working capital provided.* (Parallel forms are employed for *uses of working capital.*)
Work in process	Also called *work in progress, goods in process of manufacture.*

auditor, they simply confuse the reader. If no opinion can be offered, the auditor should imply that an unfavorable opinion is not being suggested and should state why no opinion could be made. The opinion probably should be an overall one; piecemeal opinions may confuse the reader.

Scope of the Examination and Explanations. The scope of the examination section describes the extent of the examination and introduces the audited statements and schedules. Explanations are then presented. These are essential matters, often of a material nature, that could not be expressed in the financial statements.

Exceptions. The next section, exceptions, describes the reservations or qualifications of the auditor. Exceptions often concern the following items:

▲ Limitations on the examination, such as audit procedures not done;
▲ Company departures from GAAP;
▲ Unacceptable changes in procedures from those followed in prior periods;
▲ Contingencies whose effect is at present unknown.

The significance of the exceptions is discussed, as is the effect of the causes of the exceptions on the financial statements.

Report to Management. In the report to management, also called the *comments*, the auditor discusses matters of interest to the client—often conditions that do not require disclosure in the financial statements. Problems with the audit are described, as are unusual company procedures observed by the auditor. The comments are usually developed out of notes made by the auditor as the work progressed. They are informative and directed at helping the client improve internal controls. Moreover, they ought to help create a favorable image of the auditor as someone who has given the client value for his or her money. Often the comments paragraphs are numbered for easy future reference.

In making evaluative conclusions in the comments, the auditor should emphasize future changes needed rather than past errors or failures. When some uncertainty exists regarding a conclusion, the auditor should state the conclusion if it is *probably* valid but should withdraw it if it is only *possibly* valid. Any recommendations evolving out of the conclusions should be suggestions. They should not be requests aimed at helping the auditor during the next audit.

Management Letters and Special Reports

Management letters are often memo or short reports in letter formats that auditors send to clients to comment on material weaknesses in internal controls or on special subjects. The auditor's goal is not so much to solve a problem but rather to stimulate the client's thought and action (Evans and

Miller, 1978). However, in addition to clients, the letter also may be read by credit executives. Different readers have different purposes in reading the report:

Readers of Management Letters	Reader Purposes
Client's managers	To gain information and guidance for corrective action
Credit executives	To evaluate client's control of financial information

The existence of multiple purposes among various readers creates a difficult writing chore for auditors. They must describe problems and call for solutions without seeming to be overly critical of the client. Exhibit 11.2 shows part of a management letter in which the control condition is described in a clinical, objective manner, and then a recommendation is made for improvement. Notice that evaluation is occurring, but no evaluative words (*good, bad,* etc.) are used.

Auditors should qualify their statements so that weaknesses identified are seen in context. Thus the absence of a full control system might be acceptable in a small company where the owner is in touch with the accounting, but not acceptable in a large firm. Moreover, control weaknesses should be prioritized in terms of, first, those needing attention and, second, those needing only monitoring. In this way the seriousness of the evaluation is communicated to the reader.

Exhibit 11.2 **EVALUATIONS AND RECOMMENDATIONS IN MANAGEMENT LETTER**

Quarterly Physical Inventories

The Company uses the "ABC" method of accounting for raw material inventory. This enables you to maximize control while minimizing accounting effort. The time of physically counting the "A" inventory items is minimal: the year-end physical count took four hours for two people.

We recommend that a good control measure is to physically count the "A" inventory items bimonthly or at least quarterly. This will enable you to determine the effectiveness of your material issues procedures on a timely basis.

Reconciliation of Work in Process

The accounting procedures implemented in January 1982 included a procedure for reconciling the work-in-process costs recorded on the job cost cards to the work-in-process costs recorded in the general ledger. This was done during 1982, but the

(continued)

Exhibit 11.2   (concluded)

differences that arose were not recognized as errors. They were thought to be classification differences between raw materials and work in process. Upon further investigation it was determined that the differences were due to undetected clerical errors in the job cost cards.

We recommend that the personnel who have responsibility for reviewing the completed job cost cards review them critically for missing or excess costs. In addition, any differences in excess of $500 that arise in the aforementioned reconciliation process should be researched and explained prior to the next month end. The procedure for doing so would be to maintain the general ledger accounts by cost classification, (material, sublet, labor, and overhead). This will enable you to isolate the differences in those categories as follows:

	Material	Sublet	Labor	Overhead	Total
Month-end total of all job cost cards	$ X	$ X	$ X	$ X	$ X
Month-end total of general ledger	(X)	(X)	(X)	(X)	(X)
Difference	$ X	$ X	$ X	$ X	$ X

After the difference has been isolated by cost classification, the following steps should be performed to isolate the difference further.

1. Clerically check all job cost cards where activity was recorded during the month. Do the larger, more active jobs first.
2. Research all entries for each posting source to determine that the amounts were recorded the same in the general ledger as they were on the job cost cards.

In order for these procedures to work effectively, amounts posted in the job cost cards must be identified as to the month period. This can be done by the use of color codes, dates, audit stamp, and the like.

Status Report on Jobs in Progress

During the year, we noted that on some projects management was not aware of the cost status of the jobs. We also recognize that new personnel have been hired near year end and that steps have been taken to improve this matter.

We stress the need for realistic monthly status reports on large jobs so management can take corrective steps as early as possible. This can be accomplished by having the manager in charge of the project complete a status report listing material, sublet, labor, and overhead in jobs to date (per job cost card) with estimates to complete the budget amounts listed for comparison. This would also necessitate a detailed operating budget by phase for each project prepared consistently with the status report. If such a budget is not prepared in bidding the jobs, it must be prepared soon after the contract is let.

Exhibit 11.3 **TYPES OF SPECIAL REPORTS PREPARED BY AUDITORS**

REPORT TYPE	PURPOSE	EXAMPLES
Recommendation reports	To note problems or opportunities and to suggest actions to correct problems or to take advantage of opportunities.	▲ Suggested changes in control procedures ▲ Suggested changes in organization
Items-of-special-interest reports	To alert senior management to significant information gathered during the audit.	▲ Inventory valuation issues ▲ Financing requirements
Instruction reports	To show the client how to accomplish some procedure.	▲ Methods for computing asset value ▲ Procedures for cutting inventory costs
Evaluation reports	To make a conclusion (inference, evaluation, opinion, etc.) regarding some issue or problem of the client without suggesting changes.	▲ Internal-control restructuring needs ▲ Age and general condition of facilities
Information reports	To present information requested by the client.	▲ Comparison of overhead allocation methods ▲ Models of cost accounting

The management letter should be written in a point-by-point approach to facilitate management's response, if any. Often these responses form an addendum to the letter: they deal with either acceptance of the recommendations and the corrective steps being taken or rejection of the recommendations and reasons for the rejection.

Exhibit 11.3 lists a number of types of management letters and special reports issued to clients by independent auditors.

INTERNAL AUDIT REPORTS Although internal auditing goes on regularly within companies, the resulting reports are by no means routine. Every situation is different; thus internal auditors must design their reports to be special communications of a highly context-specific kind. Nevertheless, common dimensions to internal reports do exist and are discussed in this section.

To begin with, internal auditors begin their task by seeking the answers to rather predictable research questions:

▲ Is the firm safeguarding its assets?

▲ Is the firm promoting operational efficiency?

▲   Is the firm's accounting information relevant and reliable?

▲   Are management policies being carried out?

The internal audit process involves a number of communications situations and reports transmitted among the auditors (often in teams of two or more), line management, and senior management (Johnson, 1978).

Work and Audit Plans

Often the internal audit group will operate under a general work plan that is used as a guideline in doing specific audits. For a given audit, an audit plan will be drawn up (1) outlining the scope of the work, (2) setting forth a timetable and a budget, and (3) assigning the relevant personnel.

Communications with Audited Management

Based on the work and audit plans, an initial communication (often a memo followed by a meeting) with the audited managers occurs. Here the auditors collect information on operating procedures, data processing, and the like. The managers and auditors also discuss the timing of the work and the clerical and other assistance that the auditors will require. This beginning meeting lays the groundwork for future meetings, during which the auditors alert management to problems discovered and to suggestions for change. There must be no surprises in the final audit report.

During a closing meeting one of the auditors will make an oral report to the audited managers. This report reviews the work done and informs the managers about the contents of the formal written report, an outline of which is provided. The oral report has a persuasive tone to it in that the auditor tries to build support for suggested corrective actions. It is also an information-gathering communication, as the auditor collects comments from the managers that can be transformed into issues discussed in the written report.

Within a few weeks of the oral report, a written report is developed. Often the audited managers are asked to comment on draft versions, and their more important responses are incorporated into the report with the auditors' comments on the comments. The finished report will go to the director of internal audits, with copies to the audit committee, to the concerned managers, and perhaps to the firm's independent auditors. The existence of multiple readerships makes audit reporting among the most difficult of all accounting communications (see Exhibit 11.4, which repeats and develops Exhibit 3.5).

Exhibit 11.4 **MULTIPLE READERSHIPS OF INTERNAL AUDIT REPORTS**

READER	READER NEED	INTERNAL AUDIT FOCUS
Audited management	Needs to know about deficiencies noted and auditors' negative conclusions so as to be able to prepare a defense (see below for additional need).	*Past-oriented focus:* deficiencies and conclusions are noted in a point-by-point manner to foster easy responding.
Controller and senior accounting personnel	Need to know what needs changing and how to implement changes.	*Future-oriented focus:* future states of the audited unit are described as well as how each desired state can be achieved.
Audit committee	Needs to know general internal control policies and procedures it should recommend.	*Decision-oriented focus:* relevance of audit findings to companywide policies and procedures is discussed.
Independent auditor	Needs to know in-depth information on procedures to carry out audit function efficiently.	*Description-oriented focus:* internal control and operating procedures are described in detail.

Among numerous internal audit report formats, a common short, formal presentation is organized as follows:

1. *Title Page.* The name of the organization receiving the auditor's report is often stated on the title page.

2. *Memo of Transmittal.* This cover memo identifies the report, states a general opinion, briefly notes important deficiencies, and suggests actions taken or needed.

3. *Introduction.* This section covers three topics. First, the purpose of the examination is discussed. Was it routine or the result of a special request? What specific control activities were investigated? Second, background information is given, including:

▲ The audited unit's function and controls,

▲ A description of prior audits and findings,

▲ Any special information needed by the reader.

And third, the scope of the examination and limits on the examination are described.

4. *Opinion.* Conditions as found are assessed in terms of a professional judgment.

5. *Findings.* Here support for the opinion is provided. Generally, this section covers the following topics:

▲ Each specific unit function: what is done, why, and under what authority;

▲ The audit process followed;

▲ The favorable or unfavorable condition that exists and its causes;

▲ The standards, procedures, or controls that were not followed, if any, and how they were violated;

▲ The effect of the unfavorable condition, if any;

▲ Recommended actions, if any;

▲ Actions taken already and actions contemplated by the audited managers.

6. *Details.* Various summaries, schedules, and the like, are provided as appendices to the findings.

7. *Review.* Here are provided management's responses to the auditors' findings. In addition, the auditors' rebuttal may be included, as well as a second response by management.

CORPORATE REPORTS Corporate accountants issue daily, weekly, monthly, quarterly, and special reports. These reports go to decisionmakers and to people who need to reduce uncertainty about financial matters—an important point. Corporate reports are more valuable to management when they resolve or reduce uncertainty, not when they simply document certainty. Some typical reports are listed below:

Type of Report	Examples
Operating information	Status of inventory (special)
Control information	Cost variances (monthly)
Action	Purchasing trends (monthly)
Proposal	Investment proposal (special)
Planning	Sales forecasts (special)
Evaluation	Labor efficiency report (quarterly)
Performance	Plant manufacturing expenses (daily)
Compliance	Expenditures vs. budget (monthly)

Accounting reports can be issued before the fact (forecasts, trend projections), during the fact (variances from plans), or after the fact (financial statements). They can be long for mid-level managers and shortened for senior management. Sometimes the accountant complements them with oral reports. Indeed, there are many ways of classifying corporate reports (Wilkinson, 1976). Four of the most common classifications are by scope, timing, coverage, or focus:

Scope	Timing
Company	Scheduled
Division	Requested
Department	Ad hoc
Product	Triggered (e.g., by a shortage)
Product line	
Coverage	**Focus**
Detailed	Historical
Key items	Short term (0–1 year)
Exceptions only	Long term (1–5 years)

Flash and Management Reports

Two kinds of reports may be issued on a monthly basis: flash reports, followed by a more detailed management report. The *flash report* is a handy reference of up-to-date information useful for discussions during committee meetings, staff analyses, and one-on-one conferences. Often three flash reports are issued (Joplin and Pattillo, 1969; Lewis, 1957):

▲ At day 25 of the month, a flash of estimated results;

▲ At day 5 of the next month, a flash of approximate actual results;

▲ At day 10, the actual results.

A management report would then follow the day-10 flash report.

Flash reports are responses to an almost insatiable demand on the part of managers for information to reduce uncertainty. There is a risk here in that the likelihood of early flash reports accurately representing financial reality may sometimes be doubtful. Thus managers, to reduce the uncertainty of knowing nothing, may accept information that may be invalid. As long as they treat flashed information with caution, however, managers should benefit from them.

Typically flash reports illustrate different elements of operations in terms of a series of comparisons presented in ruled or boxed tables. The current year's month is compared to last year's month and to budget. Also, the current year to date is compared with the last year to date and with budget.

Management reports, also called directors' or officers' reports, contain summaries of operations in greater depth and with more narrative interpretation than do flash reports. Each division or company unit is given its own section, which contains, first, a general summary of sales, expenses, ratios, and the like, in narrative form, followed by detailed balance sheets and supporting schedules and analyses. Trends are presented, as are rest-of-year projections. The purpose of management reports is to aid management in correcting mistakes; adjusting to change; forming policies, procedures, objectives, and programs; and evaluating the efficiency and effectiveness of operations and controls.

Report Readers

Daily and weekly reports will go to line supervisors and foremen. The information will be mostly statistics on planned versus actual performance, with variances listed as well as reasons for variances, if known. Higher-level operations managers will receive reports less frequently. These reports will summarize unit operations, emphasizing not so much compliance with but exceptions to plans. Regarding senior management, the emphasis shifts from minor variances and exceptions that trigger corrective actions to significant deviations that provoke changes in plans and controls. More narrative is included, and accrual accounting statistics (revenue, expenses, depreciation, net income, etc.) will be presented in addition to the actual aggregates (cash receipts, disbursements, etc.) that appear on the lower-level reports.

Presentation

Corporate accounting reports are reader oriented in that the information presented is tied to the responsibility of the managers reading it. Thus a senior manager is responsible for profits and needs bottom-line information, whereas a production manager is concerned with cost control and needs specific breakdowns on costs. Usually lower-level people need highly specific information before general, broad summaries are sent to senior people. Reports should be designed around a unified theme. Thus a report used to monitor ongoing activities is not the place to state recommendations for control or policy changes—a separate report ought to be written. This specificity-of-intent approach makes it easier for readers to understand a report's purpose and focus.

Emphasis on Exceptions

Most scheduled corporate reports focus on the following exceptional conditions:

- Favorable/unfavorable
- Acceptable/unacceptable
- Over/under
- Increases/decreases
- Strengths/weaknesses
- Better than/worse than
- Positive deviations/negative deviations

The idea is *not* to stress what is neutral, moderate, predicted, or planned (although such information is useful and must be mentioned) but rather to provide information that managers can act on to increase their certainty regarding the validity of past and upcoming decisions.

If exceptions reporting focuses on deviations, the accountant should ask, "Deviations from what?" Typically, information on deviations, increases, favorableness of results, and so on, is based on the following standards for comparison:

- Planned or budgeted amount
- Standard amount
- Prior-period, last-year, or multiple-year average
- Quota
- Occurrence within a range
- Trend lines
- Policy or directive
- Suggested or requested amount
- Industry average

Thus, for every category to be reported on (e.g., net sales, costs, receivables), there must be (1) a standard for comparison (e.g., quota) and (2) an expression of the comparison with an assigned evaluation (e.g., over or under):

Salesperson	CATEGORY Sales	EVALUATION Over (Under) Quota	STANDARD Quota
Smith	$ 5,500	$ 400	$ 5,100
Parker	7,300	(800)	8,100
Johnson	5,900	(200)	6,100
Total	$18,700	$(600)	$19,300

Besides telling readers that exceptions exist, accountants should indicate their importance. They should assume that the reader is asking, "Do these exceptions deserve my attention?" One way to do this is to establish an acceptable range for exceptions. Any variances outside the range are considered unacceptable and worthy of managerial attention. Graphic display is the best way to present such information:

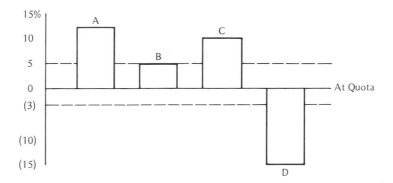

On the graph the range is indicated by the dashed lines. Within it exceptions are deemed to be random or inconsequential. Beyond the range, they merit either favorable attention (as in the case of A and C) or unfavorable attention (as in the case of D). Sometimes the range is collapsed to a line. In this case only those categories either above or below the range will be reported. Thus B would not appear on the graph. Naturally, if exceptions are not really as favorable or unfavorable as they look in a table or a graph, the accountant should explain them thoroughly.

Aiding Scanning and Comprehension

Most managers can't spend much time reading reports, so accountants should present their information in a format that helps the readers to scan the material and digest it quickly:

▲ Different-style covers can be used to identify the nature of the report (routine, special, etc., or monitoring content, evaluation content, etc.).

▲ Colored pages can be employed to identify relevant company units for which data is provided. Units can be further identified with tabs and dividers.

▲ Boxed tables should replace open and ruled tables in lengthy schedules. Where possible, graphic display (figures) should be used. Transparent overlays are sometimes useful.

▲ Exceptions ought to be highlighted. In some reports a box is drawn around the column reporting exceptions.

▲ Excessive use of dollar signs should be eliminated. The same applies to unnecessary decimal points. Also, rounding off and removing the last three digits of numbers unclutters the presentation.

▲ Computer printouts of data should not be dumped on managers who do not need to see them. They should be summarized and interpreted in a report.

237

Report Contents

The contents of corporate reports vary with their purposes. However, the following topics must be covered:

Cash Flows

Past cash flows are reported, as are current and projected flows, especially in connection with reports on needs for revolving credit financing (cash budgets). The same or other cash flow reports are used to evaluate performance of profit centers or to signal a cash surplus available for investment. The bottom line in such reports ought to reflect the purpose of the report. Thus a cash budget used to project short-term financing needs should end at the bottom of the page with the dollars needed, if any, rather than the cash flow. In this way a manager's decision on seeking credit can be facilitated. If the report ended with ending cash or a cash flow, the manager would have to probe the data to derive a financing-need figure. The following table illustrates a good decision-oriented approach in comparison with a mediocre information-oriented approach:

Information-Oriented Cash Flow		Decision-Oriented Cash Flow	
Beginning cash	_____	Cash receipts	_____
Cash receipts	_____	Cash disbursement (_____)	
Expected financing	_____	Net cash flow	_____
Cash disbursements (_____)		Beginning cash	_____
Ending cash	_____	Ending cash	_____
		Expected financing	_____

Investments

Accountants describe investments in several ways. Generally they describe investments in terms of assets or of equity/debt combinations. As assets, investments can be reported as gross assets (e.g., current assets + securities + property) or gross assets less depreciation. Sometimes they are simply viewed as net worth. More commonly, they are equity plus long-term debt (or all debt). The figures used to report investments are historical costs, inflation-adjusted costs, or replacement value costs.

A more decision-oriented approach focusing on the expected performance of investments involves projecting cash flows over the investment's life and then discounting them back to a present value (adjusted for investment costs). Given the discount rate employed, the present value can be viewed as the investment's value. This value, however, while theoretically sound, depends on the discount rate chosen. Unless a company has chosen a rate agreeable to managers, owners, and other interested parties, the valuation will inspire only a limited sense of authenticity. One way to increase confidence is to add a sensitivity analysis to the report. Different investment values are calculated for all possible combinations of a range of discount rates and a range of cash flows. The mean, median, or mode valuation is then chosen.

Still other ways exist for reporting the performance or expected performance of investments. Various rates of return can be provided, as can payback periods. The danger in reporting *all* possible values, rates of return, and payback periods, of course, is that the report will create confusion rather than a reduction in uncertainty. We would do well to remember that uncertainty is in people, not in data. Thus even limited data, if chosen in terms of reader-oriented criteria, will reduce uncertainty. These criteria, as noted in Chapter 1, require specific intent in the communication, representations of financial reality that are felt to be authentic by the reader, and unambiguous presentation at least moderately congruent with reader expectations. What these criteria demand, then, are reports tailored to specific readers and not data-laden reports targeted on *every* possible reader.

Financial Statements

Unaudited, for-internal-use-only financial statements describe assets and liabilities in varied ways. Assets may be presented at cost or lower of cost or market, but additional presentations may show current assets at net realizable value and fixed assets at price-level adjusted or replacement cost values. Liabilities may be shown at discounted present values.

Income statements can be developed in boxed tables following a highly segmented approach so that the step-by-step development of net income from revenues can be followed. One important subtotal to present is *earnings before interest and taxes* (EBIT). This figure is required for investment planning and analysis.

Among the other statements, *changes in working capital* is important. Three presentation methods are used:

1. Sources of Funds = Application of Funds. (Here increases in working capital is a balancing item in a two-column presentation.)
2. Beginning Working Capital = Increases from Sources of Funds − Decreases from Application of Funds − Ending Working Capital.
3. Sources of Funds − Application of Funds = Increase in Working Capital.

The third method, with a decision-oriented bottom line, is probably the preferred approach.

Expenses

Reports of expenses may be in terms of actual, budgeted, or standard costs. Specific breakdowns will be tied to responsibilities. Thus cost or profit center expenses will be listed, as will product costs and operating unit costs. Direct costs—labor, material, and overhead—will be given with indirect costs. Investment start-up costs will be separated from operating costs.

Inventories

Inventories are reported in dollars, items, or both. A past-oriented approach presents annual turnover for the year to date, whereas a future-oriented approach might stress number-of-months supply remaining, projected turnover, and purchase commitments and requisitions. Other analyses would stress inventory class, age, and value. Such descriptions would list obsolete, damaged, stolen, slow-moving, and frequently restocked items.

Accounts Receivable

Accounts receivable reports would provide an aging schedule; a reserve for bad accounts; and ratios of receivables as a part of sales in a period, as a turnover, or as the equivalent of so many days sales. Credit and collection reports are sometimes tied to receivables reports.

Purchasing

Reports for the purchasing department can include information on inventory positions, requisitions awaiting purchase orders, purchase commitments, purchases from vendors, and surveys of vendor performance.

Other Topics

Among hundreds of other corporate reports are personnel reports on payrolls, absenteeism, turnover, and status changes. Also useful are sales-and-profit reports in which data is classified by the following categories:

▲ Product or product line   ▲ Customer type
▲ Order size   ▲ Sales method
▲ Region   ▲ Channel of distribution
▲ Organizational unit   ▲ Delivery method
▲ Salespersons   ▲ Credit terms and payment periods

Reporting to Current or Potential Creditors

Often accountants must generate special reports for creditors, usually bankers, made up of balance sheets, income statements, cash flows, and pro formas. What the creditors want to see, however, are not so much masses of data but rather highlights that reveal measures of solvency, liquidity, and future profitability. Among many such measures examined are the following:

▲ Ratio of current assets to current liabilities
▲ Comparison of net worth to total indebtedness
▲ Ratio of sales to receivables
▲ Age of receivables
▲ Long-term debt compared to total debt
▲ Inventory compared to current assets
▲ Sales trends
▲ Gross margins
▲ Inventory-to-sales relationship
▲ Return on total sales

What the bankers are looking for are danger signals that can alert them (1) to the risks involved in making a loan and, if a loan is made, (2) to the appropriate interest rate. Note that the bankers are looking for something *wrong* as well as for something right. Accountants preparing reports for bankers should, in addition to presenting statements, schedules, and ratios, discuss danger spots and how the firm expects to cope with them. In this way they control the communication to some extent and reduce the uncertainty regarding what the bankers' response will be.

During the course of a loan negotiation, bankers will want to see a marketing plan—which incorporates the loan and describes its use. Generally they will want the loan to be used to generate profits from operations rather than to cover other loans or to speculate. They will also want to see how the profit mix stacks up. Will profits come from inventory run-off, from forecasted increases in current product sales, or both? Will profits come from expanding into new markets, increasing existing market shares, developing new products, or improving current products?

Other information in the report may include the kinds and amounts of insurance held by the company, the salaries of the company's principal managers, data on competitive pricing practices, lease-versus-buy comparisons for equipment, and investment strategies. For smaller firms bankers will ask about a "general guarantee"—which is the owner's personal guarantee that the loan will be paid even if the profits do not materialize—or about some other form of repayment if the business fails to increase revenues as expected.

Controlling Reports

Reports must be authorized, designed, prepared, reproduced, distributed, filed, and periodically consulted. This process requires a report control program in corporations. Some important elements of this program include maintaining a report catalogue, avoiding duplication of effort, developing reader-oriented formats, and assessing the effectiveness of new technologies.

Maintaining a Report Catalogue

Most firms maintain a routine report catalogue consisting of an index followed by a description of each report, including:

- ▲ Report title and objective,
- ▲ Intended use,
- ▲ Intended readers,
- ▲ Frequency of issue,
- ▲ Distribution list,
- ▲ Sample report.

Avoiding Duplication of Effort

To avoid duplication of effort and overloading of managers with data, a systematic process is required for evaluating whether or not a request for a special report can be met through an existing report.

Developing Reader-Oriented Formats

To foster uniformity, general report formats are designed that indicate trends, monitor operations, evaluate results, and reflect responsibility—all in a timely, complete, accurate, readable, and appropriate manner. Such designs should be reader oriented; they should be developed in consultation with the managers who will use the reports. As we have noted many times, if readers do not find communications authentic-seeming and congruent with their expectations, they will ignore them, reject them, or, what is worse, distort their meaning.

Assessing the Effectiveness of New Technology

Report preparation, reproduction, and distribution activities and controls are the subject of a technological revolution now in progress. The goal of this revolution is to cut communications costs and speed deliveries by employing integrated electronic systems that draw data from computer memories, that graphically represent it in reports typed on word processors by operators responding to dictated messages from report preparers, that send the reports electronically to CRT displays and printers at widely dispersed locations, and that then file the reports in computer memory to be the stuff of new reports. Although such systems are efficient, questions still remain as to their effectiveness. Indeed, accountants have been attacked for using new technology to dump even more data on already overloaded managers. Some corporate executives have even called for replacing accountants as corporate report preparers with economists and various kinds of planners who will be more decision oriented and reader oriented than accountants are. The future of internal corporate reporting, it seems, is up for grabs.

ANNUAL REPORTS In large corporations accountants will supervise the writing of the annual report and sometimes write the notes to accompany the financial statements. Appendix B of Chapter 10 provided an example of a short report that is also a good discussion of annual report communications. The data analyzed is not from a real sample, but the points made about reader orienting the annual report are worth considering. Appendix B, then, should be read in conjunction with this section.

Annual Report Readers

The annual report is not primarily a marketing tool, not an employee relations communication, and not a sociopolitical analysis of corporate responsibilities—although all these things are sometimes secondary considerations. The report is a communication to investors designed to aid them in deciding to remain or become shareholders (Dowling, 1978). The readers addressed are investors themselves, professional money managers or institutional investment specialists who represent the investor, and securities analysts who advise investors. These readers want *forward-looking information* on:

▲ The economic outlook of the industry;
▲ The place of the firm's products in the industry;
▲ The firm's current financial position (as an indicator of the firm's ability to generate future earnings).

They also want *backward looking information* on:

▲ The performance of management;
▲ Significant transactions and occurrences of the past year.

In the past annual reports were focused on the stewardship activities of management, but the modern approach is decision oriented (what Beaver [1981] calls "informational"). The modern reader looks for information mostly about the future rather than the past.

Purposes

The purposes of the annual report, based on reader needs, can be summarized as (1) to disclose financial data, (2) to describe the past year's events, and (3) to describe the company.

Disclosing Financial Data

The annual report's financial data is prepared in conjunction with the 10–K report for the Securities and Exchange Commission. The 10–K is voluminous (for a small corporation it can be well over a hundred pages), and only a part of its financial statements and schedules can appear in the annual report. Condensing the data presents a problem in that the full-disclosure focus of the 10–K supposedly should carry over to the annual report but can't because of the relative brevity of the annual report.

In some corporations the firm's legal advisers have stressed the need to comply with the SEC's full-disclosure criterion, and a kind of gobbledygook has evolved that creates the image of compliance as a hoped-for acceptable substitute for real compliance:

> Under the most restrictive of the covenants relating to dividends or other stock payments, as defined in various indentures to loan agreements to which the Company is a party, at December 31, 1982, retained earnings of $197,742,000 were available for dividends or other stock payments.

This passage (a typical rather than a specific annual report example) is certainly *full,* and the lawyer who might have written it hoped that the SEC would consider it as disclosure. Whether or not an investor could understand it was of little consequence as long as the SEC would accept it. This lack of reader orientation is disgraceful. Even worse, more than one critic has pointed out the ease with which the gobbledygook used so as to seem to comply with the full-disclosure criterion has also been used to deceive the investor. In the above example investors ought to be told more about the nature of those covenants and also just what the $197 million was used for if not for dividends—and told within the context of the discussion, not in bits and pieces buried elsewhere in the report.

Accountants and lawyers who write passages like the one cited should realize that their desire to be law-abiding citizens can lead law-abiding investors to think they are crooks! To avoid even the hint of deception, accountants should insist that full-disclosure efforts be carried out within a reader-oriented approach.

Describing the Past Year's Events

Significant transactions and events of the past year should be described with a minimum of fanfare, hyperbole, self-serving platitudes, and propaganda. Descriptions should be objective and analytical—what happened, within what context, why it happened, and what the results were or might be.

Describing the Company

In addition to giving information on products and markets, the annual report also describes management philosophies, corporate goals, and perhaps key operating policies. Sometimes a question-and-answer approach is used in which key managers respond to supposed investor questions.

Parts and Presentation

Exhibit 11.5 describes most of the sections of a typical corporate annual report. Often the report presentation is characterized by a lavish use of color, photographs, and figures. Their purpose, of course, is to foster reader retention of favorable information and feelings about the company. Needless to say, however, scores of pictures and twenty to thirty bar charts can overwhelm and confuse rather than aid memory. As we have noted earlier, "Nothing succeeds like excess" is not a communications rule to be followed (but often is).

Presentation is often two-tiered. On one level the financial information is condensed and simplified for investors who are not eager to or capable of probing more complex material. This "little old lady from Dubuque" approach is supplemented by a more extensive statistical and analytical presentation for sophisticated investors and their representatives. The report as a whole may have a theme running through it as an integrating device. The theme may be a challenge faced by the company or perhaps a continued emphasis on some highlight of the year's operations. Popular themes of recent years have revolved around the creation of a "good citizen" image. Whatever the theme, its purpose should be to tie the report together, to respond to the concerns of the financial community, and to make a point that management wants to make.

One recurring presentation problem has involved the notes to the financial statements. These often contain the most important information of the report, yet frequently they are not presented so as to gain reader attention and to foster easy comprehension. Fortunately, many companies have taken steps

Exhibit 11.5 **ANNUAL REPORT PARTS**

PART	PURPOSE	POSSIBLE CONTENTS
Financial highlights	To present condensed introductory comparison of current year with last year.	Sales, net income, earnings per share, dividends, list of year's major events
President's letter	To present comments of chairman and/or president on performance, key events, and future outlook.	Evaluation of data in highlights, statement of theme of report, identification of successes and problems
Operations	To create favorable image through description of company activities, especially in current year.	Products, services, subsidiaries, policies, employee relationships, important current year activities, change in progress
Financial information	To present relevant accrual data and aggregates that fairly describe the company's financial condition.	Management discussion and analysis, income statement, balance sheet, changes in financial position, stockholders' equity, summary of accounting policies, notes (e.g., investments, commitments, leases, long-term debt, taxes, stock issues, retirement issues, other revenue and expenses, depreciation, discontinued operations), auditor's report, five- or ten-year comparisons, earnings and selected data adjusted for changing prices
Management philosophy	To describe general protocols under which management makes decisions.	Goals, objectives, policies, procedures that direct decisions and operations
Management and corporate information	To provide list of important names and places.	Board members and affiliations, senior managers and their background, list of transfer agents, stock registrars, debenture trustees, corporate addresses

to improve the situation. Larger type is being used, as well as tabular instead of paragraph presentation of lists. More headings are being employed. Of even greater importance have been the plain-English explanations of accounting policies as if they were common-sense standards to follow rather than technical rules whose value cannot be understood by a reader of average business experience and expertise. These developments are heartening, but the cloud of full disclosure still hangs over the notes section of most reports, and only a real managerial commitment to communicating can dispel it.

FAS 33

Most firms are required to present inflation-adjusted information as set forth in FAS 33, "Financial Reporting and Changing Prices." Usually this is done in a separate section of the report, "Supplementary Data on Changing Prices." A note may explain whether the data is audited or unaudited. One way to present the data is as follows:

1. Background
   A. Need to assist readers in assessing effects of inflation (1) on results of operations and (2) on net monetary assets and liabilities.
   B. Two kinds of presentation possible regarding (1) estimates of the impact of general price changes (constant dollar presentation) and (2) estimates of the impact of specific-item price changes (current cost presentation).

2. Measurements Employed
   A. Objective of constant dollar presentation and calculation of measures.
   B. Objective of current cost presentation and calculation of measures.

3. Effects of Changing Prices on Operations
   A. Effects measured in terms of constant dollars.
   B. Effects measured in terms of current costs.
   C. Comparison of presentations.

4. Effects of Changing Prices on Net Monetary Assets/Liabilities
   A. Concept of purchasing power gain or loss.
   B. Losses on net monetary assets measured in terms of constant dollars and current costs.
   C. Gains on net monetary liabilities measured in terms of constant dollars.
   D. Comparison of gains and losses.

5. Summary
   A. Effects on operations.
   B. Effects on purchasing power gain or loss on net monetary assets/liabilities.
   C. Qualifications to estimates based on assumptions employed.

6. Statements
   A. Changes in results of operations and in purchasing power.
   B. Five-year comparisons of selected adjusted financial data.

Checkoff 11.1 **ACCOUNTING COMMUNICATIONS: REPORT WRITING: SPECIFIC**

EXTERNAL AUDIT REPORTS	**YES**	**NO**
1. Does the long-form report imply or express all the denotations and connotations of the short-form report?	___	___
2. Is the long-form report clear, complete, emphatic, objective, historical, analytical, conventional, and consequential?	___	___
3. Are the account titles in the long form as clear as possible?	___	___

(continued)

Checkoff 11.1 (*concluded*)

	YES	NO
4. Is the opinion evaluative, comprehensible, and comprehensive?	____	____
5. Are the comments future oriented rather than past oriented?	____	____
6. In management letters have I described problems and suggested solutions without seeming to be overly critical?	____	____

INTERNAL AUDIT REPORTS

	YES	NO
7. Have general work and specific audit plans been drawn up to guide reporting?	____	____
8. Have the audited managers been kept informed so that there are no surprises in the audit report?	____	____

CORPORATE REPORTS

	YES	NO
9. Do flash reports act to reduce uncertainty rather than simply to fill a void with doubtful information?	____	____
10. Are scheduled reports each generally single purpose; for example, is recommendation reporting separated from monitoring reporting?	____	____
11. Do reports focus on exceptions and their level of importance?	____	____
12. Does the report clearly state the standard or level on which the reported exception is based?	____	____
13. In reporting to creditors, does the content focus on future-oriented activities to generate solvency, liquidity, and profitability? Does the report discuss how the firm will cope with possible problems?	____	____

ANNUAL REPORTS

	YES	NO
14. Is the information in the annual report future oriented to help investors make financial decisions?	____	____
15. Are full-disclosure requirements carried out within a reader-oriented context?	____	____
16. Does the report respond to implied investor questions about the company and its transactions?	____	____
17. Does the report theme tie the parts together, respond to financial community concerns, and make a point that management deems important?	____	____
18. Do the notes explain policies and activities to readers instead of merely documenting them to comply with full-disclosure requirements?	____	____

chapter 12 Communicating Inferences

As we saw earlier, a summary in a report is not an inference, but a conclusion is one. In this chapter we examine inference making and inference communicating. We see how the accountant's inferences fit into the communications process and how he or she can influence the inference making of decisionmakers. Our theme is (1) that accountants live on the strength of their inferences, (2) that both rational and quasi-rational inference making are quite common among accountants and also among their clients or superiors, and (3) that an accountant can guide the inference making of clients or managers so that they come to conclusions and make decisions in their own best interests.

DEFINITION OF INFERENCE
Bertrand Russell somewhere says that an inference is a mix of reasonable judgment and measurable experience. Put another way, *an inference is a mix of an observation and an assumption.* Let's look at some examples.

How does a racing fan decide on which horse to bet?

The holder told Clarence the Clocker,
The Clocker told jockey McGee,
The jockey, of course, passed it on to the horse,
And the horse told me.

—Old Popular Song

This information-generating process is highly inferential. (Could the "me" be a race track auditor instead of a racing fan?)

Now consider this old rhyme:

> Billy Rose asked Sally Rand
> If she would dance without her fan.
> So Sally danced without her fan—
> Billy rose and Sally ran.

In this case Sally's observation of Billy, mixed with her assumption that he was up to no good, led her to infer that she had best leave the premises.

Finally, look at this version of another song:

> Don't throw bouquets at me,
> Don't throw bouquets at me,
> Don't throw bouquets at me,
> People will say we're in love.

The lover observes the bouquets being thrown, assumes that people relate bouquet throwing to love, and infers what people will say. The inference is a risky one, however, and not the kind an accountant ought to make. Here's what an accountant in love would say:

> Don't throw bouquets at me,
> Don't throw bouquets at me,
> Don't throw bouquets at me,
> People will say you're throwing bouquets at me.

While this version is not much in the way of love-song writing, it is excellent inference making. The accountant-lover observes bouquet throwing, assumes that people will also observe bouquet throwing, and infers that people will say that they are observing someone throwing bouquets at someone else. Common sense tells us that the probability of this inference being accepted is greater than the probability of the "we're in love" inference being true. After all, in an age of lust, the chances of bouquet throwing having anything to do with love are slim. (Note the inferential reasoning behind this explanation.)

Accounting Inferences

Here is an accounting inference. It too is made up of an observation and an assumption:

▲   *Accountant's observation*—Inventory over the past year has decreased 20 percent, while demand for our product has increased 20 percent.

▲ *Accountant's assumption*—We are probably meeting most of this new demand from inventory rather than from new production.

▲ *Accountant's inference*—Our production capacity is too small and ought to be expanded.

This inference is valid in the sense that it is logical and that other accountants would come to the same inference. However, the inference is not necessarily a statement of fact. We would have to check production figures further and then make a few calculations before we could say the probability of the inference being true was high. Even then it would still not necessarily be true because it concerns the future. Statements about the future can never be considered factual because they can't be verified in the present. The accountant probably should have inferred that production is not adequately covering all the demand. That would be a safer inference than one that deals with the future. Statements about the future should usually be made as suggestions or options to be considered rather than as inferences to be accepted as facts or near facts.

Let's look at some examples of other accounting and financial inferences:

▲ A stockholder observes that company X has reported earnings 20 percent higher than last year. She assumes that higher earnings are usually related to higher dividend payments. She infers that company X's dividend will be higher this year than last year.

▲ An accountant for a restaurant observes that the sales tally of bank card invoices does not match sales rung into the cash register under the bank card key. He assumes that employees are ringing up sales minus tips and then taking the tips out of the cash register. He infers that the difference between the sales tally and the sales rung up under the bank card key is the amount of tips.

▲ An accountant observes that inventory contains 1,000 units—he counts them himself. He assumes that 1,000 units is an extremely large inventory. He infers that the company is buffered against excess demand.

All these inferences—or conclusions—are not quite facts. Neither are they quite opinions. They are both together. Most of what accountants conclude and then communicate are inferences.

Place of Inferences in Accounting Communications

No matter what the task, every accountant follows a communications process similar to the following:

▲ Data is collected.

▲ The data is classified and analyzed. Assumptions are added that are based on accounting standards and procedures as well as on the knowledge and experience of the accountant.

▲ *The accountant makes inferences* that are communicated either in statistical form or as verbal conclusions.

▲ Decisionmakers observe the accountant's inferences as well as other data. They add assumptions.

▲ *Decisionmakers make inferences* that guide their actions.

Notice that inference making occurs twice, once by the accountant and once by the decisionmakers. Regarding inference making, then, all accountants must have two goals:

▲ They must do their best to make inferences that are as logical and as acceptable as possible.

▲ They must help decisionmakers to make inferences that are as rational and as useful to the decisionmakers as possible.

Experienced accountants know that these are their goals, but for some reason young accountants come into the profession unaware that *making* inferences is only part of their job. They must also be adept at *guiding* the inference making of others in a responsible, professional manner. We will return to this difficult guidance goal below, but for now we turn to a discussion of the special kinds of inferences an accountant makes.

TYPES OF INFERENCES The terms *logic, reason,* and *inference* are all related:

▲ Logic is the study of the method of reasoning.

▲ Reason is the method used to draw conclusions from evidence.

▲ Inference is the conclusion drawn.

Thus inferences are—or ought to be—rational conclusions that logical analysis tells us are acceptable and valid. Irrational inferences are labeled unacceptable and invalid by logical analysis.

Most accountants have no trouble avoiding irrational inferences in their communications, but that does not mean they have no trouble making rational inferences. Indeed, the problem of quasi-rational inference making (which can be acceptable or unacceptable) is one of the most troublesome communications issues in accounting. In this section we discuss rational and quasi-rational kinds of inferences.

Rational Inferences

The inferences an accountant makes involve the following activities: describing data, relating entities to each other, establishing the cause of some outcome, and predicting the outcome from some cause.

Descriptive Inferences

When an auditor selects a sample of accounts receivable, contacts the accounts and establishes their validity, assumes that a check of all the accounts would yield the same validity, and concludes that accounts receivable are as stated, she is making a *descriptive inference.* She is describing the nature of an account.

Inferences Relating Entities

When a cost accountant observes that over a five-year period the proportional increase in a production department's allocated overhead rate has matched the proportional increase of total production costs, assumes that other costs have remained stable, and concludes that production cost increases are strongly related to overhead allocation rate increases, he is making an *inference relating entities.*

Causal Inferences

When a controller observes that monthly labor costs are increasing at a 10 percent rate and that monthly gross profits are decreasing at a 10 percent rate, assumes that other costs are relatively stable, and concludes that increasing labor costs are causing decreasing profits, she is making a *causal inference.* (Note that the inference relating production cost entities above could have been stated as causal but wasn't. Perhaps the accountant didn't want to take the risk of claiming a causal relationship without more checking. Indeed, inferences relating entities are often substituted for causal inferences when the accountant is unsure of his information.)

Predictive Inferences

When an accountant observes that the interest coverage ratio of a possible acquisition firm has increased or decreased over the last decade in relation to gross sales, assumes that early estimates of this year's gross revenues being up 25 percent will be correct, and predicts that the interest coverage ratio will increase 25 percent, he is making a *predictive inference.*

Are the Inferences Rational?

Since all the inferences described above are based on assumptions that may or may not be true, the inferences themselves may or may not be true. All good accountants realize that every conclusion they make could be false, so they check and double-check their observations and examine the soundness of their assumptions. In doing so they establish the rational nature of their inferences and hope that what is rational will be accepted as true—a sensible hope in most cases.

Even though an inference rationally determined can still be dead wrong, most people will accept it as true in the absence of other rational inferences to the contrary. In establishing an acceptable truth, then, accountants examine their inferences to see whether they are rational. Such an examination could require the most sophisticated logical tests, but in fact most accountants would ask only three questions of their inference (Kelley, 1967):

▲ Is it *consistent?* Have I made similar inferences in the past based on similar observations and similar assumptions?

▲ Is it *distinctive?* Have I avoided making similar inferences when faced with dissimilar observations and dissimilar assumptions?

▲ Is there *consensus?* Given the same observations, would other accountants make the same assumptions and come to the same conclusion?

The inferences described above involved activities of describing, relating, establishing, and predicting. All of them probably are rational and thus would probably be accepted by decisionmakers as true. They would meet the tests of consistency, distinctiveness, and consensus. Let's look at how the example of establishing a causal relationship would be analyzed:

▲ *Inference*—Increasing labor costs are causing decreasing profits.

▲ *Consistency test*—In the past I have successfully concluded that increases in certain costs, with other costs perceived by me to be stable, are indeed linked to decreases in profits.

▲ *Distinctiveness test*—I have not in the past concluded that increasing labor costs are mainly causing decreasing profits when in fact all types of costs were increasing.

▲ *Consensus test*—Other accountants in the office, when presented with the data, made the same assumptions as I did and came to the same conclusion.

Notice that the truth of an accountant's inferences as perceived by decisionmakers depends on their perceptions of the reasonableness of the accountant's inferences. The accountant estimates the decisionmakers' perceptions by testing his inferences against the criteria of consistency, distinctiveness, and consensus. Notice further that the successful application of these criteria

Exhibit 12.1   **ELEMENTS OF ACCOUNTING INFERENCES**

OBSERVATION PART	ASSUMPTION PART
Observation of external data	Assumption
Inference	Cultural value
Theory (external or internal)	Business mores
Internal model	Environmental pressures
Available memory or image	Inner conviction
	Insight
	Learning
	Emotion
	Ritual behavior

depends in large part on what the accountant has done in the past and on what other accountants are doing in the present. Young and inexperienced accountants thus will usually not make acceptable inferences as often as will older and more knowledgeable accountants. Moreover, an accountant whose behavior has been predictable, conventional, and procedural will probably be able to make more acceptable conclusions than will one who, no matter how brilliant, is more willful in her actions.

The criteria can be applied to inferences, as above, or they can be applied to observations and assumptions during the inference-making process. We have looked at rather simple inferences of the observation/assumption variety. However, as Exhibit 12.1 indicates, a number of things can be substituted for or can underlie observations in the observation part of inferences, and an even larger number of substitutions or underlying bases exist for the assumptions of the assumption part. At least forty-five kinds of inferences can result from possible combinations of the items listed in the two columns of the table. These inferences are often only quasi-rational in that they often do not meet the reasonableness criteria in either the observation part, the assumption part, or both. Yet they are employed by accountants constantly and are usually accepted—but with a lowered probability of acceptance.

Quasi-Rational Inferences: Substitutions for Observations

Exhibit 12.2 describes the way in which accountants sometimes substitute nonobservational material for observations during inference making. In the exhibit inference 1 contains two observations: the bin is full and the count is 1,000. The remaining inferences substitute other things for the count.

In inference 2 an assumption is substituted for the count, and an inference results. The conclusion is thus made up of an inference plus an assump-

Exhibit 12.2 **DIFFERENT KINDS OF INFERENCES: DIFFERING BASES FOR OBSERVATIONS**

INFERENCE TYPE	OBSERVATION PART	+	ASSUMPTION PART	=	INFERENCE
1. Observation plus assumption	I observe that the inventory bin is full. I count 1,000 units in inventory.	+	I assume that 1,000 units is a large inventory.	=	I infer that the firm is cushioned against excess demand.
2. Inference plus assumption	I observe that the inventory bin is full. Based on extensive observations, I assume that a full bin contains 1,000 units. I infer that there are 1,000 units in inventory.	+	Same	=	Same
3. Theory plus assumption	I observe that the inventory bin is full. I believe that a box $20' \times 10' \times 8'$ *should* hold 1,000 units when full. I infer that there are 1,000 units in inventory.	+	Same	=	Same
4. Internal model plus assumption	I observe that the inventory bin is full. I saw a bin similar to this bin once, and when I counted the items, there were 1,000. I infer that there are 1,000 units in inventory.	+	Same	=	Same
5. Available image plus assumption	I observe that the inventory bin is full. I vividly recall last year when Jim Smith had to count every single item. He counted 1,000. I infer that there are 1,000 units in inventory.	+	Same	=	Same

tion. The reasonableness criteria probably are met, although the more we substitute inferences for observations, the less the likelihood of decisionmaker acceptance.

In inference 3 a theory held by the accountant is substituted for the count. The signal that a theory is being employed instead of an observation is the word *should*. A theory is an inference-making tool that helps the accountant to define and interpret data (Nisbett and Ross, 1980). In this case the theory defines a bin of 1,000 units as being full and as having dimensions of $20' \times 10' \times 8'$. Notice how useful a theory is: it saves the accountant the time that would have had to be spent actually counting the units. The question remains, however, as to the appropriateness of substituting a theory for actual observations. All accountants do it much of the time, but it isn't always right to do so.

The tests of rightness are consistency, distinctiveness, and consensus (in the absence of any AICPA rule or procedure governing this issue—about which we comment below). Has past experience and counting shown that the theory consistently predicts the right number of units? Does this theory predict

1,000 units only in this distinctive situation and in no other? We can assume that a good accountant would confidently answer yes to both questions. (A lazy accountant, one who carelessly employed the theory without adequate experience of its predictive power, would be much more hesitant.) As to consensus—other accountants agreeing that use of the theory instead of counting is appropriate—the answer probably would be no without further information concerning the materiality of the exact number of units and the specific past power of the theory in accurately defining the number of units.

Because the theory doesn't meet all the tests, it is not going to lead to a rational inference. But since many accountants use this and similar theories and fare quite well, we cannot say that it's irrational. The resulting inference is somewhere in between—quasi-rational.

All accountants learn from experience, and what they learn are theories that cut down work time and make them more efficient. They store these theories in their minds and use them when appropriate. The theories are *internal.*

Sometimes internal theories work and sometimes they don't. By this we mean that the inferences based on them are often accepted as rational and true by decisionmakers and often not. To increase the likelihood of acceptance, the AICPA and other bodies have developed extensive guidelines in the form of standards and procedures. We can look at these guidelines as *external* theories that accountants can use in place of or along with their own internal theories. By using the AICPA procedures, accountants can be more confident that their use of theory instead of direct observation will be acceptable and thus their inferences will be seen as rational.

When we get to inference 4, where an internal model of the accountant is substituted for observation, we have left the situation where AICPA external theories can legitimize inferences. Inferences formed from internal models are always quasi-rational. Yet even though they fail the tests of reasonableness, such inferences indeed may state the nature of reality accurately. If the accountant can get them accepted, then, she may end up saying something true. Accountants, like the rest of us, take the chance often. The benefits of increased work efficiency are great and the risks of loss of credibility bearable.

Notice that the purpose of a theory is to define the nature of data. Its goal is *accuracy.* An internal model also defines data, but its goal is *simplicity.* An internal model is simply a shortcut used to avoid effort.

We form internal models all the time. A stereotype, for example, is an internal model. Thus a male controller is charged with evaluating a female accountant. He could observe her work, add some assumptions, and infer that she was or was not performing adequately. Or he could only make a few cursory observations, invoke the information provided by a sex stereotype, add the assumptions, and make the inference. Since sex stereotypes of women in the work force often are generally unfavorable, the inference would be unfavorable—it would also be quasi-rational and unfair.

In inference 5, also quasi-rational or irrational, a vividly recalled memory substitutes for the observation. Since the inference formed from an available memory or image would fail all three tests of reasonableness, it is irrational. Nevertheless, it still could be a true and accepted statement about the data. That's why available images are used—they sometimes work.

What is usually available in an accountant's memory is what's odd, extreme, easy to retain, useful, vivid, concrete, close by, and emotionally involving.

Examples of Quasi-Rational Inferences

Below are several examples of accounting and financial situations in which different kinds of quasi-rational inferences occur.

The Aggressive Accountant

A supervisor casually observes that an accountant is aggressive in seeking information. He believes that most accountants are wildly ambitious. Thus he explains the accountant's behavior as due to ambition. Further observation would have revealed that the accountant is simply hard working and conscientious. Here is an example of an internal model substituting for observation and being used to make a false inference.

The Acquisition (A)

Let's look at an example where both an internal model and availability are working together. Consider two firms, one of which will be selected for acquisition:

▲ *Firm A*—Mean net income for last ten years (inflation-adjusted) is $10,000,000. No real growth or decline is evident. Last year the firm made $8,000,000.

▲ *Firm B*—Mean net income for last ten years (inflation-adjusted) is $8,000,000. No real growth or decline is evident. Last year the firm made $10,000,000.

Based on its better net income last year, firm B is recommended in the acquisition study. However, there is no reason to believe that firm B will continue to consistently make more net income than firm A. Indeed, the consistency test suggests that firm A consistently outperforms firm B. Thus rational inference-makers would have chosen firm A as the better firm. Why didn't they do so?

The answer is that B's net income last year compared to A's is a more vivid and thus more available image than is an image of a comparison of means. It substitutes more easily for a rigorous observation of performance over the last ten years. Moreover, B's increased net income fits our internal model of a firm on the upswing—even though the upswing could be only a simple random fluctuation. Availability and an internal model both conspire here to substitute a quasi-rational inference for a rational one. *But the quasi-rational inference could be right.* Maybe B is on an upswing and A heading down. There is no telling. All we know is that rational inferences are usually more acceptable to decisionmakers and usually ought to be communicated instead of quasi-rational inferences. (We will see exceptions to this rule below.)

The Acquisition (B)

Now let's examine another acquisition case. Assume that the company's president has assigned two accountants to do one acquisition study apiece. Here's how each study was done:

▲　*Accountant A* went through every text on acquisitions he could find in the company library. He listed every possible criterion for evaluating a possible acquisition. He then carefully compiled a list of 500 attractive firms and evaluated each firm in terms of the criteria. Based on the evaluation, he concluded that the top five candidates, in order of importance, were:

1. Acquisition V,
2. Acquisition W,
3. Acquisition X,
4. Acquisition Y,
5. Acquisition Z.

▲　*Accountant B* went to all the senior management of the company and asked, "What kind of an acquisition do you believe we should make?" From the responses she developed a list of criteria for evaluating a possible acquisition. She then began randomly looking at firms. After looking at twenty-five firms she found five that fit the criteria. In order of importance these were:

1. Acquisition Z,
2. Acquisition R,
3. Acquisition S,
4. Acquisition T,
5. Acquisition W.

Note that acquisitions V and Z made both lists, but accountant A recommended V and accountant B recommended Z. Which *should* be chosen by the president? Which *would* be chosen?

Acquisition V should be chosen. The evaluation was consistent with generally accepted standards (consistent). There were numerous observations. Most acquisition specialists would agree with the choice (consensus). The choice of V would not have been made with a radically different list of criteria (distinctive).

Which would be chosen? Probably acquisition Z. After all, accountant B was careful to learn the internal model (the responses to her question) governing the judgment of the senior management. She sensibly assumed that a recommended choice that fit their model would be acceptable. What's more, it could turn out to be a fine acquisition even though the inference making behind the recommended choice was less rational than it could have been. Thus the probability that acquisition V is the best choice is higher than that for acquisition Z in real-world terms; *but* in terms of human behavior, Z is more likely to be chosen because of the accountant's careful awareness of the way decisionmakers make inferences.

Quasi-Rational Inferences: Substitutions for Assumptions

We have seen what can take the place of observations in the inference-making process. Now we examine some of the bases for assumptions (see Exhibit 12.3).

An assumption is a belief taken for granted. Its acceptability and truth are considered self-evident. Where do accounting assumptions come from? As Exhibit 12.3 suggests, they have a variety of sources, ranging from durable cultural values to transient emotions. Naturally an accountant would want to make inferences based on assumptions acceptable to decisionmakers.

However, what an accountant often does is to draw an inference after stating an observation but not the assumption. Thus he reports that since calculations show that accelerated depreciation will lower the company's short-term taxes, the firm should consider adopting accelerated depreciation. The stated observation is the calculations. The unstated assumption is that the company seeks a decrease in taxes over the short term. This assumption may be self-evidently true, but it deserves stating.

One of the keys to successful communication of an inference is stating the assumption on which it is based. The accountant must give readers or listeners a chance to analyze the assumption's acceptability to decide whether they would make the same assumption if they were the accountant. Here is a

Exhibit 12.3 **DIFFERENT KINDS OF INFERENCES: DIFFERING BASES
FOR ASSUMPTIONS**

INFERENCE TYPE	OBSERVATION PART	+	ASSUMPTION PART	=	INFERENCE
1. Observation plus assumption	I observe that this year's taxes calculated with accelerated depreciation are less than taxes calculated with straight-line depreciation.	+	I assume that the firm seeks short-term tax savings.	=	I infer that the firm ought to adopt the accelerated depreciation method.
2. Observation plus cultural value	Same	+	Americans place a higher premium on short- rather than long-term success. I assume that the firm seeks short-term tax savings.	=	Same
3. Observation plus business mores	Same	+	A firm should pay the minimum legal amount of taxes and no more. I assume that the firm seeks short-term savings.	=	Same
4. Observation plus environmental pressure	Same	+	The firm's products are not selling well enough in the market to cover costs. Our profit is eliminated by our taxes. I assume that the firm seeks short-term tax savings.	=	Same
5. Observation plus inner conviction	Same	+	My duty is always to recommend ways of cutting costs. I assume that the firm seeks short-term tax savings.	=	Same
6. Observation plus insight	Same	+	Short-term gains may be the starting point for long-term growth. I assume that the firm seeks short-term tax savings.	=	Same
7. Observation plus learning	Same	+	Accounting training teaches how to cut taxes using accelerated depreciation. I assume that the firm seeks short-term tax savings.	=	Same
8. Observation plus emotion	Same	+	I feel that I will be liked more if I suggest short-term options. I assume that the firm seeks short-term tax savings.	=	Same
9. Observation plus commitment to ritual behavior	Same	+	We always do it this way. I assume that the firm seeks short-term tax savings.	=	Same

reason, by the way, why it is always easier to communicate with someone like ourselves or filling the same role as ours. Since we can expect similar people to make the same assumptions, we need not spend much effort in defending our assumptions.

There are risks in assumption making, even when communicating with similar people. In the first place, an accountant sometimes bases an assumption on rote behavior. Thus he assumes that a certain financial ratio needs to be calculated from a set of data simply because he has always calculated that ratio with that data. If he blindly ignores the dictates of the situation, his inference may be inappropriate. In the second place, an assumption is sometimes based on an accounting principle or standard that is misapplied. Thus an auditor's wrong assumption that an internal control problem is material can lead to an inference wrongly requiring a qualified opinion.

Accounting executives identify rote behavior and misapplied principles as major underlying causes of faulty reports. What they see are young or inexperienced accountants, in their rush to get an inference made, serving up faulty assumptions on which to ground their inferences.

ACCOUNTANTS' PROBLEMS IN MAKING INFERENCES

We have claimed that accountants should make inferences that meet the three tests of reasonableness. Such inferences will *usually* stand the best chance of being accepted by decisionmakers. However, we have also described situations in which quasi-rational inferences based on theories, models, or available images held in the minds of decisionmakers may be more acceptable than rational inferences. And we have noted that the acceptability of an accountant's assumptions often depends on how similar she is to the decisionmakers and on whether or not they perceive her to be young and inexperienced. All in all, proper inference making is a difficult task, and problems are bound to occur.

Failing to Make Observations

Look at Exhibit 12.4. Please read it carefully now.

This unfortunate situation developed because of the failures of both the accountant and the auditor to make observations. Instead of turning outward to accounting data, they both turned inward to internal models and easily available memories. Consulting data is hard; consulting our minds is easy. The result is not only faulty substitutions for observations, but also the generation of slipshod assumptions. Both inferences 5 and 6 are based on false learning and erroneous conviction developed from previous false inferences, which in turn were based on internal generation of information rather than external search. The upshot is that observation problems in inference making often lead to assumption problems. Conversely, the accountant who wants to get her assumptions accepted by decisionmakers should stick close to her data and discipline her mind to suspend judgment until sufficient observations have been made.

Exhibit 12.4   **SEVEN INFERENCES TO AN AUDIT DISASTER**

INFERENCE	AUDIT DISASTER
1. Available image replaces observation	An auditor asks an accountant to describe any internal control weaknesses he can recall. He recalls a vivid problem that occurred once but is available to him in memory. He fails to recall equally important but less vivid weaknesses that occur quite frequently. He fails to check or provide records.
2. Internal model replaces observation	The auditor believes that the internal-control problem mentioned by the accountant is common to and frequently occurring in many companies. When he hears it mentioned, he concludes that it is common to and frequent in the audited company.
3. Theory replaces observation	The auditor has a notion that X should cause the problem. He concludes that X caused it in the audited firm.
4. Available image replaces observation	The auditor once saw this problem lead to an internal-control breakdown. In an informal discussion during the audit, he tells the client the cause of the problem and that the problem is grave and may lead to an internal-control breakdown.
5. Assumption based on false learning	The client is alarmed and provides data and records showing the important causes of the problem and demonstrating that the cause X identified by the auditor is minor. The auditor, confident in what he has learned, is doubtful.
6. Assumption based on conviction	The client provides data showing that the problem occurred only once and no longer exists. The auditor disagrees. He is convinced that the problem is frequent and material.
7. Correct inference	The client provides costly but overwhelming evidence that the problem does not exist. The auditor is forced to conclude that the problem does not exist. He apologizes but points out that if the accountant had given him data instead of inferences, he would never have made the conclusions he did.
Result	The auditing firm loses the client.

Being Reluctant to Make Inferences

The ship of finance and business floats on a sea of accounting inferences. Without them decision making is impossible. Sometimes, however, an accountant is reluctant to make an inference but doesn't realize that he is. Thus his satisfaction that an aggregate is inferential is often unwarranted. When he adds up a column of figures and states a total, he has not concluded anything. He has merely added on a new piece of data, the total. But when, for example, he makes a judgment regarding the financial condition of the firm based on the total, he is then making an inference—but not before.

Some accountants see themselves as information providers, and to them providing a total to a column of figures is evidence of their professional "judgment"—of inference making. While this view has much good sense in it, and accountants many times must provide data without really judging, there are other times when judgment is required but avoided. These same accountants have been trained to see assumption making as the unprofessional imposition of their personal views on data. But accounting inferences, which are absolutely necessary to decision making, require judicious assumptions. Accountants who won't make any assumptions at any time, no matter what, are not fulfilling their modern role as well as they should. Good professional communicating, then, requires the accountant to know when to avoid inferences and when to make them.

Observing the Expected and Missing the Unexpected

Edgar Allen Poe's famous purloined letter sat on the mantlepiece in plain sight, where no one expected it to be. It was not observed, and inferences were made that it was not in the room. Experienced accountants point to the purloined letter phenomenon as one of the most troubling problems for accountants when making judgments. They look for the expected and do not observe the unexpected. Thus their inferences are all too predictable—and sometimes wrong. Some practitioners identify the ubiquitous checkoff list as the villain here, providing as it sometimes does a guide to observing what ought to be rather than what ought not to be. Whatever the case, accountants must learn to use checkoffs wisely and to keep a weather eye open for the odd or unseemly.

Making Inferences about People Instead of Situations

Research on inference making (Nisbett and Ross, 1980) suggests that people tend to judge events as caused more by people's ability and effort (or lack of) rather than by the nature of the situation or by sheer chance. Accountants, then, need to be careful to look first at situational or even chance causes of financial events before assigning praise or blame to individuals.

Putting Excessive Confidence in Inferences

Inferences can be considered as true, false, or somewhere in between. Often accountants will exhibit more certainty about their inferences than their observations and assumptions warrant. What this means is that accountants sometimes treat their inferences as facts and invite decisionmakers to do the same.

After collecting financial data, we can form two kinds of information from it:

▲ *Observations*—What we have seen, counted, experienced, heard, and so on;

▲ *Inferences*—What we observe plus what we assume or believe.

In this chapter we have been distinguishing between observations and inferences, but some accountants often do not. They may report information as if there were no difference between observations, which are usually facts, and inferences, which are not. Thus inferences seem to be more probable than they are.

Look at a net income figure. It is an inferential statistic. That means that it is derived not simply by adding or subtracting numbers but by applying accounting principles (theories) and accounting assumptions to observed data. Depreciation expense (straight line), for example, is a figure based on a theory that such expenses should be spread out over the life of the asset in equal annual amounts. The overhead portion of cost of goods sold is derived from various models and assumptions of management. Other figures in the income statement are developed in similar ways so that net income is an inference and not a fact. As an inference its truth is based, first, on its being *consistent* in its derivation with other similar net income statements and with generally accepted principles, *distinctive* in that it would be a different figure if different observations and assumptions went into it, and *consensual* in that it is similar to the figure other accountants would have derived. But as we have seen, its truth is also based, second, on its acceptability to decisionmakers; a rational inference ought to be acceptable but sometimes isn't. The truth of a fact, on the other hand, need not pass over so many hurdles, since a fact is by definition an accepted truth.

The net income figure, then, being a statement about the financial condition of the firm that is not completely factual, must be assigned some sort of measure of uncertainty. The notes to financial statements do this to some extent by stating some of the underlying theories and assumptions, thereby implying that the net income figure is an estimate and could be different given different theories and assumptions. But when accountants then state net income down to the last dollar—$55,473,567, for example—and proceed to discuss the figure as if it were real dollars instead of a best estimate, the inferential nature of the statistic disappears and it begins to look like a fact. As we will see, this is a dangerous turn of events.

Letting Observations Trail Off into Inferences

A series of accounting observations can easily trail off into inferences posing as facts without a clear demarcation being made:

Tests were performed on all accounts to determine their accuracy. We examined accounts A, B, and C. We performed tests X, Y, and Z. We believe that we covered every possible source of error or material weakness. There is no possibility that any data was overlooked.

Notice that the observations slide into an opinion (*We believe . . .*) which is the basis for an inference posing as a fact (*There is no . . .*). The writer convinced himself that his opinion was a fact, and thus he permitted himself to state his conclusion as if it were a fact instead of the obvious inference it is. Decisionmakers now can hold him responsible for his claim that no data was overlooked instead of holding him responsible for his opinion that every effort was made to examine all data. Most accountants would prefer being responsible for their opinions, which decisionmakers will treat as probable and thus more easily excused if wrong.

The accountant who gets herself in the habit of putting excessive confidence in her inferences will soon begin to treat them as if they were certain and thus the same as facts. She will then not notice in her oral and written reporting when she has let a series of statements of observed facts slide into inferences posing as facts. It is all the same to her. But the danger is that now she is assuming more responsibility for her statements than she thinks she is. She will expect to be held responsible primarily for the reliability and relevance of the data she has communicated, but decisionmakers will hold her responsible for the total accuracy of *every* inference she carelessly tossed off as a fact in company with real facts. When an inference is shown to be false, decisionmakers will not shrug their shoulders, admitting that no one can be perfect in their judgments. Instead they will want an explanation for failure. The accountant will feel put upon without understanding what is happening.

Summary: Observing versus Inferring

Accountants, as we have seen, can be too disciplined or not disciplined enough in the conclusions they make regarding data and the inferences they communicate. A highly disciplined accountant may stick solely to observing and classifying data, forcing himself to avoid judgments that he believes were not requested. He refuses to admit the possibility that decisionmakers have implicitly made requests for judgments when they have requested data. This state of affairs is not all that admirable when the accountant hides behind the role of disciplined professional to avoid making inferences that have an element of risk attached to their communication—either risk to the accountant's reputation or risk to the firm. Too much discipline, then, makes for poor communicating.

Even worse is the undisciplined accountant who lets hard observing of data go, to be replaced by easy internal theories, models, and available images. Equally bad is the accountant who lets a lack of observation force him into extreme and excessive assumptions. And worst of all is the accountant who carelessly fails to demarcate facts from inferences. All these accountants add up to the kind of professional who does not avoid risky communications but rather revels in them. Thus the undisciplined approach to inference making is also poor for communicating.

Notice the effects of both extremes:

▲ Too much data communicating without inferences leads to accountants behaving as little more than bookkeepers. They give little help to decisionmakers.

▲ Too many inferences and too little data observing leads to accountants taking on the role of the decisionmakers they are supposed to be serving.

The accountant must communicate as someone who is more than a bookkeeper but who is not a decisionmaker. It is a difficult task, and what's more, she must actively help decisionmakers to make proper inferences from what she communicates to them. Not only must she watch her own inference making, but she must watch theirs too.

DECISIONMAKERS' PROBLEMS IN MAKING INFERENCES

Decisionmakers make mistakes similar to those of accountants in analyzing information and making conclusions. In this section we examine four common errors: (1) treating accounting inferences as more certain than they are; (2) ignoring data and paying more attention to anecdotal and vivid evidence; (3) employing their own internal models, theories, and false assumptions to make conclusions about data; and (4) making judgments too fast.

Treating Inferences as More Certain than They Are

We have seen that accountants can carelessly treat inferences as facts and thus unknowingly mix inferences in with what should be only a list of facts. Essentially they treat inferences as more certain than they usually are. Decisionmakers often have a similar problem. Let's look at two examples:

▲ *The Cost Accountant and the Marketing Manager.* A marketing manager foresees a large growth in sales of a particular product, from 300 units this year to 600 units next year. She wants to price the product so as to realize a 25 percent gross margin. But she needs to know the total cost at 600 units. She asks the accountant.

The accountant predicts costs by assuming that total costs vary in a linear relationship with volume. His inferences about cost have proven to be reasonable in the past, so he tells the marketing manager the cost at 600 units based on the linear cost assumption.

Toward the end of the next year, it becomes obvious to the marketing manager that gross margin will be only 15 percent because the total cost was higher than the accountant said it would be. He storms into the accounting department and chews out the accountant, who lamely protests that he gave only an estimated cost.

▲ *The Financial Analyst and the Bond Yields.* An accountant working as a financial analyst notes that a decline in bond notes sometimes is followed by a greater availability of bank loans as banks accumulate cash by selling off old bonds at rising prices.

He informs the treasurer of this relationship as a predictive inference worth keeping in mind. He is surprised and worried, however, by a capital expansion plan that comes across his desk in which a large capital investment for next year is to be funded by loans that will be freed up because of the expected drop in bond interest rates. He is cited as the source of all expectations.

Both the cost accountant and the financial analyst have been victimized by the old proverb coming true: *A little knowledge is a dangerous thing.*

What happened was that the marketer and the treasurer both were told inferences by accountants, inferences with a measure of uncertainty about them. Yet both chose to treat them as if they were factual—as certain to occur. The managers took a little knowledge, which reduced uncertainty by some amount to another amount, and treated the information as if it reduced uncertainty to zero.

Accountants can benefit from this tendency of managers to see more certainty in accounting communications than is really there. Indeed, some lucky accountants have become gurus in their own firms or with their clients. Praised be those on whom fortune has smiled. Unfortunately, the two accountants in our examples were not so lucky. The cost accountant got chewed out, and the financial analyst will suffer when the extreme expectations of the treasurer are not borne out.

To cover themselves in situations like these, accountants would want to stress that their inferences are estimates only and cannot be treated as facts. Moreover, they might want to get in the habit of providing ranges or qualitative assessments of uncertainty with predictive inferences. Thus the cost accountant could have reported total costs as probably between two amounts instead of as one amount. The marketer could have protected herself by treating the highest amount as certain and pricing accordingly. The financial analyst could have assessed his prediction as "moderately likely" and made it clear to management that the phrase meant only a 0.50 probability.

Attending to Anecdotal Evidence over Data

Case histories, anecdotes, and other vivid, easily available information can have a greater effect on inferences than can data summaries such as annual reports. In fact, some people will make the effort to study statistical data and *still* not pay attention to it in comparison with vivid information (Nisbett et al., 1976). Thus the cost accountant who provides statistical support for a new system to increase productivity may not be credited for the change as much as the engineer who devises the demonstration project that vividly illustrates the improvement. And the financial statement showing the mediocre performance of a company may be ignored by an analyst who responds instead to a public relations effort stressing vivid but minor evidence of company successes.

Accountants can use vividness in their communications, however, to make them influential without sacrificing their professional credibility. For example, Borgida and Nisbett (1977) found that face-to-face recommendations may be more influential than statistical aggregates are. There is no reason why an accountant can't supplement her data with a face-to-face oral report. By the same token, accountants can use anecdotal evidence to illustrate financial evidence. Monthly corporate reports, then, might contain something like the following:

▲   *Financial evidence*—The total unit cost of cabinets last month declined from $39.80 to $37.30. All of this decline was attributable to a decrease in unit labor costs from $11.50 to $9.00. The decrease occurred because of a reduction in overtime labor costs in response to the increase of the work day from 7.5 to 8.0 hours.

▲   *Anecdotal evidence*—One worker, Thomas O'Toole, went from 20 hours overtime in May to 10 hours this month for a net cash savings to the company of $25. Other workers had similar experiences.

Such anecdotal evidence is the kind of thing that gets remembered—and if it is remembered, the financial evidence will be remembered and used to make managerial decisions.

Employing Models, Internal Theories, and Weak Assumptions

Decisionmakers make inferences in the same way accountants do. They too may use internally generated theories and models that ignore financial data, as well as questionable assumptions based on vague feelings or other transient bases. Accountants who realize this will endeavor (1) to communicate accurate and valid information about accounting entities *and* (2) to influence decision-makers to hold accurate and relevant theories and assumptions about those entities. The auditor, therefore, who wants to recommend to a client a change in internal audit compliance tests of off-balance-sheet property items will also want to first persuade the client that he should be interested in such items. And the auditor with a new client who has just shifted from a privately held, unaudited firm to one requiring public audit will want, before the audit, to get the client to assume that an audit is more than an act of complying with SEC rules and that it should help in developing accounting controls. Both of these auditors will be *communicating to develop the clients' internal information-processing tools before communicating information to them.*

Making Inferences Too Fast

An inference that first comes to mind may be more influential than subsequent inferences. Thus a decisionmaker who infers that a firm's financial condition is deteriorating from first-quarter statistics may hold on to that notion even though data in the remaining quarters shows a stable condition. What may occur in this situation is that the decisionmaker prematurely commits herself to an internal theory about the firm (such as, "The firm is in a downward trend") and then looks for information to confirm her theory later on, while ignoring information that would cause theory revision (Ross and Anderson, 1982).

The accountant in this case would want to emphasize the change from a downward trend to a stable condition in his corporate reports. Vivid examples of successful financial operations could offset the theory of the decisionmaker to the point where she adopted a new theory of the firm as stable.

Defining the Accountant's Duty

What we are proposing here, and what we discuss in the next section, is a view of accounting communications in which the accountant is more active than he has been traditionally. Let us pause for a moment to explore this expanded interpretation of the accountant's role.

Modern cognitive and social psychology has raised an intriguing question: Are the actions of decisionmakers the result of needs making themselves felt or are they the result of information-processing activities not necessarily related to needs? For the accountant this question translates into another question: Should he communicate (1) to aid decision making by supplying information to spur decisions that rationally satisfy the identified needs of financial decisionmakers for profit, growth, profitability, and so on, *or* should he communicate information (2) to guide information processing of decision-makers under the assumption that their information processing might lead them away from satisfying their needs without the accountant's guidance?

The theme of this chapter is that accountants can and should do both. They should continue to provide information that satisfies needs, while at the same time recognizing that they must guide decisionmakers in processing the information rationally. Their duty to make their information reliable and relevant requires accountants to do both kinds of communicating.

GUIDING DECISIONMAKERS' INFERENCES

In a large Florida firm, computer division personnel observed frayed wires in the processing machinery. Somehow they collectively assumed that a new insect species, computer lice, had invaded the machinery. They concluded that computer lice had eaten the wires. Some people even claimed that they had been bitten by the creatures. All of this occurred without anyone ever seeing one. In any case, management was appealed to. Experts were called in. They examined the machinery and announced that no lice existed. The frayed wires were routine problems. They were laughed at.

Now a net set of experts appeared. They were observed spraying the internals of the machinery and doing other activities that were assumed to involve insect killing. When they had finished, their report to management was read to the employees. The computers were pronounced free of insect activity. Actually, since there never were any insects, the computers had always been free of insects. But the employees inferred that the new experts' work had killed the computer lice. The bogus work of the bogus experts had done the trick.

We can see here an example of *an imaginary problem being solved by an imaginary solution*. The employees had each consulted an internal model of what insect-damaged wires are supposed to look like and collectively imagined that computer lice were loose. When the new set of experts behaved in ways that confirmed their internal models of what an exterminator should do, they collectively imagined that the problem was solved. Management dealt with a nonproblem by employing a nonsolution.

The point we are making is this: Management ended up guiding the inference making of the employees so that they could get back to their work without feeling threatened every time they worked on the computers. Management did not lie. In fact, the actions of management led the employees to learn the truth. There is a lesson here for accountants: If decisionmakers persist in making quasi-rational or irrational inferences based on accounting data, accountants can and should guide them to make rational inferences in their own interest.

Let's look at Exhibit 12.5, in which an accountant's rational inference is distorted by the quasi-rational inferences of decisionmakers.

The accountant in this case did a good job and made a proper inference. It is rational to conclude that design problems are related to increased costs— but this conclusion is not necessarily true. Like all inferences, the conclusion has an aspect of uncertainty about it. For the accountant the probability that his inference is true is high, given his observations and assumptions. But for the decisionmakers in the case, who are employing internal models and available vivid information instead of observations, the probability that there is *no* relationship between design and increased costs is also high.

Look at the executive's response to the accountant's report. Her internal theory is that the new plant design *should* contain costs. Her theory takes precedence over the accountant's data. Now look at the plant manager. He consults selective, available data stored in his memory and infers that the design is indeed controlling costs.

Some might read this case and say that the accountant had simply run up against two people with vested interests in knocking down his case. That could be. But let us assume that both decisionmakers have no real need to oppose the accountant's conclusion. They have come to an opposite conclusion based on the way they receive and process information. If this assumption is correct, and in similar situations it will often be correct, then the accountant cannot hope to get his conclusion accepted unless he communicates with two goals in mind:

▲ Serving the needs of decisionmakers;
▲ Guiding the inference making of decisionmakers so that they come to rational conclusions.

What could he have done in the case described to guide decisionmakers to make the most rational inference, which is that the poor design is not leading to cost control? Both before and during his report, he could have followed these four steps in his communicating:

1. *Learn the Theories, Models, Available Information, and Assumptions of Decisionmakers.* Naturally if an accountant knows how a manager or client is going to process information, the accountant will be in a better position to communicate so as to guide inference making than will one who does not know. The accountant in the case could have interviewed managers before his report, learned from their theories, and so on, and employed counterarguments, vivid evidence of his own, and acceptable assumptions to head off or at least mute the quasi-rational inference making that was encountered.

2. *Increase Credibility.* The accountant who is deemed more credible than others is in a better position to get inferences accepted. *Credibility can be*

Exhibit 12.5   **CASE: COST CONTAINMENT IN THE NEW PLANT**

1. Your firm has recently (five years ago) built a new plant specifically designed to be the most cost efficient of all the company's widget-making plants.

2. Over the last five years you have collected data on unit and average costs at all plants.

3. The data shows:
   A. New plant unit costs were greater every year than costs at other plants. (*consistent*)
   B. Management at the new plant had changed several times, yet cost over-runs did not vary. (*distinctive*)
   C. Market demand had changed several times, yet cost overruns did not vary. (*distinctive*)
   D. Management at other plants had changed also, but only the new plant had had consistent cost overruns. (*distinctive*)
   E. A similarly designed plant of a competitor had had similar cost overruns. (*consensus*)

4. You conclude that, based on consistency, distinctiveness, and consensus criteria, the design of the new plant has led to increased rather than contained costs.

5. You make a written report and follow up with an oral report to the CEO and his senior staff.

6. In the discussion after your presentation, the following occurred:
   A. One executive noted that the new plant had been designed specifically to contain costs. She found it incredible that the design could be causing increased costs.
   B. The manager of the new plant strongly noted that for the last two months unit costs had been substantially less than at the other plants. In fact, during one month last year costs were 25 percent less than the mean costs for the other plants.
   C. Others offered similar comments.

7. Your report was accepted and filed. The general feeling was that you were trying to make a name for yourself by manipulating the data. Everyone knows that accountants can prove anything with data.

---

enhanced by increased status, by increased power, or by a history of success-ful inference making. This last is the credibility enhancer over which the accountant has most control. In the case—assuming that the accountant did have such a history—he could have subtly reviewed his successes as part of his report to create his own available memories.

An easier way to increase credibility is to have assumed the role of *expert*. An expert is one whose credibility is a given and whose assumptions and rationality are less questioned than those of nonexperts. Accountants who seek to specialize or to attach specialists to them can be viewed as experts. An accountant-expert in the case above probably would not have had much trouble with his report.

Finally, credibility and more-acceptable inference making can be improved by the accountant's having developed a series of *trust relationships* with managers and/or clients. If the accountant in the case had worked over time to build relationships with the managers instead of merely carrying out assigned tasks, he would have found his report easier going.

3. *Provide Overwhelming Evidence.* Most accountants know that the next best thing to data is more data. In the case, therefore, the accountant should have collected a number of specific examples that showed concretely how poor design was negatively impacting costs.

4. *Use Persuasive Communications.* If all else fails, persuasive communicating can be employed to gain acceptance for inferences. In the case the accountant could have followed one or all of these measures:

▲ Stress the consequences of failing to accept the inference (continued cost problems) and the benefits of accepting it (possibility of taking action to cut costs by design changes).
▲ Give examples of similar managers who accepted similar inferences and successfully cut costs.
▲ Label the decisionmakers as the kind of managers who would accept rational inferences.

Naturally, persuasive communicating would be a last step, useful only where managers insist on relying on their own quasi-rational theories, models, and assumptions.

THE ACCOUNTANT AS INFERENCE COMMUNICATOR AND GUIDE

Modern accounting is communicating, and what is communicated is inferences. More than that, accounting inferences are used by decisionmakers to make their own inferences prior to acting. We have seen what can go wrong as the accountant makes and communicates inferences, and we have described how managers and clients sometimes fail to make rational conclusions based on accounting information. None of these problems needs to occur if accountants face up to the real nature of their professional activity—inference making—and act to make rational inferences and to guide their managers and clients also to arrive at rational conclusions. All too often accountants see only data processing as their job. Such a narrow view must yield.

Checkoff 12.1 **ACCOUNTING COMMUNICATIONS: COMMUNICATING INFERENCES**

	YES	NO

IDENTIFYING INFERENCES

1. Are my statements inferential—that is, are they a mixture of observations and assumptions?

2. Have I identified those of my inferences about the future that are not meant to be predictions and changed them to suggestions or options?

MAKING INFERENCES

3. Are my inferences rational—that is, do they meet the tests of consistency, distinctiveness, and consensus?

4. If my inferences are quasi-rational and used to make my work easier, will they still be acceptable?

5. Have I generally avoided quasi-rational inferences in place of rational inferences and used them only when decisionmakers obviously want quasi-rational but sensible conclusions?

6. Have I made it clear to the decisionmaker that all inferences must be assessed in terms of probability rather than certainty?

7. Am I aware that the more I get away from observing, the more important will be my assumptions and the less likely will be the acceptance of my inference?

8. Have I generally avoided consulting internal models and available memories and instead looked at external data during inference making?

9. Are the assumptions on which I base my inferences self-evident and durable?

10. Have I stated my assumptions to the decisionmaker?

11. Have I made inferences when required to and avoided them when not required to?

12. Are my inferences based on observations of the unexpected as well as the expected?

13. Have I avoided mixing inferences in with factual statements?

GUIDING DECISIONMAKERS' INFERENCES

14. Have I made it clear to decisionmakers that accounting inferences cannot reduce uncertainty to zero?

15. Have I supplemented my rational inferences with vivid face-to-face reports and anecdotal evidence when appropriate to guide decisionmaker inferences?

(*continued*)

Checkoff 12.1 (*concluded*)

	YES	NO
16. Have I learned what theories, models, available information, and assumptions are currently influencing decisionmakers?	____	____
17. Have I worked hard to increase my credibility?	____	____
18. Have I employed persuasive communicating when needed to get my conclusions accepted?	____	____

chapter 13 Oral Reporting

Special written accounting reports often require complementary oral reports to managers and clients. The oral report, however, is never simply the written report read to a group. It is a fundamentally different communication. In comparison with written reports, oral reports are:

▲ *More persuasive*—Since they are presented face to face, they allow more feedback, which in turn allows modifications of the report during delivery to meet audience needs and to motivate listeners.

▲ *Compelled to be comprehensible the first time through*—Unlike written reports, oral reports cannot be reread to gain understanding. Comprehension must be fostered by the speaker through repetition and clear presentation.

▲ *Shorter*—Only major points can be dealt with in oral reports.

▲ *More receiver oriented*—Usually a speaker has a better opportunity to tailor the report to receivers. A writer never can be as certain about who will read the report.

Oral reports, then, are and ought to be characterized by clear, simple presentation; repetition of key points; persuasive content; and a receiver-oriented approach.

Accounting oral reports will be (1) *informational*, dealing with the meaning of some financial entity or the existence or nonexistence of something; (2) *evaluative*, dealing with the value of some measure in comparison with a standard, the past, someone else's experience, and so on; and (3) *decision oriented,* focusing on what can be done, what ought to be done, or what must be done.

AUDIENCE ANALYSIS To accomplish the goals of informing, evaluating, and decision aiding, an oral report must:

▲ Gain the audience's attention and hold it;
▲ Foster easy comprehension among listeners.

The attention-getting requirement of oral reporting further differentiates it from written reporting, where attentiveness is usually assumed. But the accountant giving an oral report cannot simply expect the group to pay attention. She must actively do something to get them to want to listen and to stay listening. Usually a good introduction and the skilled use of audiovisual aids will do the trick, but the underlying basis for attention-getting activities is a knowledge of the audience or the group. If a speaker knows who they are, what they need, and what they want, she can develop the appropriate introductions and A/V aids. Here are some questions the speaker asks herself as she analyzes her group:

▲ *Are the roles that the people in the group are playing of equal, superior, or subordinate status to the role of the accountant?* It is more difficult to report to those of higher status, because recommendations and evaluations will require more supporting facts and inferences.

▲ *Were the people required to listen to the report?* People who listen voluntarily are likely to be better at it than those compelled to listen. An accountant whose audience is listening well need devote less effort to gaining attention.

▲ *What are the demographic, technological, and socioeconomic break-downs of the group?* Specifically, what are the age, the expertise, the education, the economic class, and the sex of the group? The more homogeneous the group, the easier it is to get its attention and understanding.

▲ *What is the group's attitude to the topic?* It is easy to report to a group that will be pleased to hear the accountant's remarks. If the members are not interested in the topic, however, an effort to motivate them must be undertaken. If they are hostile, the accountant should buffer his report with pleasant information or else make statements with which he knows they will agree.

Then he can gradually lead them into his unfavorable remarks. Above all, an accountant should begin on common ground with the listeners.

▲   *What is the group's attitude to the accountant (as a person or a role)?* If the group is generally hostile to the accountant or to accountants in general, the speaker can employ the common-ground approach mentioned above. Here she would try to show the group members that she is similar to them in goals, competence, and expectations. People are unlikely to remain hostile to a person who is like them in terms of needs, desires, roles, and even physical appearance (e.g., looks and clothing). If accountants follow this strategy, by the way, they will avoid wearing three-piece business suits (both male and female accountants wear them) in situations where their clients wear extremely different clothing.

▲   *What does the group want and expect to learn from the report?* Do the listeners want confirmation of knowledge? Do they want data analyzed into information? Do they want or expect evaluations, suggestions, requests, justifications, or conclusions? Do they want something they can act on? In preparing for an oral report, accountants should write down answers to the question italicized above. Moreover, if the group's expectations appear to differ from its wants and needs, a list should be made of ways to bring needs and expectations into line *before* the report. A group that wants good news from an accountant but expects the worst is likely to use quasi-rational inference making over which an accountant has little control. Conversely, if the group can be alerted to expect good news (or at least news less bad), then its wants and expectations will fall into line and it will be likely to make rational inferences. In this case the accountant's rational presentation will have the desired effect. Here are some examples of both parallel and nonparallel needs and expectations:

Need	Expectation	Inference-Making Process
A report of increased profitability	An alarming decrease in profitability	Likely to consult an internal theory that accounting data is not dependably accurate; may discount the report and the accountant's credibility
A report of increased profitability	A report of increased profitability	Likely to make rational inferences about the goodness or badness of the information without evaluating the accountant

TYPES OF ORAL REPORTS
There are four kinds of oral reports: briefing, formal, proposal, and motivating. Each has its own purpose and desired listener response:

Type of Report	Purpose	Desired Listener Response
Briefing	To provide information or instruction	"I see. I understand."
Formal	To make conclusions and offer suggestions	"I see. I agree."
Proposal	To request funds or other resources	"I see. I approve."
Motivating	To influence beliefs, attitudes, or behavior	"I see. I will."

The last two are *persuasive* reports and will be discussed in Chapter 19. The first two are the focus of this chapter and are usually referred to as *informational* reports.

Briefings update listeners, provide background, secure understanding, report on monitoring activities, explain decisions, and describe how to carry out procedures. *Formal* reports do all these things but in a more elaborate presentation. These reports are often follow-ups to a written report. They are inferential in that evaluations and conclusions are made and future actions recommended.

Briefings can be *impromptu;* that is, they can be conversational rather than prepared. Often an accountant makes briefing reports in response to questions with little time to prepare. What the report lacks in polish, however, it should make up in timeliness. If the accountant has time to prepare a briefing or any other report type, she probably ought to choose an *extemporaneous* presentation rather than a textual or memorized delivery. Extemporaneous reports employ outlines as notes. These ensure that the speaker will be able to offer a polished, structured report without having to read from a text or to consult her memory. People who read reports lose audience eye contact and cannot hold attention, while people who report from memory risk forgetting and thus must not allow listeners to distract them. They are not audience centered and do not foster comprehension with a memorized delivery. Extemporaneous, then, followed by impromptu, are the best report presentation styles.

COLLECTING AND ORGANIZING REPORT DATA
Once the accountant has thought about his listeners, their purposes, and their expectations, he begins collecting data that he will transform into the information of the report. His task is to organize the information so that it can be stored

as knowledge in his listeners' memories. Broadly speaking, every oral report exhibits the development of data into knowledge. Here are the steps he should follow:

1. *List the Knowledge to Be Acquired by the Group.* The first step in collecting and organizing report material is to make a list of specific facts and inferences that the audience should retain at the end of the report. By starting this way, report preparation will be result oriented, since the list will govern data collection and organizing.

2. *Collect the Data.* Naturally some data had to exist to make a knowledge list. The next step, then, is to gather whatever remaining data is required. Since the information reported will be data summarized and analyzed, the data collected generally should, in words, be substantially more than the words that could be delivered during the time allocated for the report. A good delivery rate is about 125 words per minute; thus a fifteen-minute report requires about 1,900 words. Perhaps 2,500–3,000 words of data will have to be collected. Above all, an accountant should not allow himself to get in the position where he runs out of data during the report because he underestimated the condensing he would do as he created the report information. If anything, he should deliberately overestimate condensing so that data is left over to be dealt with in a question-and-answer session following formal delivery.

3. *Choose an Organizing Format.* Senior accountants have complained that lack of preparation and disorganized formats are the biggest oral-report problems they encounter in subordinates. Reports must be prepared and must look prepared to listeners. Some organizing formats are as follows:

- ▲ Familiar to unfamiliar
- ▲ General to specific (not specific to general)
- ▲ Spatial
- ▲ Chronological
- ▲ Simple to complex
- ▲ Agreeable to disagreeable
- ▲ Most important to least important
- ▲ Topical
- ▲ Problem solving

The direction of most of these formats is clear. The problem-solving format, however, needs some elaboration. First, identify the problem and break it down into subproblems. Then define how to decide when the problem is solved by giving the criteria for solution. Finally, choose the best solution (define *best*) and suggest how to implement it.

4. *Develop an Introduction.* At the beginning of the report the accountant should tell the group her purpose and state generally what she wants the listeners to know when the report is finished:

▲ *Good introduction*—Today I want to report to you on our continuing efforts to improve our system documentation capabilities. Specifically, I want to show you how you can use our computer program documentation to determine the adequacy of programs.

▲ *Poor introduction*—Lack of adequate system documentation for our computer programs has been a common problem in our EDP installation. Frequently management has been frustrated in its need for such documentation to review the adequacy of programs.

Notice that the poor introduction provides the purpose in terms of historical background, whereas the good introduction tells what is going to happen *now* and what the listeners will do in the *future*. The poor introduction would make a suitable second or third "paragraph" in the report, but it is not suitable as the introduction.

5. *Develop Transitions.* After completing a major report section, the accountant should summarize what has been said and provide a forward reference to the next section. Without these transitions listener comprehension and retention of the information is unlikely; thus they are crucial report elements:

▲ *Good transition*—Let me stop for a moment to summarize where we've been. We've seen that problems exist in our providing managers with reports that facilitate operations and in the exchange of reports among our interdependent units. Our next step—and I'm going to discuss this right now—is to describe appropriate report contents and to show how these reports will travel effectively among units.

▲ *Poor transition*—Reporting problems can be solved by following four procedures . . . .

In the poor transition the listener is compelled to try to recall from memory just what the problems discussed are. But as he is doing that, he will not be attentive to and will not comprehend the first few procedures mentioned.

6. *Anticipate Threats to Attentiveness.* If the accountant rehearses some of the reasons why a group might not be attentive, she can devise strategies for coping:

Reason for Lack of Attention	Strategy
Preoccupation—Listeners may be anxious over some past or future event. As they review or rehearse their responses, they abandon interest in the speaker.	Use dramatic A/V aids; tell an interesting story; employ humor.
Indifference—The group is simply not interested in either the speaker or the topic.	Before dealing with report content, persuade the listeners to pay attention by identifying their needs, showing that the report meets their needs, and implying the problems they will have if they don't pay attention.
Fatigue and discomfort—They are tired or the room is too hot.	If they are tired, keep the report short. If the room is usually hot, get another room.
Bewilderment—The listeners lose track of what the accountant is talking about or where the talk is heading.	Show how the report points are developed out of what has been said and signal listeners as to where the report is going. Use repetition, restatement, and definition of key terms.
Resistance—An "I'm from Missouri" attitude leads to unwarranted hostility.	Stress the importance of tentatively accepting the report content. Anticipate resistance and develop arguments to talk listeners into acceptance.

7. *Prepare Adequate Notes.* Most reports should be presented from notes of the kind shown in Exhibit 13.1. On the right side of the note is the report content; on the left are presentation instructions. Regarding content, the key report sections covering the introduction, the transitions, and the ending probably should be written out and placed between quotation marks in boxes. The box reminds the accountant that the material is important and must not be overlooked. It is so important that the accountant ought not to treat it extemporaneously but rather should read it or almost read it. In this way the listeners' needs for introductions and transitions will be served. Without the boxes and the quotes, nervous speakers, anxious to discuss their topics and make their points, might tend to hurry through or even avoid such things as full introductions or smooth transitions.

Needless to say, the accountant should not read very much of a report, and the topics and points should be covered in an extemporaneous, conversational delivery. The smoothness of topic delivery is enhanced by presentation instructions on the left side of the page. In the example these instructions tell the accountant when to show A/V aids, what to emphasize, what will require

Exhibit 13.1 **EXAMPLE OF REPORT NOTES**

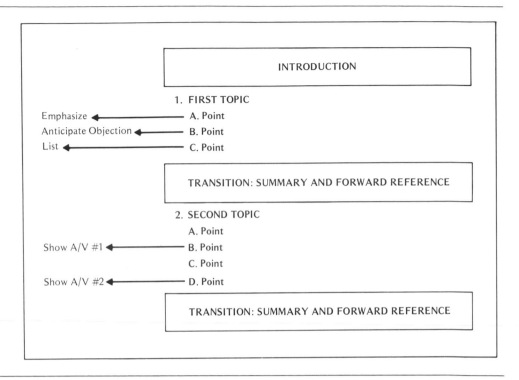

listing by counting off on the fingers, and when to anticipate and overcome expected objections and resistance.

Some people like to put report notes on 5″ × 8″ cards, while others use yellow-lined legal-size paper. Whatever is used, the notes should be written or typed large and only on one side.

PREPARING THE PRESENTATION

When delivering a report, the speaker usually should be standing and should have notes placed on a lectern. If the lights are to be turned out during the report for slides or film viewing, the lectern should have a small light, or else the speaker should carry a pocket flashlight.

The speaker should control the seating as much as possible. This control involves deciding where to place people. Each of the following arrangements has its own advantage:

▲ *In a classroom setting* — Best for informing and for viewing A/V aids.

▲ *At a long table* — Restricts a listener to interacting only with those on either side; thus hostile reactions cannot spread easily.

▲ *At a circular table*—Best for a group friendly to the report; the circle shape encourages responding.

▲ *At separate tables*—Useful if the group will break up into subgroups after the report.

▲ *In a U-shape*—Encourages responding to the speaker rather than to other group members; persuasive reports and proposals probably work well in this setting.

Handout material should be distributed prior to the report so that people can study it beforehand and not when the accountant is speaking. Moreover, such material and accompanying memos and schedules help to build group interest and can act to trigger feedback prior to the presentation ("feed forward"). An effort should also be made to place before each listener's seat (or on the seat) various required materials, such as manuals, work sheets, pamphlets, instruction sheets, outlines, or samples. By the same token, blackboard material that will not be erased during the report because of its importance ought to be drawn before the presentation.

Other things to check are electrical accessories (cords, plugs, and bulbs) and A/V accessories (chalk, felt pens, grease pencil). A speaker can lose a group's attention rapidly as he searches for a piece of chalk. He can also lose favor if he turns on a slide projector and nothing happens because of a bulb failure that should have been checked.

AUDIOVISUAL SUPPORTS A speaker's use of A/V aids makes or breaks her presentation. Good aids gain and hold attention and foster easy comprehension. But they do more. They also speed up the presentation by condensing information; such a speed up can lead to fast reporting (communications efficiency) or else to increased information flow during an allocated time span (communications effectiveness). Good aids help the accountant develop an image of an organized, thorough, competent professional; they symbolically confirm the role expectations of listeners. In this sense A/V aids help build group trust in the accountant's expertise. The result will be less support needed for conclusions, less justification for proposals, and less arguing for persuasion. Exhibit 13.2 describes the advantages and disadvantages of various A/V aids.

The drawings and illustrations that make up the content of A/V aids are tables, lists, checkoffs, line charts, bar charts, and the other aids described in chapter 10. Although these can easily be drawn on overhead transparencies with a grease pencil and a ruler, they often are more professionally prepared when used on flip charts and slides. Recent advances in computer graphics allow users to prepare highly sophisticated charts and verbal lists easily and at little cost. These computers are used extensively by corporate accountants, but auditors are only beginning to see their value.

Exhibit 13.2   **ADVANTAGES AND DISADVANTAGES OF A/V AIDS**

A/V AID	ADVANTAGES	DISADVANTAGES
Overhead projector	Room can be fully lighted; eye contact can be maintained; production of transparencies is low in cost; can be used spontaneously by drawing on transparency; overlays on transparencies can add information, develop concepts, or progressively disclose information.	Pictures and typescript must be converted into transparencies; projector may obstruct viewers; transparency must contain simple content.
Opaque projector	Can enlarge and display photos or typescript; no need to prepare visuals; color projects as color.	Noisy; darkened room needed; projector obstructs viewers; speaker must be behind audience while tending projector; projector is heavy.
Chalkboard	Good for impromptu presentation; mistakes can be erased; easy for viewers to see; easy to use to expand on information or concepts; use encourages note taking; can be used to clarify as questions arise.	Speaker must lose eye contact to use; sloppy presentation when used in haste; often used without planning; writing often too small to be read at a distance.
Flip chart/easel	Easy to refer to; displays can be drawn on; used to list important verbal points; used to outline presentation; can store specially prepared exhibits on easel, or large pieces of paper on a pad can be flipped over to reveal exhibits as needed.	Difficult to transport; useful only with small groups; poor for detailed information.
Flannelboard	Display aids with nylon flock strip on back can be stuck on 4' × 5' board with flannel stretched across; fosters progressive, vivid development of idea; formal and neat appearance; colorful and impressive.	Useful only with small groups; poor for detailed information; aids must be prepared; hard to transport.
Slides	Carousel projector with remote control allows easy prior loading and speaker presentation from in front of viewers; useful for disclosing key points in a colorful, vivid manner; arranged slides can present more than 100 pieces of information in a planned sequence; taped narration can be combined with the slides.	Dark room reduces eye contact and note taking; detailed illustrations from printed sources are not suited for slides; slides may jam during presentation; important slides cannot be kept before viewers' eyes; slide production requires skill.

(continued)

Exhibit 13.2 *(concluded)*

A/V AID	ADVANTAGES	DISADVANTAGES
Tape recordings	Can be used in conjunction with visuals; tapes can substitute for speakers when appropriate.	Listening requires a high degree of concentration; poor for reporting on how to do certain procedures.
Photographs	Vivid reinforcement to a verbal report; sequences of photos can show procedures.	Useful only with small groups.
TV tape	Simple VTR equipment allows easy preparation; emotional impact of TV is useful for stimulating discussion and persuasion; easy replay is available; can vividly demonstrate procedures.	If overused, groups may become too passive; cannot be used for large groups; producing a tape is time-consuming.
Printed material/handouts	Can be saved by listeners; foster remembering and learning.	Distract attention away from speaker if handed out during report.

Flow chart symbols (see Exhibit 13.3) are used extensively by accountants to create vivid representations of systems and processes. They are of greatest use in facilitating the analysis of complex operations. Exhibit 13.4 shows a chart using flow chart symbols. The accountant making the report most likely would have placed the aid on a handout and then gone over it in detail with his listeners.

Audiovisual aids are chosen with the communications goal in mind, be it informing, teaching, or persuading:

Goal	A/V Aids Used
Informing	Print material, handouts, tape recordings, slides, overheads, opaque projector
Teaching (procedures, principles, etc.)	Drawings, print material, handouts, TV tape, chalkboard, slides, overheads, opaque projector
Persuading	TV tape, flip chart lists, handouts

When a speaker uses an A/V aid, such as a flip chart, she should reference it in her delivery ("The flip chart next to me lists . . ."). She should turn to it, make her point, and then return to her lectern and resume eye contact with the audience. The issue here is to avoid delivering the presentation to the A/V aid instead of to the audience. Moreover, when an aid has been used, it should be turned off, covered up, or whatever. Only those aids that outline the

Exhibit 13.3 **EXAMPLES OF FLOW CHART SYMBOLS**

⬇ Starting Point in a Flow of Documents	△I	Control Point
☐ Document	△A △N △D	Permanent File of Documents Alphabetically (A), Numerically (N), and by Date (D)
→ Document Flow Direction	◇A ◇N ◇D	Temporary File of Documents
→ Information Flow Direction	☐I	Document Initialed
○ Operation or Action	☐S	Document Signed
▱ Punch Card	☐	Book or Ledger
▭ Report or Computer Printout	⬡	Source of Postings to General Ledger

presentation (which the speaker may progressively reveal by uncovering blocking material as she goes along) or make points important to the whole report should be left before a group throughout a report.

VERBAL SUPPORTS The most used of all verbal supports are statistics, analogies, narratives, and testimonies. Their functions are similar to those of A/V supports.

Statistics

Statistics should be dependable, simple, and few. No one likes to hear an accountant drone on about numbers, and listeners may come to feel that he is trying to overwhelm rather than to enlighten them. Statistics are good for expressing categorizations ("Seventy percent fell into category A . . ."), for showing relationships ("In nine out of the last ten years, the firm has had a 10 percent growth in net income and a 10 percent growth in dividends"), and of course for stating observations and inferences.

Exhibit 13.4 **USE OF FLOW CHART SYMBOLS IN AN A/V AID**

EXCEPTION PAYMENT PROCESSING ADJUSTMENTS

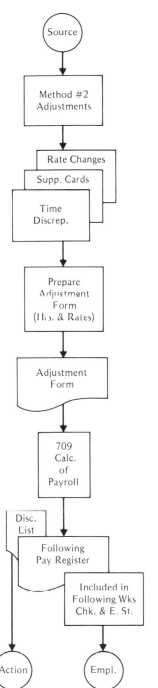

Types of payments include supplement time cards, corrected time cards, calculation errors, and rate changes under a predetermined dollar amount.

Adjustment form (per exhibit) includes identification, hours adjusted, and rate, if different from current rate.

Adjustments may be submitted for processing up to 12 noon on Monday in lieu of 4:30 p.m. the previous Friday. EDP will prepare a discrepancy list showing, in detail, adjustments that were not processed. List should be verified by Payroll and appropriate action taken.

Checks and earnings statements that include adjustments will be "sequenced" in front of the normal run of checks. These payments should then be routed to an adjustment clerk who will indicate reasons for the adjustments on the earnings statements. Checks and earnings statements are then merged with all others and disbursed.

Analogies

When a speaker points out similarities between something the group knows and something it does not know, she is using an analogy. The purpose of an analogy is to foster comprehension of the unknown. Look at the following example of an analogy:

> Now let me turn to a description of the funds flow statement. You all know that an income statement describes the flows that have occurred in a period in terms of increases and decreases—of revenues and expenses, in other words. A funds flow statement also describes a flow of funds, but from a different standpoint and with a broader focus. It describes the sources of all additional funds and the uses to which they were put. Thus a source might include an increase in long-term debt, while a use could be investment in new plant and equipment.

Analogies are among the most valuable of all verbal supports, although a speaker must know what her listeners know and don't know before using them.

Narratives

"A few weeks ago I arrived early at the office to check on the absenteeism rates for the night shift. I couldn't find them, so I walked over to the plant. On the way I met Jim Pearson, who told me that the rates hadn't been calculated because . . . ." Here the accountant is telling a story, but not necessarily to entertain his listeners. By narrating one incident involving the failure of absenteeism rates to be calculated, he can make a vivid point about why the problem exists and what can be done about it. Of course his story should be short and pointed. Garrulous accountants serve neither their own nor their superiors' interests.

Testimonies

By quoting or citing a credible or trustworthy source of information or opinion, an accountant can support his inferences. Quotes should be kept to a minimum, however, and not used to contradict observations:

▲ *Wrong*—In a survey of our stockholders, 73 percent favored our current method of presenting inflation-adjusted financial data. However, as stated in FAS 33, ". . . ."

▲ *Right*—In a survey of our stockholders, 73 percent favored our current method of presenting inflation-adjusted financial data. While this presentation departs somewhat from the spirit, but not the letter, of FAS 33, we feel that . . . .

The idea here is that a credible source should not discredit (or be discredited by) empirical data unless the data is suspect.

STAGE FRIGHT Nervousness before a group is usually one of the major problems speakers face. Stage fright, as it is known, is caused by anxiety, worry about the unknown, or the unfamiliar. Anxiety is not fear, which is worry about the known and is much less debilitating. Anxiety manifests itself in terms of sweaty palms, shaking hands, breathing problems, shaky voice, and weak voice. What specifically causes anxiety and stage fright? What can accountants do to cope with it?

Cause 1: The Unknown

What we don't know *can* hurt us. Indeed, our worries about something going wrong during a report can ruin our presentation by causing stage fright. The solution to the worry problem is to turn the unknown into the known. An accountant should rehearse in her mind before the presentation everything that could possibly go wrong, such as the following:

▲ Listener bewilderment
▲ Listener disinterest
▲ People sleeping
▲ Losing one's place during an interruption from the group
▲ Silent stolidity of the group
▲ Challenges to the validity or reliability of data
▲ Misplaced notes

▲ Loss of voice
▲ Electrical equipment failure
▲ Hostile responses from the listeners
▲ People noisily commenting to each other
▲ Demands from the group to shorten the presentation
▲ Challenges to inferences, conclusions, or suggested actions

For each problem she should determine a course of action to solve it or to soften the blow. In this way the gnawing uncertainty that can cause stage fright is dampened or eliminated.

Cause 2: The Unfamiliar

Unfamiliar environments, situations, report contents, and listeners can all create anxiety and stage fright. Most accountants would not be nervous making a report to colleagues in their own office regarding a routine situation. They might become slightly nervous making a routine report to colleagues in a conference room that they have not used before. They might become more nervous making a routine report to strangers in an unused conference room. However, a presentation on a special topic to unknown listeners in a strange room could be a gut-wrenching experience.

What is to be done? The solution is to turn the unfamiliar into the familiar, as much as possible. What this means is that the accountant must do one or all of the following:

▲ *Get to know the listeners*—He can visit or call them ahead of the presentation for trivial information. In reality he is establishing a communications channel across which will flow familiarity.

▲ *Learn the situation and the contents*—He should thoroughly learn his material and the context (past, present, likely future) in which his report is occurring.

▲ *Learn about the environment*—A short visit to a conference room that the accountant has not used before may be all it takes to gain familiarity with the report environment.

Cause 3: Lack of Status

Accountants have always had status problems in that they often do not know their status. Some people treat them as all-knowing gurus regarding everything from tax matters to stock purchases, while others see them as "mere" number crunchers and bookkeepers. There are two problems here. First, if an accountant doesn't know his status relative to his listeners because he doesn't know their evaluations of his status, he may begin to be anxious about how he should behave. Second, if he perceives his status to be low in terms of his listeners' evaluations of his status, he may worry about his inability to maintain control of his audience or even to hold eye contact with them.

The solution to both problems is for the accountant to self-define his status and not to allow his listeners to do it for him. A sense of professional worth, a trust in his experience, a belief that he knows more about the report subject than his listeners do: all of these self-perceptions create a strong aura of high status that should eliminate anxiety. Indeed, such a self-confident pose during a report usually has a favorable effect on an audience's impressions of a speaker.

Interestingly, some people get stage fright at different times during a report. Some begin a delivery with a shaky voice and then calm down as they progress. Others seem to begin calmly and confidently but then get nervous as they go on. This last group, as often as not, becomes anxious as they look out on the listeners and see what they interpret to be stolid indifference. It is as if a wall were going up between the group and the speaker. In this situation a speaker must break down the wall by reaching out to the group. She can ask for a show of hands from the audience to involve them or ask a rhetorical question and provide an answer with which she knows they will agree. She can move closer to the group by leaving the lectern and sitting on a table edge. She can ask each of them to write something down and then to tell the group what they have written. She can tell a funny story. Easiest of all, she can smile. All of these techniques get an audience involved with the speaker and break down invisible barriers that may be causing speaker stage fright. A warning: the worst response to growing stage fright is to do nothing. If the accountant simply plods on, with her voice getting progressively shakier, she will find that her listeners will begin to show signs of discomfort and then of rejection. A group will happily allow a speaker five minutes of stage fright at the beginning of a report—they've experienced it themselves—but will not tolerate a calm beginning followed by a growing display of nerves.

PRESENTATION   The response of a group to data depends more on how an accountant presents it in an oral report than on how relevant and reliable the data is. A few inexperienced practitioners start their careers believing that data tells its own story—that accountants are simply conduits from financial reality to financial decisionmakers. In oral reporting this is not the case. The presentation of data greatly influences the nature of the data in the minds of the listeners. In fact, the faulty inference making described in Chapters 2 and 12 is more likely to occur in the minds of listeners to oral reports than in any other receivers of accounting communications. Two presentation modes that will foster rational inference making are slow delivery and full analyses. A slow delivery gives the listener time to process the data. If time is lacking, processing will give way to a quick dependence on one of the ten rules discussed in Chapter 2—in other words, on a snap judgment. By the same token, if the accountant states a conclusion and then analyzes it and supports it, the listeners will usually adopt the analysis as their own. Note that conclusions, assertions, suggestions, and the like, generally should be stated first and then supported. This is a better presentation than an analytical building up of data to a conclusion.

Word Rate

The most acceptable delivery is about 125 words per minute. At faster rates listeners hear something like this:

Person A: Jeetjet?   *Person B: Nodyu?*

This exchange is New Yorkese for "Did you eat yet?" with the response, "No. Did you?" Speak slowly!

Eye Contact

The eyes send out invisible rays that hit people and mysteriously hold them attentive. Although this ancient belief is not true, accountants would do well to behave as if it were true. Many speakers avoid eye contact by concentrating on notes, on the back of the room, or on the blackboard and other aids. Others fix on one person or on one-half of the group and avoid the others. What is required, of course, is a normal, fluid movement of the head from left to right so that the eyes spread their "rays" over everyone in the room.

Body Movement and Gestures

If one's feet are close together, the body will sway. If they are too far apart, the body will look too rigid. About twelve inches apart is about right. As for body positioning and movement, a speaker should stand up straight before a lectern in a formal or semiformal report setting. Occasionally the speaker can lean on the lectern to create a relaxed image, but should not deliver the whole report slumped over it. The speaker need not stay behind a table or lectern unless a microphone requires it. If the speaker can move, he should do so. He can go to the left of the lectern to talk about problems and then to the right to propose solutions. The chosen solution can be reported back at the lectern. If A/V aids are several feet away, the speaker should approach them to make the point illustrated by the aid. If at all possible, speakers should get as close as possible to aids when they are to be discussed. Finally, the speaker can come out from behind a lectern and report while standing right before the listeners. This is a dramatic gesture, since by moving from the lectern and his notes, a speaker is abandoning his defenses, as it were, to create a bond with the audience.

Gestures should be natural and fluid—limp-wristed movements in men and women are not appropriate. If a speaker keeps his hands together at his waist, so that his lower arms are horizontal to the floor, he creates a base from which to make gestures. If gestures are made from a base of hands hanging at the side, the arm movements will be too sweeping and histrionic (try both arm positions now to see the difference).

One of the best uses of the hands is for the speaker to enumerate items by using one finger to count off the fingers on the other hand ("The points I want to make are, first . . ."). If hands are shaking from stage fright, the best place for them is behind the speaker's back. Men generally should keep their hands out of their pockets, especially if they have loose change in them. Sometimes speakers will hold a pen in their hands to check off on the notes parts of the speech as they are completed or else to point to aids. The pen is a kind of a crutch and probably should not be held throughout an entire report.

Relationship to Topic

Accountants presenting reports should make their relationship to the topic clear. Are they neutral, advocates, or critics? Are they prescribing, describing, or suggesting? A relationship, once made clear, should be maintained. One should not go from neutral to advocate or from fact provider to opinion provider without preparing listeners for the change ("Now that I've discussed the facts, let me offer several opinions based on the data"). If opinions or evaluations are to be reported, the accountant should state the criteria or standards of judgment. Does the opinion depend on personal observations, the observations of others, data analysis, previous inferences, GAAP, or various other accounting standards or procedures?

Time Allotment

The time devoted to topics should vary with their importance. Important topics should have more time in the report than less important ones. A trivial topic should not be dwelled on simply because lots of data exists on it. If time becomes a problem, a speaker should omit topics rather than attempt to cram them into the report.

Summary and Question Session

In ending a report, an accountant should summarize the key points made in the report and perhaps point toward future events in terms of their likelihood or desirability. He should then ask for questions. In answering questions, he should avoid arguing or letting someone in the audience make a speech. (Say, "I'm sorry, but some other people have questions. Perhaps you and I can get together later to discuss this.") If he doesn't know the answer to a question, he should say so and promise to get back to the questioner later with the answer. Good speakers usually keep a body of report material in reserve so that they can bring it up during the question session. In this way they are rarely at a loss for words.

Checkoff 13.1   **ACCOUNTING COMMUNICATIONS: ORAL REPORTING**

	YES	NO
PREPARING ORAL REPORTS		

1. Have I realized that oral reports are fundamentally different from written reports?   ___ ___

2. Does my oral reporting focus as much on attention getting and holding as it does on informing?   ___ ___

3. Have I analyzed my listeners in terms of their roles and status relative to my own, their demographics and expertise, their attitudes toward me and my subject, and their expectations and desires?   ___ ___

4. Are my reports usually extemporaneous? Do I avoid reading my reports at listeners?   ___ ___

5. Have I prepared my report by listing the facts and inferences I want my listeners to remember?   ___ ___

6. Have I collected more data than I need so that (1) I will have material available for questions and (2) I don't risk underutilizing my time?   ___ ___

7. Have I organized the report so that it will *sound* organized to listeners?   ___ ___

8. Is my report introduction future rather than past oriented?   ___ ___

9. Have I made the transition from one topic to another by employing a summary and a forward reference?   ___ ___

DELIVERING ORAL REPORTS

10. Have I controlled the seating of listeners, as much as possible, to facilitate my purpose?   ___ ___

11. Do my A/V aids gain and hold attention, foster comprehension, speed up the report, and create a favorable image of my competence?   ___ ___

12. In using A/V aids, have I referred to them verbally and kept them as close to my delivery station as possible?   ___ ___

13. Are my statistics dependable, simple, and few? Have I turned statistical tables and schedules into A/V figures when appropriate?   ___ ___

14. Have I used analogies, narratives, and testimonies to support verbally my assertions?   ___ ___

15. Have I coped with stage fright by identifying what could go wrong, by familiarizing myself with the environment and the situation, and by recognizing the high degree of competence I possess?   ___ ___

(continued)

Checkoff 13.1   (*concluded*)

		YES	NO
16.	Do I realize that relevant and reliable data can be ruined by a poor speaker presentation?	___	___
17.	Are my deliveries slow and my analyses full to give my listeners a chance to make rational inferences?	___	___
18.	Do I maintain *eye contact* by spraying eye "rays" across the whole group?	___	___
19.	Have I made my relationship to the report content clear?	___	___
20.	Have I devoted more time to important topics than to unimportant ones?	___	___
21.	In answering questions, do I avoid arguing or yielding control to listeners?	___	___

chapter 14

Face-to-Face, One-on-One Communicating

Every accountant engages daily in scores of face-to-face, one-on-one oral communications with other persons. These two-person encounters, generally referred to as interpersonal communications, range from informal small talk to formal performance evaluations. Most of an accountant's success as a collector of information depends on success as an interpersonal communicator. How can this success be determined, measured, or monitored? There is no adequate answer. No accountant or manager or employee can ever communicate with another person by following rules developed from a set of criteria. Even if one could, no one knows how to reliably and validly measure interpersonal communications to describe their adherence to rules and criteria.

Notice how different this kind of communicating is from written communicating. In sending out a report, for example, criteria and rules regarding grammar, syntax, style, presentation formats, timing, and content exist. Although often vague, adequate measures of comprehensibility (such as the Flesch Reading Ease Formula) and other indications of success do exist. In report writing, then, we know what to do and can usually tell when we have done it well. In interpersonal communicating, however, accountants can never be certain what to say and, having said it, whether or not they have done it well. They must fall back on cultural values, habit, and organizational policies and rituals for their criteria, and they must measure their short-term success in the visible reactions of the persons to whom they are talking—but such measures are remarkably difficult to interpret. Accountants are forced, then, to wait for the long-term consequences of their encounters to appear in the form of acceptable data collected and appropriate inferences made, good relationships maintained, tasks successfully carried out, and so on. But of course they cannot tell how much their interpersonal communications contributed to the consequences.

In sum, therefore, accountants often will not be able to tell how well they are conducting their face-to-face, one-on-one communicating. Moreover, without knowledge of the value of outcomes, they will be in the dark regarding appropriate inputs that can lead to success—which is to say that, like most of us, they will be quite uncertain how to conduct themselves in such encounters. Yet accountants and the rest of us get along. How do we do it? What kind of rules of thumb do we use to guide us?

EXCHANGE THEORIES OF INTERPERSONAL COMMUNICATIONS

Exchange theory (Thibaut and Kelley, 1959; Homans, 1961) offers the rule-of-thumb explanations that can guide accountants in their face-to-face communications. We should try to see communications between two people, say an auditor and a credit manager, as a kind of exchange. Each person communicates something to the other, and both must feel that a valuable exchange has occurred or will occur over time for the communication to be successful, for it to continue, and for it to recur. In determining the value of an exchange, a simple formula is:

$$\text{Value of Interpersonal Communication Exchange} = f(\text{Benefits of Exchange} - \text{Costs of Exchange})$$

For the communication to continue or even to occur, both parties must perceive (1) that their exchange benefits outweigh the exchange costs and (2) that the value of the exchange is roughly the same for each person. In other words, both must feel that they are getting something out of the communication and that the other person is not getting substantially more.

For an auditor the exchange value of an interview with the credit manager is high in terms of the benefits to be gained from the information received at little cost in time. For the credit manager there is little or no benefit in taking part in the interview and some cost in that it would take him away from his work. The exchange value for him is low or even negative. How can the auditor keep the communication going? Practically speaking, she can try to get the manager to perceive increased benefits or lowered costs of the exchange (or both). She can increase the benefits by:

▲ Showing that she is there to help and not solely to evaluate;

▲ Implying that cooperation can result in praise from the manager's superiors;

▲ Implying that a manager with high professional status would seek to cooperate as a matter of professional integrity.

These and other persuasive techniques (see Chapter 19) can influence the manager to perceive an increase in the exchange value (hopefully to the level of the auditor's value) through an increase in benefits that are both material and psychological.

As for lowering the costs of the exchange, the auditor can shorten the time of the exchange by using a prepared questionnaire or a checkoff (a note of caution here: slavish adherence to a checkoff can make the exchange rigid and unpleasant and thus costly to the manager). She can also lower the costs by making the communication pleasurable, perhaps by conducting it over lunch or simply over coffee.

Accountants need to realize that successful interpersonal communicating occurs not so much when they act to increase their own exchange value but rather when they seek to raise the other person's benefits and to lower his costs. For example, the manipulation of the number of meetings with a client over time can affect the client's exchange value. Thus frequent encounters between a client and the accountant may lead the client to take the accountant's advice for granted and to lower the perceived benefits and the exchange value. At some point the exchange value reaches an unacceptable level, and the client gets a new accountant. If the accountant were acting to raise the client's value by increasing benefits and lowering costs, he could have sought fewer meetings—played hard to get, as it were. By playing hard to get, the accountant might have influenced the client to value each meeting highly. Moreover, fewer meetings would have lowered time costs to the client. This exchange approach is of course risky, but at least it offers accountants some control over interpersonal communications.

The whole idea of viewing interpersonal communications as exchanges chiefly manipulated by the accountant requires that he make himself aware of the client's or manager's possible benefits and costs:

Client's Exchange Benefits

Acquiring knowledge	Solving a problem by simply talking it out
Maintaining a relationship	
Keeping a communications channel open to the accountant	Enjoying a conversation
	Venting strong feelings

Client's Exchange Costs

Taking time from more important tasks	Exposing his beliefs and decisions to contradiction
Expending energy	
Becoming bored	Revealing his poor social or communication skills
Becoming angry	

Sometimes before a communication can begin, accountants are faced with the problem of getting another person to talk with them. They need to stress the benefits of talking and the costs of not talking. Here are two exchange strategies they can follow:

▲ *Stress the costs of being unassertive and uncommitted to the issue or the task*— "You can't get a budget increase until you decide that your side of the story needs to be sold to management. Why don't you and I sit down and discuss the data from your point of view before going to management?"

▲ *Point out the benefits of talking out one's anger or anxiety*— "I realize that you're upset over my report, but let's talk it over. You can get it all off your chest, and then we can get down to solving the problem. At least we'll learn where each of us stands."

In sum, then, by looking at their daily meetings with peers, managers, clients, and subordinates as a series of exchanges of benefits (and costs), accountants can begin to learn how to control interpersonal communications instead of simply engaging in them.

FACTORS GOVERNING ONE-ON-ONE COMMUNICATIONS

What factors govern the exchange behavior of a client or a manager interacting with an accountant? Some of the key factors are these:

▲ *Beliefs*—What the client knows about the accountant and the situation;

▲ *Intentions*—What the client wants to get out of the communications;

▲ *Expectations*—What the client expects to happen;

▲ *Habits*—What the client usually does with accountants in this situation;

▲ *Processing rules*—What rational or quasi-rational methods the client is using to process information;

▲ *Communication rules*—What culture-bound rules exist for behaving and communicating in this situation;

▲ *Situational constraints*—What is required by the nature of the interaction within a given environment (e.g., stressful, noisy).

Most one-on-one communications take place without our having to analyze each of these client/manager factors to see how to behave and what to say. Experience, cultural maturity, and alertness to the client's nonverbal signals allow us to react somewhat automatically to most encounters. Yet an accountant would be unprofessional not to spend some time considering these issues when an upcoming meeting is important. Mostly the accountant would rehearse what mistakes to avoid, what assumptions can be made safely about the client and the situation, and what can be done to increase the client's exchange benefits and to lower the exchange costs.

NATURE OF ONE-ON-ONE RELATIONSHIPS One of the most complex of human activities is simply talking to another person. No amount of prior analysis can predict all that will occur when two people communicate. Luckily, we do know that certain characteristics of two people's prior relationship will help us describe what a current interaction will be like. Accountants should simply ask themselves, "Has my prior relationship with the client or manager been *equal* or *unequal, positive* or *negative, formal* or *informal, intense* or *superficial?*" (Wish, Deutsch, Kaplan, 1976). With this information they can estimate what kinds of communicating are likely in terms of five common kinds of interaction activities (Wish, D'Andrade, and Goodnow, 1980):

▲ Asking versus informing

▲ Initiating versus reacting

▲ Dissenting versus approving

▲ Forcing versus nonforcing

▲ Judging versus nonjudging

Equal/Unequal Prior Relations

Where an accountant has had a relationship of equality with a client or manager, their communication will be characterized by each person exhibiting equal amounts of asking and telling, initiating and reacting, and so on. When the client or manager is perceived to be of higher status or power, then he or she will do the informing, initiating, dissenting, approving, forcing, and judging. The accountant will mostly do the asking and reacting. When the accountant has the status or power, the reverse probably will hold true.

Obviously accountants can tell a good deal about what they will be saying to someone by assessing their power relationship. Research suggests that interpersonal communications are most successful among those who see each other as equal in power and status (Homans, 1961). Thus accountants usually should seek to create a balanced relationship with clients and managers, if possible. With too little power they will be dominated in conversations; with too much, they will be resented.

Sometimes, instead of seeking balanced relationships, accountants (like the rest of humankind) will seek to establish power over another person. Indeed, interpersonal communications are often used to send hidden messages creating influence or control over another. Farace, Monge, and Russell (1977) refer to this phenomenon as the *relational control* dimension of one-on-one communicating. For example, when an accountant praises a bookkeeper, the communication can have obvious relational control issues:

Accountant:	"You deserve praise for the work you've done."
Bookkeeper:	"I appreciate your saying that."

Here the overt message is praise and its acceptance, but the accountant may be implying, "I am in charge, and I dole out praise. Do you agree?" The bookkeeper may be acquiescing and implying, "I accept your power to dispense praise."

Through this communication and others like it, the accountant establishes a control relationship with the bookkeeper. In future interactions he will know what level of equality he can expect.

But what if the bookkeeper, whose allegiance is to another accountant in the same department, does not accept the control message? The bookkeeper might respond differently:

Accountant:	"You deserve praise for the work you've done."
Bookkeeper:	"I know Bob Mason feels that way."

The bookkeeper is signaling that the other accountant is really the one to exercise the control and that their relationship is (or ought to be) more nearly equal.

As noted above, it probably is in the accountant's interest to accept their relationship as somewhat equal, since their future communications are likely to be more successful. Without such acceptance, the accountant will waste time and energy playing status games with the bookkeeper in future encounters instead of solving problems, carrying out tasks, or building trust relationships.

Positive/Negative Prior Relations

Whether or not two people like each other will have a large impact on what they say to each other in a meeting. Obviously an accountant and a manager who like each other will avoid dissenting and forcing kinds of communications. Generally, people who like each other will agree on various issues (Newcomb,

1961). However, the reverse is not necessarily true. Liking may lead to "agreeing" communicating, but agreeing will not necessarily lead to future liking (nor will disagreeing lead to future disliking).

This finding suggests that it is more important for an accountant to base interpersonal communications on a relationship-building approach than on an agreement-seeking approach. People who get to know each other and learn to trust each other will like each other and will enjoy agreement-oriented communicating. Simply being agreeable (a "yes man" approach) will not always lead to future agreement unless an accountant works to build a relationship. By the same token, an accountant who must disagree with a client or manager need not fear future disagreements much if they have a good liking relationship.

This last point requires some explanation. People who have built up a liking relationship probably can disagree with each other at less exchange cost than can those without such a relationship. As long as the number of issues on which they disagree is small relative to the number of issues on which they agree, their relationship should remain positive (Byrne and Lamberth, 1971). Thus an accountant should not fear raising an important disagreement with a well-liked manager or client as long as he doesn't raise too many of them.

If an accountant is liked by a client or a colleague, that person will probably attribute the accountant's behavior to the most favorable causes:

Most Favorable Causes for Action   Ability and competence
       Effort
       Favorable situation or task
Least Favorable Causes for Action   Luck

An accountant who makes an exceptionally good report in a meeting with a client with whom she has a good relationship, for example, often will find that the client attributes the good report to the practitioner's ability and competence rather than to mere luck or to the simplicity of the work involved. A liking relationship is thus important for building an accountant's professional image.

Formal/Informal Prior Relations

After a prior formal relationship with a client, an accountant can expect rather predictable interpersonal communications. Out-of-the-ordinary messages will be implied rather than stated. Judgments and dissensions will not be delivered with forcefulness. The accountant will find it difficult to determine just what a client feels about something and how strong the feeling is.

A prior *informal* relationship, however, presents problems also. Interpersonal communications are likely to be unstructured, so that each party is initiating ideas and assertions without giving the other party the chance to offer reacting messages. Dissenting and judging may be more intense than they would be under more formal conditions. To avoid these pitfalls of both formal and informal relations, an accountant should seek a somewhat semiformal relationship with clients and colleagues. This middle ground offers the best environment in which to probe the feelings of the other person without prying loose a noisy landslide of verbiage.

Intense/Superficial Prior Relations

People who have had an intense prior relationship can be expected to pay close attention to what each person says. The accountant's important informing and judging will not be overlooked. Intensity, unfortunately, comes at the cost of energy, and the exchange value of the interpersonal communication to a client may be reduced if too much intensity exists. Nevertheless, some level of intensity needs to be maintained. If people do not pay attention, they will miss important points and, even worse, resort to the easy, slipshod, quasi-rational processing of financial information described in Chapters 2 and 12.

How can accountants build and maintain an element of intensity in a relationship with a client or a colleague? Certainly they can present a dynamic, enthusiastic front to a client. In addition, they can keep routine channel-maintaining communications to a minimum—too many phone calls can deaden any relationship. Obviously no single best way to create intensity exists.

BUILDING A RELATIONSHIP FOR COMMUNICATING

We saw above that the best relationship on which to base interpersonal communications is one that is characterized as somewhat intense and semiformal, that involves mutual liking, and that is shared between people of relatively equal status or power. How do accountants build such a relationship? The answer is to find shared values and mutual interests with others and to build relations on them.

Given two persons, however, their minds will be full of the following elements:

Person A (Accountant)		Person B (Manager/Client/Colleague)	
Needs	Self-images	Needs	Self-images
Desires	Data	Desires	Data
Expectations	Information	Expectations	Information
Beliefs	Feelings	Beliefs	Feelings
Values	Information-	Values	Information-
Attitudes	processing rules	Attitudes	processing rules

We can safely say that, given the complexity of mind, no two minds, like no two fingerprints, are ever alike. Thus interpersonal exchange, requiring some kind of relationship based on mutual understanding and shared values, demands a mutual effort to establish that base prior to task-oriented, problem-solving communications. In effect, *relationship-building communicating must precede task-oriented communicating*. We must learn what's in another person's mind and come to share or at least understand that mind's contents before we can work with the person.

In past centuries men and women shared knowledge, attitudes, needs, and so on, derived from an immense number of well-known cultural values, class rules, status-based behavior guides, religious beliefs, and even sentiments. They could communicate with each other easily and effectively (read the diary of Samuel Pepys for an illustration). As Matthew Arnold once said, however, the old world is dead and the new powerless to be born. What he meant was that with the decline of shared values that followed the decline of homogeneous Western culture, society would have trouble maintaining its existence. People would have grave problems communicating with each other to build that society.

Arnold exaggerated, but much truth remains in his claim. Modern accountants cannot expect that their clients will share with them the same values and beliefs; yet they must establish shared values if a relationship is to be built and interpersonal communicating over financial issues conducted. Accountants must communicate with their clients to learn what elements are mutual—a task that our ancestors of 500 years ago could have foregone.

Such communicating to build a relationship—getting to know the client or manager, as it were—is hard, and all too often silence is an easy alternative. Some accountants face up to these communications problems by hunkering down to their task without seeking to "relate" to their peers, superiors, subordinates, managers, and clients. In fact, a few accountants seek out those financial tasks that require little interpersonal communicating. They are not alone, since modern American organizational behavior falsely emphasizes a task-oriented, get-the-job-done, no-nonsense, no-skylarking approach to work. Thus organizations may reward people for avoiding relationship-building communicating. It is true that some accounting jobs involve work suitable to this approach, but most do not. The typical accountant must (1) communicate with others to build relationships before he or she can (2) communicate with them to perform tasks.

Exhibit 14.1 describes the ways in which different cultural values can influence our communications. Note that a client, for example, whose communicating is characterized as "manipulating" could exhibit that behavior because he seeks power over an auditor *or* because he communicates under the influence of a cultural value that sees humans as driven by biological urges for dominance. If the auditor had made the effort to get to know the client and

Exhibit 14.1   **A PERSON'S POSSIBLE CULTURAL VALUE FOCUS AND COMMUNICATIONS FOCUS**

VALUE CATEGORY	VALUE FOCUS	COMMUNICATIONS FOCUS
Human nature	Driven by biological drives	Controlling and directing others; manipulating
	Rational seekers of happiness	Listening to needs and offering need satisfactions; negotiating; teaching; learning
Temporal orientation	Past oriented	Evaluating; telling
	Future oriented	Planning; asking; learning
Activity	Doing	Innovating; task accomplishing; solving; seeking
	Being	Maintaining; avoiding; conserving
Human relationships	Individualism	Competing; negotiating; succeeding; asking; telling
	Group identity	Conforming; accepting; agreeing; cooperating; maintaining; responding

had recognized and understood the values influencing his behavior, she could discount the client's forceful judging, dissenting, and directing communications. Without the prior relationship she might have erroneously decided that the client was seeking to compromise her independence as an auditor.

USES OF COMMUNICATIONS STYLES

Although our values and beliefs can dominate our communications behavior, accountants and their colleagues are quite capable of choosing communications styles that are adaptive to various contexts, issues, and situations. No one communicates the same way in every situation, and an accountant's thoughtful use of a communications style can increase exchange rewards and lower costs. Exhibit 14.2 describes appropriate and inappropriate situations in which various communications styles are employed.

Accountants probably employ the controlling and structuring styles most often in their communications but could improve exchange values by shifting occasionally to the egalitarian and relinquishing approaches.

UNDERSTANDING COMMUNICATIONS RULES

The two most important kinds of interpersonal communications in which an accountant engages are interviews to obtain information (see Chapter 15) and client development interactions (see Chapter 19). In these crucial encounters

Exhibit 14.2 **COMMUNICATIONS STYLES AND SITUATIONS**

COMMUNICATIONS STYLE	APPROPRIATE SITUATION	INAPPROPRIATE SITUATION
Controlling—One-way communications that are directive, manipulating, and persuasive.	When accountant is viewed as an expert; when message receiver is unmotivated or dependent; when a stress-laden situation exists.	When receiver is resistant; when change is needed.
Egalitarian—Two-way communications that seek to create an atmosphere of mutual understanding, friendliness, trust, and warmth	When a team approach is needed to perform tasks and when time is available; when a change is needed.	When receiver is inexperienced or lacks task competence; when the situation is stress laden; when receiver has either authoritarian or dependent personality or values.
Structuring—Communications of procedures, standards, policies, rules for accomplishing tasks.	When a situation is complex and in need of system and order.	When the situation and the tasks are simple.
Dynamic—Frank, brief, pointed communications that are pragmatic and action oriented.	When the environment is rapidly changing; when contact with receiver is brief.	When receiver cannot respond quickly.
Relinquishing—Communications that accept another's viewpoint, desires, and ideas and that shift responsibility to the other person.	When receiver is being counseled; when receiver is an expert; when showing confidence in the other person.	When receiver is dependent and resists assuming control.
Withdrawing—Communications that avoid issues and further interactions with the other person.	When illegal, unethical, or threatening situations or issues occur; used in place of anger or rejection.	When accountant wants to solve a problem.

an accountant should try to learn whether unspoken but real communications rules seem to be guiding the exchange of facts, needs, ideas, and so on. An understanding of communications rules gives the accountant added control of the exchange.

In observing what a client or colleague is saying, accountants should ask themselves, "Why is she saying it in that particular way? Is she pursuing some goal (future-oriented focus) or following a communications rule (past-oriented focus)?" Simply determining whether a person is a goal seeker or a rule follower gives valuable information to the accountant.

There is more to learn. If the client is pursuing a goal, is it a personal or an organizational goal? If the client is following a communications rule, is it based on a role, on communications skill, or on habit? Exhibit 14.3 describes the process for deciding on the roots of communications behavior.

As an example, suppose an accountant interviews a controller who seems to be speaking unusually fast. To determine how best to respond to this

Exhibit 14.3   **DECIDING ON THE ROOTS OF COMMUNICATIONS BEHAVIOR**

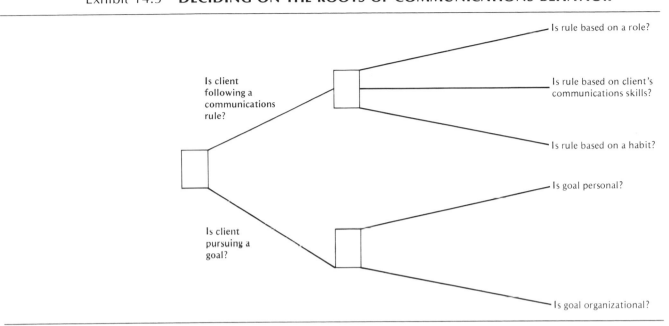

behavior, the accountant asks himself, "Why is my client talking so fast?" The root of the client's behavior suggests an appropriate response:

ROOT OF CLIENT'S BEHAVIOR	ACCOUNTANT'S RESPONSE
Personal goal—Her time is being wasted and she is conserving it.	I demonstrate my speed and efficiency in handling her problem.
Organizational goal—The organization is making many demands on her, and she must soon move on to other concerns.	I go to her boss and get him to reduce demands on her temporarily.
Role-based rule—She feels that controllers are supposed to talk fast.	I talk to her in terms of her role. I am more formal than usual.
Skill-based rule—She has learned that by talking fast she can get a lot of information communicated.	I listen carefully.
Habit-based rule—She always talks fast, no matter what she has to say.	I try to get her to slow down when complex information is being discussed.

In this situation the accountant's question posed to himself could provoke a wide variety of responses and behavior, ranging from breaking off the interview and going to the controller's boss before continuing to listening better. Of particular importance here is the accountant's recognition that the controller may have no particular goal in talking fast but is instead simply following a communications rule based on learned skills, role perceptions, or habit. Identification of rule-oriented communicating can help the practitioner explain and deal with behavior that at first may seem odd or random.

Rules are always changing, depending as they do on shifting relationships, contexts, and situations. Thus no list of rules governing interpersonal communications can be given. Yet our own experience tells us that rules often do seem to govern a number of key decisions that we must make before and during an important meeting. The following chart lists some of those decisions and the factors that may influence the generation of a rule to govern our own and our clients' behavior (in addition to the roles, habits, and skills of clients):

Decisions Based on Rules	Factors Affecting Rule Generation
Who initiates contact?	Physical proximity, open-door policy, expertise, motivation, past practice
How is contact initiated?	Previous channels used, current channels open, time pressure
What topics can be discussed?	Uncertainty, relevance, reliability
What topics should be discussed first?	Shared needs and goals, time pressure
When should a topic be dropped and another discussed?	Agreement, time pressure, understanding, compliance
How much background information needs to be exchanged?	Topic complexity, expertise level, experience, boredom level
Are controls on outside interference needed?	Availability of controlled setting, past experience, topic significance, topic complexity
Where should the communication occur?	Power relationship, level of friendship, need for privacy
When should the communication stop?	Time pressure, time of day, fatigue level, past practice, planned future meetings

BYPASSING AND FALSE CONSENSUS   Research suggests that in 20 percent of interpersonal encounters, supervisors and subordinates disagree over an issue but believe they agree (Farace, Monge, and Russell, 1976). This false consensus can lead to serious misunderstanding during a communication, which can raise the costs of the exchange. Look at the following example:

Supervisor: "Say Phil, how about that report for Production Planning? Don't they want it soon?"

What is he really saying? Is he:

- ▲ *Directing*—"You should get it to them now. That's an order"?
- ▲ *Suggesting*—"I suggest that we consider getting the report out now"?
- ▲ *Requesting*—"Can you do that report now?"
- ▲ *Describing*—"A report is needed soon by Production Planning"?
- ▲ *Questioning*—"Does Production Planning want the report soon or not?"

Let's say that the subordinate staff accountant assumes that the supervisor is simply questioning when in fact he is directing:

Staff accountant's response:	"Yes, I suppose they do. I'll check it out."
Supervisor:	"OK."

The supervisor assumes that the staff will get the report out immediately; the staff accountant assumes that the supervisor wants him to visit or call Production Planning and discuss the timing of the report. Both assume that they have understood each other's assumptions. They haven't. In fact they have *bypassed* each other—that is, they have failed to recognize each other's viewpoint and have not realized their failure (Haney, 1979).

What makes bypassing and false consensus so threatening to interpersonal communicating is the fact that communicators do not know the problem when it exists. Indeed, the symptom of the difficulty may be a pleasant smoothness in the exchange.

An accountant can test a communication for the presence of bypassing by summarizing the other's viewpoint:

Staff accountant's response:	"Are you saying that you want me to find out whether Production Planning wants the report soon or not?"
Supervisor:	"No, I want you to do the report right now and get it over to them as soon as you've finished."
Staff accountant:	"I'll get right on it."

"Are you saying that . . ." is an appropriate cue to the other person that a bypassing test is occurring. He or she usually will recognize that a communications rule prescribing participation in the test is being invoked and will comply. The result will be the identification of bypassing and misunderstanding.

When bypassing does occur, it can lead to confusion and even anger. But since both parties believe that they have understood each other, they will attribute the problem, when they finally realize that a problem exists, to personality differences, power plays, incompetence of the other, lack of special expertise of the other, and so on, instead of to misunderstanding born of bypassing.

For example, the controller and the treasurer of a medium-sized corporation are discussing at lunch current unaudited estimates of working capital in connection with advising the president on the firm's liquidity. They both agree that working capital is $50 million. Yet the controller argues that the firm ought not to increase cash contributions to a joint venture with another company. The treasurer is amazed at the controller's conservatism and says so. An argument ensues, heated exchanges occur, and bad feelings result.

Later on, one of their staff people manages to get both of them to say what their understanding of *working capital* is:

	Controller's Version	Treasurer's Version
Cash	$10 (in millions)	$10 (in millions)
Accounts Receivable	25	25
Marketable Securities	5	15
Inventories	40	40
Total Current Assets	$80	$90
Bank Loan	15	25
Accounts Payable	15	15
Total Current Liabilities	30	40
Working Capital	$50 million	$50 million

Notice that the treasurer has estimated marketable securities to be $10 million more and the bank loan to be $10 million more. She thus sees more cash available than the controller does and may assume that the loan can be rolled over. Naturally, based on her estimates, she is more willing to take a risk than the controller is. If the controller had made the same estimates, he probably would be less averse to the risk too. But the two parties have bypassed each other. Specifically, each thinks that they agree on working capital *makeup* because they agree on working capital *total*. Instead of probing each other's estimates of makeup—and an hour or so spent checking the data would have resolved the issue—they chose to see their disagreement as born of differing attitudes to the firm's risk. Bypassing turned a minor problem in definition into a major clash over corporate goals.

REDUCING INTERPERSONAL CONFLICT

If an accountant and a colleague each have goals that are incompatible, interpersonal conflict is likely to occur, and one has to learn to cope with it. But when shared goals and values exist, conflict should not occur. If it does, it is often due to a failure to break down communications barriers.

Take the case of the cost accountant who finds herself in conflict with a senior manager regarding interpretation of overhead costs allocated to his profit center. Both of them seem to share similar goals and values, yet they can't get together on the amount of overhead to be assigned. Their conflict can be resolved by following a two-step process:

- ▲ *Communicate to break down a communications barrier*—Stop arguing about the amount of overhead and discuss what each party understands overhead to be and what its purpose is.
- ▲ *Communicate to set aside an unnecessary conflict*—Use the consensus developed regarding a definition of *overhead* as a base on which to build a consensus on the amount to be allocated.

Their agreement resulted not from forging ahead to solve the conflict, but rather from pulling back to probe values and concepts mutual to both parties:

Accountant:	"We can't seem to agree on an amount to be allocated."
Manager:	"That's right."
Accountant:	"Let's approach it from another angle. Let's each say how we define the word *overhead*. Then let's talk about what we see the purpose of overhead to be. If we see that we can agree on a definition and a purpose of overhead, perhaps we can agree on an allocation."

The issue here is not so much resolving a bypassing difficulty, but it is similar to bypassing in that a word's definition is involved, What the two parties need to do is find a definition on which they agree rather than to cast off a false consensus about the definition. Nevertheless, both false consensus on definitions and lack of formulation of key definitions contribute heavily to uncalled-for conflict between accountants and others.

Besides pulling back and defining terms, conflict can also be reduced or avoided by engaging in anxiety reduction. Sometimes accountants will find that another party exhibits conflict by (1) becoming excessively defensive or (2) showing aggression as a way of deliberately making the accountant uneasy. These people may have no particular axe to grind but instead are trying, probably unconsciously, to cope with anxiety. According to Harry Stack Sullivan (1953), anxiety involves a fear of nameless and unsubstantial perceptions of threats to our self-esteem or self-image. It is a fear of some unknown that may cause a reduction of the value we place on ourselves.

A person may see the source of anxiety as coming from another person, such as an accountant, and may act to reduce or thwart the source in ways that cause conflict-ridden communicating. Defensiveness protects the self-value, whereas aggression lowers the self-value of the other person—a kind of irrational balancing act. None of this behavior needs to continue in an exchange if the accountant will simply recognize that what is occurring has little to do with hostility and everything to do with anxiety.

To counter and dampen another person's negative, anxiety-reducing behavior, accountants need to remove themselves as a threat to the other's self-esteem. Being friendly, agreeable, and even humble—even in the face of aggressive behavior—may be all it takes to signal that self-esteem is not at risk. In addition, one can be revealing of one's flaws or foibles. Telling a slightly self-deprecating anecdote about oneself can do the job quite nicely. The other person will recognize that a person with flaws has his own self-esteem to worry about and is not a threat to the self-worth of others.

In sum, interpersonal conflict that is uncalled for can be reduced or avoided by communicating to define key concepts in a mutually agreeable way and by communicating to signal to another that one is not a threat to his self-esteem and thus that there is no cause to engage in defensive or aggressive behavior. When definitional and anxiety barriers come down, smoother communications will result.

NONVERBAL COMMUNICATING

Nonverbal communicating involves voice quality and nonverbal sounds (paralanguage), body movement and facial expression (kinesics), and spatial distance between people (proxemics). Research has been ongoing for a number of years, and numerous studies tell us how to conduct ourselves nonverbally when communicating with another person. Essentially, these studies are concerned with communicating emotions, feelings, and a sense of rules being invoked or followed. An accountant probably can increase the value of an interpersonal exchange by doing the following:

▲ Conduct a meeting with another person within a four-to-seven-foot distance from the other—this is a good social distance (Hall, 1966).

▲ When seeking to influence someone, move closer or, if sitting, lean toward the person (Hall, 1966).

▲ Sitting at right angles encourages communicating more than does sitting directly across from someone (Hall, 1966).

▲ Vary voice tone and level. Talking in a monotone may be interpreted as a sign of boredom rather than deliberateness, concentration, or nervousness.

▲ Smiling is perhaps the most important way of communicating favorable feelings.

▲ Maintain eye contact (but don't stare) to signal that the interaction is pleasant. Turning away is a signal that the interaction is in trouble.

INTERPERSONAL COMMUNICATING IN CORPORATE ACCOUNTING

The aims of interpersonal communicating in corporate accounting are usually fourfold, involving (1) *coordinating* activities, (2) *directing,* (3) *maintaining* relationships, and (4) *innovating.* Often coordinating and directing predominate, but the organization will suffer if people do not communicate with each other to build and maintain friendly relations and to offer and mutually explore new ideas. Thus bull sessions, coffee breaks, lunches, short chats, and the like, are functional and necessary in an organization. Without them the organization declines in efficiency and effectiveness.

Why is this so? The answers are simple enough:

▲ People who do not communicate to get to know each other do not work well together at tasks.

▲ People who are discouraged from communicating bright ideas will become averse to risks. That is, they will not only not offer bright ideas, but they will also avoid any undirected activity in the pursuit of organizational goals. They become bureaucratic, doing only what they are told to do in the ritualized manner they have learned to do it.

Accountants, rightly or wrongly, have been accused of sometimes neglecting maintenance and innovative interpersonal communicating. If there is any truth to the assertion, it is probably the result of the accounting environment and the situations in which accountants find themselves. Thus accounting standards and procedures are highly specific, and accounting tasks highly individualized. It is easy for the accountant to see himself as a kind of lone wolf, acting alone to carry out routine and often repeated tasks. His communication needs, in this view, are solely for direction from above and for task coordination with other accountants. Experienced practitioners know that this narrow view—one might call it the view learned in many business schools—is only partly true. Accountants *must* build relationships because they cannot get the information they need without friendship. A bookkeeper, for example, will not point out an important lapse in an accounting control to a stranger. She wants to know that the problem she identifies to the accountant will be solved and not used to penalize her for informing. Such knowledge can only be the result of credibility and trust built up over a series of interpersonal communications.

Moreover, an accountant who does not innovate is the prisoner of rules and procedures. They use him rather than he using them. If he does not speculate about new ways of doing things, he essentially is saying that (and acting as if) the old ways and the book rules cover *every* eventuality. This is nonsense; yet experienced accountants identify such behavior—let's call it *blindering*—as a major problem of young accountants.

We can see, then, that accountants must be conscious of all kinds of interpersonal communications. Not only coordinating and directing communicating are required, but also maintenance and innovative communicating.

Recognizing and Crossing
Communications Boundaries

The accountant needs to realize that numerous groups of people in the firm and outside it engage in identifiable patterns of behavior. Each group's behavior pattern is the result of and reinforces the needs, values, expectations, and ways of understanding of the people in that group. We can easily sense when we have entered the domain of a group. The accountant who walks from the marketing department to the information processing department clearly senses that she has passed between groups. More important, she must also sense that she has crossed a boundary between the groups. She must listen to a kind of internal alarm that tells her that a border has been crossed and that she may need to employ a new style of communicating—just as travelers must learn to use a new language when they cross a national border.

Accountants are or ought to be among the most experienced boundary crossers in modern business and economic life. Their success at interpersonal communicating depends on their knowledge of a wide range of needs, perceptions, values, and expectations of groups of people. If the accountant can predict their needs, and so on, he can communicate with them more effectively, which in turn will lead to effective and efficient performance on his part. The start of the process, note well, is the accountant's development of the use of an internal alarm when he is about to cross an organizational boundary.

Identifying or Creating Needs

People's needs differ, and the listener-oriented corporate or public accountant must identify *or create* needs before engaging in interpersonal communications. Her chances of successfully raising the exchange value of the communication are enhanced if she is reasonably aware of the other's needs. Thus if an opportunity exists to create the needs of the other person, she should do so.

Let's look at an example. Many colleagues—call them managerial clients—do not always know what they really need from an accountant, and she must sometimes tell them what they ought to want. The general manager who wants an up-to-date statement of the cost of operating a certain production department may instead really need a forecast of operating costs after several dramatic changes in overhead allocation have been cranked in. Here the accountant would try to convince the manager of his real need before she discussed costs with him.

When the accountant is unsure what the needs of the colleague/client are, she should hold off meetings until she has had a chance to talk to associates and others who can fill her in on the client's needs that she should be

Exhibit 14.4   **SATISFYING PERSONAL NEEDS IN CORPORATE INTERPERSONAL COMMUNICATING**

NEED OF OTHER PERSON	ACCOUNTANT'S INTERPERSONAL COMMUNICATING
Need for achievement	Concentrate on providing data and information; let the other person take responsibility for solutions. Provide concrete feedback to help the other person accomplish tasks.
Need for affiliation	Seek face-to-face rather than written communications. Develop a relationship based on mutual trust rather than on fulfillment of assigned roles.
Need for power	Be willing to allow the other person to control the interactions.
Need for security	Stress probable but also possible future financial events. Be willing to risk overload to satisfy the other person's need for information to reduce uncertainty.

responding to or perhaps first creating. Of particular importance are the personal fulfillment needs of managers, which have nothing to do with organizational goals. As shown in Exhibit 14.4, these needs may involve achievement, affiliation, power, or security (McClelland, 1961; Maslow, 1954).

Naturally we should not always blindly try to satisfy needs derived from the personal quirks of others. Yet some managers do seem to be driven by these needs, and an astute accountant should pick up on them. The cost is little; the potential benefits, great.

Scripts and Plans

Within organizations—and in life, for that matter—people usually behave and communicate in predetermined ways, known as *scripts*. A script, a form of the communications rules described earlier, has been defined as an event sequence that describes what people should say and do in a familiar situation. All accountants follow scripts, as do their colleagues, and many scripts are formalized as procedures or checkoffs. But most are not. Take the case of the accountant who meets regularly with the vice president of operations to report on performance in terms of financial ratios. Over a number of meetings a script has emerged to govern their interaction. First they exchange pleasantries and reestablish their relationship. Then the accountant describes the collection of data and the ratios chosen for evaluating performance. The vice president asks predictable questions and receives predictable answers. The ratios are stated and the evaluation is made, and then more pleasantries and small talk bring the meeting to a close.

It is important to learn scripts and to follow them—except in situations where scripts are inappropriate. One should not try to make a novel situation seem routine by forcing a script. In the above case, let's assume that a serious and damaging mistake in performance evaluations was made by the accountant in his last meeting. In the current meeting he wants to bring the vice president's attention to it, explain what happened, and correct the error. The script that tells him to begin with small talk and pleasantries cannot be used here and must give way to what is often called a *plan.*

A plan is a series of projected actions and communications designed to realize a goal in a nonroutine situation. Scripts are followed; plans are developed. When we can't use a script, we should concoct a plan. Thus the accountant in the example might begin by announcing that a minor problem has come up that needs to be dealt with, instead of beginning with inconsequential talk. In this way the other person is alerted that the old script is not being followed. He will become attentive to see what kind of plan has been substituted so that he can decide what new communicating may be required. If the accountant had followed the script up to the point where the new information was transmitted, the vice president would have been taken by surprise. Nobody likes surprises, so the accountant was wise to avoid the script completely.

In sum, we follow scripts for routine, familiar interpersonal communications and develop plans for nonroutine communications. We should not employ scripts when plans are called for, and we should use the abandonment of a script as a hidden signal to a listener that he also should shift from a script to a plan. We should not attempt to make a nonroutine situation seem routine by fitting a script to it.

Little Things: Small Talk and Disclaimers

Such phrases as "How are you?" and "Lovely day, isn't it?" are part of the small talk that makes up numerous scripts within organizational life. They appear to be unimportant but in fact may be crucial in setting the stage for successful or unsuccessful interpersonal communicating. Accountants use small talk in two different kinds of scripts:

▲ Scripts that establish or keep communications links open to others.
▲ Scripts that take the place of more content-oriented communicating. These scripts are used to keep others at arm's length.

Use of the first script can be the prelude to successful communications, while overuse of the second can lead to unsuccessful communicating. Indeed, small talk as a linking device can be destroyed by extended usage of small talk as a way of keeping people at a distance. The result will be that no simple way of linking up with others will exist if small talk has been misused.

To ward off or soften possible negative effects of what we are going to say, our scripts often employ such disclaimers as the following (Hewitt and Stokes, 1975):

"I may be wrong, but . . . ."
"This may sound strange, but . . . ."
"Even though I'm not an expert on this . . . ."
"I haven't completely scoped this out yet . . . ."
"Don't get me wrong, but . . . ."

These phrases serve a number of useful purposes:

▲ They signal to a listener that what is about to be spoken is tentative.

▲ They signal that a speaker wants to avoid being labeled as odd, ignorant, inexperienced, and the like.

▲ They signal that certain rules—such as rules of logic—are about to be suspended for a good reason.

Disclaimers allow accountants to take some risks in what they tell colleagues and clients. Of course, they must not be overused; if they are, the accountant may be viewed as wishy-washy.

Giving Performance-Related Feedback to Subordinates

Accountants often have subordinates to whom they must give periodic performance evaluations. This interpersonal communication can be a trying one, especially if the meeting is poorly conducted. Here are some suggestions:

Action	Comment
Reduce potential stress in the meeting.	Set aside enough time so that the meeting is not rushed. Cut off possible interruptions.
Emphasize the future over the past.	Evaluate in terms of improving future performance rather than critiquing past performance.
Describe rather than judge. Avoid excessive use of evaluative adjectives.	Talk about the behavior of the employee, not your opinions of the behavior. Avoid "You are (adjective)" kinds of statements, such as "You are slow," "You are dynamic." Instead, give concrete examples of slowness or dynamism.

Action	Comment
Avoid dogmatic statements.	Don't say, "The policy here . . ." or "You can't do it that way." Explain the reasons behind the statements.
Avoid directives.	Don't say, "You must . . ." or "You'll have to . . ." or "You'd better . . . ." Instead say, "It's important for employees to . . ." or "Good performance usually involves . . . ."
Probe for understanding.	Say, "How do you see yourself doing?" or "If you were me, how would you describe your performance?"
Show empathy.	Say, "I can see how hard it is to . . ." or "I've been in your shoes too and I know . . . ."
Summarize the meeting.	Say, "Let me sum up . . . ."

INTERPERSONAL AUDIT COMMUNICATING

In the specialized world of auditing, face-to-face, one-on-one communicating must be both effective and efficient in terms of time spent. The auditor must quickly break down the defensiveness that a client's employees often exhibit and get on with the task of getting answers to questions without creating further defensiveness. Chapter 15 covers this subject in depth, but certain interpersonal audit encounters should be discussed in this chapter. (I am indebted to Price Waterhouse for first pointing out these problems to me).

▲ *A noisy employee tries to make the auditor look bad by ridiculing or mocking him in front of other employees.* The auditor might be tempted to argue or ridicule in return, but instead, the best strategy is to leave and reschedule the meeting either (1) when no other employees are present or (2) when the supervisor is present.

▲ *A curious employee is excessively nosey, seeking to learn what the auditor is doing and why in great detail.* The auditor could feed him a little information to satisfy him (without violating confidential material) or else ask him to do some work to keep him occupied. Announcing that the work is "confidential" wraps a cloak of secrecy around it and creates more problems than are solved.

▲ *A senior manager cannot answer the auditor's questions, won't admit ignorance, and rambles generalities.* The auditor could shift to questions that are likely to provoke answers instead of rambling. Also, she could ask for other sources of information (hidden, implied message: "You aren't helping. Please

320

show me someone who can help"). Finally, she could restate an important question, tell why the question is important, and state the general kind of answer expected. The rambling executive would have to be forthcoming or else would have to admit that he doesn't know the answer. No matter what, the auditor should never attack or insult the client ("You don't know what you're talking about" or "That's not what I asked you").

▲ *An employee puts the auditor off, refusing to make time available for a meeting.* Aside from rescheduling, the auditor could practice some persuasive role reversing. "Put yourself in my shoes," she could say. "Think about how important it would be to you for us to get together." She shouldn't be too demanding, however. As one commentator put it, "It's the auditor's ship but the employee's river. Go with the flow."

▲ *The auditor asks a question, gets an answer having nothing to do with the question, expresses displeasure with the response, and finds that the employee has become emotionally upset.* Here the auditor has created a threatening atmosphere and must reduce anxiety by saying, "Perhaps I've stated my question badly. Let me begin again." The admission that he may have made a mistake will reduce the threat to the employee's self-esteem, and the restatement of the question will allow a replay of the exchange, this time without the hostility. If misunderstanding still occurs, a third-party intermediary—perhaps another employee—can be called in to act as a translator and information source.

▲ *An employee is guarded, fearful that the auditor is evaluating him on behalf of his superior.* Avoid "Don't be silly" kinds of statements. Instead the auditor should stress the helping nature of the audit and the importance of the employee in efforts to improve the performance of the unit.

▲ *An older employee, dead-ended in his job, refuses to help. He claims that he doesn't get paid to help auditors.* Empathy is not a good response in this difficult encounter, since it implies agreement with the employee. A better approach is to label the employee as "the person everyone says I should talk to about this question." As his self-esteem increases, he may become helpful to the auditor.

▲ *An employee complains that she is bored with answering the same questions every year. She tells the auditor to consult the files.* The auditor can explain that he must check to see whether any changes have occurred and that it won't take long. However, the employee's resistance could mask a more deep-rooted problem. If the auditor senses something more at stake, he can probe ("Tell me what happened last year") for further information. If he learns the real reasons for the employee's resistance, he has a better chance of dealing with it.

These encounters and many like them require a good deal of tact on the part of accountants. They must avoid arguing or being defensive. If they must disagree, they can do so in an objective manner, using nonpersonal phrases (avoid beginning sentences with "You . . ."):

"In most of these situations an employee usually . . . ."
"Perhaps if we step back and look at the big picture . . . ."

Above all, they must not threaten the self-esteem of employees or signal aggressiveness through hidden messages or nonverbal communications. As noted earlier, the auditor's interaction with an employee should be based on an assumed positive relationship of relative equality that is moderately formal and moderately intense (at least not superficial). This kind of pose on the auditor's part should invoke employee communicating that is informational and not defensive. Contrast this with the all too common pose of an auditor as one who is an assertive, high-status person who intends to conduct a severely formal and intense interrogation of the employee. Which pose will lead to the highest exchange value and thus to the continuance of the interpersonal communication until all needs are dealt with?

Checkoff 14.1 **ACCOUNTING COMMUNICATIONS: FACE-TO-FACE, ONE-ON-ONE COMMUNICATING**

	YES	NO
EXCHANGE VALUE		
1. Have I signaled to the other person that he or she is getting something out of the meeting and that it is not substantially less than I am getting?	____	____
2. Have I lowered the other's exchange costs and/or raised his or her exchange benefits (by offering both material and psychological benefits or cost reductions)?	____	____
FACTORS INFLUENCING ENCOUNTERS		
3. Before meeting with another, have I pondered what mistakes I should avoid, what assumptions I can make safely, and what I can do to increase the other's exchange benefits and to lower his or her costs?	____	____
4. Have I analyzed my prior relationship with the other person in terms of equal/unequal, positive/negative, formal/informal, and intense/superficial relations? Have I then estimated the nature of my communications based on this prior relationship?	____	____
BUILDING RELATIONSHIPS		
5. Have I worked to build shared values and friendly relationships prior to task-oriented communicating?	____	____

(continued)

Checkoff 14.1 *(continued)*

	YES	NO

COMMUNICATIONS STYLES

6. Do I fit my communications style to the situation and context (controlling, egalitarian, structuring, dynamic, relinquishing, withdrawing)? ____ ____

COMMUNICATIONS RULES

7. Have I estimated whether the other person is a past-oriented rule follower or a future-oriented goal seeker? ____ ____

8. If the other is a rule follower, have I estimated whether her communications are based on her role, her skill, or habit? ____ ____

9. If a goal seeker, have I decided whether she is pursuing personal or organizational goals? ____ ____

BYPASSING AND FALSE CONSENSUS

10. Have I made sure that communicating of agreement does not mask fundamental disagreement? ____ ____

11. Have I checked for bypassing—that is, a failure to recognize the viewpoint of another without recognizing my failure? Have I used such phrases as, "Are you saying that . . . ?" ____ ____

12. Have I recognized that what seems to be personality problems or lack of competence of another person may be nothing of the sort but rather evidence of bypassing on both our parts? ____ ____

REDUCING CONFLICT

13. Have I avoided or solved conflicts by being willing to pull back and to probe for values, goals, and concepts mutual to both parties? Essentially, have I worked to (1) set aside communications barriers before (2) dealing with issue barriers? ____ ____

14. Have I defined the key terms I am seeking? ____ ____

15. Have I recognized hostility as often a sign of anxiety and acted to increase the self-esteem of the other person? ____ ____

CORPORATE COMMUNICATING

16. Do I recognize that maintaining and innovating communications are required as well as coordinating and directing communications? ____ ____

17. Am I capable of changing my communications style and the communications rules I follow as I travel across intraorganizational boundaries? ____ ____

(continued)

FACE-TO-FACE, ONE-ON-ONE COMMUNICATING

Checkoff 14.1 (*concluded*)

	YES	NO
18. Am I need oriented? Do I identify the needs of others *and create* their needs when appropriate?	____	____
19. Do I follow scripts when appropriate and plans when nonroutine situations occur?	____	____
Do I avoid trying to fit scripts to nonroutine occurrences?	____	____
20. Do I use small talk to maintain links to people rather than to keep them at arm's length?	____	____

chapter 15 Interviewing to Obtain Accounting Information

We have seen that the information an accountant communicates to clients and colleagues is as much as possible an isomorphism of financial reality, presented so that it is an unambiguous, authentic-seeming representation congruent (as much as possible) with the reader/listener's expectations. The task of acquiring the data that will make up the information often requires a special form of the one-on-one communication: the interview to obtain information. The objectives of an interview are (1) to discover data and information helpful in meeting a financial need or solving a problem and (2) to learn the worth of data and information already known. The interview, then, involves validating known information and uncovering unknown information. Specifically, the accountant questions respondents to learn what they know, how well they know it, what their attitude is toward what they know, and how true their knowledge is.

The advantages of an interview over written requests, surveys, or computer printouts include the following:

▲ The opportunity to motivate respondents to provide high-quality, uncertainty-reducing information;

▲ The access to immediate feedback so that questions can be modified or elaborated on;

▲   The chance to obtain nonfinancial, qualitative information that may help in developing communications that are authentic-seeming and congruent with a client's expectations.

Interviews have the disadvantages of taking up time and of becoming more of a personal interaction than an accountant might desire (sometimes, when an accountant feels that he must keep a client's employees at arm's length for various reasons, an interview may be replaced by a written survey).

PLANNING INTERVIEWS Practitioners must learn to anticipate communications barriers during interviews so that they can overcome them. To be concentrating on anticipating, accountants must not be concentrating on themselves, their roles, their self-esteem, or their status. What this means is that they must have self-confidence and commitment to their interview goals—states of mind that come from adequate planning. Planning, therefore, not only adds structure and formality to an interview, but it also frees the accountant during the interview to focus on identifying and overcoming barriers. Listed below are the planning steps to follow before interviewing:

1. *Define the Territory.*   Decide whether the respondent and the environment are friendly, neutral, or hostile to the accountant and/or to the accountant's task.

2. *Identify Permissions Needed.*   Sometimes the respondent and/or the accountant will need permission from another party before conducting the interview.

3. *Determine the Number of Meetings.*   A short, informal meeting to build rapport may be needed to precede an interview. In addition, a follow-up get-together may be required to aid in validating information.

4. *Decide on a Checkoff.*   A checkoff or a list of prepared questions can speed up an interview and ensure comprehensive coverage, but it can also lock an accountant in to an inappropriate format and can have a chilling effect on the meeting.

5. *Identify the Respondent Identifiers.*   Sometimes, before seeking out people to interview, it is better to seek out people who can tell the accountant whom to interview.

6. *Identify the Respondents.* Respondents can be special or representative. Special respondents have special information needed by the accountant. Representative respondents, on the other hand, have no special information as individuals but rather represent groups, roles, or ranks within an organization—groups whose knowledge must be sampled. In selecting respondents the accountant must also decide:

▲ Whether to seek out experts or experienced people. Supervisors may be experts due to training but lack experience. Subordinates, while lacking formal knowledge, may be a better source of facts than are experts who merely voice opinions.

▲ Who is available and willing to provide the information. Note that sometimes observers of an action—for example, the administration of a financial control—are more willing to talk about the action than are the actors.

INTERVIEWER IMAGE AND BEHAVIOR

In presenting himself to the respondent, the accountant should show familiarity with the other person's work and role. He also should try to project himself as of relatively equal status in most situations. However, a higher-status pose may be useful in influencing reluctant people to maintain contact and be forthcoming, while a lower-status image can allay the other person's perceived threats to his or her self-esteem. He should convey a sense of himself as eager to obtain information. In this way the respondent will not feel that some information is too boring or not of sufficient interest to report. Along these lines, the accountant should not by his behavior show that he already knows some of the information. The respondent may begin to withhold what he mistakenly thinks the accountant knows.

Apologetic disclaimer phrases (e.g., "This question may seem dumb, but . . ."), while appropriate in many interactions, do not work well in interviews to obtain information. Distancing statements also do not work well (e.g., "I'm supposed to find out if . . ."). Both kinds of utterance tend to create an image of one who is uncommitted to and uninvolved in the information search.

Although accountants need to establish rapport with people they interview, their role in the interview is more that of an audience member rather than a participant in an interpersonal exchange. They must concentrate on listening more than on speaking—and on active rather than passive listening (see Chapter 16). Passive participants in an encounter will respond to most statements of the other person with nods and "uh-huh's," particularly when the respondent says such things as "You know what I mean?" or "Right?" or "Got that?" An active audience-like listener, however, will probe and demand clarification.

To get good information, accountants must first give some information. Among the things that they should tell a respondent are:

▲   The kind of information needed—an example can help here;

▲   The importance of the information; note that it may be self-evidently important to the accountant but of little significance to the respondent;

▲   What led up to the need for the information (background);

▲   How the information will be used.

In sum, accountants should not sound bored, condescending, unsure of themselves, rushed, or flippant. They should sound and look of equal status to the other person, familiar with the other person's situation, eager for information, and committed to and involved in the interview.

HOW TO DO THE INTERVIEW   Careful attention to the formal process of interviewing will yield to accountants the information they seek:

1.   Give your name, work role, affiliation, your task, and any approvals of superiors.

2.   In a friendly manner explain what you want from the respondent. Explain so that none of your later questions will seem odd or surprising—such questions can cause suspicion and defensiveness.

3.   Tell the respondent why you chose her to interview (most knowledgeable, most experienced, most cooperative, etc.).

4.   Promise anonymity, if possible. If not, ask for permission to make direct quotes. If you can't get such permission, ask it for indirect quotes (such as "Miss Smith told the auditor that . . ."). If the respondent is still reluctant to be associated with the data but you can't grant anonymity, simply tell her that her name will be mentioned in your report but that she will not be named as the source of any assertion.

5.   Ask questions and take notes. Notes are a must, since accountants who depend on their memory will find that they remember their judgments and opinions rather than what was actually said by the respondent. If the respondent seems nervous about note taking, explain that it is a routine procedure and that most people have no objection to it. Notes can be in the form of checks on a checkoff, important highlights, and central points. Rarely are notes highly detailed—note taking, after all, can hinder listening. When a complex response has been noted, the accountant should summarize the note for the respondent ("Now let me see if I've got this straight . . .") to check its accuracy.

6.   After questions, a short chat to maintain rapport is in order. This is an important part of the interview, since information not given during the ques-

tioning may emerge. Moreover, a "let your hair down" chat can provide opinions and background that complement the facts collected.

COPING WITH RESISTANCE AND OTHER PROBLEMS

Exhibit 15.1 lists some responses that indicate resistance to the accountant's questions. Suggestions for dealing with these responses are also given.

If the respondent senses that the accountant might show disapproval of him or of his work, he will exhibit resistance to perceived threats to self-esteem through the following kinds of responses:

▲ *Evasive responses*—Answering a question not asked.

▲ *Depersonalized answers*—"Most inventory supervisors check on those things."

▲ *Minimization*—"That's not very important to me."

▲ *Defense*—"It's not my fault if something goes wrong."

▲ *Offense*—"What kind of a question is that?"

It is important for the accountant to realize that these responses are emotional reactions to anxiety rather than evasions or hostility. If she acts to change her image from one of threatening to one of helping, this kind of resistance should diminish.

Other response problems involve answers that express the ideal rather than the real:

Accountant:	"Do the salesmen routinely offer to take back unsold inventory at a later date?"
Respondent:	"They're not supposed to make any deals like that."

Here what ought to be has replaced what in fact is. What ought to be does not reduce uncertainty; what is does.

A related problem is the injection of hindsight into past occurrences. What should have been done becomes part of what was done:

Accountant:	"What were the details of this sale?"
Respondent:	"Let's see. In accord with policy, the machine would have been sold on an installed basis under a warranty against defects for ninety days after installation."

When the accountant hears words like *supposed to, should,* and *in accord with policy,* she should be alert to the possibility of the ideal or of hindsight being substituted for the real. A bit of probing and record checking will reveal what really is happening.

329

Exhibit 15.1 **COPING WITH RESISTANCE**

RESISTANCE RESPONSE	COPING TECHNIQUE
Time pressure or lack of interest— "I'm busy right now."	The accountant should emphasize the short time needed for the interview and stress the importance of the respondent's input. After a few questions say, "I have only a few more questions."
Ignorance, real or feigned— "I don't know about that stuff."	Say, "I see," and go on with the questions. If the respondent is really ignorant, you will soon find out.
Forgetting— "I can't remember."	Often the respondent is implying that he needs more time to remember rather than that he can't remember. Come back to the question later on.
Turning the tables— "What's your opinion as an accountant?"	Say something like, "It's a complex issue, but it's your information that is important right now." Avoid becoming the interviewee.
Aggressive bewilderment— "What's that got to do with production controls?"	Try to give an example of the relationship between the question and the topic ("Well, if I knew the answer to the question, then I could determine . . ."). Also, if the respondent was simply thrown off by the question, a simple restatement may be all that's needed.
Short answers— "The answer to your question is no."	Try silence. Respondents hate silence and will fill up the void with words.
Excessive confidence— "The project will be finished on January 15."	People often answer questions with more confidence than is warranted. Test confidence by asking, "Is that your expectation? What if . . . ?"

Sometimes respondents will give information based on the immediate past or future rather than on the long term:

Accountant:	"How much money is generally available in your bank for letters of credit and trade acceptances?"
Respondent:	"As of last week we had $1.5 million available."

The accountant was looking for a typical, usual amount (she used the word "generally") but was given the immediate past amount, which may or may not be typical. She should consider the response inadequate until she has further probed for the usual amount available.

Finally, people will often respond with evaluation when they have been asked for description:

Accountant: "What percent of bank borrowings are secured by accounts receivable? What percent by inventory?"

Respondent: "Our receivables-secured loans are a significantly greater proportion than are our inventory-secured loans. Financing has generally been on a satisfactory basis."

Instead of a description of the percentages involved, the respondent provided an evaluation of the bank financing. The interviewer will have to prod a bit to get him to be more descriptive.

ASKING QUESTIONS

Proper questioning to obtain information involves asking appropriate questions while avoiding inappropriate questions:

Appropriate Questions	Inappropriate Questions
Direct	Leading
Open	Loaded
Hypothetical	Double-bind
Clarifying	Closed-ended
Probing	Forced choice
	Why-didn't-you

Also important is questioning to avoid provoking defensiveness or resistance, using imprecise wording, and arguing while questioning.

Appropriate Questions

To gather information regarding specific events or actions, one asks *direct questions:*

"Who compiles the age of accounts? What does the report contain? How often is the report made? Who receives the report?"

These questions sound like a cross-examination by a lawyer and in a sense they are. Their purpose is to accumulate information that is not inferential. In other words, one seeks facts, not opinions.

If the accountant wanted opinions, he might ask *open questions:*

"Tell me about the reporting process of age of accounts? What do you think of the process?"

This kind of question seeks opinions, attitudes, background, or justification. It is useful in fleshing out the factual responses to direct questions and will often reveal the need for further direct questioning:

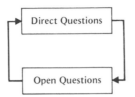

Hypothetical questions involve the respondent in the interview:

"What would you do if you were in charge of credit collections?"

"If you had the resources, what improvements to the information system would you make?"

These "What if" questions allow a reluctant interviewee to make responses that might be held back if direct or open questions ("Tell me what changes are needed in credit collections?") were employed. They are a good recourse when the direct-to-open-to-direct questioning process does not pan out:

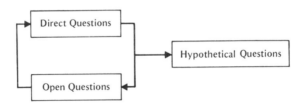

As information on facts and opinions begins to be collected, the accountant will need elaboration and details—particularly in learning the basis for opinions. *Clarifying questions* are used here:

"Are you saying that age-of-accounts reports are too infrequent for management's purposes? Why is that?"

"From your point of view, then, the problems you've seen in age-of-accounts reporting are serious? Why?"

These questions often require the interviewer to repeat or rephrase the response in order to check his perception of the response and to stimulate further responding. Clarifying questions thus help (1) to validate what the accountant hears and (2) to control what he wants to hear next.

Finally, to develop insight into responses, an accountant can ask *probing questions*. There are several types (Metzler, 1977), the most common of which are illustrated in the following dialogue:

Direct question:	"How often do you count the inventory?"
Response:	"About once every three weeks."
Responsive probe:	"Sounds fine. That seems to be an ambitious effort."
Response:	"Oh, not really. It's easy."
Developing probe:	"How so? Why is it so easy?"
Response:	"Well, we don't really count every item."
Clarifying probe:	"I don't understand. What do you mean?"
Response:	"We have a line drawn at the top of the bin. When the units get to that line, we know there must be a thousand of them."
Direct question:	"So how often do you actually count the units?"
Response:	"We've never actually counted them in the ten years I've been here."

The responsive, developing, and clarifying probes employed here were useful in getting the respondent to define what "count" meant to her. Without the probes the accountant might have simply assumed that "count" meant to *enumerate*. With the probes he learned that it meant *estimate*.

Good questioning, then, is a process involving getting information (direct, open, and hypothetical questions), making sure that what one has heard is indeed what was said (clarifying questions), and pursuing responses in depth to gain further and more precise information:

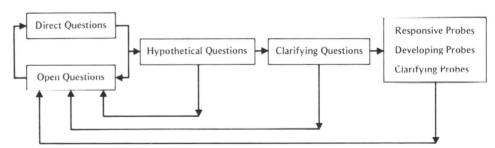

The process is circular in that as hypothetical questions, clarifying, and probing bring out issues, a new series of direct and open questions occurs and the process starts over again.

Inappropriate Questions

Loaded questions contain a signal to the respondent as to the desired or correct response:

"Don't you feel that the age-of-accounts report is poorly handled?"
"How do you rate this poor performance?"

The accountant is questioning here not to obtain information but to seek support for an opinion already held. The interview becomes a confirmation rather than a test of theories and ideas in the accountant's mind.

Leading questions are similar to loaded questions but result more from carelessness than from a desire to confirm an opinion.

Leading Questions	Direct Questions
"Your superior has told us that the cash draft system of handling cash receipts works because it matches payment date to delivery date. Do you think the system works well?" (Context is leading.)	"What problems, if any, do you see in accounting for cash receipts under the cash draft system?"
"What about this odd cash draft system? What problems do you have?" (Charged word is leading.)	Same as above

In the first example the context cues the listener as to a response. In the second the word *odd* has a negative tone to it, which suggests that problems must exist.

Double-bind questions compel the listener to choose in an either/or situation, neither of which are acceptable:

"Do you prefer X or Y as a control procedure?" (Z is really preferred.)

By the same token, the *closed-ended question* limits the response:

Closed-Ended Question	Direct Question
"Which of the following internal-control procedures do you monitor: A, B, or C?"	"Please list the internal-control procedures that you monitor."

Closed-ended questions, however, are often useful to save time, such as when the respondent doesn't have time to give an elaborate answer, or to help the respondent's memory—recognizing the points brought out by the accountant is easier than recalling them.

Finally, there is the *why-didn't-you question:*

"Why didn't you implement the purchasing control procedure?"

This question has an accusatory tone to it, which will provoke resistance and defensiveness rather than answers.

Questioning to Avoid
Defensiveness/Resistance

Unlike the why-didn't-you questions, which can be avoided with a little self-discipline, many direct questions that inadvertently provoke defensiveness are hard to avoid. Here are some examples and how to reword them:

Wrong	Right	Comment
"How soon can I have the cost data?"	"When can I have the cost data?"	*How soon* puts the respondent under pressure, which the accountant may not intend.
"What kinds of problems have you had in calculating deferred taxes?"	"What can be done to avoid difficulties in calculating deferred taxes?"	*Difficulties* causes less defensiveness than *problems*. Also, the second question is oriented toward future solutions rather than toward past problems.
"Have you stopped the increase in age of accounts yet?"	"What's been happening to the age-of-accounts situation?"	The first question presumes an unfavorable state of affairs, which may elicit defense rather than data.

Using Precise Language

The accountant needs to use precise, clearly understood terms. A term can seem precise yet be misunderstood by the listener:

Wrong	Right	Comment
"Has production improved?"	"What is the current volume of production?"	*Improved* could mean either in volume or in quality.

Even when an imprecise term is understood, however, it may provoke an imprecise response:

Wrong	Right	Comment
"Are there a lot of errors occurring?"	"What percent of current output is not salable?"	The phrase *a lot of* is imprecise. It brought forth an imprecise answer, "Quite a few."

Another common language problem having to do with precise use of terms concerns *might, could,* and *should:*

Question	Comment
"How do you think we *might* increase production?"	This question asks for a list of *possible* ways of increasing production.
"How do you think we *could* increase production?"	Here only the likely, *probable* ways from among the possible are asked for.
"How do you think we *should* increase production?"	This question seeks a statement as to *desirable* ways to increase production.

Disputing a Response Without Angering

If the accountant disagrees with a response that makes some kind of claim, she can counterargue—assuming that such counterarguing will bring out additional needed information—by imputing her position to someone else:

Question:	"How reasonable are the cost estimates made by your subordinate department heads?"
Response:	"These managers are tops in the business. What they tell me is right on target."
Disputing question:	"Some people think that the great variability in raw material quality these last few years makes cost estimating very difficult."
Response:	"That's for sure. My people do the best they can. It's not easy to hit those estimates on the button. Sometimes I kick the data back to them for reworking."

Here the disputing question brought forth a response revealing that the estimates were not always reasonable—just as the accountant suspected.

INTERVIEWING BY TELEPHONE Telephone interviewing, while not providing the nonverbal feedback of face-to-face interviewing, is nevertheless an efficient way to collect information in the sense that it costs less in time. Thus the exchange costs are reduced for the respondent, and he will be more likely to allow himself to be questioned than he would in a face-to-face exchange. Good telephone interviewing requires following these steps (Calbridge, 1976):

1. Prepare a list of questions with space below each question to write responses.
2. Identify yourself fully to whoever answers the phone.
3. If the person you seek is not available, be willing to talk to subordinates or peers.
4. State how long your call will take. If the listener cannot take part, be prepared to arrange for a call-back time convenient to both.
5. Be prepared for interruptions on the listener's end of the line.
6. If a response is unclear, say so and ask for clarification.
7. Try to let the respondent do most of the talking.
8. Don't fill up a respondent's silence with words. Let the person think.

VALIDATING INFORMATION RECEIVED

How does an accountant know if the information received is true? Senior accounting executives have noted that the collection of further information—evidence—is the best validity test available. However, such evidence is often not forthcoming. Instead, accountants test for information validity in other ways—some not as sensible as others. Among the sensible ways of finding out whether information is true or not is the skillful use of probing questions. Also important is a dependence on the reputation and competence of the respondent and on the experience of the accountant herself. Less sensible is validation by status (if they have high status, what they say must be valid), by impression (they seem like nice people), by expectation (if it's what I expected, it must be right), or by routine (if it's the same as last time, it must be okay).

In assessing information, the accountant must ask herself, "Can I make an inference about the relevance and reliability of the data and the information?" Then she must ask, "What is the likelihood of my inference being valid? What must I do to raise that likelihood?" The assessment focuses on two entities: first, the information itself; and second, the respondent who provides the information. Regarding information, respondents provide information in many forms: personal observations, assertions based on experience, the reported observations and/or experience of others, opinions and inferences, stereotypical examples, analogies of the "just like" variety, and statistics. The form of the information must be identified and then the following tests applied to it:

▲ Is the information in this form *sufficient*? Does it give me the right to make an inference? Will more information raise the likelihood that my inference is valid? Will more information raise my certainty at a bearable cost?

▲ Is the information *accurate*? Does it seem to correspond to known facts?

▲ Is the information *appropriate*? Is it the kind of information an accountant ought to use to reach a conclusion?

▲ Is the information *consistent*? Does it fit in with my developing knowledge of the situation? If not, why not?

▲ Is the information *timely?* How much need do I have for recent information?

▲ Is the information *acceptable?* Would other accountants accept the information as relevant and reliable?

These criteria are simply elaborations of those discussed in Chapter 12 concerning rational inference making. As we note in that chapter and elsewhere, the presence in the accountant's mind of theories, models, scripts, knowledge structures, and vivid but trivial data can bias her answers to the questions. Thus she must further ask of herself, "What is validating the information? Is it something within me or is it something within the information itself? Am I talking to myself or is the data talking to me?" These self-inquiries are highly important, since all of us, accountants included, are usually all too eager to listen to our inner voices rather than to the data offered us from our environment.

If the tests of information are inconclusive, as is so often the case, the accountant must turn to an assessment of the source of the information:

▲ Is the source competent? Does he or she have a right to sound authoritative about the information? What is the basis for that authoritativeness? Is it hard work? Is it a lucky guess? Is it experience or education? Is it brilliance?

▲ Is the source's air of competence due only to status or the image created by his role?

▲ What is his reputation? Does he habitually provide valid information?

▲ Does the source need to slant the information to serve his own interests?

With assessments of both the information and the source of the information, then, an accountant is in a good position to conclude whether or not the information is valid.

Checkoff 15.1 **ACCOUNTING COMMUNICATIONS: INTERVIEWING TO OBTAIN ACCOUNTING INFORMATION**

PLANNING INTERVIEWS	YES	NO
1. Do I conduct interviews so as to (a) obtain new and valid information and (b) to further validate my current knowledge?	___	___
2. In interviews do I concentrate on overcoming communications barriers rather than on myself or my role?	___	___
3. Have I decided whether I should interview special or representative respondents, experts or experienced respondents, observers or actors?	___	___

(continued)

Checkoff 15.1 (*concluded*)

		YES	NO
4.	Have I generally maintained an image (a) of equal status to the respondent and (b) of one who is eager to obtain information and who is not bored?	____	____
5.	Have I explained things to the respondent so that none of my questions will seem odd or surprising?	____	____
6.	Have I worked to establish rapport that will bring forth valuable elaboration and opinions of the respondent?	____	____
7.	In an interview, have I planned how I will deal with a respondent's ignorance, memory failings, aggressiveness, time pressure, and lack of interest?	____	____

CONDUCTING INTERVIEWS

		YES	NO
8.	Have I listened for phrases such as *supposed to, should,* or *in accord with policy*—evidence of the ideal or of hindsight being substituted for what really happened?	____	____
9.	Have I made it clear when I am looking for information about the typical or the usual rather than the immediate, the vivid, or the short term?	____	____
10.	Have I asked direct and open questions and developed further information with hypothetical, clarifying, and probing questions?		____
11.	Have I avoided questions that are leading, loaded, double-bind, closed-ended, forced choice, and why-didn't-you?	____	____
12.	Have I been careful in my use of *might, could,* and *should?*	____	____
13.	Have I tried to validate the information I have received?	____	____

chapter 16 Listening to Retain Accounting Information

If the following quotations are any indication, the modern problem of faulty listening has ancient roots:

> We have been given two ears and but a single mouth, in order that we may hear more and talk less.
>
> —Zeno of Citium, circa 300 B.C.

> The biggest block to personal communication is man's inability to listen intelligently, understandingly, and skillfully to another person. This deficiency in the modern world is widespread and appalling.
>
> —F.G. Roethlisberger, 1962

Among accountants faulty listening is noted in surveys as one of the most important communications issues facing the profession. During an interview one corporate executive noted:

> I see two listening problems. First, my purchasing agents need to learn to listen when negotiating with vendors. Second, when I give instructions to my staff accountants, they only seem to listen for the routine stuff and don't seem to hear the deviations from the routine.

Accountants, then, need to learn to listen to retain information. Moreover, they need to help people who listen to them to listen better.

Problems with listening are based in a misconception about its nature. Hearing is a physiological process, but listening is a psychological activity. Hearing is mostly automatic, but listening requires effort, discipline, and concentration—an act of will. Needless to say, too many people confuse listening with hearing and simply set themselves up as passive receptacles for spoken words. Listening, however, is an active process, requiring deliberate attending to and comprehending of words, facial expressions, body language, and other nonverbal communications. It further requires the active providing of feedback in the form of head movements, eye focusing, clarifying questions, summarizing of what has been said, and displays of empathy or sympathy.

THE GOALS OF LISTENING

Why does an accountant listen? The question seems simple enough until we probe the various listening purposes he has and recognize the conflicting goals that can occur. An accountant listens for the following purposes:

▲ *To remember*—What he hears spurs him to recall or recognize important knowledge from his memory.

▲ *To store knowledge*—The data and information he hears become the knowledge he can use later on to make inferences and decisions.

▲ *To make inferences*—Instead of storing information, he uses it on the spot to reach conclusions, to form opinions, and to make decisions.

If we are listening to make inferences, we must be forming assumptions in our mind to match against the data entering it (remember that an inference is a mix of data and assumptions). It is easy to miss information under such conditions. Take the accountant who is interviewing a client about the adequacy of automatic and/or mechanical safeguards and custody devices regarding the client's assets. As she listens to the client describe safeguards, she is also searching her mind for relevant assumptions she can make about relevant criteria to apply to what she is hearing. Being preoccupied, she misses several points the client makes explaining the absence of certain safeguards. She erroneously infers that serious problems exist in guarding assets. She listened to make an inference, not to store knowledge.

Now look at the accountant who is dutifully listening to absorb knowledge about a client's record-keeping responsibilities. He is told about several people and what they do. Suddenly he recalls that a person just named is also the custodian for some important assets. But he forces it out of his mind and concentrates on learning about record keeping. He soon forgets about the inappropriate dual record-keeping and asset-custodian problem. Instead of listening to remember, he listened to store knowledge.

Numerous other examples are easy to come by, but the point is obvious. When we concentrate on one purpose of listening, we tend to slight the other purposes and may listen poorly. Unfortunately, the solution is not simply to concentrate on remembering, storing, *and* inferring—few humans can do all three at once. The real solution is twofold: (1) to decide beforehand what our goal is in listening and (2) to be flexible enough to modify the goal when a shift in purpose is required. Thus listening involves not only three purposes, but also a fourth: *We must listen to be able to shift our purposes in listening when necessary.*

OVERCOMING LISTENING FAULTS

Listening is a learned skill, and part of any skill is knowing how *not* to do it as well as how to do it right. This section describes what accountants must avoid and must help their listeners to avoid.

Avoid Focusing on Absolutes

We tend to hear absolutes and not qualifications:

▲ *Speaker's statement*—"The principal records that reflect our financial transactions are the record of receipts, which is taken from the cash register, and our checkbook, which describes cash paid out."

▲ *What the accountant understands*—All transactions are in the record of receipts and the checkbook.

If the accountant were listening for qualifying words and phrases, she would have picked up on *principal* and asked about nonprincipal records.

Avoid Focusing on Abstractions

We tend to hear abstractions rather than facts:

▲ *Speaker's statement*—"We place incoming bills in a voucher file and follow the usual voucher system control procedure."

▲ *What the accountant understands*—My knowledge of the voucher system in common use parallels what is actually done in this case.

The accountant is abstracting when he substitutes a general class for a particular instance. In this case he should have probed for more facts, such as whether credits are made to Accounts Payable or to Vouchers Payable.

Avoid Focusing on Assertions

We tend to listen for assertions and fail to ask for evidence or reasons:

▲ *Speaker's statement*—"In accounting for capital costs we use the annuity method of depreciation. It's the most conceptually sound basis there is."
▲ *What the accountant understands*—The best way to measure assets employed is the annuity method of depreciation.

By not asking for evidence or reasons to support the assertion, the accountant has listened to and stored two kinds of knowledge when she sought only one. First, she wanted to hear what procedure the speaker used. This she learned. Second, she heard what is supposed to be the *best* procedure. This she did not seek to learn but learned it anyway. Without realizing it, she has been influenced to make an inference about accounting for capital costs in addition to accumulating knowledge about such accounting. If she had asked for reasons, she still might have made the same inference—but it would have been a conscious, controlled conclusion instead of the unconscious acceptance of a conclusion.

Avoid Careless Sympathetic Listening

When we listen to a colleague express strong feelings about the harmful, poor performance of another colleague, we may respond with a nod or else provide feedback showing that we understand the problems faced by the speaker. This is *empathetic listening*—showing understanding of but not participation in the feelings of another. Empathy in this case would encourage the communications exchange to continue. But what if we responded with signs of our own feelings of anger and frustration to match those of the speaker? This is *sympathetic listening,* in which we show that we not only understand but also are experiencing the same feelings as the speaker. Here sympathy might lead the speaker to fear that the conversation has become too emotional and to withdraw. Generally, performance evaluating should foster empathetic rather than sympathetic listening.

However, there are lots of times when sympathetic listening is in order. When a client is overjoyed after signing a big contract, his accountant probably would want to express a genuine joy as she listens to him. Indeed, in situations where the accountant has worked hard to enjoy the benefits of efficient and dependable information transfers that result from trust and mutual liking, sympathy is a cost incurred. It goes with the territory.

Avoid Rationalizing

The urge to clarify what we hear leads us to rationalize:

▲ *Speaker's statement*—"The output of our production department cannot be measured solely by the quantity and quality of the products we produce. After all, our contribution to the company's goals and objectives involves a high degree of training of supervisors for other departments."

▲ *What the accountant understands*—The current performance measures for the production department are not relevant. After all, the manager in charge says that other performance criteria are needed.

The accountant has heard a rather complex assertion regarding the need for a complex set of performance criteria. But she has simplified what she has heard by assuming that the manager has said that the current measures are not relevant. Then, to justify her oversimplification, she tells herself that this is what the manager said. He didn't. He said that *additional* measures are needed. She rationalized her simplification by thinking that he said that *new* measures are needed. The key to avoiding this kind of distortion in listening is to discipline ourselves not to simplify. We must be prepared to admit complexity when we hear it and to probe further for full understanding.

Avoid Excessive Talking

We are often overcommitted to being sources of information rather than receivers of information. Accountants, like all of us, enjoy talking more than listening. Obviously we cannot listen well if we are not disposed to listen at all. A point worth noting: high-status people do more talking than low-status people. Thus high-level accountants must be doubly careful to listen rather than to talk.

Avoid Selective Listening

We avoid hearing what we don't expect or don't want to hear. Researchers refer to this finding in terms of selective attention and perception. Among numerous causes for it are the following:

▲ *Anchoring*—We fix on the first bits of information we hear and ignore later information that contradicts it.

▲ *Anxiety*—We tend to avoid hearing whatever might threaten our self-esteem.

▲ *Goal-related listening*—We listen for what we have decided beforehand is what we need to know.

Anchoring can be avoided by disciplining ourselves to listen better at the ends of meetings. Anxiety can be controlled by raising our sense of self-worth (get a rise in status, wear more expensive clothing, extend our expertise, etc.). Goal-related listening can be muted by a firm commitment to data and evidence rather than to theories and models. (One accountant has a sign in his office that reads in large letters: "I AM AN EMPIRICIST!")

Avoid Daydreaming

We tend to let our attention wander; we daydream. A person knows when another is not listening. Eyes are seen to become glazed, and a certain lassitude becomes evident. The problem is well known, as is the cause. It seems that we speak at a rate of about 125 words per minute but can listen at a rate of about 400 words per minute. Thus when we listen to a speaker, our minds need only function at about one-third of capacity. The rest of the time our listening faculties are unoccupied. Since nature abhors a vacuum, we tend to fill up the gaps with daydreams or simply with a dazed inertia. Recognition of the problem goes a long way toward solving it, but of course some specific gap-filling actions are needed to keep the mind from wandering. These will be discussed below as steps to take to improve listening.

We allow noise and eyes to distract us. Obviously the solution to the problem of a noisy environment is to avoid it or to seek a quieter place. Eye contact problems are less easy to solve. It is important to maintain eye contact with a client or colleague, but if one concentrates on another's eyes, one will experience difficulties in processing what is heard. The mind can concentrate on maintaining eye control or on processing words, but not easily on both. One possible solution is to maintain *ear contact*. Here the accountant focuses his eyes on the eyes of the other person, but as he looks at eyes, he is concentrating on his own ears. He visualizes a stream of words entering his ears. His overt gaze is eye oriented, then, but his real concentration is ear oriented. The eyes are his tool for keeping the interpersonal exchange functioning, and his ears are his tool for accumulating the information he needs to do his job after the exchange ends.

Avoid Focusing on Rebuttals

We tend to prepare to argue instead of act to listen. When we hear a statement with which we disagree, we tend to prepare a rebuttal then and there. But a focus on a rebuttal will cause us to miss what we ought to listen to next. We lose information in our desire to start and win a brief argument. For accountants, who live on the information they collect, the cost is too heavy to bear

They must learn to curb their emotional or argumentative responses and to concentrate on accumulating data.

Avoid Stereotyping

We tend to let mannerisms and clothing excessively color our listening. Certainly an accountant must use every bit of information he can get to make judgments about the worth of the speaker as an information source. He must, in the words of the author Henry James, be one on whom nothing is lost. Yet the risk remains that odd mannerisms or unconventional clothing can lead an accountant to create a stereotypical model of the speaker in his mind that is a gross distortion of his real value. What is heard is then tested against the standard of the model rather than against more realistic evaluative criteria. Important information may be rejected unless the accountant overcomes the tendency to stereotype or else learns to form stereotypes based on more relevant data than gestures and clothes.

ACTIVE LISTENING

What does it take to be a good listener? Of course an accountant should avoid the problems described above, but success requires a more active approach. Good listening is a willed behavior, requiring commitment, discipline, and concentration. Here's what to do:

Look Interested

A listener must not only be interested in what is said, she must look interested as a signal to the speaker of approval of his effort (not necessarily of his words). A cold, impassive listener discourages speakers and may cause them to communicate less effectively.

Suspend Disbelief

The accountant listener must willingly suspend any disbelief in the speaker's message for at least the beginning of the communication. In this way he gives a fair hearing to what he opposes and at the same time collects observations and data that may be useful in strengthening his own point of view. This is not to say that the accountant should not be evaluative. Sooner or later in his listening he must test what he hears against his reason, his experience, or his standards.

Ask a Speaker to Clarify

As noted above, we tend to want to simplify a complex message to make it clear. However, clarifying is the speaker's job, not the listener's. If the message is hard to grasp, the listener should ask the speaker to restate and rephrase. What is complex will still be complex, but at least it will be understandable. Note that the listener must become the speaker in this case to help the original speaker solve a communications problem. As soon as clarification occurs, the listener again becomes a message receiver.

Listen for the Main Idea

As an accountant listens, she should be continually asking herself, "What is the main idea? What is the point of the speaker?" Good listeners also constantly summarize and condense what they are hearing as they go along. They listen to the message, not the speaker.

Separate Facts from Opinions and Feelings

When an accountant is taking notes, he should draw something like the following on his note paper:

Facts/Ideas	Speakers' Opinions	My Feelings

This classification scheme for notes is a control device that helps the accountant to decide on the spot what is a fact and what is an opinion or a feeling. Making these decisions later with only raw notes can be quite difficult.

Listen for Quantifiers and Qualifiers

Sometimes little words and phrases can make the difference between truth and falsehood. One should learn to pick out the quantifiers (*some, most, many, few,* etc.) and the qualifiers (*if, except, however, yet, but,* etc.) that can modify information so dramatically.

Anticipate

As the accountant listens, he should anticipate conclusions or inferences that he expects the speaker to make. When the conclusions do come, he can match them against his expectations. If he notes differences between what he anticipated and what he heard, he should find out why—by probing questions or by restating for the speaker what he thinks he heard.

Summarize

Periodically, a listener should sum up what she has heard so far (during a lull in the speaker's comments). The value of this activity lies in its helping the mind to store the information in memory. Chunked information, as in a summary, is easier to remember than bits and pieces of data.

LISTENING AND CERTAINTY We return here to the issue of financial information and the reduction of uncertainty (see Chapter 3). The value of such information lies in the degree to which it reduces the uncertainty of a decisionmaker. When an accountant interviews someone, she must listen to the data and information and decide how valuable it is. Essentially her task is to assess quickly how much of her uncertainty has been reduced by the information. Exhibit 16.1 illustrates the problems that can occur as the accountant hurriedly tries to assess how much she has learned and what she still must learn—in other words, how much certainty about the information she has.

In the exhibit the *effect* of listening to ever increasing amounts of data and information is shown on the level of certainty (which is the same thing as the level of acquired knowledge, the level of success in acquiring information, and so on). Two relationships are shown: (1) the accountant's perception of certainty and (2) the likely real certainty. A number of points are made here. First of all, one's confidence in acquired data is probably greater than it ought to be. Research suggests that we tend to judge the value of data as higher than an objective assessment would make it. Thus our perceptions of certainty will be higher than they should be unless we discipline ourselves to evaluate what we hear as objectively as possible.

Second, no matter how good a listener an accountant is, at some point overload can occur. This is the point at which the mind simply cannot handle all the data coming in. If he were objectively viewing what was happening, the

Exhibit 16.1   **IMPACT OF WHAT WE HEAR ON HOW CERTAIN WE ARE**

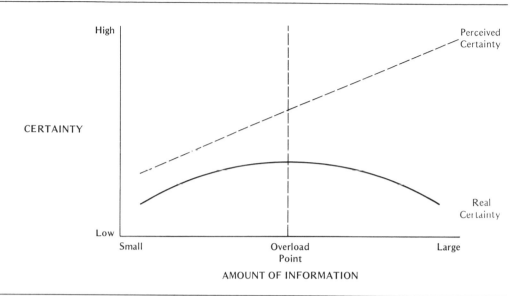

accountant would see not only that his success at acquiring good information is stagnant, but also that if he continues to seek more data, his success will decline. This fall in the level of certainty is likely because as a jumble of data comes in, contradictions are bound to occur in what is heard. One would have to start being less sure of the data. However, rarely do managers and accountants seek relief from data. Indeed, they usually seek more and more of it. The reason is that they *perceive* certainty to be always rising as data is heard. Unless they look quite clinically at what they are taking in, they will ask for more of it. And as contradictions and confusions arise after overload occurs, they will clarify and simplify through the use of internal theories, models, and stereotypes. In short, they will stop observing (active listening) and will start assuming.

Exhibit 16.1 suggests two rules that accountants must follow:

▲ Realize that your first assessment of the value of the data you hear is probably too high and ought to be lowered.

▲ Realize that even a skilled listener must stop seeking data at some point lest overload occur and a consequent false sense of certainty begin to develop about the information one thinks one is acquiring.

These two rules help accountants to avoid a kind of self-deception regarding the value of data that occurs as they listen to managers or clients. They are part and parcel of active listening.

Checkoff 16.1 **ACCOUNTING COMMUNICATIONS: LISTENING TO RETAIN ACCOUNTING INFORMATION**

PURPOSIVE AND ACTIVE LISTENING	**YES**	**NO**
1. Do I listen for deviations from the routine rather than for the routine?	____	____
2. Do I decide on my purpose in listening beforehand: to remember, to store knowledge, or to make inferences? Am I flexible enough to change my purpose if need be?	____	____
3. Do I listen for qualifying statements?	____	____
4. Do I avoid listening for abstractions and concentrate on facts?	____	____
5. Do I make conscious, controlled conclusions instead of simply accepting assertions I hear?	____	____
6. Do I exercise care in choosing to respond either empathetically or sympathetically?	____	____
7. Am I prepared to listen for complexity instead of simplifying and then rationalizing to justify my simplification?	____	____
8. Do I avoid being the source of information when I should instead be the receiver?	____	____
9. Do I avoid anchoring—fixing on the first bits of information I hear and discounting the rest?	____	____
10. Am I willing to listen for the unexpected or the undesired?	____	____
11. Do I avoid eye contact problems by visualizing words entering my ears?	____	____
12. Do I listen instead of preparing arguments in rebuttal?	____	____
13. Do I avoid letting mannerisms or clothing excessively color my listening?	____	____
14. Do I look interested to encourage the speaker to continue?	____	____
15. Do I seek data and information from the speaker if I need clarification?	____	____
16. Do I listen for main ideas?	____	____
17. Do I separate facts and ideas from the speaker's opinions and my own feelings?	____	____

(continued)

Checkoff 16.1 (*concluded*)

		YES	NO
18.	Do I listen for the important little words that can dramatically modify what I hear (e.g., *some, most, if, except*)?	____	____
19.	Do I summarize periodically and also anticipate what is coming up?	____	____
20.	Do I realize that often my first assessment of the value of what I hear is too high and in need of lowering?	____	____
21.	Am I prepared to stop seeking data when I feel overloaded?	____	____

chapter 17 Communicating in Small Groups

Accountants, particularly auditors, often work in small groups formed to deal with specific tasks or to serve a client's special needs. Why are groups needed? Why can't accountants work as separate individuals? The fact is that most accounting work does require a highly individual effort. Group work, however, must and indeed does occur for a number of reasons:

▲ A group has more knowledge than an individual does. It is not likely to make an ignorance-based mistake.

▲ People who work in groups are often more motivated, more satisfied, and better performers than those who don't (Katz and Kahn, 1978).

▲ Group work builds consensus and support for financial decisions.

▲ The spreading of responsibility across group members allows groups to take greater risks than individuals can.

This last point seems to fly in the face of the popular belief that groups and committees never do anything. On the contrary, a rich knowledge base and shared responsibility position work groups (1) to take on and (2) to make financial decisions bearing risks that individuals alone could not accept.

Accountants form work groups, then, to handle complex tasks and/or to make risky decisions. Without these stimuli there is not much incentive to form into groups, especially since group existence makes demands on the individual and on the organization that require effort and resources.

SMALL GROUP SOCIOLOGY

An accountant's work group must adapt to the situation in which it finds itself and then work to carry out its mission. But as it does so, it must satisfy its members' needs lest they withdraw their allegiance and the group disintegrates. In addition, it cannot function without following the policies and procedures of the organization. This balancing of individual and organizational needs—all within the context of the work group's attempt to do its job—can be a trying experience for group members and particularly for group leaders. Look at what an audit team must do:

- Initiate, coordinate, and evaluate auditor actions;
- Develop and enforce workable standards to govern auditor actions;
- Seek resources from the client and the accounting firm to carry out the audit;
- Develop a system for making important decisions regarding the adequacy of the client's internal controls;
- Develop the individual auditor's commitment to a team effort;
- Maintain each individual's good feelings about the group;
- Coordinate information flows so that each auditor accumulates knowledge appropriate to the task;
- Avoid or resolve conflict among group members.

These efforts are exceptionally complex and rarely carried out with perfect success. Indeed, an air of tension, stress, and even failure may hover about a group, leading its members to feel anxious and depressed. Work on audit teams thus can be one of the most trying experiences of the modern accountant. The work can be made easier if accountants understand the nature of the group process and, more important, recognize the need for and employ interpersonal communication skills of a high order.

ACCOUNTANTS AND THEIR GROUP ROLES

In Chapter 1 we described the importance of roles in communicating. Roles are patterns of behavior that people adopt or are assigned to in organizations. Accountants play different roles in different groups and even within the same group at different times. The role being played determines the communications made, which in turn influence the performance of the group. We can see then that role playing, either deliberately or unconsciously, is the key to successful group productivity. What kinds of roles can and should accountants play? What should they avoid?

Generally, roles can be viewed as blocking, building, or maintaining. Blocking roles hinder the group from doing its job, whereas building roles are useful during task activities, and maintaining roles are needed as the group members interact to keep the group functioning as a unit.

Blocking Roles

Recognizable patterns of behavior that hinder a group from carrying out its work can be described as dominant, arrogant, calculating, cold, quarrelsome, aloof, introverted, lazy, or submissive (Wiggins, 1979). People who exhibit these traits are often referred to in the following ways:

The Aggressor.   This person is uncivil, ill-mannered, uncooperative, and discourteous. If we take audit teams as our context, he is the auditor who endlessly disagrees with the other auditors or with the client's employees for the sake of being disagreeable.

The Dominator.   She is excessively assertive, domineering, and bullying, particularly toward subordinates or assigned helpers within the group. Her goal is self-aggrandizement rather than group success.

The Narcissist.   He is conceited, boastful, and cocky. He enjoys flaunting his expertise or his status.

The Withdrawer.   This person represents the "green eyeshade" stereotype of accountants. She is undemonstrative, painfully shy, meek, and forceless—a self-appointed note taker whose passivity in the face of changing demands on an audit team can make it inflexible.

The Cold Fish.   He carries out his work with an aloof, ruthless impersonality. He is distant, unsmiling, and unsympathetic. For him a group is made up of work units rather than people, and a client's employees are just so many barriers to be knocked down to acquire knowledge. He is exploitative and calculating, ignorant of or unwilling to develop rapport and trust.

In interviews accountants concede that some practitioners do indeed play all these roles in audit teams and similar groups. Obviously, their communicating will not foster good performance (or at the least will compel the group to spend more time—and thus the client's money—than is necessary to do the job). Luckily, audit seniors ought to have no difficulty both in spotting aggressors, dominators, narcissists, withdrawers, and cold fish and in directing their behavior and their communications toward more productive roles.

Building Roles

Accountants who play building roles exhibit task-oriented communications and behavior. They are persevering, innovative, industrious, self-disciplined, organized, deliberate, deliberative, and steady. People with these traits can be classified as follows:

The Innovator.   This accountant is recognizable in work groups for her suggestions. She constantly comes up with new ideas or new ways to attack a problem or implement a procedure.

The Elaborator.   When an innovator suggests a new idea, the elaborator is the one most energized by her creativity. He takes the idea and develops it, offering a sensible critique and fitting it to the work team's needs.

The Organizer/Coordinator.   He is the person who is constantly clarifying where the team stands and probing for ways to summarize the work done so far and the work remaining. He can be counted on to be deliberate and hard working without being rigid or cold.

Maintaining Roles

If an audit team is to function as a team, it must maintain itself. Accountants who are good at maintaining roles are collaborative, accommodating, friendly, cordial, approachable, trusting, and cheerful. They can be recognized as one of these types:

The Compromiser.   When a conflict arises over ways to proceed or evaluations to be made, the compromiser seeks a consensus solution rather than a personal triumph. Her goal is to keep the team moving forward.

The Encourager.   He always sees the best in people and praises them when they perform well. He is a good neighbor within a group.

The Gatekeeper.   The person who fills this role is one of the group's most important communicators. His job, as he defines it through his activities, is to keep all relevant communications channels open and in use—to keep the gates open, as it were. If a team member is not contributing, he encourages him to do more. If someone is too silent, he gets her talking again. Without the gatekeeper to facilitate the flow of information, the group cannot collect and analyze all the information it needs.

Egocentric Behavior

Recent studies on how people behave in social and work groups have revealed that individuals in groups unintentionally tend to judge themselves more responsible for a group's successful performance than in fact is warranted in terms of the assessments of the other team members (Ross and Sicoly, 1979). Without realizing it, then, accountants on audit teams may practice a kind of self-aggrandizement that can block group cohesion. This is not deliberate role playing but rather the exhibition of an egocentrism that appears to be common in Western culture. Such behavior may result in communications that seem power oriented and dominating. All team members should realize that blocking problems may be occurring, not because of individual failings but because of culture-bound behavior. Such problems do not occur as frequently in Japanese and other cultures that value the merging of the self into the group. Americans need to be alert to this conflict between our cultural and our organizational values.

COMMUNICATIONS CHANNELS Audit and similar accounting work teams can structure their communications channels in two ways:

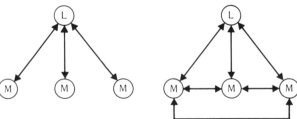

Leader-Centered Structure   Member-Centered Structure

In the *leader-centered structure* the leader acts as a central authority. All staff members perform tasks coordinated by her. They do not generally communicate directly with each other. The advantages of this approach lie in the speed with which leader directions can be transmitted and carried out. Moreover, the team leader does not have to wait for members to consult with each other before getting feedback on which to base new directives. Under time pressure, when work must be done quickly, this group structure will emerge. A disadvantage, however, is that the lack of intermember maintenance communicating may damage group cohesion. Work quality could diminish after a time as the members cease to function well together.

The *member-centered structure* allows both the leader and the members to monitor each other's work constantly. The work will take longer but probably will be done well. Often audit teams try to incorporate the best of both structures into their work. Thus in the morning the team will gather to go over what has been done and what needs to be done. During the rest of the morning the staff will carry out their tasks with little or no group communicating but with coordinating discussions held periodically by each member with the leader. Then the team will meet over lunch to discuss the work *and* to build and maintain group cohesion. In the afternoon the solitary work will begin again. Thus a shifting back and forth occurs from the efficiency-oriented leader-centered channels structure to the effectiveness-oriented member-centered approach. This middle-ground focus on the communications channels set up in a work group probably is the best method for accomplishing accounting team goals.

GROUP CONFORMITY AND ACCOUNTANTS' INDIVIDUALISM

Work groups need cohesion, but cohesion can cause conformity. In this situation a drifting of the group in a certain direction can carry all members along, even those whose competence and experience would ordinarily influence them to pull back from such a tack. A team of internal auditors, for example, under the influence of a vivid but inconsequential single instance of a control failure, may begin to evaluate negatively (and falsely) the work unit under scrutiny. Some individuals in the group may recognize that the unit is performing well but find themselves going along with the team bias anyway. What happens is that the group's will may dominate an individual's will by the group's taking on an image of invulnerability to each member.

Irving Janis (1972) has described behaviors that are based on conformity to group will. His findings enable us to list the kinds of communicating necessary to undo or avoid excessive conforming behavior:

▲ *The group should discuss as many action-oriented alternatives as possible* (e.g., a discussion of ways to conduct statistical sampling during an internal audit). In this way the group cannot drift into a focus on only one alternative without a thorough discussion based on the varying degrees of expertise of team members.

▲ *The group should not accept the past as given.* If a certain procedure has become routine, that is no reason for the group to demand that all members conform to it. What has been done in the past should be discussed as an alternative, not a rule.

▲ *The group should not demand conformity to an inference based more on assumption than on observation.* For example, suppose a group is evaluating depreciation methods to employ for a new fixed asset. The group tacitly assumes that the tax laws governing depreciation allowances will not change and compels members to consider various possible methods based on this assumption. (Many groups in 1980 probably did just this without considering the possibility of the changes that did in fact occur in 1981.) A member can fight this conformity by anticipating it and arming herself with data and arguments suggesting the need to view the assumption as uncertain rather than as a given. Data always drives out conformity-inducing assumptions.

▲ *The group should describe expected future actions in terms of probability rather than of certainty.* All possible known reasons why things could go wrong should be discussed. In this way groups will not tend to demand that individuals treat a future event as if it were a fact.

▲ *The group should discuss standards or criteria for evaluating alternatives in addition to debating the alternatives.* Thus an accounting staff working on developing a new management information system ought to discuss ways of evaluating systems (e.g., cost cutting, revenue generating, time saving) and the relative importance of each criterion. If standards are in place to govern discussion, conformity is less likely to impede successful deliberations.

▲ *Before demanding that everyone commit himself to a financial decision, the group should discuss how to implement the decision.* Excessive and unrealistic demands for conformity from some individuals should come to light.

If the danger of too much conformity is obvious, however, the danger of too little conformity is less so. Accountants are known for their highly individualistic personalities. They often work alone and like it. There is nothing wrong with this approach to work, except when working in groups. Conforming behavior, as long as it doesn't get out of hand, is necessary if groups are to be successful, so a good practitioner has to learn when to accept a general consensus and be governed by it.

GROUP COMMUNICATING PROCESS The process of a group's activities is outlined in Exhibit 17.1. All groups must first plan, then interact, negotiate, and decide. Planning involves a good deal of person-to-person communicating as group members get to know each

Exhibit 17.1 **COMMUNICATIONS DURING GROUP ACTIVITIES**

		GROUP COMMUNICATIONS				
		Maintaining Communications	Innovating Communications	Orienting Communications	Directing Communications	Control Communications
GROUP ACTIVITIES	Planning	✓	✓			
	Interacting			✓	✓	✓
	Negotiating	✓				✓
	Deciding		✓			

other and learn of each other's knowledge and assigned tasks. Audit teams often meet together for such planning before starting a new job. During the interacting stage the group's task is undertaken. The audit team sets to work, and task-oriented communicating begins to dominate. Here messages flow from each auditor to the group (represented by the senior or manager acting as leader) so that activities can be monitored, integrated, and coordinated. As the work comes to a close, the team may meet to analyze the materiality of control problems uncovered. This is a negotiating stage in which the group must tie itself together if it is to exhibit unity in its final decision. Finally, in the decision stage the group (1) decides whether its work is finished, and (2) decides on what to report to its superiors.

Exhibit 17.1 shows the kinds of communicating that occur during the various group activity stages:

▲ *Maintaining*—Seeking to know other team members as fellow workers, offering advice, giving praise, showing group solidarity, showing satisfaction with the group;

▲ *Innovating*—Suggesting, proposing, hypothesizing, pointing, integrating;

▲ *Orienting*—Providing background, clarifying, confirming or denying expectations, asking questions, providing answers;

▲ *Directing*—Assigning activities, telling when to do activities, coordinating;

▲ *Controlling*—Motivating, monitoring, evaluating.

Planning

Planning requires maintaining and innovating communications. It is important to note that these are "last hired—first fired" kinds of messages because team leaders, eager to save time, often rush into task activities without properly constituting the group. In many instances, particularly with groups performing routine assignments, this approach works. Over the long run, however, a lack of group maintenance and innovating communications will have downstream effects on negotiating and deciding activities. Without group solidarity and cohesion, personality conflicts will begin to break out. Without planned standards to govern final discussions, emotional rather than rational criteria may dominate decision making.

Interacting

During interacting, as the group's task is carried out, orienting, directing, and controlling communications occur. Most accountants are exceptionally able at handling such messages, but this skill can be a drawback if task communicating replaces maintenance communicating simply because accountants are good at one but only fair at the other. Whether done well or poorly, maintaining messages must flow.

Negotiating

Negotiating probably is the most difficult stage of all for communicating. Not only must control communicating occur to evaluate the work done, but also maintenance communicating must occur to avoid threatening the self-esteem of the people who did the work. As noted above, routine audits or audits where standards are easily applicable do not require a negotiating stage. New audit engagements, new personnel, and/or a vague relationship between standards and the audit data, however, do require such a stage. It can be an agonizing experience for those involved unless the group has developed solidarity during the planning stage and acts to maintain it during the negotiating stage.

Deciding

Finally, decision making should be the easiest stage of all if the group has communicated well in earlier stages. Decisions will emerge organically from the group. If the decisions seem artificial or wrenched from the group, the fault lies earlier, probably in the lack of communicating during planning. Indeed, the key to successful group performance is to be found not at the end of its work but rather at the beginning. An audit team on a new job probably determines how well it will do on the first day of the engagement, not on the last.

THE ACCOUNTANT AS TEAM LEADER Accountants become team leaders early in their careers, particularly in regard to both internal and external auditing. Few of them realize the complex communicating in which they must engage as leaders. Exhibit 17.2 and the following list suggest the dimensions of this task:

- Directing the work
- Deciding from among alternatives
- Gatekeeping
- Praising
- Summarizing results
- Enforcing rules
- Clarifying complex findings

- Resolving conflict
- Reporting to superiors
- Evaluating information
- Advising subordinates
- Interpreting
- Coordinating activities

Not only must leaders know how to deliver these and similar communications, but they must also know situations in which each of these communications works or doesn't work.

Fitting Communication to Situation

A number of situations are known to influence dramatically what a leader ought to say to subordinates. Some of these are listed below, with comments on the kinds of communicating to be used:

Stress. Under conditions of stress brought about by time pressure—a typical situation during audits—a team leader probably ought to concentrate on task-oriented messages rather than on maintenance messages.

Exhibit 17.2 **EXAMPLES OF LEADER COMMUNICATIONS IN TASK GROUPS**

GOAL OF THE MESSAGE	EXAMPLES
Spurring the team's awareness of its position regarding the task	"Are we agreed that . . . ?"
	"Let me summarize what we have to do . . . ."
	"Are we going too fast [or too far afield] when we discuss . . . ?"
Getting the members to participate	"Mary, what do you think of . . . ?"
	"Bob, what do you see as the implications of doing things this way?"
Maintaining the group	"We're well along and things look good."
	"I appreciate your work so far."

High Subordinate Ability. When staff are highly skilled, they need less directing. However, group cohesion problems can occur from "prima donna" behavior. Thus more group maintenance is needed than with low-skilled workers.

Leader Power. When the leader has strong power over the group by right of rank or authority, task-oriented communicating works well. When the leader's position is moderately shaky—such as when a young, low-rank auditor is put in charge of a team—then maintenance communicating should be more prominent.

Leader–Staff Relations. Little maintenance communicating is needed when an auditor is working with people he knows and likes—and people who like him in return. Only when his relationship with the team is poor or weak need he focus on socially supportive communicating. (Such a situation is of course the hardest time to do maintenance communicating.)

Task Structure. Most accounting tasks are highly structured. In these situations, a task-oriented communicator probably does best.

Generally then, task-oriented messages work best and should predominate under conditions of high stress, low worker ability, high leader power, good leader–staff relations, and highly structured tasks. Maintenance and group-cohesion communicating should be given more prominence when stress is not a problem, when staff are highly skilled, when the leader's power is shaky, when relations with the group are poor, and when tasks are unstructured.

Identifying Leader Styles

Routine audits probably ought to involve task-oriented communications by the leader. The leader of an ad hoc group formed to conduct a lease-acquisition study involving large sums of money would probably have to do a good deal of maintenance because of the unstructured nature of the task and her lack of experience with the group. If management were able to identify accountants with task-oriented communications styles, they could be assigned to audits, whereas those known to focus on socially supportive messages would generally be given the lease-acquisition group work. Can leader styles be thus identified? Do people generally fall into personality categories characterized as task oriented or maintenance oriented? No one is quite sure, but some accountants do indeed seem to exhibit a tendency to focus on one or the other kind of

Exhibit 17.3 **LEADER PERSONALITIES FROM TASK TO MAINTENANCE ORIENTED**

LEADER PERSONALITY	COMMUNICATIONS
Task oriented	Makes and announces directives and decisions with little group participation.
	Makes and announces directives and decisions and then seeks to persuade team members of her point of view.
	Suggests a course of action or a decision and seeks to generate discussion, which she controls.
	Describes the goal of the group and what can or cannot be done; lets the group determine specific courses of action.
Maintenance oriented	Lets the group determine the goal and courses of action; acts as a gatekeeper; praises good ideas; listens well; serves group needs.

behavior. Exhibit 17.3 describes the leader-communications characteristics of task- and maintenance-oriented personalities. If superiors use this description to identify an accountant's personality, they will probably be able to successfully match leader personality to the nature of the group's task—and thereby increase the chances that the leader (and the group) will perform well.

As noted above, some situations arise in which task-oriented personalities are clearly to be preferred as leaders, while other situations clearly call for socially supportive maintenance leaders. Accountants who have been identified as personality types at either end of the continuum described in Exhibit 17.3 would fit the bill in these situations. Over time superiors will learn just how accurate their judgments of personality have been and whether or not matching personality to situation improves performance. Of course, most situations are never clearly of one kind or another, just as most accountants do not clearly exhibit a recognizable personality. But when clearly defined group tasks present themselves and when easily recognized personality types are on the staff, a match of leader to task can occur.

Learning versus Performing

An accountant who is leading a group needs to know whether the group is learning or performing, since each activity requires a different communications focus on the leader's part. If the group is in need of learning, leadership should take the form of information providing. Discussions with the team need to take on a lecture form. However, when the group shifts to performing work tasks, team members need to use learned information rather than to acquire new information. The accountant now must shift from a lecture form of leader communication to a group discussion form in which all uses of the information are considered and employed. In the learning situation the leader does the talking, whereas in the performing mode he is more of a listener, a summarizer, a coordinator, and a consultant responding to technical questions.

Ordering versus Suggesting

What a leader regards as an order is quite often misinterpreted by subordinates as a suggestion (Burns, 1954). This research finding describes a form of bypassing that most managers have experienced regularly without much damage occurring. In audit team work, however, the risks of the audit not being properly done because of directives not being followed is a real one. The result can be serious legal difficulties for the audit firm. Audit team leaders, then, must take great care to differentiate their directives, which must be followed by the staff, from their suggestions, which are not binding and act to coordinate and integrate the work.

A Leader's Power Base

A leader's communications of directives to staff rest on any or all of a number of power bases. Take the example of the audit leader who tells an experienced staff member to use a sampling technique not routinely employed. What kind of power does the auditor need to communicate to the staff member to get her to comply with the directive (Etzione, 1961)? Here are the choices:

▲   *Coercive*—Comply or be punished.
▲   *Reward*—Comply and be rewarded.
▲   *Legitimate*—Comply because of my position.
▲   *Referent*—Comply because of my charisma.
▲   *Expert*—Comply because of my competence and special knowledge.

We can rule out coercive or referent power bases, which seem to be little employed in modern accounting practice. That leaves reward, legitimate, and expert power. Probably a mix of all three would be employed. The senior might try to persuade the subordinate that he possessed expert knowledge justifying the use of the technique. If resistance were encountered he might fall back on rewards (e.g., promising a tradeoff such as using another technique favored by the subordinate in another task if only she will use the senior's technique in this task). A last resort would be the exercise of authority.

Notice that the exercise of such power to gain subordinate compliance with directives requires that a senior engage in two other kinds of communications prior to issuing directives:

▲ Informal communications in which the needs and desires of subordinates become known to the leader;

▲ Formal and informal communications in which the senior makes his competence salient to subordinates.

In this approach the accountant's power as a leader rests on his skill at communicating (1) to build the trust of subordinates (so they will tell him their needs) and (2) to develop an image of expertise.

If a senior has worked to build trust and develop his image, his directives to subordinates will be viewed not as orders but rather as instructions for achieving success. He will be a valued teacher rather than simply a boss.

AVOIDING AND RESOLVING CONFLICT

What is conflict? There are several different definitions. Conflict can be viewed as a *competition* during which one party in a group seeks to dominate another. This situation emerges from the view that the desires of one party are incompatible with the desires of the other (Boulding, 1962). Less traumatic is conflict as a *maneuver* designed to increase one's power without seeking total domination. Then there is conflict that is *debate,* an ordered controversy in which both parties seek an outcome beneficial to all. Finally, conflict can be *disagreement,* a mutual exchange of opposing views that is something like a persuasive communication (Beck, 1971).

Accountants working in groups must learn when their conflict-like communications are disagreements or debates, which are valuable exchanges, as opposed to maneuvers or competitions, which are harmful to the attainment of team goals. They must also learn to distinguish between issue-oriented conflict and interpersonal conflict. The team member who argues with someone because he or she doesn't like the other person is engaging in an exchange that may be personally satisfying but will have little positive result. Better to concentrate on issue-oriented conflict rather than on interpersonal conflict. The problem is, however, that arguments over issues have a way of disintegrating into personal clashes. "I don't like your idea" can rather easily become "I don't like you."

Sources of Conflict

If there are different kinds of conflict, there are also different sources of conflict:

Resource Allocation Difficulties.   Occasionally some group members will individually command more resources (typists, computer access, subordinate staff, etc.) than do others. Conflict can result.

Strategy Problems.   Deciding which action to take or procedure to employ can lead to difficulties. Sometimes accountant members of a group may favor a strategy based on rigorous adherence to quantitatively stated criteria, while nonaccountants will favor a different strategy based on nonquantifiable feelings and judgments. The resulting argument can be particularly intense.

Misunderstanding.   The failure to define key terms or vague terms such as *some, few, many, success,* or *acceptable* can lead to bypassing and conflict.

Escalation.   A series of communications that can be characterized as view sharing may become disagreements and then competitions.

Conflicts can also arise from status differences between members; from a member's efforts to carry out a task without possessing the required authority; from personal idiosyncrasies; from unequal structures for rewarding or punishing members; from inappropriate or unworkable procedures, policies, or directives; from discrimination; from stress; from role conflicts that are natural within organizations (e.g., marketing manager versus cost-conscious accountant); from dual sources of authority (too many chiefs); and from different members having different goals for the group.

With so many possible sources one is compelled to view most conflict as inevitable. The accountant who seeks to avoid conflict, then, will probably not function effectively. A better approach is to learn to *monitor* conflict so that it can be identified and its source determined. Such analysis ought to allow an accountant to decide whether the conflict is functional or not (that is, whether it is a disagreement or a debate). A functional conflict fosters needed change, provides useful feedback, raises important issues that need airing, and may act to head off more disruptive maneuvers and competitions when they threaten.

Communicating to Avoid/Resolve Conflict

The cure for many conflicts is communications. Interpersonal exchanges within the group can create the kind of feedback that leads to consensus, tolerance, and the realization that victory can be defined as cooperation rather than domination. People who talk get to know each other. This involvement builds up trusting relationships, and people who trust each other obviously are better prepared to resolve conflict than those who do not. Some concrete approaches are listed below:

Create a Superordinate Goal. Assume that two accountants in a group are arguing over whether LIFO or FIFO inventory accounting is appropriate for a new acquisition. Both have cogent reasons for preferring one over the other, and the debate promises to escalate into harmful competition involving a personality clash. The group leader intervenes at this point. Instead of deciding anything or even moderating the debate, she directs both parties to work together to come up with a recommendation report within two weeks. Now both accountants are faced with a common goal and are forced to cooperate. The creation of this superordinate goal leads them to decide on LIFO with the further recommendation that a review of inventory accounting principles be held within five years and a change made if certain agreed-on criteria are not met. Communicating under the direction of the new goal has dampened their conflict and channeled it into a useful report.

Require Communicating at Fixed Intervals. Sometimes accountants work alone and really don't need to talk to other people to accomplish their tasks. But as we saw above, communicating to maintain the group is always required. A smoothly functioning work group will build such communicating into its schedule as a routine and required occurrence. It will foster group cohesion and will check conflict.

Require Informal Communicating First to Resolve Conflict. When an argument gets out of hand, people in groups quickly tend to fall back on their roles, their status, or their expertise for support. Usually such behavior is considered not playing fair. Instead, informal and open expression of differences on a human-to-human basis should be tried first.

Restate the Opponent's Views. Often the simple summarization of an opponent's points can clarify issues and resolve conflict.

Practice Open Gatekeeping. Conflict can emerge because people are not getting a chance to have their views considered—but such people may not realize that frustration rather than issue differences is the basis for their competition. A gatekeeper can give them what they really seek: time, not power.

Some communications strategies exist that are *not* usually effective in resolving conflict:

Don't Seek Binding Arbitration.   If two parties in a group are in conflict, they may go to a third member for a decision. This approach essentially rejects communicating as a resolution process and substitutes the normative process followed by an arbitrator. This person will impose a solution based on what rules say should occur rather than on what the situation requires—which could have been learned by increased communicating. Arbitrators in groups create enemies and thus foster rather than resolve conflicts.

Don't Withdraw.   Here one or both parties cease discussion and withdraw. Although cooling off periods are often worthwhile, an avoidance of communicating will not lead to conflict resolution. Sooner or later, preferably sooner, talk must begin again.

Don't Seek Majority Rule.   A work group that breaks up into "us" (a majority) and "them" will lose group cohesion and eventually break apart. Instead, ongoing discussions looking for consensus are a better tactic.

Don't Horsetrade.   Horsetrading involves the winning of a few points in return for losing a few. It differs from problem solving, which seeks to resolve conflict rather than merely ending it. Horsetrading is probably suitable for short tasks or ad hoc groups, such as audit teams that do their job and then disband. Over the long term, however, horsetrading will turn into competition as winners seek to hold their advantage and losers fight to catch up. Ongoing accountant groups thus should focus not on putting off differences but rather on resolving them.

PROBLEM SOLVING   When a group finds itself in one condition and recognizes that it needs or desires to be in another condition to accomplish its task, it must engage in problem solving. The process of problem solving is usually somewhat informal, but it follows several steps: problem identification, solution generation, evaluation of alternative solutions, solution choice, and solution implementation.

Identifying the Problem

Problems emerge either from within the group or from without. Inside the group, problems come up as the group recognizes that resources need to be used better, that the members are dissatisfied, that time is not being used well, and so on. External problems are caused by requests, suggestions, or orders

Exhibit 17.4   **MAKING AND BREAKING BARRIERS IN PROBLEM IDENTIFICATION**

COMMUNI-CATIONS BARRIER	DISRUPTING COMMUNICATIONS	COUNTERING COMMUNICATIONS
Hidden agenda of a member	A member defines the problem to foster the hidden preference or attacks other members' problem identifications.	The leader asks the member if he had some specific goal in mind that led him to define the problem in such a narrow way.
Self-authorized agenda	A member breaks into early delibera-tions and tries to get the group to go in a particular direction.	The leader engages in gatekeeping to fully analyze the situation before settling on one member's focus.
Negative emphasis	Despair—members dwell on the impossibility of dealing with the situation.	The leader emphasizes the positive dimensions of the situation and the skills and resources of the team.

from interested parties. Some common communications barriers and ways to counter them are described in Exhibit 17.4 (Boje, 1980).

Generating Solutions

Once the problem has been identified and stated as a question ("What is . . . ?" "How can we . . . ?" "Why did . . . ?") or as an objective ("To . . . .")—a process on which Americans generally spend too little time— possible solutions are discussed. These will involve manipulating people or things or changing the structure of the team in some way (e.g., getting more specialists on it). The team must ask itself:

▲   What policies, procedures, standards, or directives should guide us?

▲   Can another team serve as a model for us?

▲   Are we discussing the problem logically—that is, are our basic assumptions sensible?

▲   What are the sources of our opinions and feelings: experience, special expertise, observations, inferences?

Exhibit 17.5 describes some of the communications barriers that occur in generating solutions and suggests appropriate countermeasures.

Evaluating Alternative Solutions

The choice of a solution usually depends on maximizing the difference be-tween its costs and its benefits. In considering costs and benefits, the group should discuss the ease of implementing the solution—sometimes the best

Exhibit 17.5 **MAKING AND BREAKING BARRIERS IN SOLUTION GENERATION**

COMMUNI-CATIONS BARRIER	DISRUPTING COMMUNICATIONS	COUNTERING COMMUNICATIONS
Hard selling	A member stresses the obvious rightness of a solution while proposing it.	The leader points out that the rightness of possible solutions is not yet under discussion.
Making speeches	A member talks too much and says little.	The leader summarizes the speech in a few sentences to subtly make the point that brevity is in order.
Knocking proposed solutions	A member criticizes proposed solutions with too many "yes, but" communications.	The leader asks the criticizer to defend her objections or to explain why she is so critical.
Passive listening	Members simply allow others to talk without actively analyzing statements. They accept talking "at" instead of talking "with."	Gatekeeping—the leader asks each member for comments responding to statements.
Choosing the last	Members choose the alternative discussed last as the solution.	The leader summarizes all alternatives for the group at the end of the discussion.

course of action is too hard to implement. Also to be discussed is what could go wrong. What will happen if the group has made a mistake? How can a mistake be corrected? If a mistake cannot be corrected, the group might want to opt for another solution, one that can be modified if need be (see Exhibit 17.6).

Choosing the Solution

In the decision phase of a problem-solving interaction, the group must first decide whether it will settle for the optimal solution or for a satisfactory solution. When total agreement has not been reached and group consensus is at issue, a satisfactory solution may replace the optimal choice. The group must be careful to avoid a compromise that satisfies no one (see Exhibit 17.7).

Implementing the Solution

The group should not dump the solution into the lap of one member for implementation. It should discuss how the job can be done, who ought to do it, and what resources need to be committed (see Exhibit 17.8).

Exhibit 17.6   **MAKING AND BREAKING BARRIERS IN THE EVALUATION OF ALTERNATIVE SOLUTIONS**

COMMUNI- CATIONS BARRIER	DISRUPTING COMMUNICATIONS	COUNTERING COMMUNICATIONS
Tangling ideas with people	A member's evaluation of an idea turns into an evaluation of the person who generated the idea.	A third member cautions the group not to mix up ideas with people. Phrases like "John's idea is . . ." are replaced by "The proposal to contest the tax assessment is . . . ."
Groupthink	Members seek to be agreeable with one another rather than to evaluate solutions.	Someone lists the alternatives being evaluated and shows that although total agreement is unlikely, consensus is possible.

Exhibit 17.7   **MAKING AND BREAKING BARRIERS IN SOLUTION CHOICE**

COMMUNI- CATIONS BARRIER	DISRUPTING COMMUNICATIONS	COUNTERING COMMUNICATIONS
Hasty choosing	A member pushes for a solution because of time problems.	The leader proposes postponing the decision so that haste does not ruin the group's work.
Forcing a solution	A member speaks about a solution as if all were agreeable to it when in fact only a few are.	The leader asks each member to state his or her preferences.

Exhibit 17.8   **MAKING AND BREAKING BARRIERS IN SOLUTION IMPLEMENTATION**

COMMUNI- CATIONS BARRIER	DISRUPTING COMMUNICATIONS	COUNTERING COMMUNICATIONS
Passive agreement	Members who merely went along with the majority during the solution phase now begin to show passive hostility to the implementation.	The leader stops the process and requests that the group return to solution analysis. Alternatively, the leader questions hostile members to see if they will commit themselves to the implementation.
Lack of energy	The members are too tired to discuss ways of implementing the solution.	The leader postpones implementation or assigns it to another group.

MAKING A DECISION Peter Drucker (1973) makes the point that information and communication are two different entities:

Information	Communication
Objective	Subjective
Logical	Perceptual
Often formal	Often informal
Specific	General or contextual
A thing	A process

Decision making in a group is a communication process dealing with information and manipulating it in various ways. The information—especially financial information—cries out for highly formal, logical, objective treatment, but the group may process it in a highly idiosyncratic manner that can lead to seemingly irrational decisions. This is a risk every organization faces when it fosters work groups to accomplish tasks. Audit teams, for example, may decide that the internal controls of a client are sound even though the information clearly indicates problems. Perhaps the team has consulted its collective feelings and experience rather than the evidence in making its decision. Perhaps it has allowed one member, whose opinion is thoroughly wrong, to dominate its decision. Perhaps it allowed time pressure to overwhelm it so that any decision became better than no decision. For these and a hundred other reasons, groups can do dumb things with smart data. Let's look at what groups must do to govern their decision making:

▲ *Base decisions on standards, not on member positions.* When groups discuss standards or criteria for making decisions, they will analyze alternatives. When they discuss alternatives without the guidance of clear standards or procedure, they will analyze member positions. In the first instance, communications are characterized by premises, conclusions, and inferences. In the second, attitudes and demands prevail, followed by concession making and horsetrading. Standards lead to communications based on reason; a lack of standards leads to communications based on power.

▲ *Recognize that information on which to base a decision is rarely total.* A collection of competent and experienced accountants in a group can lull itself into a feeling of information mastery because of its collective feelings of expertise. As such, the group's decisions will have no stochastic dimension. That is, the group will tend to behave as if the probability were 1.0 that its decision is the right one. In these cases, no second-choice alternatives will be considered and no actions will be planned in case anything goes wrong.

A posture of information mastery can also lead to illusory unanimity in which members believe that, since the group knows all, each member must know all and therefore agree with the others regarding group decisions. The false assumption here is that total knowing leads to total agreement. Even if total information were available (which is rarely the case), total agreement need not necessarily occur, because individuals process information in different ways, leading to different opinions and conclusions. Groups laboring under the assumption that total knowing leads to total agreement will not admit the possibility of disagreement or debate. Communications within the group and decisions coming from the group will have a sense of authoritativeness, certainty, and objectivity about them—when in fact they should have been tentative, probabilistic, and somewhat subjective.

The solution to these problems is for group members to stress the importance of information gathering. As we saw in Chapter 1, accountants are both information gatherers *and* information processors. Groups that process information should also constantly focus on gathering it.

REDUCING STRESS When demands made on a group match or exceed the group's resources, stress occurs. Not all stress is bad, since a good deal of research over the years suggests that groups can operate at peak effectiveness when under stress. The problem is that when stress goes on for too long or begins to increase, groups sometimes will disintegrate. Thus while the benefits of stress are well known, the magnitude of the risks make stress-controlling communications particularly important (Kahn and Quinn, 1970; Caplan et al., 1975).

Communications that reduce or control stress in small work groups involve (1) messages that lead members to feel they are part of a network of people who understand and help each other; (2) messages that seek input regarding decisions to be made; (3) messages that increase members' certainty about the near future; and (4) messages that help reduce information overload. Essentially, then, stress control requires communications that encourage trust, participation, and a sense of belonging; that set out work schedules well ahead of time; and that condense and integrate raw data as much as possible. This last point is important for audit teams, which must depend on experts feeding them information from the base office. Instead of simply xeroxing various AICPA, SEC, FASB, IRS, and so on, pronouncements, specialists would do well to draw up summaries (properly noted) that would not overburden field people.

Checkoff 17.1 **ACCOUNTING COMMUNICATIONS: COMMUNICATING IN SMALL GROUPS**

DEVELOPING GROUP COMMUNICATING SKILLS	YES	NO
1. Does the group concentrate on building and maintaining task-oriented behavior and does it avoid blocking?	____	____
2. Does the group understand that egocentric, power-oriented behavior may not be deliberate self-aggrandizement but rather unconscious, culturally determined behavior common in America?	____	____
3. Does the group try to avoid fostering excessively conforming behavior by members without allowing anarchic individualism?	____	____
4. Has the group spent enough time in the planning phase of its task?	____	____
5. Is the group careful not to let task-oriented communicating overwhelm maintenance communicating?	____	____
6. Is the team leader aware of the complex communicating skills she must master and exhibit?	____	____
7. Does the leader realize that task-oriented communicating should predominate under conditions of high stress, low worker ability, high leader power, good leader–staff relations, and highly structured tasks?	____	____
8. Does the leader realize that maintenance communicating should be given prominence when stress is low, staff are skilled, the leader's power is shaky, leader–group relations are poor, and tasks are unstructured?	____	____
9. Does the team leader understand that in a group learning situation he does the talking, while in a performing situation he does the listening?	____	____
10. Has the leader avoided having her orders misinterpreted as suggestions?	____	____
11. Does the leader recognize that his power rests on his skill at communicating (1) to build trust and (2) to develop an image of expertise?	____	____
12. When conflict occurs, does the group differentiate between healthy (debates and disagreements) and unhealthy (competitions and maneuvers) conflict?	____	____
13. Does the group recognize the value of issue-oriented conflict and the harm of personality conflict?	____	____
14. Does the group understand that conflict is inevitable and as such should be controlled rather than avoided?	____	____

(continued)

374

Checkoff 17.1 (*concluded*)

		YES	NO
15.	Has the group based its decisions on standards rather than on member positions?	_____	_____
16.	Has the group realized that it probably does not possess total information and that information gathering should be an ongoing process?	_____	_____

Organizational Accounting Communications

chapter 18

Every accountant works within some kind of organization, be it a public accounting firm, a small business, or a giant corporation. All these entities are similar in that they are made up of various communications networks through which travel predictable kinds of messages. In this chapter we consider the flow of such messages, especially between superiors and subordinates within networks. We also discuss important issues of feedback and overload, as well as several problems associated with conflicts between organizational needs and the need for communications to be specific, realistic, authentic-seeming messages full of unambiguous content reasonably congruent with a reader/listener's expectations.

TYPES OF ORGANIZATIONAL MESSAGES Within organizations accountants send and receive several types of communications, including service, innovation, and maintenance messages.

Service Messages

Service messages are the most common type of organizational communications. These messages contain the financial and other information required to carry out the organization's goals. Among the functions they serve are:

- ▲ *Planning*—Prescribing or describing goals, objectives, policies, procedures, and controls;
- ▲ *Organizing*—Prescribing specific tasks to accomplish the organization's goals, objectives, and so on;
- ▲ *Directing*—Assigning and coordinating tasks;
- ▲ *Collecting*—Requesting information to accomplish tasks;
- ▲ *Controlling*—Requesting information on task accomplishments to measure performance;
- ▲ *Reporting*—Describing and evaluating activities;
- ▲ *Deciding*—Solving problems and making conclusions.

Innovation Messages

Innovation messages generate information used to improve services. A problem exists here in that innovation messages often do not get translated into service messages. The accountant who communicates a new way of reporting changes in fixed costs so as to reduce those costs may find that service messages directing changes in reporting do not get sent or are not sent in the way intended. Often an organization needs some kind of person, unit, or committee whose charge it is to receive innovation messages and to stimulate or issue service messages. In a controller's office, for example, that charge might be carried out by the director of accounting methods.

Maintenance Messages

Chapter 17 pointed out the importance of maintenance messages for small work groups. In the whole organization these messages serve to keep the organization functioning. They involve the establishment and maintenance of interpersonal relations and the motivation of employees (see Chapter 19 for a discussion of this activity). In addition, messages sent simply to open or to keep open a communications channel can be considered as maintenance.

As noted earlier, maintenance messages are often ignored by accountants as parts of the formal communications within the organization. They are relegated to the informal communications system and as such are not made routinely or under the direction of policy or procedure. This casual approach to maintenance is probably the biggest failing of modern management accounting. If maintenance messages are not regularly sent, the following situations are likely to occur:

▲   Personnel will not learn to trust each other. Work efficiency will decline.

▲   Personnel will not be motivated to perform effectively.

▲   Channels to key people that need to be open in a crisis will not be open.

If people do not know each other, their ability to send service messages satisfying the criteria of specificity, reality, authenticity, nonambiguity, and congruency will be severely curtailed. Without satisfying these criteria, messages will not cause the actions they are supposed to, and work will not get done as well or as fast as it should.

Take the case of the inventory manager who has calculated a reorder point for raw materials incorporating a safety stock based on past variations in the sales of the finished product. Now assume that he gets a memo from the assistant controller suggesting that safety stock should be based on production rather than on sales. If the inventory manager knows the assistant controller and has built up and maintains an interpersonal relationship with her, he will probably trust her and be motivated to comply with her suggestion for the sake of their good working relationship. However, if they do not know each other well and have not established strong channels of communication, he may refrain from complying and instead send a memo requesting justification. When her second memo comes in, he may then send a rebuttal memo. When the controller's third memo comes back, he may call and request a meeting for clarification. All of these could take weeks or even months. If maintenance communications had been a regular part of their interactions, however, the first service message would have been the only one sent. The upshot of all this is clearly that *maintenance messages make service messages effective and reduce the number of service messages that need to be sent.*

Other Messages

Service messages, innovation messages, and maintenance messages are all parts of a *formal* communications system within an organization, the object of which is to help carry out the organization's tasks. But accountants and other personnel also send other messages that satisfy personal rather than organizational needs. These messages make up part of the *informal* communications system. They are no less necessary than formal messages, because humans cannot perform adequately unless they are reasonably free to make such communications. The organization must often tolerate the following:

Belief/Attitude/Opinion Messages.   These are often sent to satisfy some personal need or desire unconnected with the organization's needs.

Power-Seeking Messages. Some people seek power in organizations for deep-rooted cultural and psychological reasons having nothing to do with the firm's needs.

Emotional Messages. Sometimes people must scream, either literally or figuratively. Women may cry and men may shout, and both ought to be acceptable as long as they do not interfere with the flow of formal messages (this is a simple and workable standard for deciding whether emotional outbursts can be tolerated or not). Indeed, most experienced managers know that emotions must usually be allowed to be vented. Interestingly, however, female accountants probably will not be allowed to shout or male accountants to cry. Thus sex roles have a great deal to do with just how tolerant the organization will be regarding emotions.

Contemplative Messages. The "what if" kinds of communications may be formally useful as innovations. Often they are simply idle speculations of no value. Yet such thinking out loud ought to be accepted as fostering the kind of informal environment out of which formal innovations can flow.

NETWORKS All formal and informal messages travel across certain groupings of channels called networks. Accountants must be members of a number of networks if they are to function within an organization.

Accounting Networks

Accountants within an organization are not free to communicate formally with anyone they wish. Well-defined networks exist, and accountants must follow the various stated and implied rules for using them.

Authority Networks

An analyst in profit planning, for example, cannot simply walk into the controller's office to offer an innovative new way to accomplish a task. She must send a written message through what can be called an authority network, and the message must travel along a channel through various hierarchical levels in the accounting department before the controller gets it. Most organizations require a rigid adherence to authority network rules—and for a good reason. If the network breaks down because few obey the rules, the chain of command also breaks down and the work of the organization ceases. Junior accountants thus violate authority network rules at their peril.

Expertise Networks

Accountants generally play the role of "expert" within their firms. As such they will be consulted by nonexperts seeking guidance. As accountants share expertise with each other so that they can respond to such requests, they form strong communication links that emerge collectively as a network. Accountants from all over an organization, from many different departments, and with many different functions may have strong ties among themselves that foster even more communicating within their expertise network than between them and their nonexpert superiors. One can see the threat to authority networks here. If the staff accountant is doing most of her talking with other accountants, she may not be talking enough with her boss.

Information Networks

Other networks involve information exchange. These are sometimes called *horizontal trading relationships.* What happens is that as accountants do most of their communicating within authority and expertise networks, they tend to lose touch with other managers of equal status and rank who are not accountants but who need accounting information. The classic case in corporations concerns financial analysts. Often they need to know changes occurring in accounting methods and procedures because the data they use in their analysis is sometimes affected by the changes. But because they are not accountants (experts) or bosses (authorities), they find it hard to learn what the accountants are doing. To improve the flow of information to them, they will begin communicating horizontally within the controller's department to establish a relationship with the accounting methods people. In return for the information they get, they may offer their own data for whatever use the accountants have for it. This trading constitutes an information network. Its function is to reduce uncertainty not reduced by authority or expert network membership. Indeed, even if such information is coming through authority networks, it may lack the sense of authenticity it gains when coming through an information network. Everyone always wants to hear things from the horse's mouth.

Friendship Networks

The least formal are friendship networks. No organizational task-oriented purpose is served by most messages within this network. Rather it serves a maintenance function. As we noted above, maintenance messages ought to be formal parts of an organization's communications system, and the degree to which friendship networks are formally established is an indicator of how seriously the senior management believes in maintenance.

Organizational Height

As accounting information travels upward within organizations, it can be changed by receivers before being passed along to higher levels; the higher it goes, the more likely it is to be changed. This phenomenon is the *serial transmission effect.* Let's say the chief systems analyst writes a memo to the manager of accounting systems that reveals a costly, time-consuming flow in a control operation. The manager in turn writes a memo to the assistant controller for systems and computers revealing the flaw and stressing the resources being consumed in carrying out the control procedure. The assistant controller writes to the controller, describing the control activity and the difficulty of carrying it out with present resources. The controller in turn requests an increased budget allocation to cover the difficult procedure. What began as a request for a change in procedure ended as a request for funds to ensure that the procedure didn't change. This is the serial transmission effect.

What causes this effect? Among the most common causes is the tendency of intermediary receivers to:

- ▲ Simplify the original information;
- ▲ Speculate to fill in gaps or incomprehensible parts;
- ▲ Accentuate or mute problems more than was originally intended;
- ▲ Add favorable connotations.

In the example above the intermediaries muted the problem and added connotations to make the situation less problematical.

What can be done? Two of the most effective ways for an individual to control for serial transmission effects are (1) to employ redundancy, so that senior people get the information either from more than one source or over more than one channel; and (2) to write different memos for different levels. The systems analyst could have sent his original memo to his manager, casually mentioned the needed change to the controller in an informal setting, and sent a separate report to the controller in addition to the memo to his boss. In this way the original message would have gotten through as intended. These procedures will work for individuals, but if *everyone* is practicing redundancy, problems will occur. We will discuss these next.

The flatness or tallness of an organizational hierarchy has much to do with the amount of message distortion that occurs. An organization of short height, such as a public accounting firm, will enjoy little distortion of messages traveling upward from staff to managing partners. The problem, however, is that communications channels and senior people can become overburdened with information as lower-level people practice redundancy. Indeed, as these lower-level accountants see that their information is having difficulty getting through, they will tend to increase messages (this is redundancy to get through, not to avoid distortion). The senior people can become deluged. This overload problem seems to be quite common in public firms. The messages are not distorted, but there are too many of them for partners to handle.

Most large organizations were once small. They grew in height in response to the problem of clogged channels and overloaded senior managers. By establishing intermediary levels to handle routine decisions, the senior people relieved themselves of message burden, but of course they opened themselves to message distortion. Some techniques to control distortion involve such things as suggestion boxes, surveys, and ombudsmen. All these techniques allow messages from below to get to the top without passing through all levels of the organization. Let's go back to the case of the systems analyst who wanted a control procedure changed to save time and money. Instead of sending duplicate messages or using informal channels, he could have simply waited for an improvement-seeking survey he knew would circulate every two months. The message would get through undistorted, and it would not have clogged channels in doing so. He would not have had to practice redundancy to avoid distortion or to complete the communication.

In sum, then, the serial transmission effect (distortion) does not occur in organizations of small height. Their problem is messages not getting through in any form. To solve the problem, lower-level people will increase messages in the hope that a trickle of information will get through. The resulting overload will lead to a growth in organizational height as authority is delegated. Now the serial transmission effect occurs as intermediary people distort messages. One solution is redundancy of messages; but a better approach is the use of surveys or suggestion boxes. In the real world, young auditors who shift from small public accounting firms to large corporations will have to learn to shift from dealing with the problem of managing and audit partners not reading their memos or not returning their telephone calls to controllers not getting the information from them as it was originally intended.

The Grapevine and Rumors

Informal communications channels are called "the grapevine" when the messages traveling on them are rumors. A rumor is simply an unsubstantiated feeling, belief, attitude, opinion, or judgment that may or may not be factual. Although they get distorted as they travel from person to person, rumors generally are realistic in that they often do reduce uncertainty about a situation. If rumors did not generally have some truth to them, they would not thrive as they do in organizations. The real problems with rumors are that:

▲ One can never tell just what parts of rumors are true and what false;

▲ Rumors travel faster than formal messages do;

▲ Rumors can link up networks better than formal linking devices can;

▲ Rumors are often exciting and thus provide a more satisfying kind of communicating than formal message sending does.

In terms of the criteria for message effectiveness described in Chapter 1, rumors are partially effective because they are congruent; that is, they tend to confirm or deal with listener expectations. The more they confirm expectations, the stronger they become, the further they travel, and the longer they last. However, they must be considered generally ineffective because rarely is there any specific intent behind their transmission. A good communication has someone behind it in control of it.

Generally rumors thrive when employee expectations are not being met or dealt with by messages traveling on formal channels. When employees expect to receive a pay raise, yet no information comes to them in memos or newsletters from senior managers, rumors will flow. When employees expect a new management information system to be developed, yet management curtly and carelessly reaffirms its commitment to the current system, rumors of glaring failures in the system may begin to circulate. In specific terms, then, rumors will be a part of an organization:

▲ Where secrecy prevails;

▲ Where formal channels are inadequate, faulty, or little used;

▲ Where mutual trust among superiors or subordinates is absent;

▲ Where employees are worried or frustrated.

All these situations involve failure to address the communication expectations of employees.

The senior people in an organization cannot tolerate excessive rumor flow. They risk the growing disuse and decay of the formal channels and networks. What accounting department, for example, could function when directives from the controller were to be obeyed only when messages received from the grapevine during coffee breaks indicated that it really was okay to go ahead and implement the formal order? When rumors become reliable and relevant, formal messages become unreliable and irrelevant. What can be done to control rumors? One solution, practiced much in Washington, D.C., is the leak—a counterrumor started to fill up the grapevine channels with factual information replacing vague or untrue rumors. At the same time or shortly thereafter, a formal message can reveal the same facts.

Another approach is to build up the trust of subordinates. People who feel that they can trust their superiors do not feel uncertain about the future and do not engage in rumor mongering to reduce uncertainty. Take the accounting manager who seeks to stop morale-destroying rumors of radical decreases being forecast in staff size. She will tell subordinates what projections have in fact been made and what alternative actions are being considered. If she has built up a climate of trust over time, her information will be accepted as reliable.

Personnel in the organization who are focal points for informal communications and rumors—secretaries, for example—can be transformed into receivers and senders of formal information. Thus the secretary often hears bits and pieces of conversations of his or her boss and carelessly passes such tidbits along to other secretaries at lunch. Rumors begin this way in the form of inaccurate and distorted information. But what if the secretary is asked to attend meetings and to take minutes or notes? Now she hears all and hears it in an official capacity. If she is authorized to pass on specific, nonsensitive information to other personnel who approach her, her messages will become formal. Rumors do not flow along formal channels.

Other rumor control activities will involve increased formal electronic communicating. Since one of the attractions of rumors is the speed at which they travel, the use of high-speed, formal electronic communicating may tend to dampen rumor spreading. In the future such innovations as teleconferencing, electronic memos, and word processing may foster increased formal message transmissions. These will get information to people that deals with their needs and expectations more rapidly and easily than catch-as-catch-can rumors do.

Uses of Informal Networks

Left to their own devices, people in organizations will create informal networks that vary considerably from formal authority networks. Exhibit 18.1 shows a typical informal audit team network that would probably emerge from the formal net in the absence of strict enforcement of communications procedures. This informal system is probably more valuable when complex, nonroutine problems must be dealt with, such as what to do about a detected defalcation. For routine matters, however, the formal system probably is best, as it protects the manager from possible overload. The skilled accountant must be able to decide when to use or not to use the informal networks in her organization. In addition to using them for complex, nonroutine messages, she should also turn to informal channels (1) to test formal messages before sending them (she can get "feedforward" and can build consensus in this way) and (2) to add redun-

Exhibit 18.1 **FORMAL AND INFORMAL AUTHORITY NETWORK**

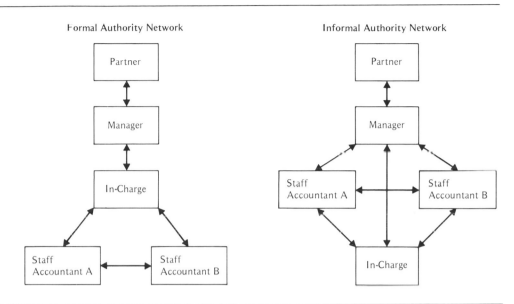

dancy to formal messages and thus to increase their chances of getting through and having the desired effect.

Group Structure

Ten people in a work group acting interdependently will communicate across forty-five different channels (person 1 with person 2, person 1 with person 3, person 2 with person 3, etc.). We can visualize their work area as filled with imaginary wires (communications channels) crisscrossing the space between all possible one-on-one communications. The potential for inaccurate, unheard, or unread messages obviously is high. If, however, the ten people are assigned to two work groups of five each, the available channels decrease to twenty:

> Group A = 10 Channels
> Group B = 10 Channels
> Total = 20 Channels
> (Potential channels $= N(N - 1)/2$, where N is the number of people in a group)

If we add on a channel from group A to group B so that the leader of A can coordinate with the leader of B, the total is increased to twenty-one, still dramatically reduced from forty-five.

The establishment of subgroups within an organization cuts available communications channels and reduces noise within the system. With less noise one could expect more accurate messages to flow and a greater part of total messages to be successfully transmitted to receivers. Every organization strives for this kind of achievement, since the possibility of key communications not getting through or not being understood correctly must be reduced if the organization is to survive. Indeed, as we will see below, organizations whose survival is or may be threatened often move to create elaborate networks of coordinators and countless work groups. One thinks of the U.S. Army or of Chrysler Corporation in this context.

We can see then that the control of communications channels and their growth is essential to organizational functioning. Saying this, however, does not imply that the organization should cut channels down to some bare minimum, since at some point the system would suffer overload—with a corresponding increase in messages not being successfully transmitted. At points on a continuum near both the maximum and the minimum numbers of channels, then, communication effectiveness is threatened. The best number of channels lies somewhere in between and is a function of the demands of the work environment. In times of threat to the organization—such as when revenues are down sharply due to a recession or loss of clients—more channels are needed than in normal times. This channel expansion probably would soon require more small-group formation and coordinating.

In an accounting firm suffering from declining revenues due to increased competition, we would expect to see channels expand as partners, seniors, managers, and staff desperately consult each other and other employees, seeking ideas for improving revenues. As communications become noisy— evidenced by telephone calls not getting through, memos running astray, and meetings being adjourned without adequate resolution—the firm would act to cut channels by forming various task groups coordinated by several levels of leaders. One group might study ways of getting new clients, while another would work on providing new services to old clients. A manager might be appointed to each group, and they would report to a partner in charge of several groups. A senior partner would receive reports from the partners coordinating all task groups. When the crisis had passed and revenues improved, the number of channels to be controlled through work group formation would diminish, and most of the groups would disband. People who rarely talked to each other before the crisis would return to their old habits of not talking to each other.

Exhibit 18.2 describes the impact of a crisis on an organization's communications channels and the corresponding change in the number of work groups and coordinators. The model can help us solve the following problem. Suppose two managers each supervise three work groups. Because of declin-

Exhibit 18.2 **THE IMPACT OF A CRISIS ON CHANNELS AND GROUPS**

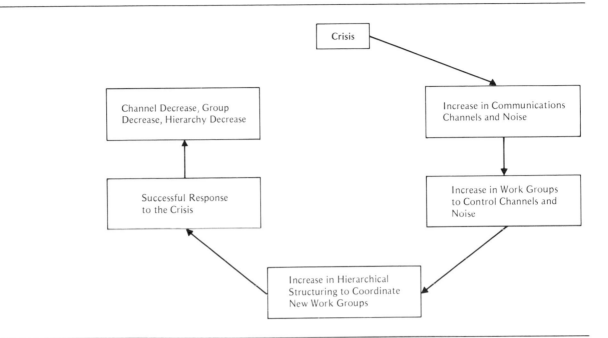

ing revenues, a layoff of accountants must occur. Should a few from each of the groups go (solution A) or should a few whole groups be eliminated (solution B)? The model indicates that work groups will be needed during the crisis to control expanded communications channels. Thus solution A (cutting a few from each group) should be followed and groups kept intact:

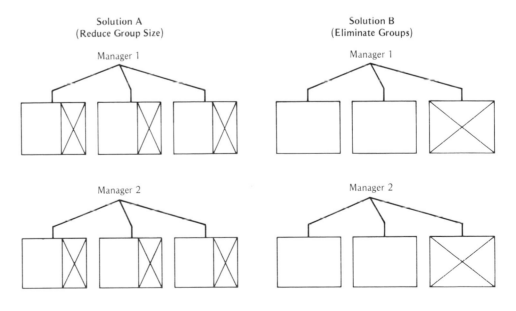

Assume that each of the six work groups has six people in it. Now let us assess the impact of a layoff of twelve people in terms of each solution:

Solution A (Reduce Group Size)	Before Change	After Change	
Interaction channels per group	15	6	
Number of groups	6	6	
Total intragroup channels	90	36	
Intergroup channels	5	5	
Total communications channels	95	41	
Reduction			54
Solution B (Eliminate Groups)			
Interaction channels per group	15	15	
Number of groups	6	4	
Total intragroup channels	90	60	
Intergroup channels	5	3	
Total communications channels	95	63	
Reduction			32

In this case reducing group size (A) is the preferred solution from an organizational communications point of view, since channels are reduced the greatest and therefore the likelihood of inaccurate, incomplete, and ineffective messages is reduced the most. As noted above, there is some minimum limit beyond which one would not want to reduce channels, but generally organizational communications are best served by reducing group size rather than by eliminating groups.

ORGANIZATIONAL SPACE

In an open field the farther apart two people get, the more difficult it will be for them to communicate. An increase in the physical space between them is the cause. In organizations it is useful to think of the concept of "organizational space," which includes several elements in addition to physical distance (Katz and Kahn, 1978):

- ▲ *Physical distance*—How far apart two people or two units are in an organization;
- ▲ *Function distance*—How different two entities are with respect to interests, tasks, terminology, and problems;
- ▲ *Position distance*—How far apart white collar is versus blue collar, staff versus line, and so on;
- ▲ *Power distance*—How far apart two entities are in the hierarchy.

The greater the "distance" between an accountant and someone else within organizational space, the less communicating they will do and the less efficient and effective will be their messages. A junior staff accountant from the head office will have a difficult time talking to a production plant manager based at a different location. The differences in space, function, position, and power (the manager is higher up) will cause enormous problems for the two of them as they try to set up and conduct meetings with each other. The organizational space between them is too great.

Organizational space problems can be dealt with in several ways. Often a reduction in one element's distance can be accomplished by manipulating another element:

▲ *Physical distance* (the accountant is based at the home office and the manager at the plant)—Change the power distance by appointing the junior accountant to an important liaison position *at the plant.*

▲ *Function distance* (the accountant's tasks are different from the production manager's)—The change in physical distance will involve the accountant more in production and the manager more in accounting controls.

▲ *Position distance* (the manager is a production person and the accountant is a staff person)—The change in physical distance attaches the accountant more to the production function.

▲ *Power distance* (the manager is higher up in the organization than the accountant is)—As the accountant's production knowledge grows and his position distance from the manager diminishes, his value as a problem-solving link to the home office will grow. He will be included in decision making, and his status will increase.

The goal of controllers should be to reduce the distance in organizational space between their accountants and the rest of the organization's personnel. There are many ways to accomplish the goal, but the end result will be the same: better communications between the controller's office and the rest of the organization.

**SUPERIOR–
SUBORDINATE
COMMUNICATIONS**

The communications that flow between accounting superiors (controllers, assistant controllers, managers, partners, seniors) and their subordinates (analysts, planners, methods specialists, auditors, systems people, consultants, secretaries) are often described in terms of (1) interpersonal relations, (2) quality of information transmitted, and (3) opportunities for communicating. In research conducted by the author, for example, computer services managers appear to have excellent relations with controllers and plenty of opportunities to communicate. What bothers them is the poor quality of information they get from their superiors. Exhibit 18.3 describes specific conditions within each category that determine the overall success of such communications.

Exhibit 18.3 **CONDITIONS INFLUENCING SUPERIOR– SUBORDINATE COMMUNICATIONS**

SUPERIOR– SUBORDINATE RELATIONS

▲ Trust and confidence are mutual.

▲ Understanding is mutual.

▲ Each respects other's competence.

▲ Each admires other's effort.

▲ Subordinate can deliver bad news without fear.

▲ Candor is mutual.

▲ Superior allows occasional emotional outburst.

▲ Superior tolerates arguing.

▲ Superior stands up for subordinate.

▲ Superior is good listener.

▲ Superior makes subordinate feel important.

▲ Subordinate welcomes performance evaluation.

QUALITY OF INFORMATION

▲ Task requirements are specific.

▲ Advance notice of change is given.

▲ Notice of goals is given.

▲ Performance evaluations are accurate.

▲ Updating is ongoing.

▲ Information is freely available.

▲ Directions are explained.

OPPORTUNITY TO COMMUNICATE

▲ Subordinate goals are requested.

▲ Subordinate input counts.

▲ Nonroutine communications are tolerated.

▲ Informal channels are used.

In the study noted above, computer services managers felt that their controllers did not exchange information freely with them, did not inform them of accounting department goals, did not provide ongoing updating of information, did not notify them early enough of relevant change, did not give them specific task instructions, and did not evaluate performance adequately. These managers apparently had been left to function almost autonomously, and while they enjoyed their freedom, they would have much preferred more direction.

Upward Communicating

Subordinates provide superiors both with information designed to reduce uncertainty during decision making and with innovative ideas for change. They initiate requests for directions, as well as signal their need for maintenance messages. Their messages will be effective, timely, and thorough to the degree that they *trust* their superior and feel *secure* in their jobs (Roberts and O'Reilly, 1974; Athanassiades, 1973). A sense of trust involves the feeling that the superior's behavior toward the subordinate will be sincere, consistent, and predictable. Moreover, subordinates who sense that no threat to their jobs exists will be more forthcoming with information than those who are worried about their position.

The information transmitted to superiors generally is data oriented and factual. Sometimes, however, inferential language is called for when a subordinate has been asked for an opinion, a judgment, an assessment, an evaluation, or a recommendation. Inferences describe feelings and assumptions in place of describing things, people, places, or processes. Unfortunately, as we saw in Chapter 12, inferences often take the place of objective observing in the same way that bad money drives out good money. Inferential communicating, whether good or bad, uses label words (*reliable, effective, efficient, successful,* etc.). These are evaluative words, not observation-oriented words.

Even when subordinates avoid careless inferences, problems can occur as their communications travel upward. For example, a staff accountant says in his memo to his supervisor:

> The inventory control clerk often takes on the duties of his manager when the manager is busy. In doing so he must put off his own work for 2–3 hours.

He is describing behavior. The accountant's supervisor, in discussing inventory control procedures and personnel with the controller, may report:

> The inventory control clerk is hard working and shows initiative.

Here a description of observed behavior became an evaluative inference as it traveled upward in the organization.

This changing of observation to inference is not necessarily bad, as concise inferences must sometimes take the place of long descriptions of observations. However, the risk of faulty communicating can be great. What if the same superior told the controller:

> The inventory clerk is often absent from his duties.

Such an inference is negative and probably faulty in that it does not reflect what was actually observed by the accountant.

The upshot of all this is that senior people receiving inferential information from subordinates should often demand support evidence in the form of observations or collected statistics. If they don't, they may eventually find that they really are not in touch with actual events occurring at lower organizational levels—too often good observations have turned into bad inferences somewhere along the path upward to them.

Downward Communicating

Superiors send messages to subordinates concerning directives, advice, instructions, suggestions, requests for information, evaluation, and maintenance of good relations. Their communications also involve motivation and indoctrination in corporate philosophy and goals. All in all, they initiate more communications with a greater number of people across a greater range of networks than subordinates do. Indeed, superiors generally receive more compensation than subordinates do because their work requires higher-order communication skills. Nevertheless, research suggests that managers often do not communicate with subordinates as well as they think they do.

Accounting managers and partners may not realize that their subordinates feel they are not receiving adequate information from above. What causes these problems for subordinates? Among many causes are (1) the habit of management only informing key people of changes, (2) routing problems of memos, (3) the managers' desire to communicate brief messages, (4) a lack of well-developed informal channels, and (5) a focus on routine message transmissions rather than on need-oriented transmissions. A competent accounting manager would want to do the following to protect herself from subordinate perceptions of poor communicating:

▲ Periodically examine memo routing to see that communications channels exist with all staff;

▲ Work to establish informal relations with staff—at lunches, training seminars, parties, coffee breaks, and the like;

▲ Analyze written communications to see that a desire for brevity does not overwhelm the goal of being reader oriented;

▲ Avoid creating small problems that cover up more serious issues;

▲ Avoid asking for advice and then ignoring or belittling it.

If subordinates know what is expected of them, they will feel that their communications with superiors are good. Sometimes, however, superiors protect themselves by being vague or ambiguous about required subordinate activities; then if problems arise, responsibility can be shifted to the subordinate:

▲ *Wrong*—"You might need to perform only a few tests on X."

▲ *Right*—"I want you to perform three tests on X: . . . ."

Every task-oriented communication from a superior must carry with it the connotation that the superior is accepting responsibility as the originator of the action to be performed. A clear statement of what is wanted not only makes the employee's task easier, but it also signals that he will not have to take the blame if it turns out that the action should not have been undertaken.

Exhibit 18.4 **THREE MANAGERIAL ATTITUDES**

TRADITIONAL ATTITUDE	HUMAN RELATIONS ATTITUDE	HUMAN RESOURCES ATTITUDE
Employees do not deliberately choose to work.	Employees will work to avoid boredom.	Employees see work as natural.
Employees need to be coerced to work hard.	Employees can be made to work hard if adequate incentives are provided.	Employees will work hard when they are self-directed and committed to do the work.
Employees do not like responsibility and want to be told what to do.	Employees do not want responsibility but do want their ideas to be listened to.	Employees seek responsibility for their actions.

Finally, a superior's communications are influenced greatly by her assumptions about employees in the workplace. Exhibit 18.4 describes three sets of attitudes that a superior might have toward workers (Peterson and Tracy, 1979).

Each of these attitudes toward subordinates will influence the accountant's communications. Thus holders of the traditional attitude will mostly tell employees what to do and warn them what may happen if the work is not done well. Accountants with the human relations attitude will talk over the work with subordinates, then issue directions, and finally offer a reward for successful performance. Holders of the human resources attitude will describe the goals and objectives of the organization and then will let employees develop concrete activity plans for carrying out the objectives.

Many accountants probably hold the human relations attitude but often communicate with employees as if they were traditionalists. If so, miscommunication is occurring, since the employees will tend to perceive the accountant as thinking less of them than he indeed does. Morale may drop. The accountant, accustomed to sending crisp, goal-directed, task-oriented messages to other accountants, may respond with bewilderment, unaware that such messages may signal nonaccountant subordinates that he has an unfavorable image of them.

The solution, of course, is for the accountant to talk over the day's tasks with his staff of bookkeepers, clerks, secretaries, and so on—seeking their ideas on the work and offering proper incentives and the chance for increased responsibility. The employees will sense his favorable attitude toward them. Moreover, they may perform well to boot.

FEEDBACK The tasks of an accounting organization involve activities that are responses to either (1) rules, procedures, standards, or schedules, or (2) to feedback communications. Rarely can an organization establish enough rules to cover every needed activity, so feedback channels must be established to tell accounting staff how they are doing and what changes they must make. An auditor's activities, for example, are highly rule directed, but her success must depend in the final analysis on how well she responds to messages from clients, peers, and superiors that evaluate and seek modifications to her past actions.

Feedback works best when it is solicited rather than imposed. An auditor would want to actively seek information concerning his future work and should be prepared to act immediately on receipt of such feedback. If he doesn't use it, the senders will become cynical regarding their importance in his scheme of things. The same holds true for all accountants, not just auditors. Feedback becomes especially useful:

▲ When new procedures are instituted,

▲ When the environment is unpredictable,

▲ When crises exist.

Generally the more feedback available (up to an overload point), the better management decisions will be implemented (Meddaugh, 1976).

SETTING POLICY Large organizations, which are not willing to suffer the risk of uncertain feedback mechanisms to control task implementation, often turn to elaborate rules, policies, and procedures to govern task activities. To maintain an image of credibility gained through formal behavior of auditors on audit jobs, small public accounting firms also may institute rules and policies. Thus feedback uncertainty and a desire to formalize employee behavior are strong underlying causes of rule and policy development. There is nothing particularly wrong in this. However, organizations with good maintenance communications, strong informal channels, superior–subordinate trust, and a highly professional staff probably do not need many policies and work rules and may well function more efficiently without them. With the exception of highly professional staffs, Japanese firms are thought to be exemplars of organizations with characteristics that eliminate the need for bureaucratic policies and rules. Ouchi (1980) calls them "industrial clans."

COPING WITH OVERLOAD Managers never cease their demands for financial information useful in making decisions, even when an overload point is reached and information processing becomes impossible. Probably the financial measures are not sought (after overload occurs) so much for analysis as they are for legitimizing guessing. If a manager has printouts and reports sitting on her desk, she will feel more confident in her snap judgments even though there are not enough hours in the day to consult all the data. The accounting staff generating such data must realize that rarely will overloaded managers admit they are not using the data provided for analysis. It is up to the staff, then, to take matters into their own hands and to dole out reports in such a way that they will be used to reduce uncertainty rather than to validate guessing born of quasi-rational, rule-of-thumb inference making.

Causes of Overload

It is remarkably easy to overload a manager. Here are some situations that can lead to overload:

▲   Sending of misplaced or misdirected messages that require correction messages;

▲   Repeating of messages to overcome channel bottlenecks;

▲   Routine sending of routine messages that do not reduce uncertainty—that state the known and the obvious;

▲   Growth in task interdependence;

▲   Sending of messages to people that ought to be sent to files;

▲   Crisis in the organization;

▲   Poorly planned technological improvements (e.g., word processing, electronic reports);

▲   Growth in organizational complexity.

Picture the plight of an assistant controller for planning. His firm has cash flow problems, and he sits in on several ad hoc groups developing cost-cutting strategies. Moreover, a new word-processing capability in the controller's organization has resulted in a speedup in the rate at which he gets reports. In addition, several of his unit chiefs routinely send him copies of memos they have written for the files as well as original memos stating that they have accomplished tasks he already knew had been done. To top it all off, the controller has found it necessary to require him to coordinate his work with the assistant controller for systems and computers. He is indeed a busy man, spending most of his day talking in small groups, reading reports and memos, coordinating with the other assistant controller on the telephone and in face-to-face meetings, reporting to the controller, and directing subordinates (with some maintenance and trust building added on occasionally). If any more information begins to arrive before his notice, he will as likely as not be unable to deal with it—yet he will make decisions as if he had dealt with it simply by resorting to rule-of-thumb behavior of the kind described in Chapter 2. He is overloaded.

Responding to Overload

Let's assume that the assistant controller is aware of the dangers of overload and decides to fight it. What can he do? Instead of substituting quasi-rational inferences for observations and analysis, he might do the following:

▲ Direct subordinates to communicate only nonroutine and uncertainty-reducing messages;

▲ Prioritize his communicating so that second-ranked communicating is not dealt with until first-ranked transmissions occur;

▲ Seek unsupported opinions of experts and trusted colleagues in place of unmanageable data and his own guesses;

▲ Delegate part of his decision making to subordinates;

▲ Postpone decisions until the data can be analyzed.

"Tragedy of the Channels" and Overload

Communications channels can be viewed as scarce organization resources owned in common by everyone. Like common resources (e.g., fish in the ocean), they can be overexploited as people seeking them rush in to get their share before depletion occurs. If one waits until tomorrow, the fish may be all gone, so one fishes for them today. This is known as the "tragedy of the commons." Let's see how this tragedy applies to communications channels.

Not everyone can gain access to a channel at all times unless one is already using it. Thus the best strategy for gaining the use of a channel is to use it as often as possible—even when it is not needed. When it is needed, one can count on having it available. The senior who drops in at the partner's office every morning for an inconsequential chat is ensuring himself an easy entreé when he needs to say something consequential. The manager who is on the telephone constantly with trivial messages for the controller knows that he has a channel open to his superior when he has something important to say. Subordinates who have not worked to establish and use channels will find (1) that it is not easy all of a sudden to drop in on or to telephone a superior if they have not regularly done so before and (2) that when they do drop in or telephone, the subordinate who has worked to build the channel is already using it.

When all subordinates learn what is happening, the boss can expect to be deluged with drop-ins and telephone calls. She will become overloaded—this is the tragedy of the channels. The solution, as in the tragedy of the commons (Hardin, 1968), is to have a central authority allocate channel usage based on criteria that identify those who can exploit the channel efficiently and effectively. Criteria based on position power or random selection (first come, first served), although used, are *not* appropriate. A better criterion is skill at communicating brief, comprehensive messages rapidly.

A partner or controller ought not to cope with the tragedy of the channels by restricting her encounters to senior people only, or even worse, to those who manage to get her attention first during the day. Instead, she can inform her staff that access will be granted only to those sending a prior short memo specifying their need for a face-to-face encounter. If this approach is too harsh, she could simply take charge of her encounters and tell her subordinates who will be seen first in the mornings. In addition, she could restrict her encounters only to those who can provide specific, unambiguous, condensed information useful for decision making. Those who could not provide such information would soon learn how to do it. A warning: These approaches are to be used only to cope with overload. Their use at any other time would seriously harm the trust-building, maintenance communicating in which every manager should engage.

CONTROLLING MESSAGE FLOW

Controllers and senior managing partners in public accounting firms must concern themselves with the flow of messages that regularly travel up and down within their units. Messages can be either too few or too many, too short or too long. Exhibit 18.5 describes the risks that poor message flow creates.

What kinds of situations cut down the risk attendant to poor message flow? Let's look at a public audit firm's organization and see how it copes with message flow problems:

Situation 1: Few, Short Messages. In this situation, characterized by brief interactions at long intervals, task coordination is difficult, and the risk is that tasks will be done inefficiently. An audit firm faces this situation regularly regarding communications among field auditors, partners, and home office staff. To cope with it, the organization fosters *task independence*. If auditors are trained to work independently of staff and partners, little communicating is necessary.

Situation 2: Many, Short Messages. Auditors do not enjoy the luxury of long conversations with clients, even when complex issues need to be dis-

Exhibit 18.5   RISKS OF POOR MESSAGE FLOW

MESSAGES

	Few	Many
Short	**1** *Risk:* Poor task coordination *Result:* Tasks are done inefficiently	**2** *Risk:* Poor handling of complex information *Result:* Only simple tasks get done well
Long	**3** *Risk:* Sporadic information input to task activities *Result:* Tasks are done haphazardly	**4** *Risk:* Manager overload *Result:* Many tasks do not get done

CONTENTS

cussed. To cope, audit firms foster *task specialization.* Specialists know what to expect and have learned to recognize real, authentic, unambiguous information without much effort. They can handle complex information quickly and get complex tasks done well.

Situation 3: Few, Long Messages. Occasionally audit firm personnel must respond to complex messages containing important changes in regulations and tax laws. If these changes are not smoothly integrated into the activities of the field personnel, tasks may get done haphazardly as some auditors put jobs off until new regulations are well known, while others try to get jobs done fast the old way before the rules force changes. The solution is high *professional competence and integrity.* Professionals know that long messages containing complex change information may occur at wide intervals. They cope by keeping up in their professional reading and contacts. In this way they anticipate change and act to keep their task behavior as predictable and consistent as possible. They do not respond to a big change with "run in circles, scream and shout" behavior, which some readers may recall as being typical in the U.S. military at one time.

Situation 4: Many, Long Messages. An auditor or a partner who must endure long meetings, long reports, and long-winded colleagues and subordinates will soon be overloaded. Some jobs will be put off or not done. The solution in most firms is to increase *hierarchical structure.* In audit firms layers of managers and seniors are placed between partners and information generated by staff. These managers can absorb some of the partner's burden *if* many, long messages begin to flow. Note the *if*. If the organization does not face frequent, long communications, then one reason for top-heavy management structure is removed.

PUBLIC ACCOUNTING FIRMS

What communications are common in public accounting firms? Certainly the firm generates audit reports, special reports, and management advisory reports for clients, but what other kinds of messages are sent?

To begin at the top, a partner communicates decisions, delegates functions, communicates to build client relationships, and so on. Audit supervisors and managers also build client relationships, but their task is mostly to coordinate audit teams in the field. As such, they plan work flow, direct seniors and in-charge staff, and report to partners. They send administrative and procedural memos, seek partner approval of work papers, and do some staff training. Together with the seniors they may write engagement letters for a partner's signature. With partners they may make proposals to clients.

Another employee is the specialist. He or she is an expert in a particular area (e.g., health services auditing) and acts as a consultant for field teams (as well as often doing field work). A specialist with outstanding skills may be called upon to advise other audit teams in the firm's offices nationwide and to prepare technical bulletins and procedure manuals.

Next are the seniors and in-charge staff members (who may be ranked in several levels). They supervise teams in the field, report problems and progress to the audit supervisor or the manager, communicate with the client to coordinate the work, assign tasks to staff auditors, and so on. In communications with their managers, they usually do the following:

▲ Seek approval for new work instructions from the client;

▲ Provide information on the scope of the work and timing issues;

▲ Estimate the completion date;

▲ Alert the manager to working papers and reports that will soon need review;

▲ Pass on client requests;

▲ Note problems in availability of data, lack of client cooperation, or poor working conditions;

▲ Describe nonroutine occurrences and irregularities;

▲ Discuss the nature of the opinion to be rendered.

In communicating with the client, they must be careful to avoid undue familiarity that might threaten independence. In addition, they must carefully avoid opinions of the client's accounting system—that is the subject of a special report issued by the firm after the audit. All in all, the in-charge has a difficult communication task.

CORPORATE AUDIT COMMITTEES

Over the years the role of the audit committee in overseeing internal controls within the corporation has grown. Committees have grown in staff, in number of outside members, and in number of meetings held. They have increased their coordination with their firms' external auditors, made more recommendations to management, and pushed aggressively for their adoption. Many committees receive weekly status reports as the yearly audit occurs. In sum, they have broadened their focus beyond simply rubber stamping management's choice of an auditor and the auditor's opinion and report.

Audit committees sometimes receive information from internal auditors on the nature of the firm's accounting principles followed and procedures implemented. They may also investigate questionable corporate activities as an in-house representative of the SEC. This activity and others like it are tending to shift audit committee communicating from receiving information to generating it—especially in the form of evaluations of the preparation of financial statements.

All of this complex communicating occurring year round requires a planned agenda. Each audit committee should have its staff draw up an annual work plan for the committee specifying meetings, topics, reports to be received, and key management personnel responsible for reports. A charge to the committee from the board should spell out its tasks and responsibilities and govern annual work plans. Of particular importance is a discussion of criteria to guide the committee in requesting reports direct from the external auditor, a step not ordinarily taken since most reports travel to management first.

Checkoff 18.1 **ACCOUNTING COMMUNICATIONS: ORGANIZATIONAL ACCOUNTING COMMUNICATIONS**

UNDERSTANDING AND COPING WITH ORGANIZATIONAL COMMUNICATIONS	YES	NO
1. Am I aware of the importance of formal maintenance messages in developing trust, motivating subordinates, keeping channels open, and reducing unnecessary service messages?	____	____
2. Am I communicating adequately in the authority, expertise, information, and friendship networks to which I belong?	____	____

(continued)

Checkoff 18.1 *(concluded)*

	YES	NO
3. Am I aware that my messages traveling upward in the organization may become distorted if the organization is hierarchically tall or lost if it is short?	____	____
4. Am I controlling the rumor mill by adequately informing employees and building mutual trust?	____	____
5. Am I using the informal network for help in dealing with complex, nonroutine problems in addition to using formal methods?	____	____
6. Am I using informal networks to get "feedforward" to build consensus and to add redundancy to formal messages when appropriate?	____	____
7. Am I aware that it is usually better, from a communications perspective, to reduce group size rather than to eliminate groups?	____	____
8. Do I understand the concept of organizational space and how I can manipulate it to improve communications?	____	____
9. Have I improved communications with my subordinates by developing their trust and their sense of job security?	____	____
10. Have I avoided careless evaluative inferences in communicating with my superiors?	____	____
11. As a superior do I avoid unnecessary secrecy, directives that are excessively brief or worded to shift responsibility to my subordinates, and ritualized communicating? Do I seek a subordinate's advice and then act on it or give a good reason for not acting on it?	____	____
12. Do I avoid using overload data to legitimize guessing and instead take appropriate actions to reduce overload?	____	____
13. Has my organization coped with message flow problems through task independence, task specialization, professional competence and integrity, and an appropriate hierarchical structure?	____	____

chapter 19

Persuading Clients and Motivating Employees

Persuasive communicating, which in this chapter concerns influencing clients and motivating employees, is probably the most difficult and least understood skill that an accountant should master. To put it into perspective, let's look at what persuasion is not and then at what it in fact is.

To begin with, persuasion is not simply the giving of data or information. An accountant who says, "If I give them the right financial measures, they will come to the decision I believe should be made" is a good information provider but is not a persuader. Persuasion requires more than objective reporting of measures—and is of course to be used only when objective reporting is not adequate, appropriate, or professionally mandated. In addition, persuasion is:

▲   Not coercion,
▲   Not the exercise of authority or rank,
▲   Not requesting,
▲   Not suggesting,
▲   Not recommending.

Obviously, then, if it is not connected with so many routine communications, persuasion must be a nonroutine, highly specialized form of message transmission.

The old term for persuasion is *rhetoric,* and both terms imply the same meaning: the use of language to influence someone to be, to believe, or to do what the persuader desires. Notice that persuasion is an active behavior—it doesn't just happen; it is planned. And note that it is not reader/listener oriented. For these reasons many people see persuasion as an uncivil activity, too manipulative and self-oriented for their taste. It certainly is these things when misused, but experienced accountants know that without persuasion as part of their personal inventory of communication skills, they simply can't always get clients to do what is in the clients' own best interests.

PERSUASION MATRIX Persuasion focuses on one or a combination of things: (1) the self-image of the person being persuaded, (2) the beliefs and attitudes of the person, and (3) the behavior of the person. What a persuader does to any or all of these things is to change them, to reinforce them, to neutralize them, or to conserve them. Exhibit 19.1 helps in defining what these terms mean.

The most difficult goal of persuasion is change, which involves moving from a negative (positive) to a positive (negative) focus. In fact, as we note later in this chapter, many persuaders approach change in an incremental fashion. First they seek to neutralize the hostile opinion (behavior or self-image) of the person being persuaded. Then they try to get the person to move from a neutral position to a slightly favorable position. If that occurs, they provide information that reinforces the favorable opinion and makes it more strongly

Exhibit 19.1 **THE GOALS OF PERSUASION**

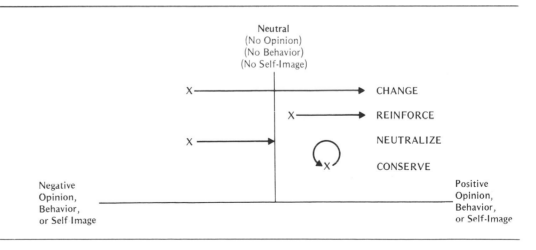

Exhibit 19.2 **PERSUASION MATRIX**

| | PERSUASION FOCUS | | |
	Attitudes	Behavior	Self-Image
Conserve			
Neutralize			
Reinforce			
Change			

PERSUASION GOAL

held. Then to get the person to keep on holding the strong opinion, they use periodic conserving messages.

Take the case of the client who has become dissatisfied with his auditor. In a meeting, the engagement partner might provide evidence to show that the client's hostile opinion probably should be replaced by a neutral, let's-hear-your-story attitude. If the client decides to take a more objective look at the situation that led to the dissatisfaction, then the partner can begin to stress all the positive things the auditor has done for the client while downplaying the unsatisfactory behavior. If the client grudgingly agrees that the audit firm has been generally favorable in its work, the stage is set to reinforce this moderately favorable attitude to make it strongly held. Perhaps the auditor will gently remind the client of the free training and consulting provided the client over the years and how these free services can now be expanded. If that gets the client feeling good about the accounting firm, the partner has succeeded in achieving opinion change. Naturally he would follow up with the services and with periodic messages to conserve the client's good opinion.

The persuasion matrix shown in Exhibit 19.2 offers a persuasion planning tool for accountants. With it accountants can identify the persuasion situation in which they are involved and then develop persuasion messages to fit the strategy. Here are some examples:

▲ *Conserving behavior*—The accountant wants to persuade a marketing manager to keep providing her with marketing policy and procedure information, information that was beginning to tail off.

▲ *Changing behavior*—The accountant seeks to persuade a client to change from LIFO to FIFO inventory accounting.

▲ *Changing self-image*—The accountant wants to persuade a client to switch capital asset planning from a short- to a long-term focus by changing the image of the

404

firm from a corporation that hustles after short-term profits to one that concentrates deliberately on long-term growth.

▲   *Reinforcing opinions* — The accountant seeks to persuade a manager who has reluctantly been providing her with labor cost data to feel more favorable toward the data-gathering work of accountants.

Once the accountant has developed an understanding of just what his persuasion involves, he can choose the appropriate persuasion message by consulting a list of compliance techniques.

COMPLIANCE TECHNIQUES

Compliance techniques, or persuasive appeals, are usually classified as rational, emotional, or ethical. *Rational appeals* are based on logical argument and are appropriate in situations where decisionmakers should or can be expected to process information analytically. *Emotional appeals* focus on meeting the desires of those being persuaded (e.g., desires for status, power, safety, or autonomy). *Ethical appeals* show that the persuader has qualities that ought to lead the person receiving the message to accept it. Such qualities involve honesty, credibility, sincerity, expertise, competence, respectability, empathy, and high status.

Rational Appeals

Persuading through rational appeals, often referred to as *argument,* involves the accountant stimulating a logical inference-making process in a client or manager so that the desired conclusion is reached after analyzing the accountant's evidence. Arguments are of several kinds.

Argument by Example

In argument by example, a statement is made and then examples (facts, observations, acceptable inferences) are given as evidence. This type of rational persuasion is effective in attitude or behavior change—the idea being that the new examples supersede the old attitude or behavior. The persuader should show that her examples are typical and occur frequently.

Argument by Generalization

A person who argues by generalization bases a statement about a whole class or group on an analysis of only a sample of the group. Such statements must be made in terms of probability rather than of certainty. The choice of a sample should be determined by either random selection or adherence to appropriate criteria.

Argument by Causal Relation

In argument by causal relation, an effect is shown to have resulted from a certain cause (e.g., an increase in personnel department costs resulting from an increase in employees). Conversely, a certain cause can be shown to lead to a certain effect. Generally, persuasion of this kind is enhanced by naming all possible causes and then showing that only one cause is likely to have produced the effect. If an accountant were trying to persuade a manager that the increased cost of the personnel department was a result of an increase in the company's employees, she would want to discuss all possible causes (such as inefficiency, special task assignments, etc.) and then to show:

▲ That as the work force has grown over time, so have the personnel department costs (the consistency test of Chapter 12);

▲ That if the firm eliminated all possible causes, the elimination of the work force increase would be the only one to reduce costs substantially (the distinctiveness test);

▲ That managers and accountants studying the issue agree that increased costs are due to increased labor (the consensus test).

Persuasion by cause-effect arguing is perhaps the most powerful form of influence available. Unfortunately, it is exceedingly difficult to do. Rarely can one argue successfully that consistency, distinctiveness, and consensus all apply. Nevertheless, if an accountant can argue using only *one* of the criteria, the consistency standard should be chosen. Consistency of cause-effect relationships over time is usually a stronger piece of evidence than the consensus of experts or the apparent absence of other possible causes.

Argument by Analogy

An accountant who argues by analogy reasons that if two things are alike in several important respects, they will also be alike in certain other respects. If two subsidiaries are alike in using LIFO inventory valuation accounting, an accountant might argue that they ought to be alike in choosing the same inventory control system. Although the argument is often quite powerful and persuasive, good professional behavior suggests that the conclusion is better stated as a hypothesis worthy of testing (say in a pilot study) rather than as a settled fact. Persuasion by analogy is arguing *before* observation and measurement rather than after. It should not be used as a substitute for information-gathering activities. In the situation above, the accountant should persuade decisionmakers to do the pilot test rather than to commit themselves to the proposed system.

Argument by Deduction

When an accountant makes a general statement and then draws conclusions from it, he is persuading by deduction. There are logical pitfalls here, however, known as "begging the question":

▲ *Wrong* (begging the question)—The bank should loan our client money because when profits begin to come in, the loan will be repaid easily.

▲ *Right*—Cash flow has generally increased over the last two years. For this reason we feel that the company will easily be able to pay back the loan it seeks from the bank.

In the first statement the implied general statement that profits will come in cannot be proven (one cannot prove the future). Any conclusions argued from it are weak. In the second, the general observation that cash has been coming in is verifiable, and the conclusion based on it is quite persuasive. When begging the question, we assume a general statement to be true with little or no evidence and then draw conclusions from it, which we try to get others to accept.

Emotional Appeals

Rational appeals are based on rules of inference external to the persuader and the person persuaded. Emotional appeals focus on the persuadee's needs, desires, and self-image. Among the most powerful of emotional appeals are the following:

▲ *Promise of reward*—Persuader promises to reward persuadee if he complies.

▲ *Threat of punishment*—Persuader threatens some kind of harm if compliance doesn't occur (note: depending on the harshness of the punishment, this form of persuasion can easily turn into coercion, which is not an influence-seeking communication).

▲ *Pregiving*—Persuader gives persuadee a reward prior to compliance, thus generating a feeling of obligation.

▲ *Hard sell*—Persuader becomes so aggressive that persuadee complies simply to escape the annoying communication.

▲ *Debt*—Persuadee is reminded of past favors and complies to relieve the debt.

▲ *Moral appeal*—Persuadee is told that compliance is the right and good thing to do.

▲ *Self-feeling*—Persuadee is told that she will feel better (or worse) about herself if she complies (or doesn't comply).

▲ *Labeling*—Persuader tells persuadee that someone of her qualities and reputation would comply.

▲ *Altruism*—Persuader throws himself on the mercy of persuadee and seeks compliance as a gesture of goodwill.

▲ *Social esteem*—Persuadee is told that people whose opinion he values will think well (ill) of him if he complies (doesn't comply).

▲ *Social conformity*—Persuader shows that since others have complied, the persuadee should comply too.

These are powerful appeals, and accountants will find many of them useful in communicating with clients and motivating employees (see below). However, the risk of unethical behavior is always present with emotional appeals, so accountants need to remember that they have an obligation to behave as the professionals they are (notice the use of labeling in this sentence).

Ethical Appeals

With ethical appeals, something good about the accountant himself becomes the base for successful persuasion. Techniques of ethical appeal may involve the following elements:

▲ *Liking*—Persuader is friendly and humorous to put persuadee in a good frame of mind.

▲ *Personal similarity*—Persuader shows how similar she is to persuadee and that therefore her message should be accepted.

▲ *Personal experience*—Persuader recounts his experiences and shows that they are similar to persuadee's. Thus his experience-based persuasion should be accepted.

▲ *Trustworthiness*—Persuader shows that she should be believed because she is credible, honest, sincere, and knowledgeable.

Rational persuasion, then, tries to convince the persuader to accept the impact of certain rules of argument or of inference; emotional appeals focus on the interests and needs of the persuadee; and ethical appeals stress the nature of the persuader. In terms of the reader/listener—oriented theory of rhetoric discussed in Chapter 1, emotional appeals ought to become more prominent in accounting communications. Although this is the case in certain activities, such as *employee motivation*, professional standards restrain their use. Accountants must communicate with their clients to meet real needs, not manufactured ones. Accountants communicate to turn the chaotic into the recognizable, the uncertain into the more certain, and the unhelpful into the helpful. Persuasion, of whatever kind, must follow these criteria.

PRESENTING A PERSUASIVE MESSAGE

In presenting a persuasive message, an accountant tries to establish herself as a credible source of information. If she has worked to develop a professional image, she will be seen as an expert, of equal or high status, trustworthy, and likable. As such, she will be paid attention to. As long as she doesn't contradict strongly held beliefs (without a great deal of preparation) and concentrates on reader/listener needs, she will continue to hold attention.

With the attention of her client, employee, or colleague, the accountant delivers the message. The nature of the message receiver has a large impact on whether or not a one-sided or a two-sided presentation is made:

One-Sided Presentation	Two-Sided Presentation
Friendly reader/listener	Unfriendly reader/listener
Receiver favorable to accountant's position	Receiver unfavorable to accountant's position
Receiver cut off from opposing argument	Receiver open to opposing argument

In proposals to clients when no competing firms are in the running, a one-sided presentation is best. When a competitor is strong and moreover is available to counterargue (perhaps their proposal is to follow immediately), then a two-sided presentation may be in order. This kind of presentation compares the accountant's position to the competing position and shows point by point why the accountant's position is best. A one-sided presentation simply deals point by point with the accountant's position.

During a presentation all favorable information should be presented first. Next comes any unfavorable information, neutral information, or background. The presentation should end with a summary of the favorable points.

Accountants can enhance the persuasiveness of their messages by choosing the communications channel with care. Electronic channels (telephone) are more persuasive than written channels, but oral channels are the most persuasive of all. And within oral channels, face-to-face, one-on-one communicating is best. The choice is simple. Maximize the likelihood of persuasion by maximizing face-to-face, one-on-one encounters.

FACE-TO-FACE PERSUASION A number of issues bear on the kind and amount of influence an accountant can exercise during a face-to-face encounter (Anderson and Zimbardo, 1979).

Information

The more information an accountant possesses or is perceived to possess, the greater will be his influence. Naturally, if the persuadee believes that he himself does not possess adequate information, the same effect occurs. The greater the ignorance of the persuadee, then, the greater the influence of the accountant. One can see that a persuasion strategy that first attempts to convince the persuadee that he is ignorant about certain matters can be quite effective. Of course, honesty demands that the accountant genuinely believe that the persuadee is ignorant.

Bonding Needs

When a person feels a need to become closer to others, she will act to increase communications. The process also involves a greater susceptibility to influence. A trade-off occurs: as a person seeks to communicate more with others because of a bonding need, she may have to accept more influence-oriented communications in return from others who recognize what is happening. This trade-off need not be considered sinister unless the influence is harmful. An accountant who builds a relationship with clients or subordinates will gain influence over them (and they over her). As long as she serves their interests, her use of the bonding relationship is appropriate.

Social Rewards

No detailed research program is needed to demonstrate that one person can communicate influence more easily to another if he employs such social reward responses as smiles, praise, personal concern, and so on. As the message receiver is rewarded with communications of praise, he becomes prepared for persuasive communicating. Once again, this process is not inherently evil. In the hands of a skilled accountant, for example, the social rewards process can be used to help persuade a client to make needed changes in internal controls. This process is of special use when formal reports (e.g., management letters) have had no impact.

Roles

As we saw in Chapter 1, interpersonal communications are deeply affected by role relationships. When persuading those of lower-status roles, an accountant can engage in more opinionated, unsupported assertions than when dealing with those of equal or higher status. Accounting "experts" or specialists are seen as high-status people and can influence others easily by offering advice that is unsupported opinion. A word of caution: Chapter 14 described the value of an accountant adopting an equal-status role in terms of developing good relationships. Here we have noted the value of adopting superior-status roles in persuasive communicating. Since one accountant can't be of both high and equal status at the same time in relation to another person, a group of accountants (e.g., auditors) needs to divide itself up into persuader specialists and relationship-building practitioners. The first group can be called on by the second when clients and other persuadees are not responding appropriately.

The Situation

We can distinguish between normal and abnormal situations—as perceived by the persuadee. Persuasion is more likely in normal situations, since the aroused attention that people give to abnormal situations tends to heighten a person's resistance and skepticism (Goffman, 1971). An accountant who seeks to influence a client or manager would do well to concentrate on communicating in the client's own office, during her routine work time, and in a step-by-step process of persuasion. This last is so that each successful influence is accepted as part of a routine ongoing activity. Radical change suggested in the accountant's office during a hastily called meeting is not the best way to influence a client or manager.

Positive Approach

The degree to which persuasion is couched in positive terms will affect the probability of impact. An accountant who is trying to get senior management to stop requiring certain inefficient accounting procedures would not so much want to push the demerits of the current system as the merits of the new system. Essentially, the accountant who is future oriented in communications will be more influential than the one who is past oriented.

Empathy

One researcher once described accountants as "financial psychiatrists," people who can influence their clients' or superiors' needs for financial growth by showing empathy. What this amounts to is showing understanding of the persuadee's plight, demonstrating that the accountant shares the client's needs, and signaling that he has been subjected to similar predicaments. As empathy grows, influence grows.

CLIENT COMMUNICATING Getting and holding a client is a four-step process followed by all public accounting firms:

1. Develop a systematic approach to communicating the firm's *image* to the public.
2. Treat the initial client contact and interview as an *attention*-getting device in which the accountant alerts the client team to the fact that his firm can meet their needs.
3. Submit a written proposal that describes the services offered and develops the client's *interest* in the firm.
4. Make an oral presentation that follows a persuasion strategy, employs compliance techniques, and creates a *desire* in the client to hire the accounting firm.

Note the incremental nature of these activities. Once a good image of the firm has been created, potential clients will pay attention to its messages. The series of messages delivered begins with interest-arousing communications and ends with solid persuasion delivered in an oral presentation.

Developing an Image

A successful public accounting firm enjoys the image of a group of people who are knowledgeable, experienced, committed to serving their clients' needs, willing to do and give a little extra for a client, and eager to build a people-to-people relationship. Specifically, such a firm is known to:

▲   Seek frequent informal meetings with clients to build trust relationships;
▲   Eagerly offer helpful advice on solving the client's problems;
▲   Volunteer help without having to be asked;
▲   Be easily available to the client.

Many of the larger accounting firms alert their potential clients to their image through regular newsletters, speeches, press releases, attendance at meetings, and seminars. These last have become quite common and are often given free or at low cost. The idea is to give the seminar participants useful information (often about taxes). In giving the information, contacts are made and the firm's image is communicated. The objective is to make the firm known—and known in a certain way controlled by the firm itself. Thus the firm's image grows in the way the firm wants it to grow. In addition, the seminar provides a mailing list and, if a survey has been conducted during the seminar, a description of each potential client's needs is available. Follow-up letters and brochures can be specifically tailored for groups of companies falling into identified segments.

Getting and Holding Attention

New clients may be referred to the accounting firm by existing clients; may refer themselves after exposure to seminars, brochures, and the like; may be developed through personal contacts of the partners; or may be referred by lawyers or bankers. The source of the initial contact is important, since it will influence the persuasion strategy employed later. A self-referred potential client will only need persuasion that reinforces existing favorable attitudes and behavior. A firm suggested to a client by a banker, however, may be a reluctant contact and thus may require attitude change messages. Another firm may not see itself as the kind of company that would use a certain kind of public accounting firm. It would need persuasion that focuses on changing its self-image.

The initial meeting and any subsequent preliminary survey/interview work should be held under an aura of the accountant's *enthusiasm* for the job. She must show how exciting it is to be offered the chance to take on a new, challenging task for the client. This is a bit more difficult than it sounds and deserves some elaboration.

Accountants in public firms must place themselves daily in new and sometimes strange surroundings as they deal with potential clients. They will probably experience many of the feelings listed below and respond to their feelings as shown:

Feelings	Compensating Behavior
Tentative	Assurance, certainty
Inadequate	Drive, dynamism
Lacking in control	Dominant, structuring
Unfamiliar with the environment and the people	Stereotyping and categorizing
Worried about one's role	Overplaying the accountant's role—deluging with jargon

The behaviors that emerge may command a client's respect, but not necessarily her warm admiration. Such behavior is that of an accountant who is enthusiastic for doing rather than helping—an end to himself rather than a means to the client's end. He is not there to aid but to direct.

The accountant who recognizes that his feelings are natural does not try to compensate for them in his behavior but instead lets his actions grow out of his feelings:

Feelings	Appropriate Behavior
Tentative	Asking questions and listening
Inadequate	Being fully prepared and well trained
Lacking in control	Cheerfully responding to the client's needs
Unfamiliar with the environment and the people	Building interpersonal relations without judgment
Worried about one's role	Adopting the behavior pattern appropriate for the situation

Receptive, prepared, responsive, personal, and adaptable: these are the qualities and behaviors that ought to characterize an accountant's enthusiastic acceptance of a new job.

Research has shown that people, when making a decision about a person, do not review previously obtained facts about the person but rather previous judgments they have made about the person (Ostrom et al., 1979). Thus a potential client will not recall the data she has collected about the accountant so much as the impressions she has formed during her initial and follow-up contacts. In this sense the good image of the firm and the accountant's carefully crafted enthusiasm are major determinants of a hire decision. Of course the services the firm offers and its price will count, but so will the impression the accountant creates during initial client meetings.

Developing Interest

The written proposal develops the interest of the potential client by describing the benefits to be gained by hiring the accountant's firm. Such benefits are shown to derive from the following factors:

▲ The firm's efficient and productive organization;

▲ Adequate geographic coverage to service such things as subsidiaries located elsewhere;

▲ Complete services in auditing, taxes, financial planning, systems planning, advisory services, and client training;

▲ A high-quality, experienced staff;

▲ Experience in the client's industry;

▲ Reasonable and competitive fees.

Below is a thorough outline of a highly successful written proposal form:

1. *Cover.* A specially developed cover lists the name of the accounting firm, the potential client, the date, and the title "Audit Proposal and Description of Services."

2. *Cover Letter.* In a one-page letter to the decisionmakers in the client's firm, the audit firm sets forth why it feels that it can best serve the client's needs.

3. *Executive Summary.* In two pages the audit firm shows how it understands the client's industry, its specific philosophy, and its needs. In somewhat more detail than in the cover letter, it describes its services within and in addition to the audit services:

▲ Financial planning for adequate capital margins and appropriate debt levels;

▲ Pricing advice to preserve the client's advantages in a competitive market;

▲ Cost utilization and control;

▲ Systems planning to maximize use of computer resources;

▲ Organizational alternatives to respond with flexibility to government regulations;

▲ Risk identification in the internal control system.

The executive summary also briefly describes the reports that will be issued in addition to the usual audit reports (such as reports on data processing procedures, on administrative issues, and on accounting procedures). Finally, the estimated man-hours to be spent and the fee are listed.

4. *Table of Contents.*

5. *Chapter 1: Who We Are.* Here the firm is described. Of particular importance, lists of clients similar to the potential client are provided. A listing of the staff is given and its technical abilities are discussed briefly in relation to the client's needs. (10–12 pages.)

6. *Chapter 2: What We Offer.* Each division is described in more detail than in Chapter 1. Brief résumés of the partners heading each division are provided. The chapter focuses on how each division can serve the client. (8–10 pages.)

7. *Chapter 3: The Client Service Team.* Partners and staff to be assigned to the client are listed, and a one-page résumé is provided for each team member. The primary team is often made up of an engagement partner, an audit manager, and an audit senior. Also listed could be a tax specialist and a management advisory specialist. Sometimes a national partner with particular expertise is listed and described. He or she is available for specific advice. (10–12 pages.)

8. *Chapter 4: Audit Approach.* The scope of the examination is described, and the reports given to the client are named. These reports, in addition to the long-form audit report and a management letter, may include a letter of compliance with a loan agreement, a special report on some important topic, and a final oral report to management or to the audit committee.

The scope of the audit is often expressed in a tabular form. Here is an example:

Activity	Time Allocated	Personnel
Planning	1 week	Senior, 2 staff
Preaudit meetings with management	2 months	Partner, manager, senior
Preliminary work	2 weeks	Senior, 3 staff
Audit work and wrap-up	3 months	Partner, manager, senior, 3 staff
Postaudit meetings	1 month	Partner, manager, senior

This schedule also may be represented in flow and time-line charts. Moreover, each specific task's share of total audit time may be listed:

Audit Tasks	Percent of Total Audit Time
1. Meet with management	1.5%
2. Write engagement letter	0.5
3. Prepare permanent files	3.0
4. Complete planning	2.5
5. Communicate with management	2.0
6. Document accounting systems (review documents, conduct interviews, develop familiarity with computer and control systems, prepare flow charts)	8.5
7. Identify internal accounting controls for testing	1.5
8. Perform tests	10.0
9. Determine validation procedures	2.0
10. Develop computer audit procedures and perform interim validations	9.0
11. Prepare management letter	2.5
12. Perform year-end validations	55.0
13. Issue reports	2.0
Total	100.0%

Chapter 4 usually also lists the fee. This may be expressed as a flat fee, but usually a discussion of monthly billings and inflation adjustments is added. A number of audit firms make it clear to the client that fees are competitive—which implies that negotiation is possible. (10 pages.)

9. *Chapter 5: Other Services.* Some firms describe their consulting services, while others list free seminars they will put on during the next twelve months. In addition to free seminars, a few firms offer "free" in-house training for some of the client's key personnel. This specially tailored training appears to be a powerful persuader for some clients.

10. *Appendices.* At the end of the proposal are attached samples of newsletters, manuals, and brochures the client will receive if the proposal is accepted.

Persuading Client Action

The oral proposal is the most persuasion-oriented part of the whole process and by far the most important. When asked why he had chosen a new auditor from among five similar written proposals, a client responded:

> It was the oral proposal. They knew everybody's name on my committee and what each person's job was. They showed how each of us would benefit from what they offered. And they had it all up on a flip chart so they made sure we got it. It was an impressive performance.

The audit firm that got this job, by the way, is noted for its commitment to communications training for its staff and partners.

Notice that the client described here was persuaded not by rational argument but by reader/listener-oriented emotional appeals and by ethical appeals based on the auditor's carefully developed image of the expert professional. The format for the persuasive oral report should look something like the following:

1. *Attention-Getting Opening.* The auditor can begin by noting one important point that will make the client team sit up and take notice (e.g., "Last year our firm handled five audits for firms within your industry, firms that face the same challenges you do"). Another attention getter is a genuine compliment to the client (e.g., "Acme Industries is generally acknowledged to be a leader in its field. Smith-Wallace is delighted to have the opportunity to offer our services to you").

Also in the opening, the auditor summarizes what his basic compliance techniques are (e.g., "I want to show you now that Smith-Wallace offers . . .

and that you will benefit in the following ways by naming Smith-Wallace as your auditor. First, . . ."). A flip chart graphic on an easel should then be revealed that lists the compliance appeals. It should remain in view of the client team throughout most of the proposal.

2. *Describing the Client's Needs.* Here the auditor discusses what he has identified as the client's needs. As much as possible, the needs and interests of each person on the client's team should be discussed. Questions should be encouraged so that the auditor gets feedback that tells him whether he has successfully identified needs (although long, involved answers that slow the presentation should be avoided; e.g., "That's an interesting question. Generally I would agree. Let me get back to you on that after the presentation").

3. *Building Credibility and Meeting Needs.* The auditor next takes each need in turn and shows that his firm can meet it. As he does so, he interjects information that builds his firm's image of competence and reputation for solid, client-oriented work (e.g., "Just last week we had a call from one of our clients over in Mason City. They were so delighted with our work that they . . ."). Once again, questions should be encouraged. Now, however, the answers should give an opportunity to demonstrate the auditor's expertise and familiarity with the client's operations. In these answers and in the prepared presentation, the persuasion strategy and compliance techniques are fully employed. For a new client the strategy might be to reinforce an existing attitude (toward a Big Eight firm) or perhaps to conserve an existing self-image (for a client that sees itself as small and thus in need of a small, non–Big Eight auditor). The compliance techniques would stress need satisfaction of various kinds and the credibility or likability of the audit firm. Rational appeals based on general industry consensus that the auditor is expert may also be used.

4. *Visualizing the Results.* Once the basic persuasive appeals have been delivered, the auditor then paints a picture of what will have occurred once the audit firm is hired and the job is completed ("Let's look at what your situation will be once we've completed our work for you . . .").

5. *Seeking a Decision.* All of the long preparation in carrying out a systematic approach to client communicating now focuses on the "call for action"—the signal to the client that a hire decision is being sought. Generally the speaker will summarize the client's needs and how his firm can satisfy those needs. Then he will ask for any final questions. Two questions that often come up concern the fee and possible conflicts because the auditor is also working for a competitor.

In discussing the fee the auditor can take the "lemons into lemonade" approach and point out that the fee is competitive, and if it is somewhat higher than in other proposals, that is because of the need to compensate a highly qualified staff. Another approach is simply to state that the fee will be no higher than the lowest proposed by the other firms. Still a third approach is to offer extras in return for a slightly higher fee. Here the importance of offered in-house training becomes manifest. It is the reward appeal that may persuade the client to hire the accounting firm.

As for questions about possible conflict, the auditor can (1) stress his reputation for independence and (2) emphasize his detailed expertise in the industry. Whatever responses are made, the auditor must remember that he is not there to win a debator's point but to persuade the client to make a hire decision. He should not argue.

Once all the questions have been dealt with, the auditor proposes his firm as the client's next auditor ("We want you to know that your needs will be met if you consider our firm as your new auditor . . ."). He then thanks the client team for the opportunity to make a proposal and withdraws. In an informal way he then asks when he can expect a decision and casually alerts the client that he will get back to him soon to learn of the decision or of further information requested by the client.

EMPLOYEE MOTIVATION The same persuasion matrix approach is useful in developing communications to motivate employees, either during informal meetings or during performance evaluation sessions. Indeed, performance evaluation should focus not on what the employees have done (although that must be discussed) but on motivating them to do better. This approach may involve changing behavior, reinforcing attitudes, conserving the employees' self-image, and so on. Exhibit 19.3 describes some of the emotional and ethical appeals that can be used to persuade employees to comply.

Systematic Approach to Motivation

The persuasive motivating communication is most effective within the context of a systematic approach to employee motivation (Myers, 1972). What this means is that an accounting firm or department should establish and maintain communications channels for the following purposes:

▲ *To tell staff the purposes of the tasks they perform.* It is not enough to tell people what to do. An accounting manager must tell her young "bean counters" why something is to be done. One thinks of the television reporter who walked into the U.S. Department of Agriculture some years ago and asked an employee what his job was. "I write reports," the man replied. "Oh," said the reporter, "and what are the reports used for?" "I don't know," said the man.

Exhibit 19.3 **COMPLIANCE-GAINING PERSUASIVE TECHNIQUES IN EMPLOYEE MOTIVATION**

TECHNIQUE	COMMUNICATION
Promise of reward	Employee is offered an incentive to comply.
Threat of punishment	Employee is threatened (1) with a loss of something desired or (2) with an increase of something undesired.
Positive/negative reasoning	Employee is presented with information showing advantages of complying or disadvantages of not complying.
Liking	Superior is friendly and warm to get employee in the right frame of mind to make a compliance commitment.
Pregiving	Employee is rewarded before compliance is sought.
Debt	Employee is reminded of special consideration shown him/her in the past.
Moral appeal	Employee is told that doing the right thing requires a compliance commitment.
Self-feeling	Employee is told he will feel better about himself after compliance and worse if he does not comply.
Labeling	Employee is told that persons with her positive qualities would comply or that only persons with certain negative qualities would not comply.
Altruism	Superior tells employee how badly he needs compliance—"I need your help."
Social esteem	Employee is told that her colleagues will think well of her if she complies or poorly of her if she doesn't comply.
Social conformity	Employee is told that everyone else complies, so why not him?
Personal experience	Superior tells of her compliance when she was in the employee's position. She shows that she and the employee are similar kinds of people.
Foot in the door	Employee is asked to comply with a small request. Later he is asked to comply with larger request, and so on.
Door in the face	Employee is asked to comply with a large request (a request that the manager knows will be refused, being too extreme). Then the employee is asked to comply with a smaller request (the request of importance to the manager).

"I only pass them on to my superior and he passes them on and so on." This man, ignorant of the purpose of his work, appeared incompetent on the television screen. In fact, the real incompetence was above him in the seniors who did not tell him why the reports were needed. Employees, indeed all human beings, need to see a direction in their activities and often seek purposive direction from their managers. An accounting manager needs to tell her staff what is to be done and why.

▲ *To convince staff that the purpose of their work is useful to accomplishing the organization's goals and to achieving their personal goals.* Here the persuasive tactics described earlier come into play. The manager assesses staff attitudes, current behavior, and self-images regarding the work and their doing it and decides what motivating appeals are needed. Typically, for example, young accountants might not see themselves as the kind of people who engage in tedious inventory counts. The manager, therefore, might show them:

> That inventory counts, though tedious, add significant information to the organization's knowledge—information useful in making crucial financial decisions.
>
> That every successful senior manager started his or her career by counting inventory.
>
> That management has chosen the accounting staff because they are the kind of people who can be expected to accept the tough jobs as a way of earning a chance to move into the top spots.

▲ *To tell staff how to do the work.* Most large public accounting firms engage in elaborate training so that staff people learn task procedures. Such is not the case in many smaller public and corporate accounting settings, where staff are expected to sink or swim on their own. This expectation is really a sign of faith in chance, because without some control (e.g., training) chance alone will determine how likely an accountant is to do a task well.

One might object at this point that the employee selection process will identify competent accountants who can perform almost any tasks assigned to them. Unfortunately, however, a firm could select Albert Einstein, CPA, and still find that he hadn't the foggiest notion of how to do or to evaluate a consolidated balance sheet for a U.S. firm with subsidiaries in Japan and Brazil. The fact is that accounting work is not so standardized that colleges and schools can teach every possible task activity.

▲ *To show staff that they will have some control over the work.* Highly intelligent accountants do not like thinking of themselves as marionettes on a string. They need to be told that each of them will have choices, within certain limitations, regarding time and effort allocations, the way the work is done, and the activities that occur after the work is done and new work must be planned.

In sum, then, motivational communications must take place within a context of informational communications (1) telling what is to be done, why, and how and (2) assuring staff that they will have some autonomy during their work.

A Motivation Scenario

In a counseling session, a manager might begin by describing what the future ought to look like rather than evaluating past actions of the subordinate. Evaluation will provoke defense rather than compliance:

▲ *Evaluation of past action*—"Your failure to implement the control procedure allowed a $500 error to occur."

▲ *Focus on future action*—"You need to direct as much attention as possible to implementing the control procedure."

The future-oriented statement focuses on a needed change in behavior. Next might come a compliance-seeking message based on labeling:

"I know that you're the kind of person who will bear down on this problem."

Finally, to reinforce the impact of labeling, the employee could be promised a reward:

"If we get through this quarter without any errors, I feel that you will be a strong candidate for the promotion we've discussed."

Checkoff 19.1 **ACCOUNTING COMMUNICATIONS: PERSUADING CLIENTS AND MOTIVATING EMPLOYEES**

PERSUASIVE COMMUNICATING	YES	NO
1. Am I aware that persuasion is *not* simply informing, requesting, or suggesting?	____	____
2. Have I learned that persuasion is the use of language to influence people to do or believe what I want them to?	____	____
3. If I focus on persuasion leading to change (as opposed to reinforcement, conservation, etc.), have I approached it in a step-by-step fashion?	____	____
4. Once I have determined a persuasion focus and goal, have I chosen suitable compliance techniques based on rational, emotional, or ethical appeals?	____	____

(continued)

Checkoff 19.1   (*concluded*)

	YES	NO
5. Does my persuasion help turn the chaotic into the recognizable, the uncertain into the more certain, and the unhelpful into the helpful?	____	____
6. Do I know when to use one-sided or two-sided persuasion presentations?	____	____
7. Do I maximize the likelihood of persuasion by maximizing face-to-face, one-on-one communicating?	____	____
8. In client communicating have I followed a systematic approach involving image building, attention getting, interest development, and compliance-gaining persuasion?	____	____
9. In communicating with a client have I shown enthusiasm for helping the client in place of enthusiasm for dominating the client?	____	____
10. Does my employee motivating focus on the future rather than on the past?	____	____
11. Does my motivating occur within a context of ongoing informing of employees what they are to do, why they must do it, and how to do it?	____	____

Selected Bibliography

ACCOUNTING COMMUNICATIONS ISSUES

Accounting Principles Board. "Basic Concepts and Accounting Principles Underlying Financial Statements of Business Enterprises." *APB Statement No. 4.*

American Institute of Certified Public Accountants. Accounting and Review Services Committee. *Compilation and Review of Financial Statements.* December 1978.

_____. *Codification of Statements on Auditing Standards, Numbers 1 to 26.* New York, 1980.

_____. *Professional Standards, Management Advisory Services.* New York, July 1979.

_____. *The Process of Communication in Public Accounting.* New York, May 1965. The communications process within the public accounting organization.

Arthur Young and Company. "Financial Reporting and Changing Prices." New York, November 1979. How to communicate FAS 33 information.

Beaver, W. H. *Financial Reporting: An Accounting Revolution.* Englewood Cliffs, N.J.: Prentice-Hall, 1981.

Bedford, N. M., and V. Baladouni. "A Communication Theory Approach to Accountancy." *The Accounting Review,* 1962, *37,* 650–659. Excellent introduction to the accounting communications process.

Bedford, N. M., and M. Onsi. "Measuring the Value of Information: An Information Theory Approach." *Management Services,* 1966, *3,* 15–22. Important discussion of data, information, knowledge, and uncertainty.

Briloff, A. J. *The Effectiveness of Accounting Communication.* New York: Praeger, 1967. Description of serious communications problems based on the absence of agreement regarding accounting standards and measurements. Read the last chapter only.

Calbridge, R. A. "Interviewing by Telephone." *The GAO Review,* 1976, *11,* 51–55. Sensible step-by-step procedures.

Chen, K. H., and E. L. Summers. "Should Accounting Data Be Single-Valued Measurements?" *The International Journal of Accounting*, 1977, *12*, 109–25. Single-valued measures versus interval measures and measures of uncertainty.

Corr, A. V. "Accounting Information for Managerial Decisions." *Financial Executive*, 1977, *45*, 40–44. The kinds of information provided by accountants to managerial decisionmakers.

Dolphin, R., and R. A. Wagley. "Reading the Annual Report." *Financial Executive*, 1977, *45*, 20–22. Lack of comprehensibility of many annual reports.

Dowling, J. H. "Main Job of the Annual Report: Wooing Investors." *Dun's Review*, 1978, *112*, 127–128, 133–134. Stewardship-oriented versus future-oriented annual reports.

Driver, M. J., and T. J. Mock. "Human Information Processing, Decision Style Theory, and Accounting Information Systems." *The Accounting Review*, 1975, *50*, 490–508. Users of accounting information seek more information than they can process.

Evans, B., and R. Miller. "Management Letters: A Source of Inside Information." *Credit and Financial Management*, 1978, *80*, 10–11, 35. Purposes and forms of management letters and special reports.

Financial Accounting Standards Board. *Objectives of Financial Reporting by Business Enterprises*. FASB Statement of Financial Accounting Concepts No. 1. Stamford, Conn., November 1978. Kinds of information communicated and goals of accounting communications.

_____. *Qualitative Characteristics: Criteria for Selecting and Evaluating Financial Accounting and Reporting Policies*. Stamford, Conn., August 1979. Concepts of relevance and reliability of accounting information.

Haried, A. H. "The Semantic Dimensions of Financial Statements." *Journal of Accounting Research*, 1972, *10*, 376–91. Criteria for establishing uniformity of meaning between senders and receivers of accounting information.

Johnson, G. H. "The Communication Process in Auditing." *Retail Control*, 1978, *47*, 53–64. Communications among the internal auditor, line management, and senior management.

Joplin, B., and J. W. Patillo. *Effective Accounting Reports*. Englewood Cliffs, N.J.: Prentice-Hall, 1969. Kinds of corporate accounting reports and how to write them.

Jordan, J. R. "Financial Accounting and Communication." *The Price Waterhouse Review*, 1969, *14*, 12–22. Problems of form and content in communications.

Lewis, R. B. *Accounting Reports for Management*. Englewood Cliffs, N.J.: Prentice-Hall, 1957. Types of corporate accounting reports and ways of preparing them.

Lindo, D. K. "Routine Reports: Who Needs Them?" *CGA Magazine*, 1978, *12*, 4–7.

Lothian, N. "Bad Language in Financial Reports." *Accountancy*, 1978, *89*, 42–44. Differences between technical language and jargon.

Mock, T. J. "Concepts of Information Value and Accounting." *The Accounting Review*, 1971, *46*, 765–78. How decisionmakers value accounting information.

Romans, D. B. "Drafting a Meaningful Annual Report." *Financial Executive,* 1979, *47,* 26–30.

Wilkinson, J. W. "Effective Reporting Structures." *Journal of Systems Management,* 1976, *27,* 38–42. Classification of accounting reports.

GENERAL COMMUNICATIONS ISSUES

Alexander, Don H. *Banking for the Non-banker.* Seattle: DHA and Associates, 1974.

Andersen, S., and P. Zimbardo. *On Resisting Social Influence.* Technical Report Z–79–01. Washington, D.C.: Office of Naval Research (Code 452). September 1979.

Anderson, D. R.; L. A. Schmidt; and A. M. McCash. *Practical Controllership,* 3d ed. Homewood, Ill.: Irwin, 1973.

Athanassiades, J. C. "The Distortion of Upward Communications in Hierarchical Organizations." *Academy of Management Journal,* 1973, *16,* 207–25.

Bales, R. F. "Task Roles and Social Roles in Problem-Solving Groups." In E. Maccoby, T. M. Newcomb, and E. L. Hartley (eds.), *Readings in Social Psychology,* 3d ed. New York: Holt, Rinehart and Winston, 1958, pp. 437–47.

Barrett, H. *Practical Methods in Speech.* New York: Holt, Rinehart and Winston, 1968.

Baskin, O. W., and C. E. Aronoff. *Interpersonal Communication in Organizations.* Santa Monica, Calif.: Goodyear Publishing Company, 1980.

Baugh, A. C. *A History of the English Language,* 2d ed. New York: Appleton-Century-Crofts, 1957.

Beck, D. C. "Communication Through Confrontation: A Case Study in Intergroup Conflict Reduction." Paper presented at the International Communication Association Convention, Phoenix, Ariz., April 22–24, 1971.

Benne, K., and P. Sheats. "Functional Roles of Group Members." *Journal of Social Issues,* 1948, *4,* 41–49.

Berdie, D. R. *Questionnaires: Design and Use.* Metuchin, N.J.: Scarecrow Press, 1974.

Bergwick, R. J. "Effective Communication of Financial Data." *The Journal of Accountancy,* 1970, *129,* 47–54.

Bodensteiner, W. D. "Information Channel Utilization under Varying Research and Development Project Conditions: An Aspect of Interorganizational Communication Channel Usage." Doctoral dissertation, University of Texas at Austin, 1970.

Boje, D. M. "Making a Horse Out of a Camel: A Contingency Model for Managing the Problem-Solving Process in Groups." In H. J. Leavitt, L. R. Pondy, and D. M. Boje (eds.), *Readings in Managerial Psychology,* 3d ed. Chicago: University of Chicago Press, 1980, pp. 445–71.

Borgida, E., and R. Nisbett. "The Differential Impact of Abstract vs. Concrete Information on Decisions." *Journal of Applied Psychology,* 1977, *7,* 258–71.

Borman, E.; W. Howell; R. Nichols; and G. Shapiro. *Interpersonal Communication in the Modern Organization.* Englewood Cliffs, N.J.: Prentice-Hall, 1969.

Boulding, K. E. *Conflict and Defense.* New York: Harper and Row, 1962.

Burgess, P. M., and L. L. Slonaker. *The Decision Seminar: A Strategy for Problem Solving.* Columbus: The Mershon Center of the Ohio State University, 1978.

Burns, T. "The Direction of Activity and Communication in a Departmental Executive Group." *Human Relations,* 1954, *7,* 73–97.

Byrne, D., and J. Lamberth. "Cognitive Reinforcement Theories as Complementary Approaches to the Study of Attraction." In B. Murstein (ed.), *Theories of Attraction and Love.* New York: Springer, 1971.

Cammann, C. "Effects of the Use of Control Systems." *Accounting, Organizations and Society,* 1976, *1,* 4, 301–13.

Campbell, D. T. "Systematic Error on the Part of Human Links in Communication Systems." *Information and Control,* 1958, *1,* 334–69.

Caplan, R. D.; S. Cobb; J. R. P. French, Jr.; R. D. Harrison; and S. R. Pinneau. *Job Demands and Working Health: Main Effects and Occupational Differences.* Washington, D.C.: U.S. Government Printing Office, 1975.

Carey, J. R. *The Concept of Management Services by CPAs.* New York: AICPA, 1959.

Carter, E. E. "The Behavioral Theory of the Firm and Top-Level Corporate Decisions." *Administrative Science Quarterly,* 1971, *16,* 413–28.

Cooper, C. R., and L. Odell. *Evaluating Writing: Describing, Measuring, Judging.* State University of New York at Buffalo: National Council of Teachers of English, 1977.

Davis, K. "Management Communication and the Grapevine." *Harvard Business Review,* 1953, *31,* 43–49.

———. *Human Behavior at Work.* New York: McGraw-Hill, 1972.

Deloitte, Haskins and Sells. *Working Paper Organization and Preparation.* 1978.

de Mare G. *Communicating at the Top.* New York: John Wiley, 1979.

Devine, C. T. "Essays in Accounting Theory." 2 volumes, unpublished typescript (University of Washington Library, Seattle), 1962.

Drucker, P. F. *Management: Tasks, Responsibilities, Practices.* New York: Harper and Row, 1973.

Dubin, R. "Stability of Human Organizations." In M. Haire (ed.), *Modern Organization Theory.* New York: John Wiley, 1959, pp. 218–53.

Etzione, A., (ed.). *Complex Organizations: A Sociological Reader.* New York: Holt, Rinehart and Winston, 1961.

Farace, R.; P. Monge; and H. Russell. *Communicating and Organizing.* Reading, Mass.: Addison-Wesley, 1976.

Ference, T. P. "Organizational Communications Systems and the Decision Process." *Management Sciences,* 1970, *12,* B83–B96.

Flesch, R. "A New Readability Yardstick." *Journal of Applied Psychology,* 1948, *32,* 221–33.

Fhaner, S. "Subjective Probability and Everyday Life." *Scandinavian Journal of Psychology,* 1977, *18,* 81–84.

Gieselman, R. D., and K. O. Locker. "Presenting Numerical Data Effectively." In R. D. Gieselman (ed.), *Readings in Business Communication*. Champaign, Ill.: Stipes, 1974.

Goffman, E. *Relations in Public: Microstudies of the Public Order*. New York: Harper and Row, 1971.

Goldhaber, G. M.; H. S. Dennis; G. M. Richetto; and O. A. Wiio. *Information Strategies: New Patterns to Corporate Power*. Englewood Cliffs, N.J.: Prentice-Hall, 1979.

Golen, S. "An Analysis of Communication Barriers in Public Accounting Firms." *The Journal of Business Communications*, 1980, *17*, 39–49.

Gordon, R. L. *Interviewing, Strategy, Techniques, and Tactics*. Homewood, Ill.: Dorsey Press, 1969.

Guetzkov, H. "Communications in Organizations." In J. March (ed.), *Handbook of Organizations*. Chicago: Rand McNally, 1965, pp. 534–73.

Guetzkov, H., and W. R. Dill. "Factors in the Organizational Development of Task-Oriented Groups." *Sociometry*, 1957, *20*, 175–204.

Hall, E. T. *The Hidden Dimension*. New York: Doubleday, 1966.

Haney, W. V. *Communication and Interpersonal Relations*. Homewood, Ill.: Irwin, 1979.

Hardin, G. "The Tragedy of the Commons," *Science*, 1968, *162*, 1243.

Heise, G. A., and G. A. Miller. "Problem Solving by Small Groups Using Various Communications Nets." *Journal of Abnormal and Social Psychology*, 1951, *46*, 327–35.

Hewitt, J., and R. Stokes. "Disclaimers." *American Sociological Review*, 1975, *40*, 1–11.

Hirsch, E. D., Jr. *The Philosophy of Composition*. Chicago and London: University of Chicago Press, 1977.

Homans, G. C. *Social Behavior: Its Elementary Form*. New York: Harcourt, Brace and World, 1961.

Huff, D. *How to Lie with Statistics*. New York: W. W. Norton, 1954.

Hunkins, F. P. *Questions, Strategies, and Techniques*. Boston: Allyn and Bacon, 1972.

Irmscher, W. F. *Ways of Writing*. New York: McGraw-Hill, 1969.

Janis, I. *Victims of Groupthink*. Boston: Houghton Mifflin, 1972.

Jensen, J. V. *Perspectives on Oral Communication*. Boston: Holbrook Press, 1970.

Kahn, R. L., and Quinn, R. P. "Role Stress: A Framework for Analysis." In A. McLean (ed.), *Mental Health and Work Organizations*. Chicago: Rand McNally, 1970.

Katz, D., and R. L. Kahn. *The Social Psychology of Organizations*, 2d ed. New York: John Wiley, 1978.

Kelley, H. H. "Attribution Theory in Social Psychology." In D. Levine (ed.), *Nebraska Symposium on Motivation*, vol. 15. Lincoln: University of Nebraska Press, 1967.

Klare, G. R. *The Measurement of Readability*. Ames: Iowa State University Press, 1963.

Koehler, J. R.; K. W. Anatol; and R. L. Applbaum. *Organizational Communication: Behavioral Perspectives*. New York: Holt, Rinehart and Winston, 1976.

Lawrence, P., and J. Lorsch. *Organization and Environment: Managing Differentiation and Integration*. Boston: Division of Research, Harvard University School of Business Administration, 1967.

Lawson, E. D. "Change in Communication Nets, Performance, and Morale." *Human Relations*, 1965, *18*, 139–47.

Leavitt, H. J. *Managerial Psychology*. Chicago: University of Chicago Press, 1958.

Lee, K. J. *Language Habits in Human Affairs*. New York: Harper and Row, 1941.

Lewis, P. V., and W. H. Baker. *Business Report Writing*. Columbus, Ohio: Grid, 1978.

Lichtenstein, S.; B. Fischoff; and L. D. Phillips. "Calibration of Probabilities: The State of the Art." In H. Jungermann and G. de Zeeuw (eds.), *Decision Making and Change in Human Affairs*. Amsterdam: Reidel, 1977.

March, J. G., and H. A. Simon. *Organizations*. New York: John Wiley, 1958.

Maslow, A. *Motivation and Personality*. New York: Harper and Row, 1954.

McClelland, D. C. *The Achieving Society*. Princeton, N.J.: Van Nostrand, 1961.

Meddaugh, E. J. "Report Frequency and Management Decisions." *Decision Sciences*, 1976, *7*, 813–28.

Metzler, K. *Creative Interviewing*. Englewood Cliffs, N.J.: Prentice-Hall, 1977.

Miller, J. G. "Information Impact, Overload, and Psychopathology." *American Journal of Psychiatry*, 1960, *116*, 695–704.

Mills, G. H., and J. A. Walter. *Technical Writing*, 4th ed., New York: Holt, Rinehart and Winston, 1978.

Moore, W. E. *Creative and Critical Thinking*. Boston: Houghton Mifflin, 1967.

Myers, M. Scott. "The Human Factor in Management Systems." *California Management Review*, 1972, *14*, 5–10.

Newcomb, T. M. *The Acquaintance Process*. New York: Holt, Rinehart and Winston, 1961.

Nichols, R. G. "Do We Know How to Listen? Practical Help in a Modern Age." *The Speech Teacher*, 1961, *10*, 119–20.

_____. "Factors in Listening Comprehension." *Speech Monographs*, 1948, *15*, 161–62.

_____. "Listening." In R. F. Reid (ed.), *Introduction to the Field of Speech*. Chicago: Scott, Foresman, 1965.

Nichols, R. G., and L. A. Stevens. "Listening to People." *Harvard Business Review*, 1957, *35*, 85–92.

Nisbett, R.; E. Borgida; R. Crandall; and H. Reed. "Popular Induction: Information Is Not Always Informative." In J. Carroll and J. W. Payne (eds.), *Cognition and Social Behavior*, 1976, *2*, 227–36.

Nisbett, R., and L. Ross. *Human Inference: Strategies and Shortcomings of Social Judgment.* Englewood Cliffs, N.J.: Prentice-Hall, 1980.

O'Connell, S. E. *The Manager as Communicator.* San Francisco: Harper and Row, 1979.

O'Hayre, J. *Gobbledygook Has Gotta Go.* Washington, D.C.: U.S. Government Printing Office, n.d.

Oliver, R. T., and R. L. Cartwright. *Effective Speech,* 4th ed. New York: Holt, Rinehart and Winston, 1961.

Oppenheim, A. N. *Question Design and Attitude Measurement.* New York: Basic Books, 1966.

Ostrom, T.; J. Lingle; J. Pryor; and N. Geva. *Cognitive Organization of Person Impressions.* Columbus: Ohio State University, Department of Psychology, August 1979.

Ouchi, W. G. *Theory Z.* Reading, Mass.: Addison-Wesley, 1980.

Palen, J. M. *Report Writing for Accountants.* Englewood Cliffs, N.J.: Prentice-Hall, 1955.

Payne, S. L. *The Art of Asking Questions.* Princeton, N. J.: Princeton University Press, 1965.

Peterson, R. B., and L. Tracy. *Systematic Management of Human Resources.* Reading, Mass.: Addison-Wesley, 1979.

Pinney, T. *A Short Handbook and Style Sheet.* New York: Harcourt Brace Jovanovich, 1977.

Porter, L. W., and E. E. Lawler. *Managerial Attitudes and Performance.* Homewood, Ill.: Irwin, 1968.

Price, R. D. *Preparing Instructional Developers for the Initial Client Conference.* Paper presented at the National Convention of the Association for Educational Communications and Technology, Kansas City, April 1978.

Redding, W. C. *Communication within the Organization.* New York: Industrial Communications Council, 1972.

Roberts, K. H., and C. A. O'Reilly. "Failures in Upward Communication in Organization: Three Possible Culprits." *Academy of Management Journal,* 1974, *17,* 205–15.

Roethlisberger, F. C. "Barriers to Communication Between Men." In S. I. Hayakawa (ed.), *The Use and Misuse of Language.* New York: Fawcett Publications, 1962.

Rosenthal, R. A., and R. S. Weiss. "Problems of Organizational Feedback Processes." In R. A. Bauer (ed.), *Social Indicators.* Cambridge, Mass.: Massachusetts Institute of Technology Press, 1966, pp. 302–40.

Ross, L., and C. Anderson. "Shortcomings in the Attribution Process: On the Origins and Maintenance of Erroneous Social Assessments." In A. Tversky, D. Kahneman, and P. Slovic (eds.), *Judgment under Uncertainty: Heuristics and Biases.* New York: Cambridge University Press, 1982.

Ross, M., and F. Sicoly. "Egocentric Biases in Availability and Attribution." *Journal of Personality and Social Psychology,* 1979, *37,* 322–36.

Roy, R. H., and J. H. MacNeill. *Horizons for a Profession.* New York: AICPA, 1967.

Schoettle, E. C. B. "The State of the Art in Policy Studies." In R. A. Bauer (ed.), *The Study of Policy Formation.* New York: Free Press, 1968, pp. 149–80.

Schwartz, G. E. *Stress Management in Occupational Settings.* National Technical Information Service Report, Yale University, 1979.

Shaw, M. E. "Some Effects of Problem Complexity upon Problem Solution Efficiency in Different Communication Nets." *Journal of Experimental Psychology,* 1954, *48,* 211–17.

Shaw, M. E., and G. H. Rothschild. "Some Effects of Prolonged Experience in Communication Nets." *Journal of Applied Psychology,* 1956, *40,* 281–86.

Stanga, K. G. "A New Look at the Language of Business." *CA Magazine,* 1977, *110,* 39–42.

Stone, M. L. "Improving Writing Skills." *The Journal of Accountancy,* September, 1971, 84–85.

Student, K. R. "Supervisory Influence and Work Group Performance." *Journal of Applied Psychology,* 1968, *52,* 188–94.

Sullivan, H. S. *Conceptions of Modern Psychiatry.* New York: W. W. Norton, 1953.

Sullivan, J. J. "The Power of the Flesch Reading Ease Formula." Proceedings of the American Business Communications Association International Convention, Washington, D.C., December 28–31, 1980.

Swenson, C. H. *Introduction to Interpersonal Relations.* Glenview, Ill.: Scott, Foresman, 1973.

Terhune, K. W. "Motive, Situation, and Interpersonal Conflict within Prisoner's Dilemma." *Journal of Personality and Social Psychology,* 1968, *8,* Monograph Supplement.

Thibaut, J. W., and H. H. Kelley. *The Social Psychology of Groups.* New York: John Wiley, 1959.

Thomas, K. "Conflict and Conflict Management." In M. D. Dunnette (ed.), *Handbook of Industrial and Organizational Psychology.* Chicago: Rand McNally, 1976.

Timm, P. R. *Managerial Communication.* Englewood Cliffs, N.J.: Prentice-Hall, 1980.

Touche Ross International. *The Touche Ross Audit Process Manual.* New York, August 1978.

Tversky, A., and D. Kahneman. "Judgment under Uncertainty: Heuristics and Biases." *Science,* 1974, *185,* 1124–31.

United States General Accounting Office. *The Language of Audit Reports.* Washington, D.C.: U.S. Government Printing Office, 1957.

Vroom, V. H. *Work and Motivation.* New York: John Wiley, 1964.

Wiggins, J. R. "A Psychological Taxonomy of Trait-Descriptive Terms: The Interpersonal Domain." *Journal of Personality and Social Psychology,* 1979, *37,* 395–412.

Wish, M.; R. D'Andrade; and J. Goodnow. "Dimensions of Interpersonal Communication: Correspondences Between Structures for Speech Acts and Bipolar Scales." *Journal of Personality and Social Psychology,* 1980, *39,* 848–60.

Wish, M.; M. Deutsch; and S. Kaplan. "Perceived Dimensions of Interpersonal Relations." *Journal of Personality and Social Psychology,* 1976, *33,* 409–20.

Witte, A. E. "Organizing to Write." *Accountancy,* September 1972, 105–06.

Wofford, J. C.; E. A. Gerloff; and R. C. Cummins. *Organizational Communication.* New York: McGraw-Hill, 1977.

Index

DATE DUE